1ST NATIONAL EDITION

SOFTWARE

DEVELOPMENT

A LEGAL GUIDE

BY ATTORNEY STEPHEN FISHMAN
CHAPTER 5 BY PATENT ATTORNEY LEIGH HUNT FIRESTONE

EDITED BY STEPHEN ELIAS, RALPH WARNER & LISA GOLDOFTAS

NOLO PRESS BERKELEY

Your Responsibility When Using a Self-help Law Book

We've done our best to give you useful and accurate information in this book. But this book does not take the place of a lawyer licensed to practice law in your state. If you want legal advice, see a lawyer. If you use any information contained in this book, it's your personal responsibility to make sure that the facts and general information contained in it are applicable to your situation.

Keeping Up-to-Date

To keep its books up-to-date, Nolo Press issues new printings and new editions periodically. New printings reflect minor legal changes and technical corrections. New editions contain major legal changes, major text additions or major reorganizations. To find out if a later printing or edition of any Nolo book is available, call Nolo Press at (510) 549-1976 or check the catalog in the *Nolo News,* our quarterly newspaper.

To stay current, follow the "Update" service in the *Nolo News.* You can get a free two-year subscription the paper by sending us the registration card in the back of the book. In another effort to help you use Nolo's latest materials, we offer a 25% discount off the purchase of any new Nolo book if you turn in any earlier printing or edition. (See the "Recycle Offer" in the back of the book.) This book was last printed in November 1994.

FIRST EDITION	
Second Printing	November 1994
EDITORS	Steve Elias, Lisa Goldoftas and Ralph Warner
BOOK DESIGN	Jackie Mancuso
COVER DESIGN	Toni Ihara
PRODUCTION	Stephanie Harolde and Dan Geller
PROOFREADER	Louis Suarez-Potts
INDEX	Mary Kidd
PRINTING	Delta Lithograph

Fishman, Stephen.
Software development : a legal guide / by Stephen Fishman. -- 1st
    national ed.
      national ed.
          p. cm.
      Includes index.
      ISBN 0-87337-209-3
      1. Computer software industry--Law and legislation--United States-
-Popular works. I. Title.
KF390.5.C6F57 1994
343.73'078004--dc20   94-2700
[347.30378004]   CIP

Printed on paper with recycled content
Printed in the U.S.A.

Acknowledgments

My sincere thanks to:

Nolo publisher Jake Warner for his invaluable editorial contribtutions, patience and support

Patent attorney Leigh Hunt Firestone, author of the chapter on software patents (Chapter 5), who made an arcane subject understandable

Nolo Editor extraordinaire Lisa Goldoftas who deftly whipped the manuscript into final shape

Stephanie Harolde who handled a difficult manuscript and numerous revisions with aplomb

Jackie Mancuso for her oustanding book design and Dave McFarland for production.

Ely Newman for his thorough proofreading

The following attorneys who provided insightful comments about software contracts (Chapter 11):

- Paul Goodman of Elias, Goodman and Shanks, P.C. (New York),
- Susan Eiselman of TeleLawyer, Inc.,
- Alan Alberts of Alberts and Associates (Placerville), and
- Andrew Weill, Esq. of Benjamin, Weill and Mazer (San Francisco)

Robert Barr of Brobeck Phleger & Harrison (Palo Alto) and David Pressman (author of *Patent It Yourself*) for their comments on Chapter 5 (Patenting Software)

Donna Demac, fellow, the Freedom Media Studies Center at Columbia University, for her comments on Chapter 13 (Multimedia Projects)

Vincent S. Castellucci, Associate Director of Licensing, Harry Fox Agency, for reviewing the material on use of music in multimedia programs (Chapter 13)

William Roberts, President, Media-Pedia Video Clips Inc. for patiently explaining the stock footage business.

Finally, I thank Steve Elias and dedicate this book to him. Steve has not only been my indefatigable editor for the past three years, but my role model as well.

About the Authors

Stephen Fishman received his law degree from the University of Southern California in 1979. After stints in government and private practice, he became a full-time legal writer in 1983. He has helped write and edit over a dozen reference books for attorneys. He is also the author of *The Copyright Handbook* (Nolo Press).

J. Leigh Hunt Firestone is a patent attorney who lives and works in Berkeley. In her free time she can be found in an art studio or poring over endocrinology books on her way to a Masters Degree.

Contents

C H A P T E R   4

Trade Secret Protection

Software Patents

Trademarks and Software

CHAPTER 7

Workers in the Software Industry: Employees vs. Independent Contractors

CHAPTER 8

Ownership of Software Created by Employees and Independent Contractors

CHAPTER 9

Employment Agreements

CHAPTER 10

Agreements With Independent Contractors

C H A P T E R   14

Help Beyond This Book

A P P E N D I X

Abstract of In re Alappat

Note on Trademarks

We have taken the liberty of putting all software trademarks in capital letters to make them easier to identify.

CHAPTER 1

How to Use This Book

Thishis book is about computer software law and contracts (written agreements). It may be used by anyone involved in the software industry, including:

- software developers
- companies and individuals who hire software developers to create software on their behalf, and
- people who work for software developers, whether as employees or independent contractors.

A. How This Book Is Organized

Conceptually, this book is divided into four parts:

Chapters 1-6 contain this overview of how to use the book, followed by a detailed discussion of intellectual property protection for software, including copyright, trade secret, patent and trademark protection.

Chapters 7-10 examine the legal relationship between a software developer and its employees and independent contractors; separate chapters cover employment and independent contractor agreements.

Chapters 11-13 cover agreements for the development of software. Included are:

- a detailed custom development agreement, which governs the development of software for a specific end-user (Chapter 11),
- a programmer's guide to software publishing agreements (Chapter 12), and
- a discussion of special legal problems involved in developing multimedia programs (Chapter 13).

Chapter 14, Help Beyond This Book, tells you how to do further research on your own and, if necessary, find a software attorney.

Icons Used in This Book

 A caution to slow down and consider potential problems.

 "Fast track" lets you know that you may be able to skip some material that doesn't apply to your situation.

 This icon lets you know when you probably need the advice of an intellectual property attorney, software specialist or other professional.

 Information regarding the forms disk included with this book.

 This icon alerts you to a tip that may help you negotiate or draft an agreement.

B. Which Parts of the Book You Should Read

Not everyone will want to read the whole book. Which parts you do want to read will, of course, depend on why you bought the book.

Most of you bought the book for one or more of these four reasons:

1. You want a contract you can use with a client, developer, employee or independent contractor.
2. You want to know how to obtain the maximum legal protection possible for your software.
3. You have a specific question or problem.
4. You want a general education in software law.

Let's look at each of these reasons in more detail.

1. You Want a Contract to Use

This book contains a number of sample software contracts. These contracts are also on the forms disk at the end of this book so you can easily load them onto your computer.

⚠️ Before you use any contract on the forms disk, read the detailed discussion about it in the book. Most of the contracts contain a number of alternate provisions and you'll need to read the book to know which ones to use. The information in the book will help you decide whether to add or delete material from a contract, or perhaps not even use it at all.

Following are the types of forms in the book and on the disk; a complete list is in Section C, below. You need only read the chapters that cover areas of concern to you:

- Trade secret nondisclosure agreements (in Chapter 4, Trade Secret Protection for Software);
- Departing employee's acknowledgment of obligations to employer (in Chapter 4, Trade Secret Protection for Software);
- Employment agreements for technical and nontechnical employees (in Chapter 9, Employment Agreements);
- Independent contractor agreement (in Chapter 10, Agreements with Independent Contractors);
- Custom software development agreement (in Chapter 11, Agreements for Development of Custom Software); and
- Multimedia license agreements (in Chapter 13, Multimedia Projects).

2. You Want Maximum Legal Protection for Your Software

Perhaps the sole reason you bought this book was to learn how to obtain maximum legal protection for the ideas and expression associated with your software. Here's how to proceed:

- First, read Chapter 2, Introduction to Intellectual Property, for an overview of the various forms of protection, and a discussion of how to implement an intellectual property protection plan.
- Next, you can read Chapters 3-6 straight through, or whatever portions of them interest you.
- Also, read Chapter 8, Ownership of Software Created by Employees and Contractors, which discusses the ownership issues involved whenever software is created by an employee or independent contractor.

3. You Have a Specific Question or Problem

If you have a specific question or problem, look for that topic in the table of contents at the front of the book. For example, suppose you want to know whether you need to get permission to use an excerpt from a book in a multimedia program you're developing. By scanning the Table of Contents, you would discover Chapter 13, Multimedia Projects—probably the place to start. And by examining the section headings under Chapter 13, you would find that Section B is the place to start reading. If you didn't find what you were looking for in the Table of Contents, you could search in the index under such terms as "multimedia" and "permissions."

4. You Want a General Education in Software Law

Perhaps you bought this book because you want to learn all about software law. It may come as a surprise to discover that there really is no such thing as software law. Instead, there is a vast body of different state and federal intellectual property and contract laws that, taken together, are used legally to protect software and govern software transactions. Read Chapter 2 for an overview of intellectual property law and then delve into whatever chapters interest you.

C.   How to Use the Forms Disk

All of the forms in this book are included on a 3-1/2" forms disk formatted for the PC (MS-DOS).

1.   System Requirements

To use the disk, you'll need an IBM PC or compatible, PC/MS-DOS 2.0 or higher, and a 3-1/2" disk drive that reads 720K disks. You will also need some type of word processing or text editing application.

COMPUTER DISK WITH CONTRACTS AND FORMS

A 3-1/2" PC/MS DOS computer disk containing files for all the contracts and agreements is included with this book.

These files are provided in the standard ASCII file format that can be opened, completed, and printed with your PC word processing program.

Macintosh developers will need a super disk drive and Apple File Exchange® or similar utility to read a DOS disk. For specific instructions on using contracts and agreements on the disk, see the README.TXT file included on the disk (insert the disk in your A: drive and type A:READ<E.TXT or MORE<A:README.TXT at the DOS prompt to view this file on the screen).

2. Choosing a File

Each form document covered in this book is provided in a separate computer file. The accompanying chart, "Files Provided on the Forms Disk," lists all computer files as well as the form titles and corresponding chapter and section in the book. Before you open any of the files, turn to the chapter of the book that discusses that particular form. Where there are several forms available, make sure you choose the form that applies to your situation.

FILES PROVIDED ON THE FORMS DISK

Chapter	Form Name	File Name
4, Section G5a	General Nondisclosure Agreement	NONDISC1.TXT
4, Section G5b	Nondisclosure Agreement (Prospective Customers)	NONDISC2.TXT
4, Section G5c	Nondisclosure Agreement (Beta Tester)	NONDISC3.TXT
4, Section G5d	Visitor's Nondisclosure Agreement	NONDISC4.TXT
4, Section H8a	Acknowledgment of Obligations	ACKOBLIG.TXT
4, Section H8b	Letter to new employer regarding former employee's access to trade secrets	LTRSECRT.TXT
9, Section F	Employment Agreement for Nontechnical Employees	EMPLOY1.TXT
9, Section G	Employment Agreement for Technical Employees	EMPLOY2.TXT
10, Section B	Independent Contractor Agreement	INDPCONT.TXT
11, Section D	Sample clauses for custom software agreement	CLSCUST.TXT
11, Section D	Custom Software Development Agreement (Model 1)	CUSTSFT1.TXT
11, Section D	Custom Software Development Agreement (Model 2)	CUSTSFT2.TXT
11, Section D	Custom Software Development Agreement (Model 3)	CUSTSFT3.TXT
11, Section D26	Assignment of Intellectual Property Rights	ASSIGN.TXT
12, Section B	Sample clauses for software author's publishing agreement	CLSPUB.TXT
13, Section F4	Multimedia Publicity/Privacy Release Form	MULTIREL.TXT
13, Section H2	Multimedia License Agreement	MULTILIC.TXT

3. Editing the Forms

The disk contains files that are formatted in text-only (ASCII). You may access and edit the forms in most word processing programs. The files have double spacing at the end of each paragraph (two pairs of Carriage Return/ Line Feed codes).

See your word processing application's documentation for instructions on how to open (load, retrieve, import) ASCII text files.

Note. *A line of ^@'s (a string of O's) may appear as the last line of the text files. Simply delete this line prior to saving the text file as a word processing document.*

 As with any software, it's prudent to make a backup copy of the disk before you begin. In accordance with copyright laws, remember that copies of the disk are for your personal use only.

Because the forms are not set up in a stand-alone program, you'll need to edit various clauses to suit your particular circumstances and needs. Use the regular word processing functions you would use for any text (such as cut, copy, paste, delete and insert).

When customizing the forms, or selecting clauses from a clause-only file, follow these simple rules:

- *Follow the instructions in this book.* This book explains key features of all forms and guides you through the process of completing them.
- *Look for instructions in brackets and capital letters.* The forms on disk indicate where information must be filled in by short instructions contained in brackets, such as "[DATE]." You may want to search for a left bracket ("[") to find the beginning of each item that must be completed. Remember to delete (or replace) the bracketed instructions after you've read them.
- *Modify and delete text only as directed.* The clauses are legally sound as designed. If, however, you change important terms, you may affect their legal validity.

- *Select alternatives as directed and delete alternatives that don't apply.* When you have a choice between two or more provisions, these are referred to as "alternatives." Read the discussion of the alternatives in the book; the text of all alternatives is on the disk only. Each alternative is clearly marked at the beginning "[ALTERNATIVE 1]," "[ALTERNATIVE 2]," and so on. Each alternative ends with a similar marking: "[END ALTERNATIVE 1]," and so on. Delete the markers as well as the alternative(s) that you did not select.
- *Optional clauses are marked* "[OPTIONAL]." That means it's up to you as to whether or not to include them. Delete the word "[OPTIONAL]" and the subsequent "[END OPTION]" marker if you use the clause. Delete the entire clause and markers if you choose not to use it.

D. Putting the Agreement Together

After the parties have decided what to include in their agreement, there are some technical details that have to be dealt with. Usually, one party handles this and submits the finished agreement to the other for review and signature.

1. The Process of Reaching a Final Agreement

One of the parties will create a first draft of the agreement. This and all subsequent drafts should be dated and numbered (e.g., "draft #1, October 6, 1993"). In addition, a legend like the following should be placed at the top of the draft to make clear that it is not the final agreement:

**PRELIMINARY DRAFT FOR DISCUSSION PURPOSES ONLY—
NOT INTENDED AS A LEGALLY BINDING DOCUMENT.**

The draft should be sent to the other party to review. Often, the other party will want to make changes. This can be done in several ways. The other party can discuss the changes with the original drafter in person or by telephone; the original drafter will then make the agreed changes and send a second draft to the other party for review. Alternatively, the other side may suggest its changes in writing; this can be in the form of a letter, interlineations to the original draft, or by completely revising the original draft. The original drafter will then review the changes, perhaps make more changes, and then send another draft back to the other side for review. It is common for contract drafts to go back and forth among the parties many times before a final agreement is reached.

a. Keeping Track of Changes

Care must be taken to alert the other side to all changes made in each draft. The normal practice is to underline all additions and to indicate deletions either by leaving them in place with a line drawn through them or using a caret or other sign indicating omissions. This can be easily done with many word processing programs.

2. Print Out and Proofread the Final Agreement

Print out the final agreement on regular 8-1/2 x 11-inch paper. Make sure the pages are consecutively numbered (either at the top right corner or the bottom of each page). Read through the entire agreement to make sure it is correct and complete. Minor changes can be made by hand (in ink only) and initialed. However, it's probably just as easy (and neater) to make any changes on your computer and then print out the agreement again. When you're finished proofreading, print out at least two copies of the agreement.

3. Attach All Exhibits

Attach a complete copy of all exhibits, if any, to every copy of the agreement. Each exhibit should be consecutively numbered or lettered ("A,B,C" or

"1,2,3"). Make sure that your references to the exhibits in the main body of the agreement match the actual exhibits.

4. Signing the Agreement

Each party should sign both copies of the agreement (both are originals). The parties don't have to be in the same room when they sign and it's okay if the dates of signing are a few days apart.

If either or both of the parties is a corporation, the agreement should be signed in their corporate capacities. For example, if Joe Jones is President of AcmeSoft Corporation, he should sign on AcmeSoft's behalf, like this:

AcmeSoft Corporation,

By: _____
Joe Jones, President

It's best that a corporation's president or chief executive office (CEO) sign the agreement, since he or she will have clear authority to sign for the corporation. For the same reason, if a party is a partnership, it's preferable that a partner sign. If this is not possible, the signature should be accompanied by a corporate resolution or partnership resolution stating that the person signing the agreement has authority to do so.

5. Save the Agreement

Each party should keep one original signed copy of the agreement. Make sure to store it in a safe place. You might want to make additional photocopies to ensure against loss.

E. Registration Form

We hope you are pleased with *Software Development: A Legal Guide*. If you complete the tear-out Registration Form included at the back of this book (we pay postage), we will add your name to our mailing list and notify you of future updates to our disks, publications and programs. We promise never to sell or give your name and address to anyone else. ■

CHAPTER 2

Introduction to Intellectual Property

In this chapter we introduce the concept of intellectual property and discuss how a software developer may implement a simple plan to preserve and protect its intellectual property.

A. What Is Intellectual Property?

"Intellectual property" is a generic term used to describe products of the human intellect that have economic value. Computer software is just one of the many forms of intellectual property. Other examples include such works as books, music, movies, photographs, artwork, records and other works of authorship, as well as certain inventions.

Intellectual property is "property" because, over the past 200 years or so, a body of laws has been created that gives owners of such works legal rights similar in some respects to those given to owners of real estate or tangible personal property (such as automobiles). Intellectual property may be owned and bought and sold the same as other types of property. But in many important respects, ownership of intellectual property is very different from ownership of a house or a car.

Anybody who develops real estate would be a fool not to know something about real estate law. Similarly, everyone who creates software, or hires others to do so, should have a basic understanding of intellectual property laws. These laws define exactly what a software developer owns and doesn't own, what it can sell and what it can and cannot legally take from others.

A software developer or owner that makes wise use of the intellectual property laws maximizes the value of its software. In contrast, a developer or owner that pays little or no attention to intellectual property may end up throwing away potentially valuable assets or find itself at the wrong end of an expensive lawsuit.

B. Using Intellectual Property Laws to Protect Software

There are more ways to legally protect computer software than virtually any other product of the human brain. This is because software can be viewed as a work of authorship, a commercial product and a part of a machine. As we'll discuss briefly in this chapter, there are four separate bodies of law that may be used to protect software. These are:

• trade secret law,
• copyright law,
• patent law, and
• trademark law.

Each of these bodies of law may be used to protect different aspects of computer software, although there is a great deal of overlap. In most cases, both copyright and trade secret law can and should be used together to protect the same piece of software. Patent law is used much more rarely than copyright or trade secrecy to protect software; but, when it is used, it can provide the most powerful protection of all. State and federal trademark laws are used to protect product names, logos, slogans, packaging and other symbols used to market software.

Let's take a brief look at each type of intellectual property law. (All four types of protection are covered in more detail in later chapters.)

1. Trade Secret Law

A trade secret is information or know-how that is not generally known in the business community and that provides its owner with a competitive advantage in the marketplace. The information can be an idea, written words, formula, process or procedure, technical design, list, marketing plan or any other secret that gives the owner an economic advantage.

If a trade secret owner takes reasonable steps to keep the confidential information or know-how secret, the courts of most states will protect the owner from disclosures of the secret to others by:

- the owner's employees,
- other persons with a duty not to make such disclosures,
- industrial spies, and
- competitors who wrongfully acquire the information.

This means that the trade secret owner may be able to sue the infringer and obtain an injunction (a court order preventing someone from doing something, like infringing on another's trade secrets) and/or damages. However, the trade secret owner must truly take steps to preserve the trade secret; the more widely known a trade secret is, the less willing the courts are to protect it.

Example: *AcmeSoft, a small software developer, decides to create a program designed to automate and improve the manufacture of widgets. AcmeSoft knows that several of its competitors are working on similar programs, but its star programmer has devised a revolutionary new method to computerize widget making.*

AcmeSoft doesn't want its competitors to know about the new method, or that it's developing a new widget manufacturing program, so it keeps this information as a closely-guarded trade secret. It requires its employees to sign employment agreements in which they promise not to disclose valuable information to outsiders without AcmeSoft's permission. AcmeSoft also implements other trade secrecy measures (discussed in detail in Chapter 4, Sections G and H), such as marking documents with sensitive information "confidential." All of these measures are designed to:

- *prevent outsiders from learning about AcmeSoft's development activities; and*
- *give AcmeSoft legal grounds to stop the information from being used by a competitor if the competitor learns about them illegally (by hiring away or bribing an AcmeSoft employee). By relying on trade secrecy principles, AcmeSoft gets a leg-up on its competition, all of whom are pursuing different, less original and imaginative designs for their own widget manufacturing programs. When AcmeSoft distributes its program, AcmeSoft can continue to maintain the program as a trade secret by providing customers with copies in object code form only (which cannot be easily read) and by requiring them to sign license agreements by which they promise to keep the program confidential.*

Trade secrecy is increasingly being seen as the most important form of protection for most software, in part because of the limitations on copyright protection (discussed briefly below).

(For a detailed discussion of trade secrets, see Chapter 4.)

2. Copyright Law

Virtually all software qualifies for protection under the federal copyright law, at least to some extent. The copyright law protects original works of authorship. Computer software is considered to be a work of authorship, as are all types of written works (books, articles, etc.), music, artwork, photos, films and videos.

A copyright costs nothing, is obtained automatically and lasts a very long time—over 50 years. But copyright protection for software is relatively weak. Here's why. The owner of a copyright has the exclusive right to copy and distribute the protected work, and to create derivative works based upon it (updated versions, for example). However, this copyright protection extends only to the particular way the ideas, systems and processes embodied in software are expressed by a given program. Copyright never protects an idea, system or process itself. In other words, copyright protects against the unauthorized duplication or use of computer code and, to some extent, a program's structure and user interface, but copyright never protects the underlying functions, methods, ideas, systems or algorithms used in software.

Example: *AcmeSoft's widget program is automatically protected by copyright as soon as it's written. This means no one may make or sell copies of the program without AcmeSoft's permission.*

In addition, it is illegal for anyone to create new software very similar to AcmeSoft's using a substantial amount of AcmeSoft's program. Nonetheless, AcmeSoft's competitors are free to independently create a new program accomplishing the same purpose.

Because of the complexity of the law and confusion in the courts, the extent of copyright protection for such aspects of AcmeSoft's program as its structure and interface is not entirely clear. However, by treating the program as a trade secret, AcmeSoft can not only definitely protect these items, but also the program's underlying ideas, inventive functions, methods, systems and algorithms.

(For a detailed discussion of the copyright law, see Chapter 3.)

3. Patent Law

The federal patent law protects inventions. By filing for and obtaining a patent from the U.S. Patent and Trademark Office, an inventor is granted a monopoly on the use and commercial exploitation of an invention, typically for 17 years. A patent may protect the functional features of a machine, process, manufactured item or composition of matter, the ornamental design of a non-functional feature, or asexually reproduced plants. A patent also protects improvements of any such items.

To obtain a patent, the invention must be:

- novel—unique over previous technology in one or more of its elements, and
- nonobvious—that is, surprising to a person with ordinary skills in the relevant technology.

Most software is not sufficiently novel and/or nonobvious to qualify for a patent. When a patent is appropriate, obtaining it can be a difficult, expensive and time-consuming process. It usually takes about two to three years.

As mentioned above, a computer program can be viewed as part of a machine or process as well as a work of authorship, and computer programs may be patented if they meet the underlying requirements. A patent provides broad protection for the ideas, inventive functions, methods, systems and algorithms that, taken together, constitute the invention, not just the computer code used to express or implement them. In effect, patent protection gives the patent holder an absolute 17-year monopoly over the use of its invention as described in the patent. Where available, patent protection is so strong that it takes the place of both copyright and trade secret protection.

Example: *Certain features of AcmeSoft's widget manufacturing program are quite revolutionary and have never been used before. If AcmeSoft applies for and obtains a patent on these features, it will have a monopoly on their use in widget manufacturing for 17 years. In other words, no one else may use the patented features of AcmeSoft's program to manufacture widgets without AcmeSoft's permission. If they do, AcmeSoft could successfully sue for patent infringement.*

(See Chapter 5 for a detailed discussion of software patents.)

4. Trademark Law

Trade secret, copyright and patent laws do not protect names, titles or short phrases. This is where trademark protection comes in. Under both federal and state laws, a manufacturer, merchant group or individual associated with a product or service can obtain protection for a word, phrase, logo or other symbol used to distinguish that product or service from others. If a competitor uses a protected trademark, the trademark holder can obtain a court injunction (a court order preventing the infringement) and money damages.

Example: *AcmeSoft markets its program under the name "WIDGETEER" and registers this trademark with the U.S. Patent and Trademark Office. None of AcmeSoft's competitors can use its name on a widget manufacturing program without AcmeSoft's consent. If they do, AcmeSoft could get a court to order them to stop and sue for damages.*

(See Chapter 6 for a detailed discussion of trademarks.)

C. Implementing an Intellectual Property Plan

Every software developer, no matter what the size, needs to create and implement an intellectual property plan. This consists primarily of using forms and procedures to identify, establish ownership and protect the developer's intellectual property.

1. Using the Intellectual Property Forms in This Book

Following are the basic forms any software developer should have. Samples of most forms are included in this book.

a. Employment Agreement

Every employee engaged in the creation of software and other intellectual property, or who may be exposed to company trade secrets, should sign an employment agreement. Ideally, each employee should sign the agreement no later than the first day of work on the project. The agreement should assign (transfer) to the employer ownership of all software and other work-related intellectual property the employee creates within the scope of employment. The agreement should also include nondisclosure provisions designed to make clear to the employee that she has a duty to protect the company's trade secrets. Existing employees who have not signed such agreements should be asked to do so. (See Chapter 9 for a detailed discussion and sample agreements.)

b. Independent Contractor Agreement

Every independent contractor—that is, each nonemployee who performs work for the company—should sign an independent contractor agreement, ideally no later than the start of work. This agreement includes trade secrecy provisions and provisions designed to make it clear that the worker is an independent contractor, not an employee. (If you're not sure whether a worker is an employee or an independent contractor, see Chapter 7.) Most importantly, the agreement should assign ownership of the contractor's work product to the company. This is absolutely vital. Without such a provision, the company may not end up owning the copyright in the contractor's work product, even though it paid for it! (See Chapter 10 for a detailed discussion and sample agreements.)

c. Custom Software Development Agreement

It is in the best interests of both a software developer and its clients that a detailed development agreement be negotiated and signed before custom software is developed. This agreement should, among other things, describe the software to be developed, contain payment provisions, state who will own the software when it is completed and contain any desired warranties. (See Chapter 11 for a detailed discussion and sample clauses.)

d. Nondisclosure Agreements

No software developer should ever reveal its trade secrets to an outsider unless he or she signs a nondisclosure agreement promising to keep them confidential. "Outsiders" can include potential customers, beta testers and even office visitors. (See Chapter 4, Sections G4 and G5, for a detailed discussion and sample agreements.)

2. Taking Trade Secrecy Measures

In addition to using the form agreements outlined above, certain physical security measures should be taken to prevent outsiders from obtaining access to company trade secrets. For example, documents containing trade secrets should be marked confidential and kept locked in desks, filing cabinets or safes when not in use. (See Chapter 4, Section G, for a detailed discussion.)

3. Exploring Patenting

Most software cannot be patented. However, if a program contains a truly innovative approach to a problem that is a significant advance in the field or that has long stymied other programmers, it may qualify for a patent.

If a company is serious about obtaining patents, its employees should be encouraged to bring any potentially patentable inventions to management's attention. In addition, all employees engaged in research and development should keep an inventor's notebook documenting when and how their software inventions were developed. The United States has a first-to-invent patent system, and such notebooks can be critical both in obtaining a patent and in defending against patent infringement claims. (See Chapter 5 for a detailed discussion.)

4. Copyrighting Software

Relatively little has to be done to preserve copyright protection—it begins automatically the moment a protectible work is created. However, it is highly advisable—but not mandatory—to register the copyright in all software with the Copyright Office in Washington, D.C. For maximum protection, this must be done no later than three months after the software is published. A copyright notice should also be placed on all copies of published software and documentation. (See Chapter 3 for a detailed discussion.)

5. Registering Trademarks

The company should conduct a trademark search before adopting a trademark to see if any similar trademarks are already in use. This is done by checking state and federal trademark registration records and other sources of trade name listings, such as industry directories.

All trademarks on software that is marketed in more than one state or territory, or overseas, should be registered with the U.S. Patent and Trademark Office. Although trademarks are protected to some extent by state law, substantial rights can be lost by not obtaining federal registration. (See Chapter 6 for a detailed discussion.) ■

CHAPTER 3

Copyright Protection for Software

Copyright law provides one of the two major vehicles by which most software is protected (the other being trade secrecy). The importance of copyright law in the software industry cannot be overemphasized. Copyright law is used to allocate contractual rights and responsibilities—who will own the program code, who has the right to develop and market the product and so forth. To protect the rights of everyone involved, these commercial relationships should be carefully described in software development and publishing contracts.

The copyright law will also usually serve as your first line of defense against software pirates. However, as discussed below, there are significant limitations on the scope of copyright protection for software. As a result, in most cases software owners need to supplement their copyright protection with the stronger protection afforded by trade secrecy. (See Chapter 4.)

This chapter provides an overview of copyright protection for software. For a far more detailed discussion of these issues, including step-by-step guidance on how to register a software copyright with the Copyright Office, refer to Fishman, *Copyright Your Software* (Nolo Press).

A. What Is a Copyright?

A copyright is a legal device that provides the creator of a work of authorship the right to control how the work is used. If someone wrongfully uses material covered by a copyright, the copyright owner can sue and obtain compensation for any losses suffered, as well as an injunction (court order) requiring the copyright infringer to stop the infringing activity.

In this sense, a copyright is a type of intangible property—it belongs to its owner and the courts can be asked to intervene if anyone uses it without permission. And, like other forms of property, a copyright may be sold by its owner, or otherwise exploited by the owner for economic benefit.

1. Author's Exclusive Rights

The Copyright Act of 1976—the federal law providing for copyright protection—grants creators (called "authors") a bundle of intangible, exclusive rights over their work (17 U.S.C. 101 et seq.). These rights include:

- *reproduction rights*—that is, the right to make copies of a protected work;
- *distribution rights*—that is, the right to sell or otherwise distribute copies to the public;
- *the right to create adaptations* (or "derivative works")—that is, the right to prepare new works based on the protected work; and
- *performance and display rights*—that is, the right to perform a protected work or display a work in public.

Subject to some important exceptions discussed below, an author's copyright rights may be exercised only by the author or by a person or entity to whom the author has transferred all or part of her rights.

2. Who Is an Author?

The exclusive rights outlined above initially belong to a work's author. However, for copyright purposes, the "author" of a work is not necessarily the person who created it; it can be that person's employer—a corporation, for example. There are four ways to become an author:

- An individual may independently author the work.
- An employer (whether a person or business entity such as a corporation or partnership) may pay an employee to create the work, in which case the employer is the author under the work made for hire rule. (See Section G1, below, for a detailed discussion.)
- A person or business entity may specially commission an independent contractor to create the work under a written work made for hire contract, in which case the commissioning party becomes the author.

- Two or more individuals or entities may collaborate to become joint authors.

The majority of software is created by employees or independent contractors under work made for hire agreements. As a result, most software is owned by businesses, not by the people who actually created it.

The initial copyright owner of a work is free to transfer some or all copyright rights to other people or businesses, who will then be entitled to exercise the rights transferred. (See Section G2, below, for a detailed discussion.)

B.   What Can Be Protected by Copyright?

Copyright protects all kinds of original works of authorship. This includes, but is not limited to:

- literary works;
- motion pictures, videos and other audiovisual works;
- photographs, sculpture and graphic works (paintings and drawings, for example);
- sound recordings;
- pantomimes and choreographic works; and
- architectural works (architectural drawings, blueprints and the design of actual buildings).

1.   Computer Programs Are Protectible Literary Works

Literary works are very broadly defined to include any work "expressed in words, numbers, or other verbal or numerical symbols or indicia" (17 U.S.C. 101). This includes all types of written works, including software documentation and computer databases. It also includes computer programs, which are defined as "sets of statements or instructions to be used directly or indirectly in a computer to bring about a certain result" (17 U.S.C. 101).

This means the owner of the copyright in a computer program has all of the exclusive rights discussed in Section A, above.

Example: *Kay, a veterinarian and avid bird breeder, writes a program that helps owners of pet birds diagnose and treat bird diseases. As the owner of the copyright in the program, Kay has the exclusive right to copy it, to distribute it to the public and to create derivative works based upon it (new or enhanced versions, for example). Subject to some limited exceptions discussed below, no one else can exercise Kay's copyright rights without her permission. If they do, Kay is entitled to sue them in federal court for copyright infringement both to make them stop the infringing activity and to pay damages.*

2. Screen Displays Are Protectible as Audiovisual Works

The copyright law defines audiovisual works as "works that consist of a series of related images" intended to be shown through the use of a machine or device (17 U.S.C. 112). Computer screen displays may constitute an audiovisual work that is separate and distinct from the "literary work" comprising the actual computer code. For example, several early software copyright cases held that the computer screen displays contained in videogames such as *Pac Man* were protectible as audiovisual works. In more recent years, audiovisual copyrights have been claimed with varying degrees of success in the "look and feel" of computer programs such as *LOTUS 1-2-3* and in the *Apple Macintosh* graphical user interface. (See discussion at Section D1, below.)

A separate audiovisual copyright might also be claimed for visual and/or audio elements of multimedia programs.

C. Three Requirements for Copyright Protection

Not every work of authorship receives copyright protection. A program or other work is protected only if it satisfies all three of these requirements:

- fixation,
- originality, and
- minimal creativity.

    Let's look at each in more detail.

1. Fixation

The work must be fixed in a tangible medium of expression. Any stable medium from which the work can be read back or heard, either directly or with the aid of a machine or device, is acceptable. For example, a work is protected when it is written or drawn on a piece of paper, typed on a typewriter or recorded on tape. However, copyright does not protect a work that exists in your mind but that you have not saved on disk, set to paper or otherwise preserved.

Computer software satisfies the fixation requirement the moment it is stored on magnetic media such as discs or tapes; imprinted on devices such as ROMs, chips and circuit boards; or, of course, written down on paper. Fixation also occurs when a program is loaded into computer RAM (volatile random access memory). Thus, copyright infringement may occur when a program is loaded from a permanent storage device into computer RAM. *Mai v. Peak*, 991 F.2d. 511 (9th Cir. 1993).

Copyright protection begins the instant you fix your work. There is no waiting period and it is not necessary to register the copyright. (But, as discussed below, very important benefits are obtained by registering the work with the Copyright Office.) Copyright protects both completed and unfinished works, as well as works that are widely distributed to the public or never distributed at all.

2. Originality

A work is protected by copyright only if, and to the extent, it is *original*. But this does not mean that copyright protection is limited to works that are novel—that is, new to the world. For copyright purposes, a work is "original" if at least a part of the work owes its origin to the author. A work's quality, ingenuity, aesthetic merit, or uniqueness is not considered. In short, the Copyright Act does not distinguish between the most complex and innovative multimedia project and a high schooler's first efforts in *BASIC*. Both are protected to the extent they were not copied by the author—whether consciously or unconsciously—from other software.

a.   Independent Creation—A Defense to Copyright Infringement

One effect of the originality requirement that has significant implications for the software industry is that so long as a work was independently created by its creators, it is protected, even if other highly similar works already exist. In other words, a programmer cannot infringe upon a pre-existing program she has never seen or otherwise been exposed to.

Example: *Tom, a paleontologist at a midwestern university, writes a software program that helps identify and date dinosaur fossils. Unbeknownst to Tom, Jane, a paleontologist in another part of the country, has written a program of her own that accomplishes the same task. Tom and Jane never had any contact with each other or each other's work. Nevertheless, since their programs were designed to accomplish the same purpose, they closely resemble each other. However, since they were independently created, both programs are entitled to copyright protection despite the similarities.*

This means that no matter how hard you work to create a program, someone else is perfectly free to create a similar program as long as he didn't copy it from you. (We'll discuss the impact of this independent creation defense in more detail in Section F3, below.)

3.   Minimal Creativity

A minimal amount of creativity over and above the independent creation requirement is necessary for copyright protection. Works completely lacking creativity are denied copyright protection even if they have been independently created. However, the amount of creativity required is very slight. A work need not be novel, unique, ingenious or even any good to be sufficiently "creative." All that's required is that the work be the product of a very minimal "creative spark." The vast majority of software—even the simplest of computer programs—easily make the grade.

But there are some types of works that are usually deemed to contain no creativity at all. For example, telephone directory white pages are deemed to lack even minimal creativity and are therefore not protected by copyright. Other alphabetical or numerical listings of data may also completely lack creativity.

COPYRIGHT DOES NOT PROTECT HARD WORK

In the past, some courts held that copyright protected works that may have lacked originality and/or creativity if a substantial amount of work was involved in their creation. For example, these courts might have protected a telephone directory if the author had personally verified every entry. However, the Supreme Court has outlawed this "sweat of the brow" theory (*Feist Publications, Inc. v. Rural Telephone Service Co.*, 111 S.Ct. 1282 (1991)). It is now clear that the amount of work put in to create a program (or other work of authorship) has absolutely no bearing on the degree of copyright protection it will receive. Copyright only protects fixed, original, minimally creative expressions, not hard work.

D. Scope of Copyright Protection for Computer Software

Creating a new and useful computer program requires an investment of a great deal of time and intellectual labor. Understandably, programmers (and those that hire them) would like to be able to exercise the exclusive copyright rights outlined in Section A, above, for every element of their software.

However, this is not possible. Copyright protection is limited in scope because the copyright laws are intended to promote the advancement of knowledge, not to enable copyright owners to maximize their profits. Too much copyright protection for works of authorship would end up retarding, not promoting, this larger purpose.

Perhaps the greatest difficulty with copyrights is determining just what aspects of any given work are protected. This problem exists with all types of works of authorship—for example, books, music, artwork—but it has proved particularly vexing for computer software.

All works of authorship—particularly computer programs—contain elements that are protected by copyright and elements that are not protected. Unfortunately, there is no system available to precisely identify which aspects of a given work are protected by copyright. The Copyright Office makes no such determination when software is registered. The only time we ever obtain a definitive answer as to how much any particular program (or other work of authorship) is protected is when it becomes the subject of a copyright infringement lawsuit. In this event, a judge or jury will have to make a determination. (See Section E, below.) Of course, such litigation is usually very expensive and time-consuming.

Over the past dozen years, federal courts all across the country have been deciding an ever-increasing number of software copyright infringement cases. Their legal opinions are the only concrete guidance available on how, and to what extent, software is protected by the copyright law. Studying these opinions is the only means available (short of filing a lawsuit) to determine the extent to which a given work is protected. To make matters worse, because this is a difficult and complex area of the law, subject to varying interpretations, courts in different parts of the country disagree on the extent of copyright protection for software. For example, the scope of software copyright protection seems to be narrowing in California and New York, while remaining relatively broad in New England and Pennsylvania.

All this means that studying court decisions probably won't allow you to definitively assess how much of a given work is protected. At best an educated guess can be made.

If you've been accused of infringing or you suspect someone has infringed on your software, you're best off seeing a copyright attorney who has had experience in deciphering the relevant court decisions. But keep in mind that even an attorney will often be unable to provide you with a definite "yes" or "no" answer; only a lawsuit and court decision will be definitive.

The bottom line: There are few sure answers when it comes to copyright protection for software. The more you stay away from someone else's creation, the better your chances of staying out of trouble.

To appreciate the dilemma faced by the courts, attorneys, software copyright owners and programmers in trying to decide how much any program is protected by copyright, you must understand the following two basic rules of copyright law:

- *Rule One.* Copyright only protects "expressions," not ideas, systems or processes.
- *Rule Two.* The scope of copyright protection is proportional to the range of expression available.

Let's look at both rules in more detail.

1. Rule One: Copyright Only Protects "Expressions," Not Ideas, Systems or Processes

Copyright only protects the tangible expression of an idea, system or process—not the idea, system or process itself. Copyright law does not protect ideas, procedures, processes, systems, mathematical principles, formulas or algorithms, methods of operation, concepts, facts and discoveries (17 U.S.C. 102(b)). Remember, copyright is designed to aid the advancement of knowledge. If the copyright law gave a person a legal monopoly over ideas, the progress of knowledge would be impeded rather than helped.

Example: *Grace writes a book about gardening that describes a revolutionary new method of growing vegetables with minimal amounts of water. The words in Grace's book are protected by copyright—no one can copy and publish them without her permission. But the ideas contained in Grace's book are not protected. This means that anyone is free to read Grace's book and employ her method for low-water gardening. In addition, anyone else is free to write his own book describing Grace's system—so long as he doesn't copy a substantial portion of Grace's book.*

This idea-expression dichotomy also applies to software. Consider the following real-life example:

Example: *While a student at the Harvard Business School in the late 1970s, Daniel Bricklin conceived the idea of an electronic spreadsheet—a "magic blackboard" that recalculated numbers automatically as changes were made in other parts of the spreadsheet. Eventually, aided by others, he transformed his idea into VISICALC, the first commercial electronic spreadsheet. The program, designed for use on the Apple II, sold like hotcakes and helped spark the personal computer revolution. Of course VISICALC was protected by copyright. Nevertheless, others were free to write their own original programs accomplishing the same purpose as VISICALC. The copyright law did not give Bricklin any ownership rights over the idea of an electronic spreadsheet, even though it was a revolutionary advance in computer programming. The copyright in VISICALC extended only to the particular way VISICALC expressed this idea—to VISICALC's actual code, its structure and organization, and perhaps to some aspects of its user interface.*

Very soon, many competing programs were introduced. The most successful of these was LOTUS 1-2-3 originally created by Mitchell Kapor and Jonathan Sachs. Building on Bricklin's revolutionary idea, Kapor and Sachs expressed that idea in a different, more powerful way. Designed for the IBM PC, 1-2-3 took advantage of that computer's more expansive memory and more versatile screen display capabilities and keyboard. In short, 1-2-3 did all that

VISICALC did, only better. VISICALC sales plunged and the program was eventually discontinued.

LEGAL PROTECTION FOR IDEAS AND SYSTEMS

What if Bricklin, in the above example, had wanted to protect his idea or system of an electronic spreadsheet itself, not just *VISICALC*? He would have had to look to laws other than copyright. If the electronic spreadsheet had qualified as a patentable invention, it could have been protected under the federal patent law.

With a patent, Bricklin would have had a 17-year monopoly on its use. Anyone else seeking to write a program implementing the spreadsheet idea would have had to obtain Bricklin's permission or been liable for patent infringement. Bricklin did not apply for a patent, and it is far from clear whether, at the time, he could have obtained one had he done so. (See Chapter 5 for a detailed discussion of software patents.)

Of course, it's easy to say that "copyright does not protect ideas, only expression." But what does this mean in the real world? Almost all computer programs embody "systems" or "processes." When does the unprotectible system end and the protectible expression begin? In point of fact, it can be very difficult to tell the difference between an unprotected idea, system or process and its protected expression. This is particularly true for computer software. Although some courts have tried, no one has ever been able to fix an exact boundary between ideas and expression; probably nobody ever can. Nevertheless, let's look at what aspects of computer software have been found to constitute protectible expression by courts in recent years.

a. Program Code Is Protected Expression

A program's code clearly constitutes the programmer's expression of the ideas embodied in the program. To the extent code is fixed, original and minimally creative, it is protected by copyright. This is true both for "source code" (code written in high-level computer languages consisting of English words and symbols readable by humans, such as *BASIC, C, COBOL* and *Pascal*) and "object code" (the series of binary ones and zeros read by the computer itself to execute a program, but not readable by ordinary humans).

Subject to the limitations discussed below under Rule Two, copyright protects the code for:

- applications programs (programs that perform a specific task for the user, such as word processing, bookkeeping or playing a video game), and
- operating systems programs (programs that manage a computer's internal functions and facilitate use of applications programs).

Example: *Franklin Computer Corp. manufactured a computer that was compatible with the Apple II. To achieve such compatibility, Franklin copied verbatim 14 separate programs comprising the Apple II's operating system. Apple sued Franklin for infringing on its copyright in these programs and won. The court held that operating system program code constituted protectible expression, not unprotectible methods, processes, systems or ideas (Apple Computer v. Franklin, 714 F.2d 1240 (3rd Cir. 1983)).*

b. Program Structure, Sequence and Organization

There are many different ways to design a program, both in terms of its modular structure and dynamic behavior. A program's structure is an important factor determining its efficiency. Much of the expense and difficulty in creating a new program is attributable to developing its structure, logic and flow, not in creating the literal program code. It is generally agreed by courts today that a program's structure, logic and flow can constitute protectible "expression," even though these elements are not entirely visible and concrete, either in the program's code or screen displays.

Example: *Whelan created a program called Dentalab written in the EDL computer language and designed to automate the bookkeeping functions of dental offices. Jastrow created a very similar program in the BASIC language. He did not* *directly translate the Dentalab code into BASIC. Rather, he copied the way Dentalab instructed the computer to receive, assemble, calculate, hold, retrieve and communicate data, and the way data flowed sequentially from one program function to another.*

Whelan sued Jastrow for infringing on the copyright in her program and won. The court held that the protectible expression of a computer program includes "the manner in which the program operates, controls and regulates the computer in receiving, assembling, calculating, retaining, correlating and producing useful information either on a screen, print-out or by audio communication" (Whelan v. Jastrow, 797 F.2d 1222 (3rd Cir. 1986)).

The *Whelan* decision has been criticized by many legal experts and other courts, but it established the principle that copyright *can* protect more than a program's literal code. Whether copyright *will* provide such protection in any given instance depends on the application of Rule Two, discussed below.

c. Protection for User Interfaces ("Look and Feel")

The "user interface" of a computer program is the way a program presents itself to, and interacts with, the user. It consists principally of:

- the sequence, flow and content of the display screens that appear on a computer's monitor and permit the user to select various options and/or input data in a prescribed format, and
- the use of specific keys on the computer keyboard to perform particular functions.

The "look and feel" of a program's interface can be very important to the user (a well-designed interface makes a program much easier to use) and therefore very valuable to the program's owner.

User interfaces can be copied without literally copying any code. Several courts have held that all or part of a user interface can constitute protectible expression. One of the best known of these cases involved the popular electronic spreadsheet program *LOTUS 1-2-3*. In order to compete with Lotus, Paperback Software created and marketed an electronic spreadsheet of its own, called *VP-PLANNER*, designed to be compatible with *1-2-3* so that *VP-PLANNER* users could easily transfer spreadsheets created on *1-2-3* to *VP-PLANNER*. *VP-PLANNER*'s creators admitted that to achieve such compatibility they copied *1-2-3*'s user interface virtually verbatim. Lotus sued for copyright infringement and won. The court held that, although the idea of an electronic spreadsheet itself was not protectible, the user interface of *1-2-3* taken as a whole was protected. The court found that *1-2-3*'s menu structure—including the choice of command terms, the structure and order of those terms, and their structure and presentation on the screen—constituted protected expression (*Lotus Dev. Corp. v. Paperback Software Int'l.*, 740 F.Supp. 37 (D. Mass. 1990)).

Perhaps the most important look and feel case to date involved the Apple Macintosh graphical user interface. Apple sued Microsoft, claiming that the user interface of Microsoft's "Windows" system violated Apple's copyright in the Macintosh user interface. Ultimately, all of Apple's claims were dismissed and the case was on appeal when this book went to press. The trial court held that the "desktop metaphor" underlying the Macintosh user interface—suggesting an office with familiar office objects such as file folders, documents and a trash can—was an unprotectible idea.

The court also ruled that most of the individual elements of the user interface at issue in the case were not protectible, either because Apple had licensed them to Microsoft, because they were not original to Apple or because of the factors discussed under Rule Two, below. However, the court found that the interface *as a whole* was protected by copyright. In other words, although most of the individual elements of the interface were not protectible standing alone, they formed part of a larger arrangement or selection (a "compilation") that was protected expression. But the scope of copyright protection given to such a compilation consisting of largely uncopyrightable elements is very limited. The court held that the interface would only be protected from *virtually identical* copying—that is, copying substantially the entire interface (*Apple Computer v. Microsoft Corp.*, 717

F.Supp. 1428 (N.D. Ca. 1989), 779 F.Supp. 133 (N.D. Ca. 1992), CCH Copyright Law Dec. ¶27,086 (N.D. Ca. 1993)).

The bottom line: No one knows what the bottom line is on copyrightability of user interfaces. However, the clear trend is to limit their protection. But this does not mean you can feel free to copy a competitor's interface wholesale. Verbatim or very close copying of all or a very substantial part of a user interface—the type of copying present in the *LOTUS 1-2-3* case above, for example—would probably be considered copyright infringement by any court.

⚠ Don't overlook other ways to protect user interfaces. Copyright may not be the only means available to protect user interfaces. It may be possible to protect screen icons by obtaining a design patent. (See Chapter 5 for a detailed discussion.)

2. Rule Two: The Scope of Copyright Protection Is Proportional to the Range of Expression Available

We've seen above that copyright *can* protect program code, structure and even user interfaces, albeit to an unclear extent. But whether these elements *will* be protected in any given instance depends on application of our second rule: The scope of copyright protection is proportional to the range of expression available.

As we've already stated, the copyright law only protects original works of authorship. Part of the essence of original authorship is the making of choices. Any work of authorship is the end result of a whole series of choices made by its creator. For example, the author of a novel expressing the idea of love must choose the novel's plot, characters, locale and the actual words used to express the story. The author of such a novel has a nearly limitless array of choices available.

However, the choices available to the creators of many works of author-ship are severely limited. In these cases, the idea or ideas underlying the work, and the way they are expressed by the author, are deemed to "merge." The result is that the author's expression is either treated as if it were in the public domain (given no protection at all) or protected only against virtually verbatim or "slavish" copying. If this were not so, the copyright law would end up discouraging authorship of new works and thereby retard the progress of knowledge.

Example: *A jeweler wanted to create a jewelry pin in the form of a bumblebee. Bumblebees have a particular form, so there aren't many different ways to design such a piece. If another jeweler wanted to create a bumblebee pin, chances are it would look similar to the first jeweler's pin. This actually happened, and the first jeweler sued the second for copyright infringement. The court held there was no infringement because there are only a limited number of ways to design bumblebee pins. The idea of a bumblebee pin and its expression—the actual pin—were deemed to merge. If this were not so, no one other than the first jeweler could ever create a bumblebee pin. To prevent the first jeweler from having a monopoly over bumblebee pins, the court held that his design was not protected by copyright (Herbert Rosenthal Jewelry Corp. v. Kalpakian, 446 F.2d 738 (9th Cir. 1981)).*

The merger doctrine also applies to computer software. The fewer choices a programmer has when setting out to create a given element of a piece of software, the less copyright protection that element will receive. Or, to put it another way: *The scope of copyright protection is proportional to the range of expression available to articulate the underlying ideas communicated by the program.*

In recent years, the courts have been finding that more and more elements of computer programs are not protectible because of the merger doctrine. The seminal court decision of *Computer Associates Int'l. v. Altai, Inc.* identified the following constraints on the range of software expression (this list is not necessarily exclusive):

- elements dictated by efficiency,
- elements dictated by external factors, and

• standard programming techniques and software features
(*Computer Associates Int'l. v. Altai, Inc.,* 982 F.2d 693 (2d Cir. 1992)).

a. Elements Dictated by Efficiency

Programmers usually strive to create programs that meet the user's needs as efficiently as possible. The desire for maximum efficiency may operate to restrict the range of choices available to a programmer. For example, there may only be one or two efficient ways to express the idea embodied in a given program, module, routine or subroutine. If a programmer's choices regarding a particular program's structure, interface or even source code are necessary to efficiently implement the program's function, then those choices will not be protected by copyright. No programmer may have a monopoly on the most efficient way to write any program. Paradoxically, this means that the better job a programmer does—the more closely the program approximates the ideal of efficiency—the less copyright protection the program will receive.

Example 1: *As discussed above, the court in the LOTUS 1-2-3 case concluded that the structure, sequence and organization of 1-2-3's command system was protectible. The court stated that there was no merger problem because a menu command structure is capable of being expressed in many different ways. However, the court also held that 1-2-3's basic spreadsheet screen display resembling a rotated "L" was not protected because there are only a few ways to make a computer screen resemble a spreadsheet; nor was the use of "+," "-," "*" and "/" for their corresponding mathematical functions, or use of the "enter" key to place keystroke entries into cells. The use of such keys was the most efficient means to implement these mathematical functions (Lotus Dev. Corp. v. Paperback Software Int'l., 740 F.Supp. 37 (D. Mass. 1990)).*

Example 2: *Another court held that a cost-estimating program's method of allowing users to navigate within screen displays by using the space bar to move the cursor down a list, the backspace key to move up, the return key to choose a function and a number selection to edit an entry was not protectible. The court* *noted that there were only a limited number of ways to enable a user to navigate through a screen display on the hardware in question while facilitating user comfort. The court also found that the program's use of alphabetical and numerical columns in its screen displays was not protectible. The constraints of uniformity of format and limited page space (requiring either a horizontal or vertical orientation) permitted only a very narrow range of choices (Manufacturers Technologies, Inc. v. Cams, 706 F.Supp. 984 (D. Conn. 1989)).*

b. Elements Dictated by External Factors

A programmer's freedom of design choice is often limited by external factors such as:

- the mechanical specifications of the computer on which the program is intended to run,
- compatibility requirements of other programs with which the program is designed to operate in conjunction,
- computer manufacturers' design standards, and
- the demands of the industry being serviced.

   Example 1: *Intel Corp. charged that NEC Corp. had unlawfully copied the microcode to Intel Corp.'s 8086/88 microprocessor chip to create compatible microprocessor chips of its own. ("Microcode" is a series of instructions that tells a microprocessor chip how to work.) NEC sued Intel to obtain a judicial declaration that it did not infringe on Intel's microcode. The court held that NEC had not committed infringement. Although some of the simpler microroutines in NEC's microcode were substantially similar to Intel's, the court held that machine con-straints were largely responsible for the similarities; that is, NEC's programmers had very limited choices in designing their microcode to operate a chip compatible with Intel's 8086/88. Given these constraints, Intel's microcode was protected only against "virtually identical copying" (NEC Corp. v. Intel Corp., 10 U.S.P.Q.2d 1177 (N.D. Ca. 1989)).*

   Example 2: *A cotton cooperative developed a program for mainframe comput-ers called Telcot that provided users with cotton prices and information, accounting* *services and the ability to consummate cotton sales transactions. Former employee-programmers of the cooperative created a PC version of the cotton exchange program. The two programs were similar in their sequence and organization. The cooperative sued for infringement and lost. The court held that many of the similarities between the two programs were dictated by the externalities of the cotton market. The programs were designed to present the same information as contained in a cotton recap sheet, and there were not many different ways to accomplish this (Plains Cotton Cooperative Assoc. v. Goodpasture Computer Service, Inc., 807 F.2d 1256 (5th Cir. 1987)).*

Example 3: *Q-Co Industries created a program to operate a TelePrompTer—a device that displays the text read by a television announcer or performer while on camera. The program was written in Basic and Atari to run on an Atari 800-XL. Hoffman created a program accomplishing the same purpose, written in another programming language and designed to run on the IBM PC. All four modules of Hoffman's program corresponded closely to four of the 12 modules contained in Q-Co's program. Q-Co sued for copyright infringement. The court held there was no infringement because "the same modules would be an inherent part of any prompting program." In other words, the four modules in question were necessary to operate a TelePrompTer program; any programmer wishing to create a TelePrompTer program would have no choice but to include the four modules (Q-Co Industries, Inc. v. Hoffman, 625 F.Supp. 608 (S.D.N.Y. 1985)).*

c. Standard Programming Techniques and Software Features

Certain programming techniques and software features are so widely used as to be standard in the software industry. To create a competitive program, a software developer may have no choice other than to employ such techniques and features because users expect them. Courts treat such material as being in the public domain—it is free for the taking and cannot be owned by any single software author even though it is included in an otherwise copyrightable work.

Example 1: *The court in the Apple v. Microsoft case (see Section D1c, above) held that these basic elements of the Macintosh user interface were unprotectible because they were common to all graphical user interfaces and were standard in the industry:*

- *overlapping windows to display multiple images on a computer screen,*
- *iconic representations of familiar objects from the office environment, such as file folders, documents and a trash can,*
- *opening and closing of objects in order to retrieve, transfer or store information,*
- *menus used to store information or control computer functions, and*
- *manipulation of icons to convey instructions and to control operation of the computer.*

(See Apple Computer v. Microsoft Corp., 779 F.Supp. 133, 779 (N.D. Ca. 1992)).

Example 2: *The owner of an outlining program called PC-OUTLINE sued the owner of a competing program called GRANDVIEW for copyright infringement. GRANDVIEW had nine pull-down menus functionally similar to those of PC-OUTLINE. Nevertheless, the court held that GRANDVIEW did not infringe on PC-OUTLINE. The court reasoned that use of a pull-down menu was "commonplace" in the software industry. The court declared that a copyright owner cannot claim "copyright protection of an...expression that is, if not standard, then commonplace in the computer software industry" (Brown Bag Software v. Symantec Corp., 960 F.2d 1465 (9th Cir. 1990)).*

3. Works Copyright Never Protects

There are some categories of works that copyright can never protect.

a. Purely Functional Items

Copyright only protects works of authorship. Things that have a purely functional or utilitarian purpose are not considered to be works of authorship and are not copyrightable.

Thus, those elements of a computer program that are purely functional may be denied copyright protection. For example, certain aspects of the Apple Macintosh graphical user interface were found by the court to be purely functional, the same as the dials, knobs and remote control devices of a television or VCR, or the button and clocks of a stove. These functional aspects included the ability to move a window part on and part off the screen and the presence of menu items allowing a user to create a new folder within an existing folder.

b. Words, Names, Titles, Slogans and Other Short Phrases

No matter how highly creative, novel or distinctive they may be, individual words and short phrases are not protected by copyright, and will not be registered by the Copyright Office (37 C.F.R. 202.1(a)). For this reason, the use of words and short phrases in the menus and icons of the Macintosh user interface—"Get Info" and "Trash," for example, were found not to be protectible by copyright.

This words and short phrases rule may be applied to source code, as well as to words. For example, a court has stated that a security code used with the Genesis videogame system was "of such *de minimis* (minimal) length that it is probably unprotected under the words and short phrases doctrine" (*Sega Enterprises, Ltd. v. Accolade, Inc.,* 977 F.2d 1510 (9th Cir. 1993)).

Names (whether of individuals, products or business organizations or groups), titles and slogans are also not copyrightable. These items may, however, be protectible under the trademark laws. (See Chapter 6.) Titles are also protected under state unfair competition laws—that is, you can't use a title similar or identical to one already in use on a product for the purpose of confusing consumers in order to get their business.

c. Blank Forms Designed Solely to Record Information

Blank forms that contain no valuable material and are designed solely to record information are not protected by copyright. This applies to such items as time cards, graph paper, account books, bank checks, scorecards, address books, diaries, report forms and order forms.

This rule may also apply to computer screen templates designed to fit with electronic spreadsheets or database programs. If such templates are designed solely to record information, and convey no valuable material, they probably are not protected.

However, it can be difficult in many cases to determine if a form is designed solely to record information. Even true "blank" forms—that is, forms consisting mainly of blank space to be filled in—may convey valuable information. For example, the columns or headings on a blank form may be interlaced with highly informative verbiage. Moreover, the configuration of columns, headings and lines itself may convey information.

d. Typeface Designs

Copyright protection is currently unavailable for typeface styles or fonts on the grounds that they are purely utilitarian. However, this rule is currently being challenged in court.

Copyright can protect typeface software (computer programs designed to produce fonts), but the end product of such programs—the typeface designs themselves—are not protected under current law.

E. Copyright Infringement

Following is a brief overview of the complex subject of copyright infringement. For a detailed discussion of this subject, refer to Fishman, *Copyright Your Software* (Nolo Press).

If you believe your software has been infringed upon, or are worried about infringing someone else's work, you should seek the advice of an experienced intellectual property attorney. This section should give you an idea of some of the things you need to discuss if you see an attorney.

1. What Is Copyright Infringement?

Copyright infringement occurs when a person other than the copyright owner exploits one or more of the copyright owner's exclusive rights without the owner's permission.

Infringement of software usually involves the unauthorized exercise of a copyright owner's exclusive rights to reproduce and distribute the work or prepare derivative works based on it. In plain English, this means that someone incorporates the protected expression contained in your software into their work without your permission.

Here are some examples of infringement:

Example 1: *A large accounting firm buys one copy of TaxEze, a tax prepara-tion software package, and makes 100 copies for its employees without the copy-right owner's permission. The purchaser of a computer program may legally make only one copy of the program for archival purposes without the copyright owner's permission. (See sidebar below.) Thus, the making of 99 unauthorized copies constitutes infringement on the copyright owner's exclusive right to reproduce and distribute TAXEZE.*

Example 2: *Without authorization, Larry creates a Mac version of a popular PC video game and sells copies by mail order. Larry has infringed on the video game owner's right to create derivative works from its game—that is, the right to create new works based upon or derived from the PC game.*

Example 3: *BigTech, Inc. creates a database program for medical records. In doing so, it obtains a copy of the source code for a pre-existing similar program owned by Medidata, Inc. from a former Medidata employee. BigTech copies* *hundreds of lines of code from Medidata's program. BigTech has infringed Medidata's exclusive right to reproduce (copy) the code in its program.*

SOFTWARE PURCHASERS' LIMITED RIGHT TO MAKE COPIES AND ADAPTATIONS

There is an important exception to the rule that a software copyright owner has the exclusive right to reproduce its work and create adaptations ("derivative works"). A purchaser of a computer program may load the program onto his hard disk, computer RAM or otherwise copy or adapt it to get it to run on his computer. In addition, a person who legally purchases a program may make a single back-up copy for archival purposes, provided that the copy is made and kept only by the person who owns the legally purchased copy (17 U.S.C. 117.)

This limited right to make a back-up or archival copy is not really very generous. Since the copy is for back-up purposes only, it cannot be used on a second computer. This means, for example, that if you own a desktop computer and a laptop, and want to use your word processor on both, legally you must buy two copies—or you just remove the program from one computer and load it onto the other each time you switch computers.

In an effort to make their customers happy, some large software publishers are now including provisions in their license agreements permitting their customers to use a program on two different computers. For example, Microsoft permits purchasers of *Microsoft Word* to use the program on both an office and home computer, as long as one computer is being used the majority of the time.

2. Penalties for Infringing

The Copyright Act doesn't prevent copyright infringement from occurring, just as the laws against auto theft do not prevent cars from being stolen. However, the Copyright Act does give copyright owners a legal remedy to use after an infringement has occurred: they may sue the infringer in federal court.

A copyright owner who wins an "infringement suit" may stop any further infringement, get infringing software destroyed, obtain damages from the infringer—often the amount of any profits obtained from the infringement—and recover other monetary losses. This means, in effect, that a copyright owner can make a copyright infringer restore the author to the same economic position she would have been in had the infringement never occurred. And, in some cases, the copyright owner may even be able to obtain monetary penalties that may far exceed her actual losses. (See Section I2 , below.)

SOFTWARE PUBLISHERS ARE GOING AFTER COPYRIGHT PIRATES

Of course, many companies and individuals make unauthorized copies of the programs they purchase. This practice is copyright infringement. Software publishers, along with their trade organization, the Software Publishers' Association (SPA), are making an active effort to stop unauthorized copying by corporate users. Investigators are actively seeking out companies that routinely make illegal copies, and the SPA maintains a toll-free hotline to which people can report violations (this is often done by disgruntled employees or ex-employees). Once evidence of illegal copying is obtained, the SPA or company whose software has been copied can take the violator to court or even seek to have it criminally prosecuted by the government.

3. Proving Infringement Can Be Difficult

The three examples of copyright infringement in Section E1, above, all involve rather extreme cases of wholesale or extensive unauthorized copying of all or most of a work. These types of copying present very clear cases of copyright infringement. However, extreme cases like these are increasingly rare. Most software infringement involves subtler forms of copying—for example, copying part of a program's structure, elements of its user interface or relatively few lines of code. Proving copyright infringement in cases such as these can be difficult.

Copyright infringement is usually proven by showing that the alleged infringer had access to the copyright owner's work and that the protected expression in the two works is *substantially similar*. What does one compare to see if the two works are similar? The federal appeals court in New York addressed this question in a very important copyright decision that may help set the standard for the entire nation. In *Computer Associates Int'l. v. Altai, Inc.*, 982 F.2d 693 (2nd Cir. 1992), the court held that the person who claims his work was infringed upon (the "plaintiff" in a copyright infringement suit) must subject his work to a rigorous "filtering" process to find out which elements of the work are and are not protected by copyright. In other words, the plaintiff must filter out from his work ideas, elements dictated by efficiency or external factors, or taken from the public domain (see discussion in Section D2, above). After this filtration process is completed, there may or may not be any protectible expression left. If there is, this core of protected expression is compared with the allegedly infringing program of the defendant (which is not subjected to filtration) to see if there has been impermissible copying. The defendants in many, if not most, software copyright infringement actions will doubtlessly claim that any alleged similarities relate only to elements of the plaintiff's program that should be "filtered out" as unprotectible.

The effect of *Computer Associates Int'l. v. Altai, Inc.* is that it may be very difficult indeed for a plaintiff to establish substantial similarity and win an infringement case unless there has been extreme, wholesale copying. Some copyright experts predict that the flood of software copyright cases brought in the 1980s will slow as copyright owners encounter the challenges created by *Computer Associates Int'l. v. Altai, Inc.*

The legal tests for determining whether copyright infringement has occurred are very complex, and we've hardly touched the surface of this topic here. However, what usually happens in infringement cases is that the judge or jury do what they think is fair. In other words, if they think the person or company accused of infringement has done something wrong, they will usually conclude that copyright infringement has occurred. This is illustrated by the fact that no matter what legal rules have been applied, companies that have engaged in wholesale unauthorized copying to create "clone" programs—the type of copying that occurred in the *LOTUS 1-2-3* case discussed in Section D1c, above, for example—have almost always been found to have committed copyright infringement.

WAYS TO HELP PROVE COPYING

Map publishers often include nonexistent streets on their maps (in remote areas). This way, the publisher can prove that copying has occurred; if the nonexistent street appears on someone else's map, they must have copied it. Software authors can do the same thing—that is, include unnecessary codings, unique identifying notations or intentional "errors" in their computer programs. If a competitor's program contains such features, it will be easy to prove that it copied the program.

F.   Defenses to Copyright Infringement Claims

One of the most important events in the continuing evolution of software copyright law occurred in 1992, when a trio of court decisions held that certain defenses long available to defendants accused of infringing on books, music and other traditional works of authorship may be available in the realm of software as well. These decisions have had the effect of weakening copyright protection for software.

1. Fair Use

The fair use privilege is a very significant limitation on all copyright owners' rights. Simply put, the fair use privilege permits a person to make limited use of a copyright owner's work without asking the owner's permission. Before we see how the fair use privilege might apply to software, let's examine the basics of fair use law.

a. Fair Use Factors

In deciding whether an unauthorized use of a copyrighted work constitutes a fair use, courts primarily consider the following four factors:

- the purpose and character of the use, including whether such use is of a commercial nature or is for nonprofit educational purposes,
- the nature of the copyrighted work,
- the amount and substantiality of the portion used in relation to the copyrighted work as a whole, and
- the effect of the use upon the potential market for or value of the copyrighted work.

b. Typical Fair Uses

The following types of uses are generally considered to be fair uses:

- *Criticism and comment*—for example, quoting or excerpting a work in a review or criticism for purposes of illustration or comment.
- *News reporting*—for example, summarizing an address or article, with *brief* quotations, in a news report.
- *Research and scholarship*—for example, quoting a short passage in a scholarly, scientific or technical work for illustration or clarification of the author's observations.
- *Nonprofit educational uses*—for example, photocopying by teachers for classroom use.

c. Commercial Uses Are Less Likely to Be Fair Uses

Note that the uses listed above, with the possible exception of news reporting, are primarily for nonprofit educational purposes. The fact that a work is created primarily for private commercial gain weighs against a finding of fair use. This would seem to mean, at first glance, that the fair use has relatively little application to the commercial software industry, where new programs are created primarily for financial gain. However, as we'll see below, this is not entirely true.

2. Reverse Engineering as a Fair Use

"Reverse engineering" is the process of taking a product or device apart and reducing it to its constituent parts or concepts to see how it works. Reverse engineering has long been used by manufacturers of all types of products to help them create new products. Reverse engineering is perfectly legal so long as it doesn't violate another's patent or copyright rights.

Computer hardware may be reverse engineered by unscrewing the box and looking inside. The best way to reverse engineer a computer program is usually to read the source code. To prevent competitors from reading their valuable source code, software owners normally distribute their programs in object code form only while the source code is kept locked away. However, it is possible, though often difficult, to reverse engineer object code by translating it into human-readable assembly language, which programmers then read to understand the object code. This process is called "decompilation" or "disassembly."

The information gained by reverse engineering can be put to a variety of uses, each with a different economic effect on the owner of the original program. For example, the information can be used to develop a competitive product. In other cases, decompilation can be used to create a "clone" program that is functionally compatible. Decompilation can be used to help develop a program that is not competitive, but "complementary" to the original program—for example, creating a videogame cartridge to run on a videogame system like Nintendo or Genesis.

a. Is Decompilation Copyright Infringement?

Decompilation and disassembly involve the making of at least a partial reproduction or derivative work of the object code. Typically, a copy of the original program is made on a disk, and decompiler software is used to load the program into computer memory. The copy is then transformed into human-readable form, which is then fixed on disk and/or paper.

Of course, we know that both source and object code may be protected by copyright, and that a copyright owner has the exclusive right to copy and create derivative works from his protected material. Does this mean that decompilation and disassembly constitute copyright infringement? These issues are decided on a case-by-case basis. In 1992, two courts apparently gave the green light to decompilation and disassembly, at least under certain circumstances.

The most important of these cases involved Sega Enterprises, manufacturer of the Genesis videogame system (*Sega Enterprises, Ltd. v. Accolade, Inc.,* 977 F.2d 1510 (9th Cir. 1992)). Accolade, Inc. wanted to manufacture a videogame cartridge to be used with the Genesis system. Rather than pay Sega for a license to do so, Accolade reverse-engineered the Genesis system. It disassembled the object code stored in commercially available ROM (read-only memory) chips in Sega's games to learn the requirements for creation of a Genesis-compatible game cartridge. This process required that Accolade make unauthorized copies of Sega's code for study and analysis (called "intermediate copies"). Sega sued Accolade for copyright infringement, claiming that Accolade's copying violated its copyright. Sega lost.

The federal appeals court held that disassembly of object code is a fair use if:

- it is the *only* means (other than getting permission from the copyright owner) available to obtain access to the unprotected elements of a

computer program—ideas, functional principles and so forth (see
Section D, above), and

- the copier has a legitimate reason for seeking such access.

In applying the fair use factors discussed above, the court found "the
purpose and character of the use" to be noncommercial, despite the fact that
the copying was being done to create competing game cartridges. The court
reasoned that the interim copies were not themselves sold. The court also
said that the copying would not harm the market for Sega's videogames
because consumers "might easily" purchase both Sega-made and Accolade-
made game cartridges. The court also stressed that if disassembly like
Accolade's were prohibited, Sega would, in effect, enjoy a monopoly over the
unprotected ideas and functional principles contained in its code, since the
only way to obtain access to those ideas was through disassembly.

b. Limitations on Decompilation as a Fair Use

The *Sega* case did not create a blanket rule permitting all decompilation.
Rather it demonstrated that decompilation may be a permissible fair use
when necessary to develop compatible or complementary programs that do
not cause the copyright owner economic harm. If a copyright owner can
establish that decompilation of its object code has caused or will cause it
economic harm, a court should conclude that the decompilation was not a
fair use.

Furthermore, decompilation can be a fair use only when it is the *only*
available means to study the unprotected elements of a program (other than
asking the copyright owner for permission). Often, there are means available
other than decompilation to study such elements—simply studying the
screen display will reveal the ideas and concepts of many programs. The *Sega*
court stated that the need for disassembly "arises, if at all, only in connection
with operations systems, system interface procedures, and other programs
that are not visible to the user when operating" (*Sega Enterprises, Ltd. v.
Accolade, Inc.,* 977 F.2d 1510 (9th Cir. 1992)).

The fair use factors discussed above are subject to varying interpretations, and it is often difficult to predict the outcome of any particular case. This fact is illustrated by another court decision on fair use, involving decompilation of security system source code for the Nintendo videogame system by Atari Games. The court reached the same legal conclusion as the *Sega* decision—decompilation can be a fair use in the proper circumstances. But the court held that Atari's decompilation was not a fair use because Atari obtained the Nintendo source code from the Copyright Offices under false pretenses. Atari's bad faith and lack of fair dealing obviated a finding of fair use (*Atari Games Corp. v. Nintendo Of America, Inc.*, 980 F.2d 857 (Fed. Cir. 1992)).

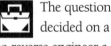 The question of whether a use qualifies as a fair use must always be decided on a case-by-case basis. For these reasons, anyone wishing to reverse engineer a program to create a new product should first consult with a qualified intellectual property attorney.

3. Independent Creation Defense

We discussed above that so long as a program or other work is independently created, it is entitled to copyright protection even if other similar works already exist. This means that if a programmer can prove she independently created a program, she cannot be guilty of infringing on a pre-existing program, even if it is very similar to the pre-existing program.

Of course, proving that a program was independently created can be difficult. The creators of the program must be able to show they did not have access to the pre-existing program; or, even if they could have had access to it, they never saw it. One approach taken by some software developers who wish to create programs similar to and/or compatible with pre-existing software is the use of "clean room" procedures to establish independent creation. "Clean room" procedures are used to isolate the people who actually develop the software. In some cases, such developers are denied access to any information about the pre-existing software. In other cases, they may be given only information about the pre-existing program's purpose or functions.

The important decision of *Computer Associates Int'l. v. Altai Inc.*, discussed in Section E3, above, shows that clean room procedures can really work and serve as a good defense to copyright infringement claims. Here's what happened in that case: Altai hired a programmer formerly employed by Computer Associates Int'l. (CAI) to create a job scheduling program. Unbeknownst to Altai, the programmer used substantial chunks of CAI code to create Altai's software. When Altai learned what happened, it decided to create a "clean" version of its scheduling program. Altai hired eight new programmers to create the new version. They were denied access to the infringing version of the software and forbidden to talk to the programmer who created that version. The new programmers were only provided with a specification developed from an earlier noninfringing version of the software. It took about six months to create the new program. It accomplished everything the prior version did, but used none of CAI's code. Altai was sued for copyright infringement by CAI, but the court held that this version of the program did not infringe on CAI's copyright.

For clean room procedures to be effective, great care must be taken not to give the clean room personnel information protected by copyright. For example, an overly specific description for a user interface might contain protected expression which, if used, could "taint" the clean room.

 Before implementing a clean room procedure of your own, you should consult with a knowledgeable intellectual property attorney.

G. Copyright Ownership

The basics of copyright ownership are discussed in this section. For a detailed analysis of the ownership issues involved when software is created by employees or independent contractors, see Chapter 8.

1. Initial Copyright Ownership

A computer program or other work that satisfies the three criteria for copyright protection discussed in Section C, above (fixation, originality and minimal creativity) is protected automatically upon creation. At that same moment, the author or authors of the work become the initial owner(s) of the copyright in the work.

There are several basic ways to author a work and thereby become its initial copyright owner:

- An individual may independently author the work.
- An employer may pay an employee to author the work, in which case the employer is the author under the work made for hire rule. (See Section G1b, below.)
- A person or business entity may specially commission an independent contractor to author the work under a written work made for hire contract, in which case the commissioning party becomes the author.
- Two or more individuals or entities may collaborate to become joint authors.

a. Independent Authorship by an Individual

The individual author of a work is the initial owner of its copyright when the work made for hire doctrine doesn't apply (see Section G1b, below) and when there is no joint authorship (see Section G1c, below). The individual may exercise any of her copyright rights herself. For example, she may reproduce and sell the work herself, or authorize others to do so—that is, license a publisher. She may also transfer her ownership in whole or in part to others. (See Section G2, below.) An individual copyright owner may do whatever she wants with her copyright in the United States; she is accountable to no one.

IMPACT OF COMMUNITY PROPERTY LAWS ON COPYRIGHT OWNERSHIP

In states that have community property laws, property that is acquired while people are married is usually considered to belong to both spouses equally. This means that individual software authors who reside in Arizona, California, Idaho, Louisiana, Nevada, New Mexico, Texas, Washington and Wisconsin may be required to share ownership of their copyrights with their spouses.

b. Works Made for Hire

Not all works are initially owned by the person or persons who actually create them. If you create a program or other protectible work on someone else's behalf, that person (or entity) may be considered the work's author and thereby initially own the copyright in the work, not you. These types of works are called "works made for hire." There are two different types of works made for hire:

- works prepared by employees within the scope of their employment, and
- certain works prepared by non-employees that are specially ordered or commissioned where the parties both agree in writing that the work shall be considered a work made for hire.

The owner of a work made for hire is considered to be the "author" of the work whether the owner is a human being or a business entity such as a corporation or partnership. As the author, the owner is entitled to register the work with the Copyright Office, to exercise its copyright rights in the work (such as marketing the work), to permit others to exercise these rights and to sell all or part of its rights. The actual creator of a work made for hire has no copyright rights in the work. All he receives is whatever compensation the hiring party gives him, whether a salary or other payment. (We discuss works made for hire in greater detail in Chapter 8.)

c. Jointly Authored Works

When two or more individuals collaborate to create a work that is not a work made for hire, the work is normally jointly owned by its creators—that is, each contributing author shares in the ownership of the entire work. A work is jointly authored automatically upon its creation if:

- two or more authors contributed protectible material to the work, and
- each of the authors prepared his or her contribution with the *intention* that it would be combined with the contributions of the other authors as part of a single unitary work.

We'll refer to such works as "joint works."

Example: *Adam and Dave decide to create a new database program. Adam designs the structure, logic and flow of the program and Dave does the actual coding. The resulting program is a joint work by Adam and Dave.*

The respective contributions made to a joint work by its authors need not be equal in terms of quantity or quality. But, to be considered a joint author, a person must contribute more than a minimal amount of work to the finished product. For example, a person who merely beta tests a program created by others is not a joint author of that program. In addition, a joint author must contribute protectible expression, not just ideas.

Unless they agree otherwise, joint authors each have an undivided interest in the entire work. This is basically the same as joint ownership of a house or other real estate. When a husband and wife jointly own their home, they normally each own a 50% interest in the entire house—that is, they each have an undivided one-half interest. Similarly, joint authors share ownership of all the exclusive rights that make up the joint work's copyright. For example, they may each reproduce and market the work or permit others to do so; but they also each have a duty to account for any profits and share them with the other joint authors in accordance with their ownership interests or other agreed formula. (For a detailed discussion of joint author-ship, see *The Copyright Handbook*, by Stephen Fishman (Nolo Press), Chapter 8.)

2. Transfer of Copyright Ownership

An author of a computer program or other protectible work automatically becomes the owner of a complete set of exclusive rights in any protected expression he or she creates. These include the right to:

- reproduce the protected expression,
- distribute copies of the work to the public by sale, rental, lease or otherwise,
- prepare "derivative works" using the protected expression (that is, adapt new works from the expression), and
- perform and display the work publicly.

These rights are "exclusive" because only the owner of one or more particular rights that together make up copyright ownership may exercise it or permit others to do so. For example, only the owner of the right to distribute a program may sell it to the public or permit others to do so.

Original copyright owners seldom hang on to all their copyright rights. Rather, all or part of the copyright ends up in the hands of different people and business entities.

A transfer of copyright ownership rights must be in writing to be valid. There are two basic types of copyright transfers:

- exclusive licenses, and
- assignments.

Although these terms are often used interchangeably, there are some differences.

SALES OF COPIES DO NOT TRANSFER COPYRIGHT OWNERSHIP

Ownership of a copyright and ownership of a material object in which the copyrighted work is embodied, such as a floppy disk or hard copy print-out, are entirely separate things. The sale or gift of a floppy disk or other media containing a computer program does not transfer the copyright owners' exclusive copyright rights in the program. A copyright owner's exclusive rights can only be transferred by a written agreement. For example, a person who buys a software package in a computer store owns the physical material in the package—the floppy disks containing the program and the manuals—but acquires no copyright rights in the software itself.

---

a. Exclusive Licenses

The term "exclusive license" is usually used when a copyright owner transfers one or more of her rights, but retains at least some of them. The transfer of rights via an exclusive license must be in writing to be valid.

The holder of an exclusive license becomes the owner of the transferred right(s). As such, unless the exclusive license provides otherwise, the license holder is entitled to sue anyone who infringes on that right while she owns it, and is entitled to transfer her license to others. She may also record (file) the exclusive license with the Copyright Office, which provides many valuable benefits. (For a detailed discussion, see *The Copyright Handbook*, by Stephen Fishman (Nolo Press), Chapter 9.)

Example: *Cathy develops a new electronic spreadsheet called CathyCalc and gives Mammoth Software Co. an exclusive license to market the program in the*

United States. She retains all her other copyright rights. As Cathy's exclusive licensee, only Mammoth has the right to market Cathy's program in the United States and may sue anyone else who does so without its permission, including Cathy.

A copyright owner's exclusive rights can be divided and subdivided and transferred to others in just about any method imaginable: by geographical area, computer language, operating systems, hardware, time or virtually any other way.

Example: *StickySoftware, a small start-up software developer, develops a new program and gives Behemoth Distribution, Inc., a software distribution company, an exclusive license to distribute the program for use on PCs in the United States. StickySoftware gives CDS, Inc., another distributor, the right to bundle the program with personal computers in Europe. (This type of exclusive license is called an "exclusive territorial license.") StickySoftware also grants an exclusive license to DigiTek Co., a mainframe computer manufacturer, to bundle the program with its mainframes.*

b. Assignments ("All Rights Transfers")

If an owner of all the exclusive rights in a copyright transfers the entire bundle of rights that make up his copyright simultaneously to a single person or entity, the transaction is usually called an "assignment" or sometimes an "all rights transfer." An assignment must be in writing to be valid.

Example: *Assume that Cathy in the example above grants Mammoth Software Co. all her copyright rights in CathyCalc, including the right to sell it anywhere in the world and create new versions. This is an assignment of the entire bundle of copyright rights originally owned by Cathy. For all practical purposes, Mammoth now owns the copyright in CathyCalc, not Cathy.*

RIGHT TO TERMINATE COPYRIGHT TRANSFERS AFTER 35 YEARS

We've all heard sad stories about authors or artists who sold their work for a pittance when they were young and unknown, only to have it become extremely valuable later in their lives or after their death. In an effort to protect copyright owners and their families from unfair exploitation, the Copyright Act gives individual authors or their heirs the right to terminate any transfer of their copyright rights 35 to 40 years after it was made. This special statutory termination right may be exercised only by individual authors or their heirs and only as to transfers made after 1977. This right can never be waived or contracted away by an author. The owner of a work made for hire, whether an individual or a business entity, such as a corporation, has no statutory termination rights.

Example: Art, a teenage videogame enthusiast, creates a new and exciting computer arcade game. He sells all this rights in the game to Fun & Gameware, for $500 in 1980. The game becomes a best seller and earns Fun & Gameware millions. Art is entitled to none of these monies, but he or his heirs can terminate the transfer to Fun & Gameware in 2015 and get back all rights in the game without paying Fun & Gameware anything.

This statutory termination right may be important to visual artists (painters and sculptors, for example), but, the fanciful example above aside, it probably doesn't mean much in the software world. Given the pace of development in the software industry, it is likely that little or no software will have any economic value 35 years after its creation.

c. Nonexclusive Licenses

A nonexclusive license gives someone the right to exercise one or more of a copyright owner's rights, but does not prevent the copyright owner from giving others permission to exercise the same right or rights at the same time. A nonexclusive license is not a transfer of ownership; it's a form of sharing. As with exclusive licenses, nonexclusive licenses may be limited as to time, geography or in any other way. For example, a copyright owner may grant a non-exclusive license to use a program on one particular microcomputer in one country for a set period of time.

Nonexclusive licenses can be granted orally or in writing. The much better practice is to use some sort of writing; this avoids possible misunderstandings as to the scope of the license.

Example: *Assume that instead of transferring her rights in CathyCalc, Cathy gives nonexclusive licenses to 10 different accounting firms permitting them to use the program for a fee. This means that all 10 firms may use their copy of CathyCalc simultaneously subject to any restrictions Cathy writes into the agreement.*

REGISTER COPYRIGHT AND RECORD TRANSFER AGREEMENT WITH THE COPYRIGHT OFFICE

Any document effecting a transfer of copyright rights should be recorded with the Copyright Office. Recording simply involves sending a copy of the agreement to the Copyright Office and paying a fee. The agreement is then filed and becomes a public record. By recording the agreement, the copyright owner is protected if the other party attempts to re-sell or license the software to someone else, even though it doesn't own it.

Example: The Apollo Moving Co. hires MoveWare, a small software developer, to develop custom scheduling program for its fleet of moving vans. MoveWare does so and transfers all its rights in the program to Apollo. Apollo registers the copyright and records its agreement with MoveWare with the Copyright Office. A few months later, MoveWare "sells" the program to the Vulcan Moving Company, even though it doesn't own it. Since Apollo registered its copyright in the software and recorded its agreement with MoveWare, it is clearly entitled to legal priority over the later purported transfer by MoveWare. In other words, Apollo is considered the owner of the program, not Vulcan. Had Apollo not registered its copyright and recorded the agreement, Vulcan would have been considered the software's rightful owner if it had recorded its transfer agreement with MoveWare and been unaware of MoveWare's prior relationship with Apollo.

For a detailed discussion of recording copyright transfers, see *Copyright Your Software,* by Stephen Fishman (Nolo Press), Chapter 10.

H. Copyright Duration

One of the advantages of copyright protection is that it lasts a very long time—far longer than will ever be needed by the vast majority of software copyright owners. The copyright in a program or other protectible work created after 1977 by an individual creator lasts for the life of the creator plus an additional 50 years. If there is more than one creator, the life plus 50 term is measured from the date the last creator dies.

The copyright in works created by employees for their employers (probably the majority of software) lasts for 75 years from the date of publication, or 100 years from the date of creation, whichever occurs first. This term also applies to works created by individuals who are not employees, but choose to remain anonymous or use a pseudonym (pen name) when they publish their work.

It has been said that computer years are like dog years, except that you multiply by 50 instead of seven. If that's true, no owner of a software copyright ever need worry about the copyright expiring.

I. Formalities for Obtaining Maximum Copyright Protection

There are certain simple technical formalities that must be attended to obtain maximum copyright protection.

1. Copyright Notice

Before 1989, all published works had to contain a copyright notice (the "©" symbol followed by the publication date and copyright owner's name) to be protected by copyright. This is no longer necessary; use of copyright notices is now optional in the United States. Even so, it is always a good idea to include a copyright notice on all works distributed to the public so that potential infringers will be informed of the underlying claim to copyright ownership. Besides deterring potential infringers, inclusion of a copyright notice makes it impossible for an infringer to claim she didn't know the software was copyrighted, which may enable the copyright owner to obtain greater damages if a copyright infringement suit is brought. In addition, copyright protection is not available in some 20 foreign countries unless a work contains a copyright notice.

It has never been necessary to include a copyright notice on unpublished works—unpublished works have always been protected by copyright whether or not they contain a copyright notice. A work is "published" for copyright purposes when copies are sold, rented, lent, given away or otherwise distributed to the public on an unrestricted basis. Software that is distributed to the public without a signed license agreement is normally considered "published." Software that is under development or licensed to a limited number of users under a signed license agreement is usually considered "unpublished." However, since unpublished copies of your work may receive limited distribution—to beta testers for example—it is a good idea to include a notice on them as well.

Following are the basics you need to know about copyright notices. (If you have additional questions, see *Copyright Your Software*, by Stephen Fishman (Nolo Press), Chapter 3, for a far more detailed discussion.)

a. Form of Notice for Published Works

There are strict technical requirements as to what a copyright notice must contain. Follow these rules exactly or your notice may be found to be invalid and may not accomplish its intended purpose.

A valid copyright notice must contain three elements:

- *The copyright symbol.* You should use the familiar "©" symbol—that is, the lower-case letter "c" completely surrounded by a circle. The word "Copyright" or the abbreviation "Copr." are also acceptable in the United States, but not in many foreign countries. So if your work might be distributed outside the U.S., be sure to always use the "©" symbol.

Often, you'll see the word "Copyright" or the abbreviation "Copr." followed by—or preceding—the © symbol—for instance, "Copyright ©." Technically, this is not required—the "©" symbol alone is sufficient. However, it is a good idea to include the words anyway because they will further clarify that the work is protected by copyright.

- *The year in which the work was published.* You only need to include the year the work was *first* published. However, if the work is substantially revised after its original publication, it is common practice to include additional dates as well.

- *The name of the copyright owner.* Briefly, the "owner" is: 1) the author or authors of the work, 2) the legal owner of a work made for hire, or 3) the person or entity (partnership or corporation) to whom *all* the author's exclusive copyright rights have been transferred. If there are multiple owners, they should all be listed in the copyright notice. The owners' names may appear in any order.

Although the three elements of a copyright notice need not appear in a particular order, it is common to list the copyright symbol, followed by the date and owners.

Example: *A computer program owned by AcmeSoft, Inc. and published in 1994 should contain a copyright notice like this: Copyright © 1994 AcmeSoft, Inc.*

b.   Form of Notice for Unpublished Works

If a program is unpublished, you can't include a publication date in the copyright notice. Instead, the notice should indicate the work's unpublished status. A copyright notice for an unpublished work should be in one of the following forms:

- *Copyright © John Smith (this work is unpublished),* or
- *Copyright © John Smith (work in progress).*

In addition to a copyright notice, be sure to include a trade secret notice on your unpublished work. Here's an example: "THIS IS AN UNPUBLISHED WORK CONTAINING JOHN SMITH'S CONFIDENTIAL AND PROPRIETARY INFORMATION. DISCLOSURE, USE OR REPRODUCTION WITHOUT WRITTEN AUTHORIZATION OF JOHN SMITH IS PROHIBITED."

c. Where to Place the Notice

According to Copyright Office regulations, the copyright notice must be placed so as not to be concealed from an ordinary user's view upon reasonable examination. This can be accomplished in any one of several ways:

- by printing the notice in or near the title of the program or at the end of the program,
- by displaying the notice when the program is first activated (on the opening screen or in an "about" or credit box),
- by displaying the notice continuously while the program is being used, or
- by placing the notice durably on a label affixed to the diskette, box, cartridge or container in which the program is distributed (37 C.F.R. 201.20(g)).

A proper copyright notice should also be included on all manuals and promotional materials. Notices on written works are usually placed on the title page or the page immediately following the title page.

Display your copyright notice often and obviously. A good rule is to display it on the screen at the beginning and end of a program, as well as every time the program title is displayed. In addition, it should be prominently included on any packaging.

2. Registration

Copyright registration is a legal formality by which a copyright owner makes a public record in the U.S. Copyright Office in Washington, D.C. of some basic information about a protected work, such as the title of the work, who wrote it and when, and who owns the copyright. When people speak of "copyrighting" a work, they usually mean registering it with the Copyright Office. Following is a brief overview of registration; for detailed step-by-step instructions and all the necessary forms, refer to Fishman, *Copyright Your Software* (Nolo Press).

Contrary to what many people think, it is not necessary to register to create or establish a copyright. As mentioned earlier in this chapter, copyright protection begins automatically the moment an original work of authorship is fixed in a tangible medium of expression. However, registration is required before a copyright owner may file a lawsuit to enforce her rights. In addition, timely registration in the U.S. Copyright Office makes a copyright a matter of public record and provides three very important advantages if it is ever necessary to go to court to enforce it:

- *Benefit 1.* The copyright owner may obtain attorney fees if he successfully sues someone for infringing his work. However, the work must be registered before the infringement occurred or within three months of publication.

- *Benefit 2.* The owner may elect to receive special statutory damages up to $100,000 from an infringer. However, the work must be registered before the infringement occurred or within three months of publication.

- *Benefit 3.* So long as the work is registered within five years of the date of first publication, it is presumed to be protected by a valid copyright, and the people and/or entities named in the certificate of copyright registration issued by the Copyright Office are presumed to be the copyright owners.

IMPORTANT CHANGES TO COPYRIGHT LAWS ARE PENDING

As this book went to press, important copyright legislation was pending in Congress that would eliminate the need to register to obtain statutory damages and attorney fees. Even if this legislation is enacted into law, registration will still be worthwhile to establish the validity of the copyright and ownership. This is the greatest benefit of registration. It means that the alleged infringer has the burden of proving your program is not protected by copyright or you are not the lawful owner. This presumption also helps a copyright owner obtain a quick injunction against an alleged infringer.

If the proposed legislation is enacted, the main effect will be to eliminate the need to rush the registration process. Instead of having to register within three months of publication, copyright owners will be able to wait as long as five years after publication or until an infringement occurs.

a. Registration Procedure

Copyright registration is a relatively easy process. You must fill out the appropriate pre-printed application form (usually Form TX is used for software), pay an application fee (usually $20), and mail the application and fee to the Copyright Office in Washington D.C. along with one or two copies of the work being registered (called the "deposit").

The deposit requirement can be a problem. The deposit and application form become a public record, available for inspection at the Copyright Office by anyone—including your competitors. To avoid this, the Copyright Office has adopted special rules for registration of source code designed to preserve its trade secret status. Instead of submitting all of your code, you may deposit the first and last 25 pages with trade secrets blacked out or even deposit object code instead. For a detailed discussion, refer to Fishman, *Copyright Your Software* (Nolo Press).■

C H A P T E R   4

Trade Secret Protection

This chapter is divided into two parts. Part I (Sections A through E) provides an overview of the law of trade secrets. Part II (Sections F through H) then discusses in detail the practical steps a software company should take to identify and protect its trade secrets.

If you want to immediately implement a trade secret program for your company, you can go straight to Part II. You may, however, want to refer back to Part I for an explanation of the legal concepts underlying any protection program. You'll also need to refer to Chapters 9 and 10 for sample trade secret agreements for use with employees and independent contractors.

PART I. INTRODUCTION TO TRADE SECRET LAW

Trade secrecy is basically a do-it-yourself form of intellectual property protection. It is based on this simple idea: By keeping valuable information secret, one can prevent competitors from learning about and using it. Trade secrecy is by far the oldest form of intellectual property, dating back at least to ancient Rome. It is as useful now as it was then. Trade secrecy should be an integral part of any software developer's intellectual property protection program.

A. What Is a Trade Secret?

A trade secret is any formula, pattern, physical device, idea, process, compilation of information or other information that 1) is not generally known by a company's (or individual's) competitors, 2) provides a business with a *competitive advantage*, and 3) is treated in a way that can reasonably be expected to prevent the public or competitors from learning about it, absent improper acquisition or theft.

Trade secrecy may be used to:

- protect ideas that offer a business a competitive advantage, thereby enabling a software developer to get a head start on the competition,
- keep competitors from knowing that a program is under development and from learning its functional attributes,
- protect source code, software development tools, design definitions and specifications, manuals and other documentation, flow diagrams and flow charts, data structures, data compilations, formulas and algorithms embodied in software, and
- protect valuable business information such as marketing plans, cost and price information and customer lists.

Unlike copyrights and patents, whose existence is provided and governed by federal law that applies in all 50 states, trade secrecy is not codified in any federal statute. Instead, it is made up of individual state laws. Nevertheless, the protection afforded to trade secrets is much the same in every state. This is partly because some 26 states have based their trade secrecy laws on the Uniform Trade Secrecy Act (UTSA), a model trade secrecy law designed by legal scholars. (For a text of the UTSA and a list of those states adopting it, refer to volume 14 of the *Uniform Laws Annotated* published by West Publishing Co.)

TRADE SECRETS COMPARED WITH COPYRIGHT PROTECTION

If you've read Chapter 3 on copyright protection for software, you know that it can be very difficult to tell what elements of a program are and are not protected by copyright. This is because copyright only protects a programmer's expression of the ideas embodied in a program, not the ideas themselves. Copyright does not protect ideas, systems, facts, methods, discoveries or algorithms. There are no such limitations on trade secrets. That is, an idea *can* be a protected trade secret. When dealing with trade secrecy, there is no need to make the often Jesuitical distinctions between idea and expression that courts make in the copyright realm. Moreover, copyright only protects works that are fixed in a tangible medium of expression (written down, saved on disk, etc.). A trade secret need not be written down or otherwise fixed.

Stated simply, trade secrecy can protect everything copyright can protect *and* everything copyright cannot protect (provided the requirements discussed in this section are satisfied).

1. No Protection for Generally Known Information

Information that is public knowledge or generally known in the software industry cannot be a trade secret. Things that everybody knows cannot provide anyone with a competitive advantage. However, information comprising a trade secret need not be novel or unique. All that is required is that the information not be generally known by people who could profit from its disclosure and use.

Most software qualifies as a trade secret. Computer programs usually contain at least some elements or combination of elements that are different from other programs and are not generally known in the software industry. Thus, for example, trade secret protection has been extended to accounts receivable programs, database management software, time-sharing systems and communications programs, even though similar software already existed.

2.   Ownership of Trade Secrets

Only the person or entity that owns a trade secret has the right to seek relief in court if someone else improperly acquires or discloses the trade secret. Also, only the trade secret owner may grant others a license to use the secret.

As a general rule, any trade secrets developed by an employee in the course of employment belongs to the employer. However, trade secrets developed by an employee on her own time and with her own equipment can sometimes belong to the employee. To avoid possible disputes, it is very good idea for employers to have all employees who may develop new technology sign an employment agreement. The agreement should assign in advance all trade secrets developed by the employee during her employment. Courts generally will enforce such agreements. (See Chapter 9 for a detailed discussion.)

3.   Multiple Trade Secrets for the Same Information

Because trade secrets are by definition kept secret, a software developer cannot know what trade secrets are already possessed by others. The result is that, without even knowing it, a software developer may create trade secrets identical to trade secrets currently possessed by others. This has no effect on trade secret protection. So long as a trade secret provides its owner with a competitive advantage, it can be identical to other existing trade secrets if it was independently conceived and not generally known by others in the relevant industry.

Example: *SoftWays devises a new method of coordinate tracking for a graphics program it's developing. Unbeknownst to SoftWays, DataTek, Inc., has already devised the same method for its own graphics program, and has kept it secret. Both SoftWays and DataTek are entitled to trade secret protection for their coordinate tracking techniques, so long as they are not generally known in the software industry.*

4. Reasonable Secrecy Must Be Maintained

Software or other information qualifies as a trade secret only if precautions are taken to keep it secret. Absolute secrecy is not required—it is not necessary to turn your office into an armed camp. A trade secret owner's secrecy precautions need only be *reasonable under the circumstances*. What precautions are "reasonable" will vary from case to case, depending on the size of the company, the nature and value of the information and other factors. After reading this material, you should have a pretty good idea of how to judge what is reasonable secrecy under your particular circumstances. (We discuss the details of setting up trade secrecy programs in Part II of this chapter.)

5. How Trade Secrets Are Lost

A trade secret is lost if either of these conditions is met:
* the product in which it is embodied is made widely available to the public through sales and displays on an *unrestricted* basis, or
* the secret can be discovered by reverse engineering (see Section D1, below) or inspection.

   This means that trade secrecy will be lost if a program's source code is made available to the public on an unrestricted basis through such means as a Copyright Office deposit, listing in a computer magazine, or distribution on a floppy disk or other medium. For this reason software is normally distributed only in object code form, which is difficult to reverse engineer. All object code can be reverse engineered, but because of the difficulty, the code can still qualify as a trade secret unless it actually is reverse engineered. It is also the reason why limited distribution software is normally licensed rather than sold outright—that is, purchasers and other end users are required to sign license agreements in which they promise not to use or disclose the trade secrets embodied in the program without permission. Publishers of mass-marketed software often attempt to impose the same restrictions on consumers by including "shrink-wrap licenses" with their products, but the effectiveness of such licenses is very much in doubt. (See Section B1c, below.)

6. Duration of Trade Secrets

Trade secrets have no definite term. A trade secret continues to exist as long as the requirements for trade secret protection remain in effect. In other words, as long as secrecy is maintained, the secret does not become generally known in the industry and the secret continues to provide a competitive advantage, it will be protected. Some trade secrets have lasted for a very long time indeed. For example, the formula for Coca-Cola has been maintained as a trade secret by the Coca-Cola Company for over 100 years.

B. Trade Secret Owner's Rights

A trade secret owner has the legal right to prevent the following two groups of people from using and benefiting from its trade secrets or disclosing them to others without the owner's permission:

- people who are bound by a *duty of confidentiality* not to disclose or use the information, and
- people who steal or otherwise acquire the trade secret through improper means.

For example, if an a software developer's employee signs an agreement establishing a duty of confidentiality (see below) but later discloses the developer's trade secrets to a competitor without the developer's permission, the developer will be able to sue both the employee and competitor for damages. In addition, the developer may be entitled to obtain a court order preventing the competitor from using the information. The developer would have the same rights against an industrial spy and her employer.

But note carefully that a trade secret owner's rights are limited to the two restricted groups of people described above. In this respect, a trade secret owner's rights are much more limited than those of a copyright owner or patent holder. The owner of a copyright or patent receives a set of exclusive rights that everyone in the United States is legally bound to respect.

1. Duty of Confidentiality

Persons who learn about a trade secret through a confidential relationship with its owner may not use or disclose the trade secret without permission. A duty of confidentiality may be deemed by the courts to arise automatically (is "implied in law") from certain types of relationships, including those between employers and employees who routinely receive trade secrets as part of their jobs. (See the sidebar below.) But by far the best way for a trade secret owner to establish a duty of confidentiality is to have each person to whom he discloses trade secrets agree in writing to preserve their confidentiality. This type of agreement is called a "confidentiality agreement" or nondisclosure agreement.

a. Employees

The cornerstone of any trade secret protection program is to have all employees who are exposed to trade secrets read and sign nondisclosure agreements. Such an agreement should require the employee to treat as confidential any trade secrets he or she learns in the course of employment. If the employer later tries to prevent the employee from using information considered to be a trade secret, the existence of a signed nondisclosure agreement will establish that the employee knew that he owed a duty of confidentiality toward his employer.

Many courts consider the use of employee nondisclosure agreements the single most important reasonable precaution an employer can take to establish and maintain the secrecy of confidential information. In other words, confidential information may not be deemed to be a trade secret where an employer does not use such written agreements. (Nondisclosure agreements are discussed in detail in Section G4, below.)

However, there are limitations on the effectiveness of nondisclosure agreements with employees. In particular, the general knowledge, skills and experience an employee acquires during her term of employment are *not* trade secrets and therefore are not covered by a nondisclosure agreement.

Difficult and costly disputes can develop as to whether information constitutes a trade secret or merely an employee's general knowledge. For this
reason, some employers utilize noncompetition agreements with their
employees in addition to nondisclosure agreements. (See the discussion in
Section G4a, below.) Some employees also use other methods to help ensure
their employees' loyalty, such as stock-options or other benefits that fully vest
only if the employee stays with the company for several years.

EMPLOYEES HAVE A DUTY OF CONFIDENTIALITY IMPOSED BY LAW

All may not be lost if an employer fails to have an employee sign a
nondisclosure agreement. Even if an employee has never signed such an
agreement, she will usually be deemed by the courts to have a confidential relationship with her employer if she routinely comes into contact
with the employer's trade secrets as part of her job. Such an employee is
duty bound not to disclose or use, without her employer's permission,
information that:

- the employer tells her is confidential (preferably in writing), or
- the employee knew or should have known was confidential because
  of the context in which it was disclosed, the measures the employer
  took to keep the information secret and/or the fact that the information was of a type customarily considered confidential in the industry.

However, an employer's failure to use nondisclosure agreements
will tend to show that the employer was not protecting any trade secrets
and will surely not impress a judge if the company goes to court to
enforce its claimed trade secret rights. Employers have won trade secret
cases against employees in the absence of nondisclosure agreements, but
it is much easier to do so with them.

b. Independent Contractors and Consultants

People who perform services for a trade secret owner but who are not employees—freelance programmers, technical writers or beta testers, for example—may have a duty of confidentiality implied by law just as employees may (see the sidebar above). However, as is the case with employees, independent contractors should always sign nondisclosure agreements. (See the detailed discussion in Chapter 10.)

c. End Users and Other Third Parties

A trade secret owner can protect his trade secrets from unauthorized disclosure and/or use by end users and other third parties by having them agree not to disclose or use the information without permission. Such nondisclosure agreements are legally enforceable contracts. This is accomplished in the typical software transaction by licensing the software to the user, rather than selling it outright. The license gives the user permission to use the software under the terms of the license, which includes a nondisclosure provision. Nondisclosure agreements work best for programs that are distributed to a specialized market where licenses can be negotiated and signed with each individual end user.

Example: *AcmeSoft develops and markets a highly specialized program used to automate the manufacture of widgets. AcmeSoft negotiates and signs license agreements with all the purchasers of the program (about 50 in all). Each license includes a nondisclosure provision stating that the existence and attributes of the program are not to be disclosed to persons other than those employees of the manufacturer that use the program. The widget manufacturers do not have a confidential relationship with AcmeSoft, but are contractually bound by the license agreements.*

SOFTWARE MARKETING TRENDS

Negotiating and signing a software license agreement takes time and inevitably slows down the software sales cycle. To improve sales in an increasingly competitive environment, some vendors are abandoning trade secret protection. They don't ask the buyer to sign a license agreement containing a nondisclosure provision. Instead, they sell the software outright and rely on copyright (and perhaps patent) protection. This is designed to make sales quicker and easier and thereby improve business.

Let's assume that there are only about 200 widget manufacturers in the whole country, so it was easy for AcmeSoft to have all the manufacturers who purchased its widget manufacturing program sign license agreements. But what about mass-marketed software? A software publisher cannot negotiate and sign a nondisclosure agreement with every end user of a widely distributed program.

In an attempt to get around this problem, mass marketed programs often contain "shrink-wrap licenses." These are purported license agreements that are usually printed on or inside the mass-marketed software package. Such licenses attempt to convert what would appear to the average person to be a simple purchase of a piece of software into a licensing transaction. The shrink-wrap license typically provides that, by opening the package and using the program, the purchaser agrees to possess the software under the terms of the license. Agreement to the license's terms is also often elicited from the user on screen when the program is first used. Among other things, a shrink-wrap license usually prohibits the purchaser from disclosing any trade secrets learned from the program and contains various limitations on the seller's liability.

There are serious questions as to whether shrink-wrap licenses are enforceable in court. (See the sidebar below.) Moreover, many experts believe it is unlikely that a court would find that a shrink-wrap license constituted reasonable efforts on the part of the trade secret owner, under the circumstances of mass-marketing, to keep the information secret. Distributors of mass-marketed software must rely principally on distributing the software in a form that makes reverse engineering difficult (compiled code), copyright protection and, where available, software patents. Of course, up to the time a program is made available to the public, it can and should be protected by an effective internal trade secrecy program.

ARE "SHRINK-WRAP LICENSES" ENFORCEABLE?

The enforceability of shrink-wrap licenses has not been specifically tested by any court. However, many experts believe that, for a variety of reasons, shrink-wrap licenses are not worth the paper they're printed on. For one thing, they are "contracts of adhesion"—a person who wants to purchase the software has no choice but to agree to the shrink-wrap; he cannot negotiate its terms. Others view shrink-wraps as unconscionable and violative of state consumer protection legislation.

Two states, Illinois and Louisiana, have adopted laws providing that shrink-wrap licenses meeting certain requirements are enforceable. However, a federal court held that major portions of the Louisiana law were invalid because they were preempted (superseded) by the federal copyright laws (*Vault Corp. v. Quaid Software Ltd.*, 847 F.2d 255 (5th Cir. 1988)).

In any event, shrink-wraps would more likely be enforceable if they were printed in bold letters on the outside of the packaging in which software is sold. This way, the consumer could read the license before deciding to buy the product. Apparently for marketing reasons, few software publishers currently do this.

2. Obtaining Trade Secrets by "Improper Means"

Even in the absence of a confidential relationship (whether implied by law or created by contract), a trade secret owner is protected from persons who discover a trade secret by "improper means." This includes anyone who:

- obtains trade secrets through theft, bribery, fraud or misrepresentations or industrial espionage,
- knowingly obtains or uses trade secrets that have been improperly disclosed by a breach of a nondisclosure agreement or breach of a confidential relationship, or
- obtains trade secrets by inducing someone (an employee, for example) to breach an express or implied agreement not to disclose them.

The prohibition on a third party's knowingly obtaining or using trade secrets that have been improperly disclosed is of particular importance in the software industry, where there is a high degree of job mobility. It means that if an employee who has had access to trade secrets goes to work for a competitor, the new employer cannot obtain or use the employee's trade secrets if it knows that doing so would breach the employee's confidentiality obligation to the prior employer. One way to ensure that the new employer is on notice is to inform it in writing that the new employee has knowledge of the former employer's trade secrets and is duty bound not to disclose them to the new employer. (See detailed discussion in Section G4, below.) If the new employer obtains trade secrets from the former employee, the old employer may sue and be able to obtain an injunction prohibiting their use and enacting other legal remedies. (See Section C1, below.)

C. Enforcement of Trade Secrets

A trade secret owner may enforce her rights by bringing a trade secret infringement action in court. Such suits may be used to:

- prevent another person or business from using the trade secret without proper authorization, and
- collect damages for the economic injury suffered as a result of the trade secret's improper acquisition and use.

All persons responsible for the improper acquisition, and all those who have benefited from the acquisition, are typically named as defendants in trade secret infringement actions.

The most common situations that give rise to infringement actions include:

- An employee having knowledge of a trade secret changes employment and discloses the secret to her new employer in violation of her duty of confidentiality.
- Improper use or disclosure of trade secrets is made in violation of a nondisclosure agreement—for example, by an independent contractor or licensee.
- A theft of trade secrets occurs through industrial espionage.

To prevail in a trade secret infringement suit, the plaintiff (person bringing the suit) must show that the information alleged to be secret is actually a trade secret. (See the discussion in Section A, above.) In addition, the plaintiff must show that the information was either improperly acquired by the defendant (if accused of making commercial use of the secret) or improperly disclosed—or likely to be so—by the defendant (if accused of leaking the information).

AVOIDING TRADE SECRECY CLAIMS WHEN HIRING NEW EMPLOYEES

Software companies have frequently been sued for trade secrecy violations when they hire competitors' employees. This is particularly likely to occur where a company hires a large number of employees from a single competitor to obtain a competitive advantage (a practice known as "raiding"). Of course it is improper to hire anyone for the purpose of gaining access to another's trade secrets.

To prevent or defeat trade secrecy claims, it's important to hire employees in a way that shows that you did not hire any particular person for the purpose of obtaining access to trade secrets. In other words, you want to be able to show that all your employees were hired because of their qualifications and expertise, not because they knew competitors' trade secrets.

Here are some simple steps a company should take when hiring its employees:

- Spread your hiring around—avoid targeting a specific company.
- Place advertisements for new employees that list the required qualifications and expertise; consider using a professional recruiter for particularly sensitive positions.
- Make all job applicants complete an employment application and present a resume.
- Interview all job applicants, even if you already know them.
- Maintain thorough records of your hiring program.
- If you hire someone who has been exposed to a competitor's especially sensitive information, consider placing him in a position where that information will not be used for a period of time—this helps show that you did not hire the person to steal trade secrets.
- Require all employees to sign employment agreements containing a promise that they will not use or disclose their prior employer's confidential information (the employment agreements in this book contain such a clause).
- Make sure new employees don't bring any confidential records or other materials from their old job.

1. Preliminary Relief for Threatened Trade Secret Infringement

Once a trade secret is improperly disclosed to others, the harm done may be impossible to adequately remedy. For this reason, it is not necessary to wait until a competitor actually learns a trade secret through an improper disclosure and/or uses it before filing suit. Rather, where there is an imminent threatened unauthorized disclosure or use of a trade secret, the trade secret owner may file suit before the disclosure actually occurs. The owner may obtain a temporary court order preventing the defendant from disclosing or using the trade secret.

Courts are authorized to issue immediate court orders (temporary restraining orders and preliminary injunctions) prohibiting the defendants in a trade secret infringement action from disclosing or using a trade secret without permission. This allows an injured business to obtain immediate and continuous protection pending a final court determination of the case. To obtain a preliminary injunction, the plaintiff must demonstrate to the court that:

- there is a substantial imminent likelihood that plaintiff's trade secrets will be disclosed or used without its permission,
- irreparable injury will occur unless a preliminary injunction is issued (usually easy to show in trade secret infringement cases), and
- the plaintiff will probably prevail in the end.

These preliminary orders are often viewed by the parties as harbingers of the case's final outcome, and accordingly lead to settlement in advance of trial in the majority of trade secret cases.

The most difficult task the trade secret owner faces in obtaining an injunction is convincing the court that there is a real imminent threat of an unauthorized disclosure or use. Mere suspicions not backed up by any facts are not sufficient. An imminent threat of disclosure can be shown by direct evidence—for example, where a departing employee tells his ex-employer he can say good-bye to his trade secrets as he walks out the door. But, more often, a threat of disclosure is shown by circumstantial evidence—facts from which it can be reasonably inferred that an unauthorized disclosure or use is imminent.

Example: *Space Age Robotics Inc. (SARI) has spent three years developing a computer security system that visually recognizes a small group of people and responds only to their voice commands. SARI has been in a race with its chief competitor, Universal Systems, Inc., which has been working around the clock to build a similar system. Having solved most of the bugs in the system, SARI plans to make a product announcement in about a month.*

Universal Systems hires Fred, SARI's chief engineer at twice what SARI paid him. Before Fred leaves, SARI's personnel officer conducts an exit interview with him in which he asks him to sign a statement acknowledging his obligation not to disclose SARI's trade secrets. Fred refuses to sign.

After Fred leaves, SARI discovers that a number of confidential documents dealing with the security system are missing from his old office. SARI is convinced that Universal hired Fred and agreed to pay him such a high salary because he will disclose SARI's trade secrets. SARI immediately files a trade secret infringement action against Universal and Fred and asks the court to first grant a temporary restraining order and then a preliminary injunction preventing Fred from disclosing any confidential information about SARI's system to Universal.

The court concludes that, based on this circumstantial evidence, there is an imminent threat that Fred will disclose SARI's trade secrets to Universal and immediately issues a 14-day restraining order. The court later holds a hearing on whether to grant a preliminary injunction to last until the case is tried. The judge then decides to issue a preliminary injunction because it is necessary to preserve SARI's trade secrets and because, when the case is tried, SARI probably will win.

2. Permanent Relief for Trade Secret Infringement

If the plaintiff is able to establish that a trade secret was or will be improperly used, disclosed or acquired by the defendant, the court can enjoin its disclosure or use. Such injunctions can last forever. More commonly, the courts will employ the "head start rule." This gives the rightful owner of the trade secret a "head start" in commercially exploiting it by prohibiting its disclosure or use by the competitor for as long as it would have taken the competitor to independently develop the information.

Example: *SARI wins its case against Universal and Fred. The court grants SARI an injunction prohibiting Fred from disclosing any confidential information about SARI's security system to Universal for one year—the time in which Universal could perfect its own system independently.*

In addition to injunctive relief, a court may award damages to a plaintiff who wins at trial. Damages can consist of lost profits resulting from the sales by the trade secret infringer, profits realized by the infringer from the wrongfully acquired trade secret, and, occasionally, substantial punitive damages designed to punish and make an example of the defendant in particularly egregious cases. The availability and amount of punitive damages differs from state to state.

CRIMINAL PENALTIES FOR TRADE SECRET INFRINGEMENT

Intentional theft of trade secrets can constitute a crime under federal and state laws. Trade secret misappropriation may violate the federal National Stolen Property Act, which prohibits transferring or transporting stolen goods worth more than $5000 in interstate commerce (18 U.S.C. 2314). Where the phone or mails are used, trade secret infringement may constitute wire fraud or mail fraud.

Most states have enacted laws making trade secret infringement a crime. For example, in California it is a crime to acquire, disclose or use without authorization "any scientific or technical information...computer program or information stored in a computer...which is secret and is not generally available to the public, and which gives one who uses it an advantage over competitors" (Cal. Penal Code § 499c). In one of the first prosecutions under this law involving software, a former vice president of Borland International was indicted for allegedly passing Borland trade secrets to Symantec Corp. via electronic mail. (Symantec's president was also indicted.)

D. Limitations on Trade Secret Protection

There are two important limits on trade secret protection: It does not prevent others from discovering a trade secret through "reverse engineering"; nor does it apply to persons who independently create or discover the same information.

1. Reverse Engineering

One of the most significant limitations on trade secret protection is that it does not protect against "reverse engineering." This is the process of taking a product or device apart and reducing it to its constituent parts or concepts to see how it works and to learn any trade secrets it contains. Any information learned through reverse engineering is considered to be in the public domain and no longer protectible as a trade secret. Reverse engineering is an accepted business practice and is perfectly legal so long as it does not violate anybody's copyright or patent rights. (See Chapter 3, Section F2, for a discussion of whether reverse engineering constitutes copyright infringement.)

Any trained person who has access to a program's source code can readily learn any trade secrets it contains. "Source code" consists of the specific instructions written by a programmer to tell a computer what to do. It is usually written in a computer language such as BASIC, FORTRAN, C and Pascal, consisting of English words and common mathematical notations. It is easily read and understood by properly trained humans.

For this reason, computer programs are normally distributed in "object code" form only, while the source code is kept locked away. Object code, or machine language, is the code actually read and executed by the computer. The computer creates object code by translating (compiling or interpreting) the source code into a series of binary ones and zeros. Object code cannot be understood by even the most experienced programmers. However, it is possible, though often difficult, to reverse engineer object code. The object code may be translated back into source code, often by using a decompiler. It can also be possible to deduce a program's trade secrets simply by running it on a computer and seeing how it interacts with the computer, the data and the user.

To prevent end users from reverse engineering object code, software licenses often contain a provision prohibiting the practice. For example, the standard IBM license agreement states that the "customer shall not reverse assemble or reverse compile the licensed programs in whole or in part." Some view such restrictions as invalid because they attempt to preempt (replace) the federal copyright and patent laws. For example, one court has held invalid on ground of federal preemption a Louisiana state law providing that restrictions on reverse engineering contained in "shrink-wrap licenses" were enforceable (*Vault Corp. v. Quaid Software Ltd.*, 847 F.2d 255 (5th Cir. 1988)). Even if enforceable, it is unclear how effective such provisions are. They may not be binding on anyone who has not signed the license agreement—for example, a freelance programmer invited to work on the licensee's premises who obtains access to the object code program.

2. Independent Creation

The other significant limitation on trade secrecy is that it does not protect against independent creation. A trade secret owner has no rights against a person who independently discovers or develops his trade secret. Moreover, if such person makes the information generally available to the public, it will lose its trade secret status.

Example: *New Ideas, Inc. develops a new method of translating data from 5-1/4" to 3-1/2" floppy disks regardless of the format. New Ideas, Inc. markets its NewConversion program to the public, but keeps the conversion method as a trade secret. Dave, a freelance programmer, independently develops the data conversion technique and writes an article describing it in a computer programming journal. New Ideas, Inc. has no claim against Dave. In addition, its conversion method is no longer a trade secret because it is now generally known in the software industry.*

E.   Using Trade Secrecy In Conjunction with Copyright and Patent Protection

Trade secrecy is a vitally important protection for software, but, because of the limitations discussed in Section D, above, it should be used in conjunction with copyright and, in some cases, patent protection.

1.   Trade Secrets and Copyrights

Trade secrecy and copyright are not incompatible. To the contrary, they are typically used in tandem to provide the maximum legal protection available for most programs. (Patents provide far greater protection than either trade secrets or copyright, but are available only for a small minority of software; see Chapter 5.)

a.   Development Phase

Typically, trade secrecy is most important during a software product's development phase. As discussed in Chapter 3, the copyright laws grant a copyright owner the exclusive right to copy, distribute, adapt or display protected expression, but not ideas. The moment a program or other information is fixed in a tangible medium of expression (saved on disk or other media, written down, etc.) it is protected by the federal copyright laws to the extent it is original (independently created). Provided that secrecy is maintained, trade secret protection can still continue. Because an item is automatically protected by copyright upon its fixation, rather than when it is first published, there usually is a substantial time period during which both trade secret and copyright protection apply. This is because a program is usually tested and modified for some time after it is first "fixed," but before it is distributed. As long as it is maintained as a trade secret during this period, the program enjoys both trade secret and copyright protection.

b. Distribution Phase

Once a program is distributed, it will lose trade secret status unless steps are taken to preserve secrecy. Such steps may include distributing the program only in object code form and having each person who receives the work sign a license restricting disclosure of the secrets it contains. Of course, it is impossible to have the purchasers of mass-marketed programs all sign licenses. Pre-printed shrink-wrap licenses must be relied upon to establish a duty of nondisclosure for mass-marketed software. But, as discussed in Section B1c, above, the effectiveness of shrink-wrap licenses is very much in doubt. Thus, copyright protection alone may have to be relied upon once software is widely distributed to the public.

2. Trade Secrets and Patents

The federal patent laws provide the owner of a patentable invention with far greater protection than that available under trade secrecy or copyright laws— in effect, a total 17-year monopoly on the use of the invention as described in the patent. To obtain a patent, the inventor must file a lengthy application with the U.S. Patent Office, fully disclosing the ideas underlying the invention.

Trade secret protection is not lost when a patent is applied for. The Patent Office keeps patent applications secret unless or until a patent is granted—a process that usually takes two to three years. However, once a patent is granted and an issue fee paid, the patent becomes a public record. Then all the information disclosed in the patent application is no longer a trade secret. This is so even if the patent is later challenged in court and invalidated.

However, in most cases a software patent applies only to certain isolated elements of a computer program. The remainder of the program need not be disclosed in the patent and can remain a trade secret. (See Chapter 5 for a detailed discussion of patents and software.)

PART II. SETTING UP A TRADE SECRET PROTECTION PROGRAM

In Part I of this chapter, we introduced you to the concept of trade secret—the common sense notion that keeping information close to the chest can provide a competitive advantage in the marketplace. But simply saying that a computer program or other information is a trade secret will not make it so. The information must actually be kept secret.

Some companies go to extreme lengths to keep their trade secrets secret. For example, the formula for Coca-Cola (perhaps the world's most famous trade secret) is kept locked in a bank vault in Atlanta, which can be opened only by a resolution of the Coca-Cola Company's board of directors. Only two Coca-Cola employees ever know the formula at the same time; their identities are never disclosed to the public and they are not allowed to fly on the same airplane.

Fortunately, such extraordinary secrecy measures are seldom necessary. You don't have to turn your office into an armed camp to protect your trade secrets, but you must take *reasonable* precautions to prevent people who are not subject to confidentiality restrictions from learning them.

How much secrecy is "reasonable"? This depends largely on two factors:
- the physical and financial size of your company, and
- the value of your trade secrets.

A small start-up company need not implement the same type of trade secrecy program as a Microsoft or IBM. A trade secret's value also affects how much secrecy will be deemed reasonable by the courts. For example, more care should be taken to protect extremely valuable source code than relatively unimportant information.

Someone needs to be in charge of a company's secrecy program. In some companies, management devises a security plan and then designates someone to serve as the company's security officer to manage and enforce it. Another approach taken by some hi-tech firms is to have the employees involved with each new project devise and enforce their own security plan. Either approach can work. The key to any trade secret protection program is to devise a secrecy plan you and your employees can live with—and then stick to it.

F.   Identifying Your Trade Secrets

The first step in any trade secret protection program is to identify exactly what information and material is a company trade secret. As discussed in Part I, above, a "trade secret" can be any information used by the company that gives it an advantage over competitors who do not know or use the information. For a software company, trade secrets typically include:

- unpublished computer code—both source code and object code,
- design definitions and specifications,
- flow diagrams and flow charts,
- technical notes, memoranda and correspondence relating to the design and development of computer code,
- software development tools,
- formulas and algorithms embodied in software,
- system and user documentation,
- data structures and data compilations,
- product development agreements and other related agreements,
- business plans,
- marketing plans,
- sales data,
- unpublished promotional material,
- cost and pricing information,
- customer lists, and
- pending patent applications.

It makes no difference in what form a trade secret is embodied. Trade secrets may be stored on computer hard disks or floppies, written down, or kept only in employees' memories.

> **NOT EVERYTHING IS A TRADE SECRET**
>
> Some companies make the mistake of assuming that virtually all information about the company and its products is a trade secret that must be protected from disclosure to outsiders. They then find that attempting to protect such a morass of information is very expensive and burdensome, and may end up abandoning their protection program. Use your common sense in deciding whether disclosure of a particular item of information to a competitor would really harm the company.

G. Basic Trade Secret Protection Program

Trade secrecy measures take time, cost money, can result in aggravation and in some cases lower employee morale and/or productivity. Don't adopt an overly ambitious security program that you'll be unable or unwilling to follow. It is much better to have a modest security program that you and your employees will stick to rather than an extravagant program that will be ignored or resented.

Presented below are the absolute minimum safeguards a software company should take to protect its trade secrets. Such a basic secrecy program is adequate for small companies, particularly start-ups. In other words, if you file suit in court to prevent unauthorized disclosure or misappropriation of your trade secrets, a judge would likely conclude that you took the minimum reasonable precautions to prevent the public or competitors from learning about your secrets absent improper acquisition or theft. (See Section A4, above.)

As your company grows, you'll want to implement some or all of the advanced secrecy measures discussed in Section H, below.

1. Maintaining Physical Security

Although trade secrets are most often misappropriated by employees or ex-employees, not industrial spies, courts usually require that a company take at least some steps to ensure the physical security of its trade secrets. At a minimum, a software company should implement a "clean desk" and "locked file cabinets and desk drawers" policy. Documents containing trade secrets—such as hardcopy printouts of source code—should not be left hanging about on desks when not in use; rather, they should be locked in desk drawers or filing cabinets. Your office should also be securely locked at the end of the day. Also, consider making periodic copies of valuable source code and place them in an office safe or bank safety deposit box for security and back-up purposes.

2. Computer Security

Because software is normally created and stored on computers, it's a good idea to take reasonable measures to prevent unauthorized people from gaining access to your computer system. Here's a list of some of the security measures that can be employed; you can probably think of others:

- Use secret passwords for on-line access to source code (the passwords should be periodically changed).
- Place computers, terminals and other peripherals in a physically secure location to which access is restricted.
- Put "fuses" into software to detect unauthorized access and to stop or erase the program if unauthorized access occurs.
- Program your computers not to duplicate or reproduce software unless special programming instructions are inputted.
- Keep software in coded or encrypted form so it can't be read by outsiders.

- Include secret codes in software identifying the employee(s) who created it.

    The more valuable your software, the more of these security measures you'll want to take.

3. Marking Documents "Confidential"

The best way to alert employees and others that a document contains trade secrets is to mark it confidential. Obtain rubber stamps with the following wordings:

CONFIDENTIAL

THE CONTENTS OF THIS MATERIAL ARE CONFIDENTIAL AND PROPRIETARY TO [YOUR COMPANY NAME] AND MAY NOT BE REPRODUCED, PUBLISHED, OR DISCLOSED TO OTHERS WITHOUT COMPANY AUTHORIZATION.

Any person who generates a document containing trade secrets should stamp it confidential. Be sure to mark all copies of source code (including disks and disk jackets), specifications, technical documentation, development materials and so forth with the confidentiality notice. Also, when you create source code, flow charts or data compilations on your computer, include the confidentiality notice at the beginning and end of the program and a few places in between. This way, the notice will appear both on-screen and when a printout is made.

Workers should, however, be admonished not to go overboard and stamp everything in sight. If virtually everything is stamped "confidential," including public information, a court may conclude that nothing was really confidential. Indeed, it is better not to stamp anything than to stamp everything.

4. Using Nondisclosure Agreements

A nondisclosure agreement is a document in which a person who is given access to trade secrets promises not to disclose them to others without permission from the trade secret owner. Before you give *any* person access to your trade secrets, make sure that he or she has signed a nondisclosure agreement. This includes people both inside and outside your company.

 Don't neglect the important step of preparing nondisclosure agreements. Using nondisclosure agreements consistently is the single most important element of any trade secret protection program.

Using a nondisclosure agreement accomplishes these basic purposes:
* It conclusively establishes that the parties have a confidential relationship. As discussed in detail in Part I, above, only persons who are in a confidential relationship with a trade secret owner have a legal duty not to disclose the owner's trade secrets without permission.
* Signing such an agreement makes clear to a person who receives a trade secret that it is to be kept in confidence. It impresses on him or her that the company is serious about maintaining its trade secrets.
* If it's ever necessary to file a lawsuit, it precludes a court from concluding that the company didn't bother to use nondisclosure agreements because it really didn't have any trade secrets.

a. Employees

All employees who may have access to trade secrets should be required to sign nondisclosure agreements before they begin work, or on their very first day of work. If you have employees who have not signed nondisclosure agreements, you should ask them to do so if they are given access to any trade secrets. A nondisclosure agreement may be part of an employment agreement, which covers all aspects of employment, including confidentiality issues. Chapter 9 contains a sample employment agreement including a nondisclosure provision.

Top management should sign nondisclosure agreements as well. Although such individuals owe a duty of loyalty to their company, which includes a duty not to disclose information that would harm the business, it's prudent to put it in writing. Potential customers or investors may wish to have the extra safeguard of a signed nondisclosure agreement before buying your product or investing in your company. If your business is a partnership, all partners should sign a partnership agreement containing a nondisclosure provision.

NONCOMPETITION AGREEMENTS WITH EMPLOYEES

In addition to having employees exposed to trade secrets sign nondisclosure agreements, many employers have them agree to noncompetition restrictions (also called "covenants not to compete"). A covenant not to compete is used to prevent an employee with access to confidential information from directly competing with his employer within a given geographic area for a limited time period after he quits or is fired.

A covenant not to compete is usually much easier to enforce than a confidentiality agreement because the ex-employer need only show that the ex-employee went to work for a competitor or started his own business in violation of the agreement's terms. Moreover, an employee who can't work for a competitor or start his own competitive business will have no incentive or opportunity to use or disclose his ex-employer's trade secrets. However, there are many restrictions on noncompete agreements; they are unenforceable in California, for example. (See Chapter 9 for a detailed discussion.)

---

b. Independent Contractors (Consultants)

The consultant you hire today may end up working for a competitor tomorrow. Never expose a non-employee consultant to trade secrets without having a signed nondisclosure agreement on file. The nondisclosure agreement may be contained in an independent contractor agreement, which covers all aspects of the work relationship. This is discussed in detail in Chapter 10; sample forms are included.

Our sample form in Chapter 10 limits the consultant's confidentiality obligation to information in writing that is marked confidential, or information orally disclosed that is later reduced to writing and appropriately marked. We believe this is a reasonable limitation because it enables the consultant to know exactly what is and is not a trade secret. However, it means that whenever trade secrets are orally disclosed to a consultant, a follow-up letter must be sent stating that the information is confidential. If you're an employer, make sure that your employees understand this policy and confirm all oral disclosures to outside consultants in writing.

c. Licensees and Purchasers

Nondisclosure provisions are routinely included in software license and sale agreements. However, the enforceability of such provisions is questionable when they are included in "shrink-wrap" licenses for mass-marketed software. (See the detailed discussion in Section B1c, above.)

d. Other Outsiders

Have any other outsider who may be exposed to your trade secrets sign a nondisclosure agreement as well. This may include suppliers, outside beta testers, product reviewers, potential investors, bankers, accountants and outside auditors, as well as people who visit your company.

5. Preparing Nondisclosure Agreements

Following are instructions and samples of four nondisclosure agreements:
- General Nondisclosure Agreement;
- Nondisclosure Agreement with Prospective Customers;
- Beta Tester's Nondisclosure Agreement, and

- Visitor's Nondisclosure Agreement.

For nondisclosure agreements to be used with employees, use the employment agreements in Chapter 9. For independent contractors, use the independent contractor agreement in Chapter 10.

a. General Nondisclosure Agreement

The General Nondisclosure Agreement can be used with any outside individual or company to whom you grant access to your trade secrets.

In some cases, both parties may agree to disclose confidential information to each other. This may occur, for example, where the parties are considering a joint development project or a merger. In this event, two General Nondisclosure Agreements can be used, with the parties switching roles as Discloser and Recipient.

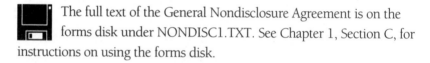 The full text of the General Nondisclosure Agreement is on the forms disk under NONDISC1.TXT. See Chapter 1, Section C, for instructions on using the forms disk.

The General Nondisclosure Agreement is self-explanatory, with the following clarifications.

Introductory Paragraph

Fill in the date. Next, fill in the disclosing company's name (the "Discloser"). Finally, fill in the name of the outside individual or company being granted access to your trade secrets (the "Recipient"). Remember to have everyone who will have access to your trade secrets sign a nondisclosure agreement.

Trade Secrets

Select either Alternative 1 or 2 (the full text of both alternatives is on disk), and delete the alternative you are not using. Here's how to choose:

- *Alternative 1.* It's best to specifically identify the trade secrets covered by the agreement; use this clause if you can individually list the material being provided.

• *Alternative 2.* Use this clause if it's not possible to specifically identify the trade secrets—for example, if the information to be disclosed does not exist when the agreement is signed. This clause contains a general description of the types of information covered.

Purpose of Disclosure

Describe the reason for disclosing trade secrets. For example, this may be to evaluate software for use, to explore joint marketing possibilities or to further the parties' business relationship.

Return of Materials

In this clause, the Recipient promises to return original materials you've provided, as well as copies, notes and documents pertaining to the trade secrets. The form gives Recipient 30 days to return the materials, but you can change this time period if you wish.

Term of Agreement

The forms disk includes two alternative provisions dealing with the agreement's term. Select the clause that best suits your needs and delete the other:

• *Alternative 1.* This provision has no definite time limit—in other words, the recipient's obligation of confidentiality lasts until the trade secret information ceases to be a trade secret. This may occur when the information becomes generally known, is disclosed to the public by the disclosing party or ceases being a trade secret for some other reason.

• *Alternative 2.* Use this clause if the Recipient prefers to have the agreement state a definite date in which the agreement, and the Recipient's confidentiality obligations, expires.

Applicable Law

Fill in the state in which the Discloser has its principal office.

Signature

The parties don't have to be in the same room when they sign the agreement. It's even fine if the dates are a few days apart. Each party should sign at least two copies, and keep at least one. This way, both parties have an original signed agreement. (Instructions on preparing and signing documents are covered in Chapter 1, Section D.)

SAMPLE
GENERAL NONDISCLOSURE AGREEMENT

This is an agreement, effective June 11, 199X, between The Accountant's Own Software Company (the "Discloser") and Sandra Miller (the "Recipient"), in which Discloser agrees to disclose, and Recipient agrees to receive, certain trade secrets of Discloser on the following terms and conditions:

1. Trade Secrets: Recipient understands and acknowledges that Discloser's trade secrets consist of information and materials that are valuable and not generally known by Discloser's competitors. Discloser's trade secrets include:

(a) Any and all information concerning Discloser's current, future or proposed products, including, but not limited to, unpublished computer code (both source code and object code), drawings, specifications, notebook entries, technical notes and graphs, computer printouts, technical memoranda and correspondence, product development agreements and related agreements.

(b) Information and materials relating to Discloser's purchasing, accounting and marketing, including, but not limited to, marketing plans, sales data, unpublished promotional material, cost and pricing information and customer lists.

(c) Information of the type described above which Discloser obtained from another party and which Discloser treats as confidential, whether or not owned or developed by Discloser.

2. Purpose of Disclosure: Recipient shall make use of Discloser's trade secrets only for the purpose of evaluating Discloser's software for use in Recipient's business.

3. Nondisclosure: In consideration of Discloser's disclosure of its trade secrets to Recipient, Recipient agrees that it will treat Discloser's trade secrets with the same degree of care and safeguards that it takes with its own trade secrets, but in no event less than a reasonable degree of care. Recipient agrees that, without Discloser's prior written consent, Recipient will not:

(a) disclose Discloser's trade secrets to any third party.

(b) make or permit to be made copies or other reproductions of Discloser's trade secrets, or

(c) make any commercial use of the trade secrets.

Recipient will not disclose Discloser's trade secrets to Recipient's employees, agents and consultants unless: (1) they have a need to know the information in connection with their employment or consultant duties; and (2) they personally agree in writing to be bound by the terms of this Agreement.

4. Return of Materials: Upon Discloser's request, Recipient shall promptly (within 30 days) return all original materials provided by Discloser and any copies, notes or other documents in Recipient's possession pertaining to Discloser's trade secrets.

5. Exclusions: This agreement does not apply to any information which:

(a) was in Recipient's possession or was known to Recipient, without an obligation to keep it confidential, before such information was disclosed to Recipient by Discloser;

(b) is or becomes public knowledge through a source other than Recipient and through no fault of Recipient;

(c) is independently developed by or for Recipient;

(d) is or becomes lawfully available to Recipient from a source other than Discloser; or

(e) is disclosed by Recipient with Discloser's prior written approval.

6. Term of Agreement: This Agreement and Recipient's duty to hold Discloser's trade secrets in confidence shall remain in effect until the above-described trade secrets are no longer trade secrets or until Discloser sends Recipient written notice releasing Recipient from this Agreement, whichever occurs first.

7. No Rights Granted: Recipient understands and agrees that this Agreement does not constitute a grant or an intention or commitment to grant any right, title or interest in Discloser's trade secrets to Recipient.

8. Warranty: Discloser warrants that it has the right to made the disclosures under this Agreement. **NO OTHER WARRANTIES ARE MADE BY DISCLOSER UNDER THIS AGREEMENT. ANY INFORMATION DISCLOSED UNDER THIS AGREEMENT IS PROVIDED "AS IS."**

9. Injunctive Relief: Recipient recognizes and acknowledges that any breach or threatened breach of this Agreement by Recipient may cause Discloser irreparable harm for which monetary damages may be inadequate. Recipient agrees, therefore, that Discloser shall be entitled to an injunction to restrain Recipient from such breach or threatened breach. Nothing in this Agreement shall be construed as preventing

Discloser from pursuing any remedy at law or in equity for any breach or threatened breach of this Agreement.

10. Attorney Fees: If any legal action arises relating to this Agreement, the prevailing party shall be entitled to recover all court costs, expenses and reasonable attorney fees.

11. Modifications: All additions or modifications to this Agreement must be made in writing and must be signed by both parties to be effective.

12. No Agency: This Agreement does not create any agency or partnership relationship between the parties.

13. Applicable Law: This Agreement is made under, and shall be construed according to, the laws of the State of Nevada.

Discloser:
The Accountant's Own Software Company

By: _____
            (signature)

_____
      (typed or printed name)

Title: _____

Date: _____

Recipient:
Sandra Miller

By: _____
            (signature)

_____
      (typed or printed name)

Title: _____

Date: _____

b. Nondisclosure Agreement with Prospective Customer

The following nondisclosure agreement is specially designed to be used when a software company provides a copy of a finished software product to a prospective customer for evaluation.

The full text of the following agreement is on the forms disk under NONDISC2.TXT. See Chapter 1, Section C, for instructions on using the forms disk.

The Nondisclosure Agreement (Prospective Customer) is self-explanatory, with the following clarifications.

Introductory Paragraph

Fill in the date. Next, fill in the disclosing company's name. Finally, fill in the name of the outside individual or company being granted access to your trade secrets (the "Customer"). Remember to have everyone who will have access to your trade secrets sign a nondisclosure agreement.

Purpose of Agreement

Describe the software or other information disclosed or provide its name.

Nonexclusive License

Fill in the number of days you are allowing the Customer to use the software for evaluation purposes.

Term of Agreement

Again, fill in the number of days you are allowing the Customer to use the software for evaluation purposes. This must be identical to the time period you listed in the Nonexclusive License clause, above.

Applicable Law

Fill in the state in which the Company has its principal office.

Signature

The parties don't have to be in the same room when they sign the agreement. It's even fine if the dates are a few days apart. Each party should sign at least two copies, and keep at least one. This way, both parties have an original signed agreement. (Instructions on preparing and signing documents are covered in Chapter 1, Section D.)

S A M P L E
NONDISCLOSURE AGREEMENT
(PROSPECTIVE CUSTOMER)

This is an agreement, effective March 22, 199X between EfficientSoft (the "Company") and Mazes, Inc. (the "Customer").

1. Purpose of Agreement: This Agreement is entered into for the purpose of authorizing Customer to receive from Company and evaluate certain proprietary computer software and documentation known as EfficientWork, hereafter referred to as "the Software."

2. Nonexclusive License: Company hereby grants Customer a nonexclusive license to install the Software on its computer system and use the Software for a period of 30 days from the date of delivery only for the purpose of evaluating the performance of the Software and not for a productive purpose. Customer shall acquire no other intellectual property rights under this Agreement.

3. Software a Trade Secret: Customer acknowledges that the Software is proprietary to, and a valuable trade secret of, the Company and is entrusted to Customer only for the purposes set forth in this Agreement.

4. Nondisclosure: In consideration of the Company's disclosure of the Software to Customer, Customer shall treat the Software with the same degree of care and safeguards that it takes with Customer's own trade secrets, but in no event less than a reasonable degree of care. Customer agrees that it will not, without the Company's prior written consent:

(a) reverse engineer, decompile or disassemble the Software or any portion of it;

(b) copy any portion of the Software;

(c) download the Software in a retrieval system or computer system of any kind except as authorized by this Agreement; or

(d) disclose any portion of the Software to any third party.

Customer shall limit use of the Software to those employees, agents and consultants of Customer who are performing the evaluation for Customer.

The restrictions and obligations contained in this clause shall survive the expiration, termination or cancellation of this Agreement, and shall continue to bind Customer, its successors, heirs and assigns.

5. Term of Agreement: This Agreement shall last for a term of 30 days from the date the Software is delivered to Customer, or until the Software is returned by Customer to the Company, whichever occurs first. Further, the Company may terminate this Agreement immediately upon written notice to Customer.

6. Return of Software and Materials: Customer shall promptly return the Software and all related materials to the Company and erase all copies and portions thereof from computer memory upon:

(a) termination of this Agreement;

(b) the Company's request; or

(c) the Customer's decision not to purchase or license the Software.

7. Limitation of Liability: Customer understands and acknowledges that the Software is being provided to Customer only for the purpose of evaluating the performance of the Software and not for any productive purpose. Accordingly, the Company shall not be responsible for any loss or damage to Customer or any third parties caused by Customer's use of the Software.

THE COMPANY SHALL NOT BE LIABLE FOR ANY DIRECT, INDIRECT, SPECIAL, INCIDENTAL OR CONSEQUENTIAL DAMAGES, WHETHER BASED ON CONTRACT OR TORT OR ANY OTHER LEGAL THEORY, ARISING OUT OF ANY USE OF THE SOFTWARE OR ANY PERFORMANCE OF THIS AGREEMENT.

8. Injunctive Relief: Customer recognizes and acknowledges that any breach or threatened breach of this Agreement by Customer may cause the Company irreparable harm for which monetary damages may be inadequate. Customer agrees, therefore, that the Company shall be entitled to an injunction to restrain Customer from such breach or threatened breach. Nothing in this Agreement shall be construed as preventing the Company from pursuing any remedy at law or in equity for any breach or threatened breach of this Agreement.

9. Attorney Fees: If any legal action arises relating to this Agreement, the prevailing party shall be entitled to recover all court costs, expenses and reasonable attorney fees.

10. Entire Agreement: This Agreement contains the entire understanding and agreement of the parties relating to the subject matter hereof. Any representation, promise, or condition not explicitly set forth in this Agreement shall not be binding on either party.

11. Modifications: All additions or modifications to this Agreement must be made in writing and must be signed by both parties to be effective.

12. Applicable Law: This Agreement is made under, and shall be construed according to, the laws of the State of Massachusetts.

The Company:
EfficientSoft

By: _____
                    (signature)

_____
                (typed or printed name)

Title: _____

Date: _____

Customer:
Mazes, Inc.

By: _____
                    (signature)

_____
                (typed or printed name)

Title: _____

Date: _____

c. Beta Tester's Nondisclosure Agreement

Here is a nondisclosure agreement to be used with all outside persons or companies that beta test software that is under development.

The full text of the following agreement is on the forms disk under NONDISC3.TXT. See Chapter 1, Section C, for instructions on using the forms disk.

The Nondisclosure Agreement (Beta Tester) is self-explanatory, with the following clarifications.

Introductory Paragraph

Fill in the date. Next, fill in the disclosing company's name. Fill in the name of the outside individual or company that is beta testing your software (the "Tester"). Finally, fill in the name of the software being tested.

Company's Obligations

Typically, a beta tester is given a free copy of the software as payment. That is what this agreement provides, although some other payment provision can be agreed to—for example, hourly payment or a fixed fee.

Term of Agreement

Fill in the time frame during which you are allowing the beta tester to test the software.

Applicable Law

Fill in the state in which the Company has its principal office.

Signature

The parties don't have to be in the same room when they sign the agreement. It's even fine if the dates are a few days apart. Each party should sign at least two copies, and keep at least one. This way, both parties have an original signed agreement. (Instructions on preparing and signing documents are covered in Chapter 1, Section D.)

SAMPLE
NONDISCLOSURE AGREEMENT
(BETA TESTER)

This is an agreement, effective November 12, 199X, between Earth Dreams (the "Company") and Lewis Industries (the "Tester"), in which Tester agrees to test a software program known as Heavenly Power (the "Software") and keep the Company aware of the test results.

1. Company's Obligations: The Company shall provide Tester with a copy of the Software and any necessary documentation and instruct Tester on how to use it and the desired test data to be gained. Upon satisfactory completion of the testing, the Company shall furnish Tester with one free copy of the production version of the Software, contingent upon the Company's decision to proceed with production of the Software. Tester shall be entitled to the same benefits to which regular purchasers of the Software will be entitled.

2. Tester's Obligations: Tester shall test the Software under normally expected operating conditions in Tester's environment during the test period. Tester shall gather and report test data as mutually agreed upon with the Company. Tester shall allow the Company access to the Software during normal working hours for inspection, modifications and maintenance.

3. Software a Trade Secret: Tester acknowledges that the Software is proprietary to, and a valuable trade secret of, the Company and is entrusted to Tester only for the purpose set forth in this Agreement. Tester shall treat the Software in the strictest confidence. Tester agrees that it will not, without the Company's prior written consent:

(a) disclose any information about the Software, its design and performance specifications, its code, and the existence of the beta test and its results to anyone other than Tester's employees who are performing the testing;

(b) copy any portion of the Software or documentation, except to the extent necessary to perform the beta testing; or

(c) reverse engineer, decompile or disassemble the Software or any portion of it.

4. Security Precautions: Tester shall take reasonable security precautions to prevent the Software from being seen by unauthorized individuals. This includes locking all copies of the Software and associated documentation in a desk or file cabinet when not in use.

5. Term of Agreement: The test period shall last from November 12, 199X, until December 12, 199X. This Agreement shall terminate at the end of the test period or when the Company asks Tester to return the Software, whichever occurs first. The restrictions and obligations contained in Clauses 3, 6, 7, 8 and 9 shall survive the expiration, termination or cancellation of this Agreement, and shall continue to bind Tester, its successors, heirs and assigns.

6. Return of Software and Materials: Upon the conclusion of the testing period or at the Company's request, Tester shall promptly (within 10 days) return the original and all copies of the Software and all related materials to the Company and erase all portions thereof from computer memory.

7. Disclaimer of Warranty: Tester understands and acknowledges that the Software is a test product and its accuracy and reliability are not guaranteed. Owing to its experimental nature, Tester is advised not to rely exclusively on the Software for any reason. Tester waives any and all claims it may have against the Company arising out of the performance or nonperformance of the Software.

THE SOFTWARE IS PROVIDED AS IS, AND THE COMPANY DISCLAIMS ANY AND ALL REPRESENTATIONS OR WARRANTIES OF ANY KIND, WHETHER EXPRESS OR IMPLIED, WITH RESPECT TO IT, INCLUDING ANY IMPLIED WARRANTIES OF MERCHANTABILITY OR FITNESS FOR A PARTICULAR PURPOSE.

8. Limitation of Liability: The Company shall not be responsible for any loss or damage to Tester or any third parties caused by the Software or by the Company's performance of this Agreement.

THE COMPANY SHALL NOT BE LIABLE FOR ANY DIRECT, INDIRECT, SPECIAL, INCIDENTAL OR CONSEQUENTIAL DAMAGE, WHETHER BASED ON CONTRACT OR TORT OR ANY OTHER LEGAL THEORY, ARISING OUT OF ANY USE OF THE SOFTWARE OR ANY PERFORMANCE OF THIS AGREEMENT.

9. No Rights Granted: Tester understands and acknowledges that the Software is provided for its own use for testing purposes only. This Agreement does not consti-tute a grant or an intention or commitment to grant any right, title or interest in the Software or the Company's trade secrets to Tester. Tester may not sell or transfer any portion of the Software to any third party or use the Software in any manner to produce, market or support its own products. Tester shall clearly identify the Software as the Company's property.

10. No Assignments: This Agreement is personal to Tester. Tester shall not assign or otherwise transfer any rights or obligations under this Agreement.

11. Entire Agreement: This Agreement contains the entire understanding and agreement of the parties relating to the subject matter hereof. Any representation, promise or condition not explicitly set forth in this Agreement shall not be binding on either party. All additions or modifications to this Agreement must be made in writing and must be signed by both parties to be effective.

12. Applicable Law: This Agreement is made under, and shall be construed according to, the laws of the State of Illinois.

The Company:
Earth Dreams

By: _____
(signature)

_____
(typed or printed name)

Title: _____

Date: _____

Tester:
Lewis Industries

By: _____
(signature)

_____
(typed or printed name)

Title: _____

Date: _____

d. Visitor's Nondisclosure Agreement

This is a nondisclosure agreement that can be used with visitors to your office who might have access to company trade secrets.

The full text of the following agreement is on the forms disk under NONDISC4.TXT. See Chapter 1, Section C, for instructions on using the forms disk.

The Visitor's Nondisclosure Agreement is self-explanatory, with the following clarifications.

Introductory Paragraph

Visitor's Name. Fill in the name of the outside individual who is visiting your company. Remember to have everyone who visits your company and may have access to your trade secrets sign a nondisclosure agreement.

Affiliation. Fill in the name of the company or organization the individual represents.

Place Visited. Fill in your company's name and address.

Date Visited. Fill in the date or dates of the visit.

Clause 1

Fill in your company's name.

Signature

Each visitor should sign and date the agreement, preferably before he or she is exposed to trade secrets. (Instructions on preparing and signing documents are covered in Chapter 1, Section D.)

SAMPLE
VISITOR'S NONDISCLOSURE AGREEMENT

Visitor's Name (print): _____

Affiliation: _____

Place Visited: _____

Date(s) Visited: _____

1. I understand that I may be given access to confidential information belonging to _____ (the "Company") through my relationship with the Company or as a result of my access to the Company's premises.

2. I understand and acknowledge that the Company's trade secrets consist of information and materials that are valuable and not generally known by the Company's competitors. The Company's trade secrets include:

(a) Any and all information concerning the Company's current, future or proposed products, including, but not limited to, unpublished computer code (both source code and object code), drawings, specifications, notebook entries, technical notes and graphs, computer printouts, technical memoranda and correspondence, product development agreements and related agreements.

(b) Information and materials relating to the Company's purchasing, accounting and marketing; including, but not limited to, marketing plans, sales data, unpublished promotional material, cost and pricing information and customer lists.

(c) Information of the type described above which the Company obtained from another party and which the Company treats as confidential, whether or not owned or developed by the Company.

(d) Other: _____

3. In consideration of being admitted to the Company's facilities, I agree to hold in the strictest confidence any trade secrets or confidential information which is disclosed to me. I agree not to remove any document, equipment or other materials from the premises without the Company's written permission. I will not photograph or otherwise record any information to which I may have access during my visit.

4. This Agreement is binding on me, my heirs, executors, administrators and assigns; and inures to the benefit of the Company, its successors and assigns.

5. This Agreement constitutes the entire understanding between the Company and me with respect to its subject matter. It supersedes all earlier representations and understandings, whether oral or written.

Visitor:_____
                    (Signature)

Date: _____

H.   Advanced Trade Secret Protection Program

Presented below are some additional security precautions that will help ensure the safety of your trade secrets. As your company grows and you develop increasingly valuable trade secrets, you'll want to consider making some or all of these precautions a part of your security plan.

1.   Limiting Employee Access to Trade Secrets

Obviously, the fewer people who know a trade secret, the less likely it will leak out. In very small companies, particularly start-ups, it may not be possible or desirable to limit access to trade secrets, since everyone is involved in every facet of the company's operation. However, as a company grows larger, it's a good idea to restrict access to trade secrets only to those employees who really need to know them.

One way to control employees' access to trade secrets is to use project logs. Start by making a list of which employees need to have access to confidential materials for each of your company's ongoing projects. Create a log for each project and have every employee sign in and out each time they use confidential materials. The log should contain room for the date, the employee's name, the time in, the time out and perhaps additional information, depending on the project. The log can be maintained manually or via computer. Consistent use of logs will help ensure that unauthorized employees don't get their hands on company trade secrets.

2.   Additional Physical Security

In larger companies, additional security precautions can be taken. Company trade secrets can be kept in a specified protected location or even in geographically separate facilities. Access to these areas can then be restricted.

3. Not Writing Down Trade Secrets

Perhaps the best way to maintain a trade secret is not to write it down at all. Particularly in small companies, a good deal of sensitive information—marketing plans, for example—can be transmitted orally to those who need to know.

4. Restricting Photocopying

If trade secrets are written down, one of the principal means by which they can be lost is through unauthorized photocopying. Try to restrict access to photocopiers, particularly at night. Keep a logbook next to the copier and require anyone who copies a document marked "confidential" to record the following information: the date, name of person making the copy, name of the person for whom the copy is made, number of copies, and the subject matter and name of the document. In addition, a record should be kept of anyone who receives confidential copies—for example, the names could be written on a cover transmittal sheet. As always, those people should sign nondisclosure agreements.

5. Noncompetition Agreements With Employees and Consultants

We've already discussed above that all employees and consultants should be required to sign nondisclosure agreements before being exposed to trade secrets. However, nondisclosure agreements are not a panacea. It can be very difficult for an employer to know whether an ex-employee has disclosed trade secrets to a competitor. Moreover, even if the employer is sure trade secrets have been disclosed, it can be difficult to obtain court relief for violations of a nondisclosure agreement. The ex-employer must prove that the employee actually disclosed confidential information. This can be an onerous task, especially where the ex-employee claims that the information allegedly disclosed didn't qualify as a trade secret.

One way to avoid these problems is to have employees and consultants sign noncompetition agreements. These are agreements by which an employee or independent contractor promises not to compete with the employer's business for a stated time period (usually no more than two years).

It's usually easy to discover whether an ex-employee has gone to work for a competitor. To enforce a noncompetition agreement in court, the ex-employer need only show that the ex-employee went to work for a competitor in violation of the agreement's terms. But, the best part about a noncompetition agreement from an employer's point of view is that it will deter both the employee from seeking employment with a competitor and the competitor from hiring him or her. This significantly reduces an employee's incentive and opportunity to divulge trade secrets.

From the company's point of view, this all sounds great, but there is a down side. Noncompetition agreements are very unpopular with many employees and consultants, and some will refuse to sign them. You could lose an outstanding prospective employee or consultant by insisting on it. Moreover, they are unenforceable in a number of states, including California. Even in those states where such agreements are enforceable, they must be carefully drafted to withstand judicial scrutiny. (For a detailed discussion and sample forms, see Chapters 9 and 10.)

6. Screening Employee Publications and Presentations

A trade secret is lost if it is disclosed to the public on an unrestricted basis. For example, the trade secret status of valuable source code will be lost if it is published in a computer magazine. Trade secrets also may be lost through disclosures in speeches and presentations at trade shows and professional conferences. Trade secrets can even be lost through advertising—for example, a software company that lists its clients in an advertising brochure cannot claim later that its customer list is a trade secret.

Companies with advanced trade secret programs screen all papers, articles and advance texts of speeches and presentations. This screening process can be done by a formal screening committee consisting of members who, taken together, are familiar with all the company's products and trade secrets, or by individuals who may specialize in a particular area.

Special care must be taken to avoid disclosing patentable inventions in articles or other publications. Patent protection in some foreign countries can be lost through such inadvertent disclosures, and disclosure in all countries starts running the one year period during which a patent application must be filed or the right to do so is lost forever. (See Chapter 5.)

7. Controlling Visitors

Visitors to your company should not be allowed to wander unsupervised in areas where confidential materials are kept. Larger software companies should require all visitors to sign a log book, including the visitor's name, address, affiliation, reason for visit, person being seen at the company and times of entering and leaving. Visitors who might be exposed to trade secrets should be asked to sign a nondisclosure agreement before leaving the reception area. (See Section G4d, above, for a sample visitor's nondisclosure agreement.)

8. Dealing With Departing Employees

The primary source of trade secret leaks are former employees. Thus, it's important to take special precautions when an employee decides to leave or is fired.

a. Exit Interviews and Acknowledgment of Obligations Form

Before an employee leaves, the company's security officer or other person in charge of the trade secrecy program should conduct an exit interview. This opportunity should be used to remind the employee of her obligation not to disclose the company's trade secrets to others, particularly her new employer. Wherever possible, prepare a list generally describing the specific trade secrets the employee was exposed to during her employment. Review this list with the employee and give her a copy. Also, make sure the employee understands that she must return *all* company documents and materials before leaving. If the employee wants to take a work sample with her, make sure it contains no confidential information. Finally, try to find out as much as possible about the worker's new employer and what the worker's job responsibilities will be. This will help you determine whether the employee might be tempted to reveal trade secrets to her new employer. If so, you may want to send the new employer the letter in Section H8b, below.

Give the employee a copy of the employment agreement she signed when she started work. (See Chapter 9.) Go over the confidentiality and, if applicable, noncompetition restrictions. Make sure the employee understands the provisions and appreciates that the company is serious about protecting its trade secrets. Finally, ask the employee to sign an acknowledgment of her obligations (a sample form is shown below). If the employee refuses to sign, be sure to note that in her personnel file. The refusal may be helpful if you later attempt to obtain an injunction to prevent the employee from disclosing company trade secrets.

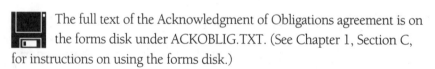 The full text of the Acknowledgment of Obligations agreement is on the forms disk under ACKOBLIG.TXT. (See Chapter 1, Section C, for instructions on using the forms disk.)

SAMPLE
ACKNOWLEDGMENT OF OBLIGATIONS

1. I understand and acknowledge that during my employment with Mystery Software, Inc. (the "Company") I have received or been exposed to trade secrets of the Company including, but not limited to, the following: those listed on Exhibit A to this Agreement.

2. I acknowledge that I have read, signed and been furnished with a copy of my Employment Agreement with the Company. I certify that I have complied with and will continue to comply with all of the provisions of the Employment Agreement, including my obligation to preserve as confidential all of the Company's trade secrets.

3. I certify that I do not have in my possession, I have not retained copies of, nor have I failed to return: any system documentation, user manuals, modification reports, training instructions, formulas, compilers, data structures, algorithms, computer source code, notebooks, notes, drawings, proposals or other documents or materials (or extracts thereof), or equipment or other property belonging to the Company.

4. During my employment I contributed to the development of the Company's trade secrets. I acknowledge that, as provided in my Employment Agreement, all right, title and interest in and to any programming conceived or developed by me, whether in whole or in part, during the course of my employment by the Company belongs to the Company.

_____

Employee's typed or printed name

_____

Employee's signature

_____

Date

b. Informing New Employer About Nondisclosure Agreement

If, as a result of your exit interview or otherwise, you're concerned that a departing employee may reveal company trade secrets to his or her new employer, send a letter to the new employer to let it know that your ex-employee has signed a nondisclosure agreement and that you are serious about enforcing it. Your letter serves two purposes:

1. It may help deter both the employee and new employer from breaching the nondisclosure agreement.

2. If a breach does occur, it will establish that the new employer knew that the employee possessed your trade secrets and had a duty not to disclose them without your permission. This will make the new employer liable for their unauthorized disclosure along with your ex-employee. It also will enable you to obtain a court order barring the new employer from using any of your trade secrets if the ex-employee makes an unauthorized disclosure. (See Section C, above.)

Be careful how you write this letter. Avoid unnecessary accusations or personal inferences; just stick to the facts. Otherwise, if your ex-employee loses his new job as a result of your letter, he might sue the company for defamation or slander. Also, don't describe the trade secrets involved in detail; a general description of the subject matter is sufficient.

The full text of this sample letter is on the forms disk under LTRSECRT.TXT. See Chapter 1, Section C, for instructions on using the forms disk.

Send this letter by certified mail, return receipt requested. A copy should also be sent to the former employee.

SAMPLE
LETTER TO NEW EMPLOYER

July 12, 199X

To Whom It May Concern:

We understand that Olivia Williams has decided to join your company. We would like to inform you of the following facts:

1. During her employment by us, Olivia Williams had access to our trade secrets including, but not limited to, advanced information about robotic visual scanning algorithms.

2. In connection with her employment, Olivia Williams signed an Employment Agreement in which she promised not to disclose or utilize any of our trade secrets without our permission.

3. Olivia Williams has been expressly informed that the disclosure of our trade secrets to others, whether our company's competitors or its customers, either actual or potential, or any other individual, either by words or conduct, can cause irreparable harm to our company.

We are confident that you are aware of, and will comply with, your duty not to use or disclose, directly or indirectly, any trade secrets learned from Olivia Williams.

Our company will view any unauthorized disclosure of our trade secrets by Olivia Williams as extremely serious. We will monitor the situation and hold all parties responsible for any violation of their duties to us to the full extent of the law.

If you have any questions regarding these matters, we will be happy to clarify them for you. In addition, if at any time you wish to know whether information provided you by Olivia Williams is a trade secret owned by us, we will be happy to work out a procedure for providing you with this information.

Very truly yours,

_____

Jane Matthews

cc: Olivia Williams ■

CHAPTER 5

Software Patents

This chapter addresses software patents—one of the hottest legal issues of the day and one of the most difficult to understand. Fortunately, difficult isn't the same as impossible. If you carefully read this material, you should be able to:

- decide whether your software innovation might qualify for a patent;
- take the appropriate actions to protect your rights as the inventor of the innovation;
- interpret and evaluate patents issued on other software-based innovations in order to avoid legal trouble; and
- make some sensible decisions if you are accused of patent infringement.

Also, if you conclude your innovation likely does qualify for a patent, you will be well prepared to do your own patent work, using David Pressman's excellent self-help primer on patenting, *Patent It Yourself* (Nolo Press), or the *Patent It Yourself* computer program based on the book (Nolo Press).

A. Who Needs This Chapter?

Even 10 years ago there was no apparent reason for a software developer to worry about software patents. Only a tiny number of highly specialized patents had ever been issued on software innovations. The general legal view was that software innovations weren't patentable, because software technology itself did not appear to fit comfortably within any of the patentable subject matter groups.

All that has long since changed. It is estimated that between 10,000 and 15,000 software and software-related patents have been issued. Clearly, anyone who develops software needs to be aware of what patents are and how the patenting process works, so that they can tell whether their innovation qualifies for a patent, or whether they might be infringing someone else's patent.

⚠️ Despite the seemingly large numbers of patents being issued for software-related advances, many software inventions do not qualify for patents, primarily because they are not considered to be innovative enough. We explain why in Section E.

THE MULTIMEDIA PATENT

On August 31, 1993 the PTO issued a stunningly broad patent on the basic search and retrieval technology used in virtually all interactive multimedia products (Reed et al., patent number 5,241,671). The patent took the software development world by surprise, primarily because few thought that this type of technology could be patented at all. Here is how the invention is described in the patent abstract:

"A database search system that retrieves multimedia information in a flexible, user friendly system. The search system uses a multimedia database consisting of text, picture, audio and animated data. That database is searched through multiple graphical and textual entry paths. Those entry paths include an idea search, a title finder search, a topic tree search, a picture explorer search, a history timeline search, a world atlas search, a researcher's assistant search, and a feature article search."

Because patent applications are confidential and this one took four years to process, hundreds of companies reportedly spent billions of dollars developing a wide variety of multimedia products without a clue that their efforts might be governed by someone else's patent.

As it turned out, the PTO decided to re-examine the patent on the basis of information it received—from other multimedia developers—to the effect that the technology covered by the patent wasn't novel or unobvious (both are qualifications for patentability). Upon reexamination, the PTO decided that the patent's main claim was far too broad given previous developments in the field, and ruled it unpatentable. However, that's not the end of the story. The owners of the patent in question are still attempting to obtain a patent on at least part of the multimedia technology covered by the former patent, and are expected to submit a new and narrower main claim for consideration.

1. Why Worry About Software Patents?

If in the course of your software development activity you produce a patentable invention, you may have an asset worth many thousands or even millions of dollars. This is because a patent provides a 17-year monopoly over the use of the innovation covered by the patent. Obviously, failing to understand the basics of software patents may mean that you inadvertently throw these rights away and have to rely instead on trade secret protection or less powerful copyright protection. Although relatively few software innovations qualify for patent protection, you definitely want to know whether yours is one of them.

Even if it turns out that your innovation isn't eligible for a patent, you—and all software developers—should be concerned with the possibility of inadvertently infringing a patent belonging to someone else. This is not a concern you should easily dismiss. If you are accused of using someone else's patented invention without the patent owner's permission, you may have to discontinue use, pay the patent owner a royalty in exchange for a license to use the invention, pay damages for the infringement (the amount of the patent owner's lost profits) or fight the matter out in court. Not only is a court battle very expensive, but if you lose, you may be liable for all the profits you made using the invention. In "exceptional cases," a court can even triple the damages and make you pay the patent owner's attorney fees.

2. Patents Compared With Copyright, Trade Secrets and Trademarks

A patent on a useful invention—a utility patent—grants a 17-year monopoly over the technology employed by the invention. Although this chapter is about software patents, it is important to remember that there are other ways to protect products of the intellect. The main ways are:

• *Copyright laws*. These protect the expressive aspects of intellectual property and are discussed in Chapter 3.

- *Trade secret laws.* These protect information that both is maintained as a proprietary secret and that provides its owner with a competitive advantage in the marketplace. Trade secret law is discussed in Chapter 4.
- *Trademark laws.* These laws protect original names, symbols and slogans that are used to distinguish goods and services in the marketplace. Trademark law is discussed in Chapter 6.

Each of these protection schemes has its limitations when it comes to protecting pure ideas.

Copyright does not protect ideas per se, but only the way ideas are expressed. If there are only one or two ways in which a particular idea can be expressed, then the idea and the expression are said to "merge" and no copyright protection is allowed. Also, copyright only protects against copying. If someone else independently produces an expression that is very similar to yours, but didn't result from copying, there is nothing you can do about it. Also, copyright does not protect procedures, processes, systems or methods of operation—all items that may be protectible in a patent.

Unlike copyright, trade-secret law does protect ideas, but only as long as they are kept secret. If the ideas are legally accessible to the public, either because they are obvious from the innovation itself or because someone discovers the ideas by reverse engineering or decompiling the innovation, protection ends. But it is possible to preserve trade secrets in software that is selectively distributed on a one-on-one basis to large customers—rather than sold in the mass market. This is done by requiring the purchaser to sign an agreement binding the purchaser to keep confidential any secrets that are discovered while using the software.

Trademark law protects marketing ideas that are reduced to symbolic form (words, logos, slogans, etc.), but does not protect either the ideas or the expression in the software innovation itself. Although branding software (for example, LOTUS 1-2-3) can be an effective marketing technique in the short run, if a competitor introduces a similar or better product at a lower cost, branding doesn't provide much in the way of long term protection.

In contrast to these other software protection schemes, utility patents do the best job in that the patent owner can keep others from using the idea covered by the patent for the 17-year life of the patent. But utility patents for most software innovations are hard won and even where a patent is possible, the application process can be costly and the enforcement process can be difficult.

 There are other types of patents that usually don't apply to software. There are two other types of patents—design patents and plant patents. Plant patents never apply to software, and so far, design patents have only applied to computer screen icons.

3. How to Use This Chapter

Whether or not you are likely to seek a patent on your software innovation, we recommend that you at least read Sections B, C and D of this chapter. These sections provide a basic grounding in patent law and procedure. In addition they explain in general terms what makes a software-based innovation patentable and assuming yours is, how to protect your patent rights once a patent is acquired.

If you want more specific information as to when a software innovation qualifies for a patent, read Section E. You'll find detailed examples of software innovations for which patents have issued and explanations of why these innovations qualified for patents.

Section F tells you how to search for patents already issued on software-based innovations. Read Section G if you want to know more about how the courts determine whether one patent has infringed another; you'll find some tips on what to do if you are accused of infringement—and some guidelines on how to avoid it.

B.　A Quick Look at Whether You May Have a Patentable Invention

To decide with some degree of confidence whether your software-based invention qualifies for a patent, you will need to thoroughly study the information presented in this chapter. However, because many readers may wish a quicker answer on the issue of patentability before deciding whether to read every word, here are some suggestions for making a preliminary assessment of your situation.

1.　How to Identify Software Patentability

Keeping in mind that quick answers risk oversimplification, you should consider your software a possible candidate for a patent if:

- The software produces a new and useful interpretation of data fed into the computer.

    Example: *A software program that converts seismic data into a useful number for comparing different seismic activity is combined with the machine that collects the original seismic data and a computer hardware system that runs the algorithm and produces an analytical report.*

- The software, through the computer, controls a device that performs a new and useful function.

    Example: *A software program calculates the time needed to cure a certain type of rubber in a certain type of mold, and then directs the mold to open when the curing is completed.*

- The software solves a computer-related problem that has been identified but not yet solved.

    Example: *The software program organizes access to files for a system that involves multiple users.*

- The software makes existing computerized processes work better.

Example: *The software program processes data from analog to digital form without the need for a step that previously involved using hardware that was expensive and time-consuming.*

Conversely, if your software relies on well known principles and routines and creates products or results that, while marketable, aren't really new, it is probably not patentable.

⚠️ **Does your software pass the "ooh and aah" test?** Although it may seem simplistic, it will help if you ask yourself whether seeing your program would cause other knowledgeable computer programmers or software developers familiar with your field to ooh and aah. If the answer isn't a resounding yes, your code is probably not sufficiently innovative and therefore not patentable.

WHEN TO WORRY ABOUT PATENT INFRINGEMENT

If you feel that your innovation is on the technological cutting edge, you should be concerned about whether someone else at an equal place on that cutting edge has already legally locked up the innovation in the form of a patent. But if your software is more conventional, the ideas that it employs probably have been around for awhile and you can relax a bit. Even if there are patents out there that in least in theory apply to one or more aspects of your code (an amazing amount of now common software is covered by one or more patents), it is unlikely that the patent owners will come after you seeking reimbursement for their lost profits. This is primarily because enforcing a software patent is like enforcing a copyright against photocopy machine users; infringement is so widespread and the economic injury suffered from each infringement is so small, that enforcement is just plain economically unfeasible. On the other hand, if your software visibly shows up in the marketplace in competition with the patented software innovation, you may have an infringement suit on your hands.

2. Should You Apply for a Patent?

The fact that your software-based innovation may qualify for a patent doesn't necessarily mean that you should apply for one. There are at least two practical reasons to hesitate.

a. Patents on Software-Based Inventions Are Suspect

Because the United States Patent and Trademark Office (PTO) has had problems deciding what kinds of software really are patentable, patents on software-based inventions are suspect. The fact that the PTO issues a patent doesn't mean the patent is valid. It only means that a particular examiner has decided that a patent should issue on your invention. If you should later go to court to enforce the patent, the infringer may be able to successfully prove that the patent never should have issued in the first place. In other words, a judge can (and often does) second guess the patent examiner and—assuming your adversary appeals—an appellate judge can second guess the first judge.

This second-guessing routine, which is potentially a problem for all patents, is especially troublesome for patents on software-based innovations. This is primarily because the PTO lacks:

- sufficient personnel who are qualified to examine software-related applications,
- comprehensive information about previous software developments, and
- a consistent understanding of when patents should and should not be issued on software-based innovations.

Simply, it's well known that many software patents have been and continue to be improperly issued. The fact that you get a patent on your software may be little more than an invitation to spend piles of money on lawyers and courts in an unsuccessful effort to enforce it against attacks on its validity.

On a more positive note, however, the courts have recently been more willing to uphold the validity of patents issued by the PTO. Also, if your patent ends up in court, it is presumed to be valid until your adversary proves the opposite—a bit like a person accused of a crime being presumed innocent.

b.   Only the Powerful (or Very Determined) Can Play the Patent Game

Seeking and then enforcing a patent can cost a bundle. Therefore you will want to make a cost-benefit analysis, weighing the costs of obtaining and maintaining the patent over its 17-year life (several thousand dollars) against the probability that you really will be able to commercially profit from it.

As a general rule, seeking a software patent is unwise unless you are reasonably sure that your invention deserves a patent and at least one of the following is true:

- You are economically strong enough to fund patent litigation should the need for it arise (patent litigation is hellishly expensive because you must hire lawyers—commonly in excess of $100,000).
- You are stubborn and savvy enough to take time to understand how the patent system works and willing to do some or all of your own legal work (a good-sized hill to climb but others have done it, with huge rewards).
- The innovation is sufficiently important to another company to cause it to come to terms with you if you have the patent (by purchasing your patent rights or paying you for a license to use the innovation).
- You own a lot of patents and are a big enough player in the industry to wheel and deal with other patent holders by trading them the right to use your patents in exchange for your being able to use theirs.
- You know your idea will change the course of a particular field, and without a patent on it you risk forfeiting the credit and profit from the idea to others, who may then obtain their own patent and freeze you out.
- You think the patent will impress prospective financial backers that your business really is special (venture capitalists have been known to

tell start-ups to come back and see them after they have obtained a patent).

- You are looking ahead to possibly selling your business and want to increase its value. But remember, the value of patent ownership must be considered in the context of the two to three years it takes to get the patent as well as the 17 years of the patent's life. In short, for a patent to add real value to your business, you need to feel confident that the invention you are patenting will not soon be out-dated by newer technology.

C.   An Introduction to Patent Law and Procedure

In this section we provide a basic grounding in patent law, especially in relation to software-based inventions. Without this grounding you will have difficulty in following the discussion about software-based inventions that comes later.

1.   What is an Invention?

So far we have used the term innovation to describe something that might be patentable. Now it's time to formally introduce you to the word "invention," the term used for "innovation" in the patent world. Generally, an invention is any device or process that:

- is based on an original idea conceived by one or more inventors, and
- is useful in getting something done or solving a problem

An invention may also be a non-functional unique design (on which a design patent may issue) or a plant (on which a plant patent may issue). But when the word invention used out the real world, it almost always means a device or process.

2. What Is a Software-Based Invention?

Start by understanding that patents don't issue on software itself (for reasons discussed in Section E, below). Rather, they issue on inventions that use innovative software to produce a useful result, that is, "software-based" inventions. And when we use the term "software patent," it is these software-based inventions to which the term applies.

Software-based inventions that have qualified for a patent are often ones that involve software connected to and running hardware components, such as a computer controlling a rubber molding press, a computer attached to a machine that receives analog seismic activity data, and a computer attached to a machine that receives electric signals that represent the activity of a heart. The essence of these inventions is found in the functional combination of their software and hardware. It's also worthy of note that a number of software-based inventions such as these transform analog data into digital information that then can be put to some diagnostic, analytic or other use.

3. Unpatentable Inventions May Be Valuable

Many inventions, while extremely clever, do not qualify for patents, primarily because they are not considered to be sufficiently innovative in light of previous developments.

The fact that an invention is not patentable does not necessarily mean that it has no value for its owner. While it is true that anyone is free to use an unpatented invention, they have to know about it first. If the invention can be maintained as a trade secret (as we describe in Chapter 4) and used by its owner to obtain a competitive advantage, the invention's owner may be better off than if the invention were disclosed to the world in a patent. This is because once the details of a patented invention are disclosed, it is often possible to "design around" the patent and thereby, as a practical matter, neutralize its economic impact.

Example: *An employee at Zoetics Software invents a method for using a computer to produce a detailed and legally-sound estate plan based on a person's personal data. However, due to previous knowledge and activity in this field, Zoetic's employee won't be able to obtain a broad, basic patent—only a narrow one. Thus, if Zoetics applies for and receives a patent on this invention, another company could review the patent and very likely design a competing estate planner that used a different (non-infringing) method. Or, in the words of the trade, they could design around the patent. Zoetics might be better off maintaining its method as a trade secret and operating a centralized estate-planning service itself.*

4. What Is a Patent?

We've been talking about patents as if you know exactly what one is. Just to be sure this is true, let's define the term. A patent is an official document—issued by the U.S. government, or another government—that describes an invention and confers on the inventors (in the case of a U.S. utility patent) a 17-year monopoly over the use of the invention. This monopoly allows the patent owner to go to court to stop others from making, selling or using the invention without the patent owner's permission.

The patent document contains:

* a title for the invention and the names and addresses of the inventors,
* details of the patent search made by the PTO,
* an abstract that concisely describes the key aspects of the invention;
* a detailed narrative description of the invention,
* drawings or flowcharts of the invention,
* very precise definitions of the invention covered by the patent (called the patent claims), and
* a brief summary of the invention.

Taken together, the various parts of the patent document provide a complete disclosure of every important aspect of the covered invention. When a U.S. patent issues, all the information in the patent is readily accessible to the public in the PTO and in patent libraries across the U.S. and through on-line patent database services (see Section G, below).

5. How Do You Get a Patent?

Here we provide a brief overview of the patent process. If you are interested in actually applying for a patent, obtain a copy of *Patent It Yourself*, by David Pressman, or the software based on that book (also called *Patent It Yourself*), by EDS/Nolo Press. Both are published by Nolo Press.

U.S. patents are obtained by submitting to the PTO:

- a patent application, and
- as of 1994, an application fee of $355, if you are a small entity—that is, an individual, a small company of less than 500 persons or a nonprofit organization under no obligation to assign the invention to a for-profit company with over 500 employees. For-profit companies with 500 employees or more must pay $710 to apply for a patent.

Once your application is received, the PTO assigns it to an examiner who is supposed to be knowledgeable in the technology underlying the invention. For example, for a software invention, the examiner may have a B.S. in computer science, or a degree in electronics with some knowledge of computers as well, of course, as on-the-job experience.

The patent examiner is responsible for deciding whether your application meets all the technical requirements of a patent application, whether the invention qualifies for a patent, and assuming it does, what the scope of the patent should be. Usually, back and forth communications—called patent prosecution in the jargon of the patent world—occur between the applicant and the examiner regarding these issues. Clearly the most serious and hard-to-fix issue is whether the invention qualifies for a patent.

Eventually, if all of the examiner's objections are overcome by the applicant, the invention is approved for a patent. Then, the applicant pays a patent issue fee of $585 (for small entities), or $1,170 (for large entities), and receives an officially ribboned copy of the patent deed. Three additional fees must be paid over the 17-year life of the patent to keep it in effect. The total patent fee for a small entity, from application to issue to expiration, is currently $3,750. (For a large entity, it is roughly twice this amount).

> Patent fees have been going up every year, sometimes substantially. Before you assume the numbers you read here are still current, call the PTO at 703-308-HELP.

APPEALING A DECISION: WHO EXAMINES THE PATENT EXAMINER?

What happens if a patent examiner decides that an invention does not qualify for a patent, and you disagree? First, an unsatisfied patent applicant can appeal the examiner's final decision to another part of the PTO, called the Board of Patent Appeals and Interferences, which follows procedural rules that are beyond the scope of this book. After the "Board" (as it is called) makes a decision, either the patent application is returned to the examiner and the patent issues (sometimes with adjustments suggested by the Board), or the examiner's final decision to deny a patent is affirmed (that is, the patent application is again rejected).

Following rejection from the Board, the unsuccessful patent applicant has two options: bring a civil lawsuit against the Commissioner of Patents in the District Court for the District of Columbia, or bring a direct appeal in the U.S. Court of Appeals for the Federal Circuit. If the lawsuit in the District Court is unsuccessful, the applicant can then still appeal to the U.S. Court of Appeals for the Federal Circuit.

The U.S. Court of Appeals for the Federal Circuit, also called the Federal Circuit or CAFC for short, is a special federal court created to handle appeals in patent and customs matters. Because this court specializes in patent law, its decisions are generally considered to be knowledgeable. The next step after a ruling in the Federal Circuit is to appeal—petition for cert as it is called in the legal trade—to the U.S. Supreme Court. Because the Supreme Court hears only a fraction of the cases appealed to it, chances are it won't agree to hear the case, meaning that the Federal Circuit Court of Appeals' decision will be final.

6. Protecting Your Rights As an Inventor

If two inventors apply for a patent around the same time, the patent will be awarded to the inventor who came up with the invention first. This may or may not be the inventor who was first to file a patent application. For this reason, especially in the software field, it is vital that you carefully document your inventive activities. If two or more pending patent applications by different inventors claim the same invention, the PTO will ask the inventors to establish the date each of them first conceived the invention and the ways in which they then showed diligence in "reducing the invention to practice."

Inventors can reduce their inventions to practice in two ways:

- by making a working model—a prototype—which works as the idea of the invention dictates it should, or
- by constructively reducing it to practice—that is, by describing the invention in sufficient detail for someone else to build it—in a document that is then filed as a patent application with the PTO.

The inventor who conceived the invention first will be awarded the patent if he or she also showed diligence in either building the invention or filing a patent application. However, if the inventor who was second to conceive the invention was the first one to reduce it to practice—for instance by filing a patent application—that inventor may end up with the patent.

A key point to understand is that it's often the quality of an inventor's documentation (dated notes in a notebook that show the conception of the invention and the steps that were taken to reduce the invention to practice) that determines which invention ends up with the patent. To create good documentation, use a lab notebook that precludes the insertion of pages after the fact (spiral binding or hard-bound for example). Each page should be dated and signed by the inventor and by a witness. Details for doing this are in David Pressman's *Patent It Yourself*. Also, Nolo Press publishes *The Inventor's Notebook,* by David Pressman and Fred Grissom, which not only serves as lab notebook, but also provides a structured step-by-step approach to documenting an invention.

There is a chance that in the next couple of years the patent system will switch from the present "first-to-invent" system to a "first-to-file" system used in other countries. If the switch occurs, it will be irrelevant who invented first because the first to file an application on an invention will automatically be considered the inventor. As a result, the need to document the steps of the invention process may be reduced. Until the law changes, however, we strongly suggest you meticulously document your inventive activity.

D.   What Qualifies a Software-Based Invention for a Patent?

An invention must meet several basic legal tests in order to qualify as a patent. Here we provide an overview of these tests, specifically as they apply to software-based inventions.

1.   The Invention Must Consist of Patentable Subject Matter

As mentioned, there are three basic types of patents:
- utility patents,
- design patents, and
- plant patents.

Virtually all patents that have been obtained on software-based inventions are utility patents, although some design patents have been issued on computer screen icons. (See Section D6, below).

The most fundamental qualification for a patent is that the invention consist of patentable subject matter. The patent laws define patentable subject matter as inventions that are one of the following:
- a process or method,
- a machine or apparatus,
- an article of manufacture,

- a composition of matter (for instance, a new glue or chemical compound), or
- an improvement of an invention in any of these classes.

Historically, software was viewed as a law of nature or mathematical algorithm and thus not in any of these categories. But now, as we describe in more detail below, a software-based invention can usually qualify as both a process and a machine, or in the more commonly used patent-speak synonyms, as a "method" and an "apparatus." Software-based inventions may also be improvements of existing software-based inventions (see Section D5, below).

a. Historical Rejections of Software-Based Inventions as Mathematical Algorithms

When first faced with applications for patents on software-based inventions in the 1950s, the PTO routinely rejected the applications on the grounds that software consists of mathematical algorithms. Mathematical algorithms had long been considered to be unpatentable as abstract methods for solving problems and not tied to a particular use or tangible structure. Also, they were considered to be akin to laws of nature and unpatentable on that ground as well.

There were and are good reasons for not granting patents on mathematical algorithms or laws of nature. Allowing a patent on a bare mathematical algorithm would create too huge (and fundamental) a monopoly. To understand why this is so, consider the Heisenberg uncertainty principle, a well known law of nature that states that you cannot design an apparatus to simultaneously determine the location and momentum of a subatomic particle. This principle is relevant to many scientific and electrical engineering applications and a patent on it would give exclusive control of the development of these applications to the owner of the patent. Effectively, this would either bring progress in any field where the principle applies to a halt, or tax all other would-be developers by forcing them to pay license fees to the patent holder.

b. Current Practice

The PTO no longer rejects all patent applications based on the algorithm/law of nature argument. Today, the fact that the Heisenberg uncertainty principle can't itself be patented (because it is considered a mathematical algorithm or "law of nature") no longer means that the principle itself can't be used as a part of a patentable invention. Now the PTO is willing to issue patents on software (software by definition employs algorithms and therefore could be a "law of nature" if that algorithm is mathematical) if the patent application describes the software in relation to computer hardware and related devices, and limits the software to specific uses. If the software is limited to specific uses, it follows that the mathematical algorithm of the software is limited to specific uses. In this way the potential "law of nature" problem—specifically for software: the tying up of a broad mathematical principle—is averted.

Example 1: *Consider a specific use of the Heisenberg uncertainty principle. Assume that this principle is made use of in an invention that analyzes the movements of tiny particles in nuclear accelerators. This practical application of the principle might receive a patent if the other qualifications for patentability are met. That is, while the Heisenberg principle itself is not patentable, the specific application of the principle would be.*

Example 2: *A software patent was issued on an invention based on the Arrhenius equation ($\ln V = CZ + X$) that calculates the length of time necessary to cure rubber (Diamond v. Diehr, 450 U.S. 175, 101 S. Ct. 1048, 67 L.Ed.2d 155 (1981)). Although the equation (an algorithm) itself was not patentable, an invention that combined it with hardware designed to open a rubber-making mold at the correct time did qualify as a patentable invention.*

Most software-based inventions for which the PTO has been willing to issue patents fall into either or both of two categories. In some ways these two categories are different sides of the same coin. The categories are:

A method or process: The invention involves feeding information into a computer and acting on that information so as to transform it into instructions that produce a specific action by the computer—or by a machine linked to the computer—that in turn produces a useful result. Emphasis in this category is on the useful result.

Example: *Raw information from a heart monitoring device is fed into a computer. The software program analyzes the information according to a set of principles and causes the results of this analysis to be displayed in a format that shows whether the person is at risk for a heart attack.*

A device or machine: The invention involves software that is described in the patent application as an integral part of the specific invention rather than as a general principle that could be applied to other inventions. Emphasis in this category is on the specific application.

Example: *(The same above invention described as a method or process.) The patentable invention is a device (consisting of a monitor, a computer, some software and a display device) that analyzes the results transferred from a heart monitor and converts these results to information that is used to predict heart attacks.*

None of these components individually could likely qualify for a patent (the physical items have already been invented and the algorithm itself is unpatentable). But the overall invention did qualify, even though the software was the key aspect of the invention.

Let's consider another, more fanciful, example, to make sure that the basis for patenting software is clearly understood. Imagine the following invention:

Example: *A machine that monitors brain waves is hooked up to a device that converts the brain waves into digital format. The digitized brain waves are then fed into a computer and run through a program that uses sophisticated algorithms which decipher them and display the result—what the person was thinking—on a screen.*

Most likely, this invention would receive a patent if it were described carefully. But why? The only part of the invention that can be said to be new are the algorithms, and algorithms by themselves do not qualify for patent protection. However, the invention can be described as a method which achieves a specific useful result and/or as an apparatus which is a specific device consisting of a combination of software and hardware that produces this particular result. Thus, the patent could issue on the apparatus or on the method, or on both.

c.   Examples of Software Patents

To give you a feel for the types of software-based inventions that have received patents, we provide some brief examples below (along with the patent numbers, if you're inclined to look them up after reading Section G about searching for patents).

The invention:

- operates a system of manufacturing plants (Deutch); controls and optimizes the operation of a system of multi-unit plants (oil refineries) at different geographic locations, where each plant has a different, unique cost function in producing the product,
- controls a computerized method and apparatus for curing molded rubber — (Diehr),
- translates between natural languages — #4,502,128 (Toma),
- determines boundaries of graphic regions on a computer screen — #4,788,438,
- governs removable menu windows on a computer screen — #4,931,783,
- generates and overlays graphic windows for multiple active program storage areas in the computer — #4,555,775,
- qualifies and sorts file record data in a computer — #4,510,567,
- compresses and manipulates images in a computer — #4,622,545,
- handles the data structure and search method for a data base management system — #4,468,728,
- automates spelling error corrections — #4,355,471 — as in some form of a spell-checker system,
- sets up a securities brokerage-cash management system — #4,346,442,
- evaluates geological formations traversed by a borehole— #4338,664,
- operates a system that valuates stocks, bonds and other securities — #4334,270,
- automatically makes a two-dimensional portrayal of a three-dimensional object (Bernhart); specifically, it transforms a 2-D drawing of an object into a computer-presentable 3-D drawing — in the simplest case, a box would be transformed into a cube,

- sets up an information storage and retrieval system — #4,068,298 — system allows information to be stored on a hard drive and retrieved by multiple users at different locations,
- measures the performance of a general purpose digital computer — #3,644,936, and
- analyzes electrocardiographic signals in order to determine certain characteristics of heart function — #4,422,459

2. The Invention Must Be Useful

Almost always, a software-based invention must be useful in some way to qualify for a patent. Fortunately, this is almost never a problem, since virtually everything can be used for something.

DESIGN PATENTS

In some instances, software inventors can apply for what is known as a design patent. A design patent provides a 14-year monopoly to industrial designs that have no functional use. That is, contrary to the usefulness rule discussed just above, designs covered by design patents must be purely ornamental. The further anomaly of design patents is that while the design itself must be primarily ornamental, as opposed to primarily functional, it must at the same time be embodied in something people-made. For example, you can't get a design patent on rock dug up from the ground. In patent terms, the design has to be embodied in an "article of manufacture." This "article" can, however, be something non-functional, like a doll or a decorative water fountain. (See the discussion in Section D6 for more on design patents.)

3. The Invention Must Be Novel

As a general rule, no invention will receive a patent unless it is different in some important way from previous inventions and developments in the field, both patented and unpatented. Or to use patent jargon, the invention must be novel over the prior art.

As part of deciding whether an invention is novel, the U.S. patent law system focuses on two dates:

- when the patent application is filed, and
- when the invention was first conceived

a. The Date of Filing

The filing date is important because of the one-year rule. For an invention to be considered novel, an application for a patent on the invention must be filed *within one year* of the time the invention is first offered for sale or commercially or publicly used or described. Otherwise, the invention will be considered no longer novel at the time the application is filed.

File your software patent application promptly. Once you understand the one-year rule it should be clear why it is so important that you file your patent application as soon as possible but in any event no later than one year after the invention has become known to the public in some way. As a general rule, the limited testing of software by the public in a structured beta test program should not start the one-year period running. But the year period might start running if the beta test release were widespread enough, or if one of the testers posted it on a widely accessed bulletin board and as a result it became well known. In any event, you are always better off to assume the worst and get your patent application in as soon as possible.

b. The Date of Conception

The date of conception is important in judging whether any previous inventions or developments—termed prior art—preclude your invention from being considered novel. If another invention can be shown to have existed when you first conceived of your invention, your invention will not be novel. This bar is different than the one-year rule, which commonly strips an invention of novelty because of the inventor's delay in filing a patent application (although technically the one-year rule also applies to somebody else's identical invention that has become known to the public more than one year prior to your patent application (even if the other invention came into existence after you conceived of your invention).

4. The Invention Must Not Be Obvious

In addition to being novel, an invention must have a quality that is referred to as "nonobviousness." Translated into regular English, this means that the invention would have been surprising or unexpected to someone who is familiar with the field of the invention. And in deciding whether an invention is nonobvious, the PTO may consider all previous developments (called "prior art") that existed when the invention was conceived. Like obscenity, obviousness is a quality that is difficult to define but supposedly a patent examiner "knows it when she sees it."

As a general rule, an invention is considered nonobvious when it does one of the following:

- solves a problem that people in the field have been trying to solve for some time,
- does something significantly quicker than was previously possible, or
- performs a function that could not be performed before.

Most software-based inventions are rejected at least in the first response from the PTO because they can't pass the nonobviousness test. This makes sense as it has been estimated that less than 1% of all software contains nonobvious innovations. However, if people familiar with similar technology are impressed with your advancement, you have a better chance to establish its nonobviousness. As a patent applicant, if you are persistent with the PTO and your invention is different from the prior art inventions that have come before it, you stand a good chance of success.

NOVELTY AND NONOBVIOUSNESS COMPARED

Slow down a minute now and be sure you understand the important difference between novelty and nonobviousness. An invention may be novel because it has one or more elements that are significantly different than any particular previous invention. But that same invention may not be considered nonobvious because the differences between the current invention and previous inventions (separately or in combination) are not sufficiently surprising to someone familiar with the particular technology.

Example: An invention eliminates one step from an existing 12-step process that enables the computer to determine the originality of art works. The elimination of the step does not dramatically speed the process up and, upon reflection, is a fairly routine improvement. Although the new invention is considered novel—because one of its elements is different from the previous process—the advance might well be considered obvious and a patent denied on that ground. If, however, the new invention reduces the original 12-step process to five steps through an innovative parallel processing approach that greatly increases the speed of the program and the accuracy of the diagnosis, the invention would probably be considered both novel and nonobvious and could be awarded a patent.

5. The Invention May Be an Improvement (of an Existing Invention)

Earlier we noted that to qualify for a patent an invention must fit into at least one of the statutory classes of matter entitled to a patent: a process, a machine, a manufacture, a composition of matter, or an improvement of any of these. We also have noted that software-based inventions usually fall into one or both of two of these classifications—a method and an apparatus. But software-based inventions can also be patented if they constitute improvements of invention, patented or unpatented.

Example: *You have a program that allows the computer user to control access to a datafile. You conceive a similar program that controls access to multiple datafiles by multiple users. This invention is an improvement of the single file access program and might qualify for a patent on that basis.*

As a practical matter, this statutory class is not very important since even an improvement on an invention in one of the other statutory classes will also qualify as an actual invention in that class. Put differently, an invention will be considered as patentable subject matter as long as it fits within at least one of the other four statutory classes—whether or not it is viewed as an improvement or an original invention.

Computer software is extremely adaptable to what is known as "improvement patenting." Because computer technology is still in a period of rapid development, programs that make operations on the computer run faster, easier or better are almost routine as innovators continue to improve the state of the art.

6. The Invention May Be a Design

Design patents are granted to new, original and ornamental designs that are a part of articles of manufacture. Articles of manufacture are in turn defined as anything made by the hands of humans. In the past design patents have been granted to items such as truck fenders, chairs, fabric designs, athletic shoes, tires, toys, tools, artificial hip joints, flatware, and even the shape of the spray coming from a water fountain.

a. What Qualifies for a Design Patent

The key to understanding this type of patent is the fact that a patentable design is required to be primarily ornamental and an integral part (ornamentally not functionally) of an item made by humans (an article of manufacture). A truck fender makes a good example. Any truck is an article of manufacture or a machine. Just as clearly, the truck fender is an integral part of the body of the truck since it partially encloses a wheel and abuts the hood. To qualify for a design patent, a truck company would need to come up with a novel (original) design for the shape of the fender that was visually pleasing (interesting), and as such, primarily ornamental as opposed to primarily functional.

So far, design patents have not played much of a role in the software field. For further discussion of this point, see Section F6c, below.

b.   Design Patents Compared With Utility Patents

Design patents are easy to apply for because they do not require much written description. They require drawings of the design, a short description of each figure or drawing and one claim that says little more than: "We/I claim the ornamental design depicted in the attached drawings." Other important differences are that design patents:

* are less expensive to apply for than utility patents,
* last for 14 instead of 17 years, and
* require no maintenance fees.

c.   Design Patents for Computer Screen Interface Elements

In 1988, 22 design patents were issued to Xerox corporation for items, including:

* icon for virtual floppy disk,
* icon for application program,
* icon for property sheet,
* icon for freehand drawing softkey display, and
* icon for broken document.

A year-and-a-half later, the PTO rejected four similar applications for design patents to software icons. The decision was appealed within the PTO. The rejection was upheld, but the PTO issued specific guidelines on how to be successful with a design patent application related to a software-based invention.

The guidelines are these:

- The design patent's drawings shall include the article of manufacture. For example if the design is an icon, include in the drawing a computer display screen that shows the icon; do not just show a picture of the icon by itself. The PTO wants to grant design patents on ornamental aspects of useful items, not for the ornamental aspects by themselves, untied to a context. (See the sample below.)

No:

or

Yes:

- Include with the design patent's application declarations (written statements from the inventor) that demonstrate that the design (for example, an icon) is an integral part of the operation of a programmed computer, even though it is ornamental and does not have a function of its own. For example, if you are attempting to patent the design of an icon for a computer display, describe how the user points and clicks on the icon to open a window on the display screen. This will show the PTO that the design is not merely a displayed picture, but an integral and active part of an operational component.

E.   Does Your Software-Based Invention Qualify for a Patent?

To help you assess whether your software-based invention is patentable, we now explain, in some detail, what makes a software-based invention qualify for a patent.

To aid in doing this, we first introduce you to two court decisions that, taken together, do much to define the parameters of when a software-based invention qualifies for a patent. Then we review in more detail what the PTO is looking for when assessing the patentability of software-based inventions.

Then, in Section F, we introduce you to the art (language, really) of drafting patent claims for software-based inventions. Even if you never have occasion to use this language yourself, familiarity with it will help you understand the precise aspects of software-based inventions that are patentable, and reduce any intimidation you might feel about patents.

1.   Court Decisions

The following three court decisions underlie all PTO decisions as to which software-based inventions are patentable. If you have read this chapter from the beginning, you have already encountered brief discussions about two of them (*Diehr* and *Arrythmia*). Here we go into more detail.

a.   Diamond v. Diehr

In *Diamond v. Diehr*, the U.S. Supreme Court first interpreted patent law to allow the patenting of a software-based invention (*Diamond v. Diehr*, 450 U.S. 175, 101 S.Ct. 1048, 67 L.Ed.2d 155 (1981)).

The case involved an invention consisting of a process for curing synthetic rubber. To do this, the invention used a known mathematical algorithm as part of a computer program to determine the proper length of time for curing the product and, when curing was complete, to open the mold automatically. The PTO refused to issue a patent because:

- the invention was based on a mathematical algorithm, and
- mathematical algorithms are unpatentable as laws of nature.

The Court of Appeals for the federal circuit upheld the PTO, but the Supreme Court disagreed and ordered that the applicant was entitled to obtain a patent on the invention. The Court based its decision on the fact that the steps of the mathematical algorithm were tied to a computer-controlled process during which tangible material (here, the synthetic rubber) is changed from one form (a molten glob) into another form (a molded piece of rubber). The Court specifically ruled that inventions using a mathematical algorithm may be patented when the algorithm is applied to a structure or process that, when considered as a whole, performs a function that the patent laws were designed to protect. Put differently, an invention that transforms or reduces an article to a different state or thing may be patented, even if an otherwise unpatentable algorithm is used to make it work. An even more basic way to summarize the Court ruling in this case is to say that an algorithm is patentable if it works in connection with a specific apparatus and is described that way in the patent claims (the precise statements of what the patent actually covers).

b. The Arrythmia Case

Following the Supreme Court's decision in *Diamond v. Diehr,* a series of cases decided by the Court of Appeals for the Federal Circuit (and its predecessor, the Court of Custom and Patent Appeals) helped to shape the current scope of what software-based inventions are patentable. One of those cases is *Arrythmia* (958 F.2d 1053 (1992)). This is a patent infringement case in which the validity of an existing patent was challenged.

The invention in the *Arrythmia* case involved a computer program that analyzes heartbeat signals in an effort to determine which heart attack victims are most at risk for complete heart failure. In stating its decision that the patent was valid, the Court first reiterated that inventions consisting solely of an abstract mathematical formula or equation, including the mathematical expression of a scientific truth or law of nature, are not proper subject matter for patents. But the Court then pointed out that under the *Diamond v. Diehr* case, an invention that involved a specific process or apparatus might qualify for a patent, even if it was implemented in accordance with a mathematical algorithm.

The Court stated that the patent claims did not result in patenting a mathematical formula, but only foreclosed others from using that formula in conjunction with the diagnostic and computer run steps of the particular invention. In the context of analyzing heart performance, those steps included converting a series of signals to time segments, analyzing the time segments, assigning an arithmetic value to that analysis, and comparing that value with a predetermined level. The comparison allowed a diagnosis to be made as to whether the individual tested was at high risk for heart failure in the future. If so, precautionary care could be undertaken to try to reduce this risk.

The Court further commented that the number obtained at the end of the computer program processing was not an abstraction, but rather was both a measure in microvolts of heart activity, and an indicator of the risk of ventricular tachycardia (the indication of complete heart failure mentioned earlier). In conclusion the Court stated that the claims were properly patented because they were directed to a specific diagnostic apparatus (a computer plus a heart monitor) that had a use (diagnosis of heart patients), and in this case was specifically used to diagnose those heart patients who might be at risk for another heart attack.

c. In re Alappat

In re Alappat is the most recent important court decision on the patentability of software based inventions (decided in July of 1994 by the U.S. Circuit Court of Appeals sitting en banc). The court held that a rasterizer, which converts analog sound data to a digital waveform that can be read on an oscilloscope screen, constitutes patentable subject matter. In reaching its decision, the court read the claims "as a whole," declining to decide whether they contained any mathematical subject matter which standing alone would not be entitled to patent protection. The court concluded that, as claimed, the invention consisted of a combination of interrelated elements which combined to form a machine. An abstract of this case is included in the Appendix.

2. The PTO's Response to the Courts

For unexplained reasons, the PTO and the Federal Circuit Court differ in their points of view on which software-based inventions should be patented. However, with persistence, the PTO can often be convinced to grant patents to software-based inventions. If, however, the PTO finally rejects the application, that denial can then be appealed to the Federal Circuit Court. There, if the invention otherwise meets the criteria discussed in Section E1, above, chances are fairly good that the court will order the PTO to issue the patent. On a positive note, it's also fair to say that, as compared to five years ago, the PTO now appears slightly more favorably disposed towards issuing patents for programs that:

- run computers that in turn run machines that then make something you can touch or visually identify—for instance, a two-dimensional picture plotted as a three-dimensional picture, or
- use an algorithm to translate one set of numbers into another set of numbers where the second set of numbers is used for diagnosis or analysis—for instance, when numbers produced by analog measurements of an earthquake are digitally manipulated to analyze the strength and characteristics of the earthquake.

F. The Patent Claims

Here we introduce you to the odd and wonderful world of the specific language used to write a patent claim—the precise definition of the invention covered by the patent. It helps to be adept at reading patent claims if you ever need to understand precisely what a particular patent covers.

1. An Overview of Patent Claims

Patent claims are the part of the patent application that precisely delimits the scope of the invention—where it begins and ends. Perhaps it will help you understand what patent claims do if you analogize them to real estate deeds. A deed typically includes a description of the parcel's parameters precise enough to map the exact boundaries of the plot of land in question, which in turn can be used as the basis of a legal action to toss out any trespassers.

With patents, the idea is to similarly draw in the patent claims a clear line around the property of the inventor so that any infringer can be identified and dealt with. Patent claims have an additional purpose. Because of the precise way in which they are worded, claims also are used to decide whether in light of previous developments the invention is patentable in the first place.

Unfortunately, to accomplish these purposes, all patent claims are set forth in an odd, stylized format. But the format has a big benefit. It makes it possible to examine any patent application or patent granted by the PTO and get a pretty good idea about what the invention covered by the patent consists of.

While the stylized patent claim language and format have the advantage of lending a degree of precision to a field that badly needs it, there is an obvious and substantial downside to the use of this arcane patentspeak. Mastering it amounts to climbing a fairly steep learning curve.

It is when you set out to understand a patent claim that the rest of the patent becomes crucially important. The patent's narrative description of the invention—set out in the patent specification—with all or many of the invention's possible uses, and the accompanying drawings or flowcharts, usually provide enough information in combination to understand any particular claim. And of course, the more patent claims you examine, the more adept you will become in deciphering them.

Software babble combined with patentspeak can cause trouble.
Although the stylized language and format of patent claims helps make them precise, never forget that they consist of a string of words which, because of their very nature, are always open to some interpretation. And, of course, in the software area, where words in common use are often themselves recent and sometimes imperfect inventions, this problem is compounded. The result is that claims for software-based inventions can be harder to interpret than is the case for claims involving a traditional technology. The downside of this imprecision is that it can be more difficult to tell whether a new software product invention infringes any prior software patent.

2. Method and Apparatus Claims

A software-based invention is usually patented either as a method, or as an apparatus, or both. What this really means is that the patent claims (the precise legal descriptions of the invention) submitted with the application for approval by the PTO describe the algorithms inherent in all software as:
- steps that run a computer (the method claim) and/or
- integral working parts of a computer that perform specific functions under direction of the software, so that these parts working together form a machine-like entity (the apparatus claim).

The greatest advantage to an inventor in terms of breadth of patent coverage is usually achieved when a software-based invention is presented in a patent application as both a method and an apparatus. This cannot always be achieved, but it is something to shoot for.

3. A Closer Look at Software-Based Invention Claims

Now let's look more closely at the types of patent claims that will result in a successful patent. By understanding how these claims work, you will get a good feel for both the types of software-based inventions being patented and how these inventions have been described. In addition, you should be better positioned to determine if your software-based invention infringes an existing patent.

Below are examples of an apparatus claim and a method claim taken from different software-based inventions. Following each claim we translate some key terms—the ones underlined in the claim—into English.

HELP IN PREPARING A PATENT APPLICATION

Telling you how to draft claims and otherwise prepare a patent application to submit to the PTO is beyond the scope of this chapter. *Patent It Yourself*, by David Pressman (Nolo Press), has an excellent chapter on claim-drafting technique, as well as step-by-step instructions for actually preparing a patent application. This same information is available in the *Patent it Yourself* software, which automates the patent drafting process. If you are ready for action, we strongly recommend that you purchase the book or software, both available from Nolo Press and most bookstores and software outlets. (For a discussion of available professional help, see Chapter 14.)

---

a. An Apparatus Claim

The following is an apparatus/machine claim to an invention that is "a system of typesetting alphanumeric information using computer-based control system in conjunction with phototypesetter of conventional design"; in English: a word processing program for printers. (We have shortened the claim a bit for space considerations.)

Example of an Apparatus Claim *(from Freeman, 573 F.2d 1237 (1978)):*

A computer display system *comprising,*

a. *a display device for generating relatively-positioned symbol images in response to applied sequences of signals specifying the shape and position of said images,*

b. *a data processor comprising*

1. *means for storing a first plurality of data sequences, each describing individual symbols, and a second plurality of data sequences corresponding to a control program,*

2. *means responsive to said control program for nondestructively reading from said means for storing and transferring to said display device selected ones of said first plurality of data sequences,*

3. *control means comprising means responsive to said control program for generating and transferring to said display device data sequences specifying the desired position of symbols corresponding to said selected data sequences.*

Here is how to decipher the claim set out above.

"a computer display": These words tell you that the claim is an apparatus/machine claim; the apparatus/machine in question is a computer display. This first line is called the preamble, and is intended to identify the type of claim (process, machine, improvement, etc.) but does not limit the nature of the invention beyond that.

"comprising": This is the standard word to use before going into the elements or parts of an apparatus. It denotes inclusion of everything in the list of elements that follows, and maybe more.

"a display device...": This is the first element or component of the apparatus/machine claim and is defined by its role in the invention, that is, its purpose is for: "generating...symbol images...." The adept among you will instantly recognize that the element described here is a computer terminal. Understand that the claim is not trying to patent the computer terminal, but only using it as one element of the overall apparatus/machine invention in the same way as an invention showing a new type of auto transmission would probably still use standardized (unpatentable) gears.

Claim language note: Notice that the element as introduced is modified with the article "a," but if it is later mentioned again it will be modified with the article "the" or more stiffly with "said." This is so that the first time an element is mentioned is distinguished from the subsequent times.

"a data processor comprising 1. means for storing...": This clause introduces a second element, a data processor. As with the first element, the intent here is not to obtain a patent on a data processor; rather, the intent is to show the role of the data processor in the overall invention. However, the clause that modifies the data processor is telling us something very important: that the data processor, to work in this invention, must have a physical structure that will permit storage of data in the manner described.

Clauses (2) and (3) provide a further definition of the structure that, together with clause (1), comprise the invention.

plurality: This word is commonly used in patent claims to indicate more than one, without committing the claim to exactly how many. This makes your claim broad rather than narrow, since if you provide a number you limit the invention to that number and another invention might escape infringing yours by using a different number.

b.   A Method Claim

The following claim is for an invention that translates spherical wave information into cylindrical wave information, something significant and useful in seismology. (*In re Taner,* U.S. Court of Customs and Patent Appeals, 681 F.2d 787 (1982)).

Example of a Method Claim:

A *method* of seismic exploration by simulating from substantially spherical seismic waves the reflection response of the earth to seismic energy having a substantially continuous wavefront over an extent of an area being explored having at least one dimension that is large relative to a seismic wavelength, *comprising the steps of*:

a) <u>imparting</u> the spherical seismic energy waves into the earth from a set of seismic sources at source positions spaced in an array over an extent having at least one dimension that is large relative to a seismic wavelength;

b) generating a reflection signal at a received position in response to each of the seismic energy waves; and

c) summing the reflection signals to form for the receiver position a signal simulating the reflection response of the earth to seismic energy having substantially continuous wavefront over at least one dimension that is large relative to a seismic energy wavelength.

First, notice that neither software nor hardware parts are specifically mentioned in this claim, yet we know the claim is talking about a software-based invention because the terms "imparting," "generating," and "summing" are described as happening in a computer-related context in the patent specification (the longish narrative description of the invention—not shown in this example).

The essence of the invention is unscrambling some seismic signals, converting them into digital form, and then subjecting the digital information to several mathematical operations that help to accurately interpret the seismic activity.

Here are some key terms:

"method": use of this word at the beginning of the claim indicates that it is a method claim. The entire section of the claim from the word method through the next five lines to the words "comprising the steps of" is the preamble and sets the stage for the rest of the claim. The rest of the claim, not the preamble, consists of the limiting (defining) description of the invention.

"comprising the steps of": this is the same use of "comprising" we saw in the apparatus claim, except that since the elements of method claims are delineated as "steps" the phrase here appears as "comprising the steps of." This phrase could also be "including the steps of" and have the same meaning.

"imparting": when describing a process/method, the claim must use a gerund—a verb ending in "ing" that acts as a noun but that can be qualified

by adverbs—to describe the action of the step. Thus, method steps are always stated as "combining," "selecting," "calculating," "mixing," "separating" and the like. Method steps are also commonly modified by including more details about the step and how it is performed, making the invention narrower by restricting it to the modification. Further narrowing could be accomplished by further breaking down the steps of the claim into even more steps. For example, the step of "imparting" above could be subdivided into two sub-steps:

1. collecting the spherical seismic energy waves from a set of seismic sources at source positions spaced in an array over an extent having at least one dimension that is large relative to a seismic wavelength, and

2. imparting the spherical seismic energy waves into the earth from the set of seismic sources.

G.   Searching the Prior Art

If you have read the previous sections of this chapter, you should have a basic idea of what a patent is, what qualifies a software-based invention for a patent, how the invention must be described to obtain a patent and how to read a patent claim to comprehend the underlying invention.

But you also may very likely feel somewhat confused. Maybe it's some consolation to know that you aren't alone. The software patent field is inherently confusing, even to most experienced patent attorneys. Partially this is because, unlike the more settled technologies, the basic technological principles applicable to software-based inventions are subject to rapid and fundamental change. Additionally, the confusion arises from the fact that a new technology is very quickly being forced upon a patent law system that has developed slowly via the accumulated innovations and applications of older technologies.

No matter. If you are a software developer, you should put these difficulties aside and learn how to search through existing software patents and other software-related materials to become familiar with the prior art in the field—that is, references to previous related developments contained in patents and other written materials. Doing this will:

- help you draft sound claims if you decide to apply for a patent, and
- expose you to related advancements and inventions in the field. This not only will help you assess how innovative your invention really is, but should give you ideas about possible new inventions.

You can also pick up from the prior art some of the terminology and phraseology appropriate to that technological area in case you decide to prepare your own patent application.

Unfortunately, as a general rule, searching software-related prior art can be like looking for a needle in an enormous haystack. To understand why, it is important to remember that the relevant prior art consists of all previous developments worldwide. This means that a thorough search for prior art may involve looking at all relevant expired and in-force U.S. and foreign patents, as well as all relevant literature and scientific papers (in English and other languages) that might describe the invention.

Although U.S. and foreign patents are readily available for searching, other published references to innovative software developments are located in thousands of technical and academic journals, published academic theses and commercial publications. See Section G.4 below for how to search for non-patent references.

A patent search will not find pending applications. It is only possible to search for patents that have issued. Patent applications pending in the PTO are not available for searching and are considered strictly confidential. Unfortunately, the PTO is two to three years behind in examining software patent applications, which means that many cutting-edge developments in software and related fields for which patents are being sought currently exist as patent applications and are not available to be searched as prior art (because they are confidential). Yet, they will operate as prior art against your invention when they issue as patents during the time that the PTO is examining your patent application.

Given these problems with searching prior art in the software patent field, you may well ask whether a search is necessary. Can't you simply submit your application and let the PTO worry about the search? Technically you can. But because of the money and time involved in pursuing a patent application, it is better for you that you find out up-front whether your invention is likely to be rejected on account of the prior art. You significantly reduce the chances of success for your patent application if you do not search the prior art before you file it.

1. Search Methods

There are several approaches to searching for prior art:

- *You can hire a professional search firm.* Many searchers can be found in the Washington D.C./Arlington, Virginia area by looking in the yellow pages or by calling the PTO and asking them for a listing. Professional search firms will charge anywhere from $120 to $300 or more ($60 per hour), plus patent copy costs ($3 per patent), for a preliminary patentability search, which usually only uncovers possibly relevant patents. Charges for broader searches relating to the validity of a patent, or an infringement search, begin at $600 (for a minimum of 10 hours of searching) and can be limited by advance request when you place the order with the searcher.

- *You may visit the PTO or a Patent Depository Library (PDL) and do the search yourself.* Visits to the PTO in Arlington, Virginia, are difficult for most software inventors. Fortunately searches can also be done at regional patent depository libraries (PDLs). In Section G2, below, we describe in some detail how to use a PDL to conduct a basic search for relevant software-based patents.

- *You may do at least part of the search from your business or home computer over the phone lines, using available databases.* It is beyond the scope of this book to describe these databases or how they are used. A partial list is set out in Section G3, below.

⚠ The learning curve for on-line patent databases is high. Almost without exception, using the on-line databases to do a patent search involves a steep learning curve, and can cost you far more money than your results will justify unless you become adept in database searching. Our recommendation is to seriously consider one of the other options first.

SEARCHING FOREIGN PATENTS

Remember, relevant prior art can come from anywhere in the world. Patents issued by other countries are accessible from within the U.S. through the PTO, at its PDLs, and in special database collections. As an inventor searching the prior art in order to determine the patentability of your invention, you should include in your sweep of what's out there both European and Japanese patents, at a minimum, as well as U.S. patents.

It is an open question as to whether a more exhaustive foreign patent search is worthwhile. If you don't do it, you risk the loss of your patent application fees and costs because of a rejection based on foreign prior art. However, by foregoing a foreign patent search, you obviously save the time and expense associated with it. Probably the best approach is to search for prior art in any country that you have reason to believe is home to work similar to yours.

The PDLs have sets of CD-ROM discs with English language abstracts of Japanese patents. There are six discs, each for one of the past six years, and discs for years before that are still being prepared. The database JAPIO has English language of Japanese patent abstracts back to 1976, and can be accessed through Orbit. (See Section G3, below.) JAPIO's updating is about six months behind the issuance of the patents. Recent counts estimate upwards of 200,000 inventions related to computers (from 1986 to 1990) on the database.

Other databases exist that have software-related inventions patented in other foreign countries. For example, the database WPAT includes patents from 31 PTOs, providing English language titles and abstracts, and can be accessed through Dialog. (See Section G3, below.)

2. Searching for Patents in the PTO or in a Patent Depository Library

As noted, United States and foreign patents can be searched at the PTO in Arlington, Virginia, and at the 70 PDLs located across the U.S.

a. The PTO

The best place to search for patent prior art is in the PTO itself, located in Virginia. However, distance considerations eliminate this option for most do-it-yourself searchers. For more information about the PTO search facilities, call 703-308-HELP.

b. Patent Depository Libraries

Here is a list of the 70 Patent Depository Libraries across the country that keep copies of all patents issued. The "*" symbol next to a library's name means it's participating in a pilot test of providing remote access to the PTO through a computer-based full text search system. If you are using one of these libraries, ask for instructions on how to use this very useful service.

Alabama:	Auburn University* 205-844-1747
	Birmingham 205- 226-3680
Alaska:	Anchorage 907-261-2916
Arizona:	Tempe* 602-965-7607
Arkansas:	Little Rock 501- 682-2053
California:	Los Angeles* 213-612-3273
	Sacramento 916-322-4572
	San Diego 619-236-5813
	Sunnyvale 408-730-7290
Colorado:	Denver 303-640-8847
Connecticut:	New Haven 203-786-5447
Delaware:	Newark 302-451-2965
Dist. of Col.:	Washington 202-806-7252

Florida:	Ft. Lauderdale 305-357-7444
	Miami* 305-375-2665
	Orlando 407-823-2562
	Tampa 813-974-2726
Georgia:	Atlanta 404-894-4508
Hawaii:	Honolulu 808-586-3477
Idaho:	Moscow 208-885-6235
Illinois:	Chicago 312-269-2865
	Springfield 217-782-5659
Indiana:	Indianapolis 317-269-1741
	West Lafayette 317-494-2873
Iowa:	Des Moines 515-281-4118
Kansas:	Wichita 316-689-3155
Kentucky:	Louisville 502-561-8617
Louisiana:	Baton Rouge 504-388-2570
Maryland:	College Park 301-405-9157
Massachusetts:	Amherst 413- 545-1370
	Boston* 617-536-5400 ext. 265
Michigan:	Ann Arbor 313-764-7494
	Detroit 313-833-1450
Minnesota:	Minneapolis* 612-372-6570
Mississippi:	Jackson (Miss. Lib. Comm'n)
	not operational yet
Missouri:	Kansas City 816-363-4600
	St. Louis 314-241-2288 ext. 390
Montana:	Butte 406-496-4281
Nebraska:	Lincoln* 402-472-3411
Nevada:	Reno 702-784-6579
N. Hampshire:	Durham 603-862-1777
N. Jersey:	Newark 201-773-7782
	Piscataway 908-932-2895
N. Mexico:	Albuquerque 505-277-4412

N. York:	Albany* 518-473-4636
	Buffalo 716-858-7101
	New York 212-714-8529
No. Carolina:	Raleigh* 919-737-3280
No. Dakota:	701-777-4888
Ohio:	Cincinnati 513-369-6936
	Cleveland* 216-623-2870
	Columbus 614-292-6175
	Toledo 419-259-5212
Oklahoma:	Stillwater 405-744-7086
Oregon:	Salem* 503-378-4239
Pennsylvania:	Philadelphia 215-686-5331
	Pittsburgh 412-622-3138
	University Park 814-865-4861
Rhode Island:	Providence 401-455-8027
So. Carolina:	Charleston 803-792-2372
Tennessee:	Memphis 901-725-8876
	Nashville 615-322-2775
Texas:	Austin 512-471-1610
	College Station 409-845-2551
	Dallas* 214-670-1468
	Houston 713-527-8101 ext. 2587
Utah:	Salt Lake City* 801-581-8394
Virginia:	Richmond 804-367-1104
Washington:	Seattle 206-543-0740
Wisconsin:	Madison 608-262-6845
	Milwaukee* 414-278-3247

c. The Patent Classification System

The trick to using the patent depository libraries is to understand how patents are classified. Software-based inventions will almost always fall within one of these main classes:

Class 395   Information Processing System Organization,

Class 364   Electrical Computers and Data Processing Systems,

Class 371   Error Detection, Correction and Fault Recovery, or

Class 340   Displays and Communications.

Each of these classes is itself broken into numerous subclasses. The goal is to use these subclasses as an index to the patents that are most likely to relate to your invention.

Unfortunately, the PTO is in the midst of reclassifying software-based patents. Most new software-based patents issued since the fall of 1991 are contained in Class 395, "Information Processing System Organization." And software-based patents dating from 1971 to 1991 that were previously in other classes but also fit into Class 395 can be found under Class 395 (although the PTO records also retain the class and subclass these older patents used to be in). Patents issued before 1991 and that do not fall into Class 395 are still listed in the older classes (as of September 1993).

As a general rule, you should first use Class 395 to search for software-based inventions. However, the classes listed above—Class 364, Class 340 and Class 371—may also contain relevant patents, since these were previously the classes used by the PTO for patents on software-based inventions.

So far, Class 395, Information Processing and System Organization, has 19 primary subclasses. Very broadly, the subject matter of Class 395 is defined as:

1. general purpose programmable digital computer systems and miscellaneous digital data processing systems,
2. artificial intelligence, and
3. static presentation or display processing.

The following 19 primary subclasses all fit more or less into these three subject matter categories:

1	artificial intelligence
100	data presentation/computer graphics (for example, image, graphics, text)
200	transmission of information among multiple computer systems
250	buffering functions
275	I/O processing
325	system interconnections
375	instruction processing
400	storage address formation
425	storage accessing and control
500	compatibility, simulation, or emulation or system components
550	timing
575	reliability
600	database or file management system
650	processing (task) management
700	system utilities
725	access control processing
750	power control
775	internal control
800	processing architecture

A complete list of the subclasses of Class 395 is much longer than this list of the primary subclasses. (In Section G2d, we tell you how to find the class for your particular type of software-based invention.)

d. Steps to Searching

USE THE REFERENCE LIBRARIAN

Although we tell you here how to conduct a search in a PDL, you should remember that each PDL is staffed by librarians who are generally quite helpful. The trick here is to undertake your own search and only use the librarian when you get stuck. The librarian is not paid to do your search for you.

Here now is an overview of the search process. The steps you will take are:

Step 1. Assess the likelihood of patents listed in a particular subclass operating as prior art against (directly relating to) your invention. The type of inventions contained in each subclass are described in two looseleaf booklets at the patent depository libraries called the Index to the U.S. Patent Classification, and the Manual of Classification.

Step 2. Through a process of elimination, narrow the list of subclasses down to those most likely to be relevant.

Step 3. Photocopy the list of patent numbers in each subclass you have chosen.

Step 4. Update this list with recent information for the last six months. To help you do this, some PDLs keep a looseleaf binder that updates these lists for the previous six months. This binder, which is not named, includes photocopies of the indexes of a weekly publication called the Official Gazette (OG) for the most recent six months. You may find the same information by looking through the indexes of the last 26 issues of the OG. Look for new patents added to the subclasses that concern you by checking in this binder or the OG indexes for each of the 26 weeks preceding the week that you are conducting the search. Copy these patent numbers.

What you should have achieved by following Steps 1-4 is a complete list of the patents that exist in the classes and subclasses that pertain to your invention up to the present week.

Searching Jargon Note: An 'X' after the patent number indicates that the invention is categorized in more than one subclass. Patent numbers preceded by RE and a five digit number are reissue patents—basically, patents that were issued, had minor problems that warranted that they be altered and then reissued in a corrected form.

INTRODUCING CASSIS: A PDL COMPUTER TOOL TO HELP CLASSIFY YOUR INVENTION AND LOCATE PATENTS

Most PDLs offer their users a CD-ROM patent searching tool known as Cassis. Cassis comes in two CD-ROMS: Cassis/BIB and Cassis/CLSF.

Cassis/BIB contains bibliographic data (the year of issue, inventor's state or country of residence, and so on) for patents issued between 1969 and the present. Abstracts are also provided, but only for patents issued within the previous three years. Also, you can display on the screen the contents of the manual of classification file that contains the titles for the classes and subclasses of the U.S. Patent system.

Cassis/CLSF contains the current patent classification information for all U.S. patents issued from 1790 to present. Indexing of the classification information has been optimized for rapid retrieval.

For more information about Cassis, contact your nearest PDL.

Step 5. Armed with your list of possibly relevant patents, locate copies of the weekly Official Gazette (OG) that includes in it the titles, sample claims and drawings of the patents that issued that week. Look up each patent in the appropriate OG by patent number.

Step 6. On the basis of the information in the OG, decide whether a particular patent might relate to your invention (that is, be relevant prior art). If not, move on. If yes, you will need to examine the full patent. (See Step 7.)

Step 7. You can examine the full patent right in the PDL. Depending on the library and the date of the patent, the patent will be available:

* in hardcopy form,
* on microfiche,
* from a CD-ROM database, or
* by using an on-line database.

Step 8. Once you have identified which patents you want copies of (to refer to when drafting your patent application), you may:

1. photocopy them at the PDL,
2. order them from the PDL (at some but not all PDLs),
3. order them from the PTO located in Arlington, Virginia, or
4. order them from a private patent retrieval company.

Copying patents yourself at the PDL. This can get expensive, especially if the patent is stored by the PDL in microfiche form. Also, it may be difficult to gain access to the copying machine, due to the number of people using the PDL. However, once you have copied the patents, you have them in your hands. Any other system will involve at least some wait.

Ordering patents from the PDL. Depending on the PDL, you may obtain patents within 24 hours or less by paying a hefty premium. For instance, the Sunnyvale Patent Information Clearinghouse (a PDL) charges $3.40 per patent, plus $ 0.85 a page, plus postage, for 24-hour turnaround. Same day service costs the same plus a special handling fee of $8.25 per patent plus express charge, and so on.

Ordering patents from the PTO. The reason why you might want to obtain copies from the PTO is that they cost only $3 per patent, which is often less than using the PDL copying facilities, The downside to using the PTO is that you will have to wait four to six weeks for the patents to arrive. Faster service from the PTO may be obtained through electronic ordering. See the sidebar below.

Ordering patents from a private patent retrieval company. A private retrieval firm may be even less expensive than the PTO but will probably charge extra if the patent is over a certain number of pages. However, the wait may be only a matter of days instead of weeks. We will mention four private U.S. located patent retrieval companies; no endorsement is intended:

FAXPAT
2001 Jefferson Davis Highway, Suite 302
Arlington, VA 22202
Tel: 800-866-1323
Fax: 800-666-1233

PATService
2001 Jefferson Davis Highway, #1209
Arlington, VA 22202
Tel: 800-336-7575

REED FAX
275 Gibraltar Rd.
Horsham, PA 19004
Tel: 800-422-1337

Research Publications, Inc.
1921 Jefferson Davis Highway, Suite 1821D
Arlington, VA 22202
Tel: 800-336-5010

⚠ The information in this chapter may be dated by the time you read it. Call your local PDL and ask for information about their services and any others they know of.

GETTING PATENTS FROM THE PTO THROUGH ELECTRONIC ORDERING

The PTO provides an electronic ordering service (EOS) and will get you the patent in two weeks, or with a larger fee, within two days. Call 202-377-2535 for more information about the EOS, and 202-603-0696 for opening an EOS account, a necessary prerequisite for using the EOS system.

You may also order foreign patents from the PTO, at a higher rate.

Note: You would have determined that you needed a copy of a foreign patent from exploration on one of the databases that catalog foreign patents. Contact the Foreign Patents Division, Scientific Library, USPTO, Washington, D.C. 20231. The patents will be sent to you in four weeks. Orders may be placed by fax 703-308-9808. Further information may be obtained from 703-308-1076. The PTO also maintains a helpline for search-related and other questions: 703-308-HELP.

3. On-Line Databases

Instead of using the PTO or PDL, you may search for patents directly from your computer by using one of the many on-line patent databases. As we stressed earlier, this searching can get quite expensive, and most of these databases involve a steep learning curve.

Nevertheless, if you plan on doing a lot of patent searching, it may benefit you to become familiar with one or more of these resources. Most of these services have a manual that you can buy for anywhere from $30 to $100, which will aid in the searching process. Be sure to inquire as to search aids available with the service.

Here is a partial list.

Dialog Information Services, Inc.
3460 Hillview Avenue
Palo Alto, California 94304
Tel: 800-334-2564; 415-858-3758
Fax: 415-858-7069

Engineering Information, Inc.
345 East 47th Street
New York, NY 10017
Tel: 800-221-1044; 212-705-7635
Fax: 212-832-1857

IFI/Plenum Data Corporation
302 Swann Avenue
Alexandria, Virginia 22301
Tel: 800-368-3093; 800-331-4955; 703-683-1085

Information Access Company
362 Lakeside Drive
Foster City, CA 94404
Tel: 800-441-1165
Fax: 415-378-5369

INSPEC
IEEE Service Center
445 Hoes Lane
Piscataway, New Jersey 08850
Tel: 201-562-5549
Fax: 201-981-0027

Maxwell Online, Inc.
8000 Westpark Drive
McLean, Virginia 22102
Tel: 800-456-7248 / 703-442-0900
Fax: 703-893-4632

Mead Data Central
9393 Springboro Pike - DM
P.O. Box 933
Dayton, Ohio 45401
Tel: 800-346-9759; 513-859-5398

National Technical Information Service
U.S. Department of Commerce
5285 Port Royal Road
Springfield, VA 22161
Tel: 703-487-4600
Fax: 212-832-1857

Orbit Search Service Division
Derwent Publications Ltd.
128 Theobalds Road
London WC1X 8RP, England
Tel: 011 44 71 242-5823
Fax: 011 44 71 405-3630
U.S. Office: 800-451-3451; 703-790-0400
U.S. Office Fax: 703-790-1426

Predicasts
Online Services Department
11001 Cedar Avenue
Cleveland, OH 44106
Tel: 800-321-6388
Fax: 216-229-9944

SOFTWARE PATENTS ON CD-ROM

If your company does a lot of software development you may be interested in purchasing a CD-ROM titled *Computer Software Index,* an EDS product distributed by Rapid Patent. This product contains the full text (but not the drawings) of virtually all the patents issued on software-based inventions between 1972 and 1993, plus an easy to use search interface that greatly increases your chances of finding the relevant prior art. The product sells for $1795 and can be ordered by calling 1-800-336-5010 or writing Rapid Patent at 1921 Jefferson Davis Hwy, Suite 1821D, P.O. Box 2527 EADS Station, Arlington, VA 22202.

4. Searching Nonpatent Prior Art

Inventors searching the prior art to see if their invention is precluded by earlier developments must search not only patent prior art, but, to be thorough, also prior art in trade and academic publications (called references), as well as marketed items. Remember from Section D, that when assessing the novelty and obviousness of an invention the PTO will examine all prior developments, not just prior patents.

To make it possible to search efficiently for the nonpatent prior art, Software Patent Institute (SPI), a part of Industrial Technology Institute (ITI), has been founded by Dr. Bernard Galler and Dr. Roland Cole. Organized as a nonprofit corporation, SPI is not affiliated with the U.S. PTO or any Government agency. SPI, which has an executive committee made up of individuals from prominent companies and the computer science community, is recognized by the U.S. Patent and Trademark Office, the Office of Technology Assessment, the U.S. Advisory Commission on Patent Law Reform and the Software Publishers Association.

SPI has finished its start-up phase and is now running. Contact the organization to get on their mailing list:

Software Patent Institute
c/o Industrial Technology Institute
2901 Hubbard Street / PO Box 1485
Ann Arbor, MI 48106-1485
Tel: 313-769-4083
Fax: 313-769-4064
Internet: spi@iti.org

H. Is There Patent Infringement?

Patent infringement occurs when someone makes, uses or sells a patented invention without the patent owner's permission. Defining infringement is one thing, but knowing when it occurs in the real world is something else. Even with common technologies, it can be difficult for experienced patent attorneys to tell whether patents have been infringed. And with software, the problem is even worse.

Following is a cursory overview of how patent attorneys decide whether a particular device infringes a patent. Although we have tried to simplify the process and terminology as much as possible, it still may be difficult going. At the very least, by becoming familiar with this material you will be able to better communicate with any patent attorney you hire for an analysis of an infringement situation.

Here are the steps to deciding whether infringement of a software-based patent has occurred:

Step 1. Identify the patent's independent apparatus and method claims.

Step 2. Break these apparatus and method claims into their elements (elements are explained below).

Step 3. Compare these elements with the alleged infringing device or process and decide whether the claim has *all* of the elements that constitute the alleged infringing device or process. If so, the patent has probably been infringed. If not, go to Step 4.

Step 4. If the elements of the alleged infringing device or process are somewhat different than the elements of the patent claim, ask if they are the same in structure, function and result. If yes, you probably have infringement. Note that for infringement to occur, only one claim in the patent needs to be infringed.

Let's take a closer look at how all this works.

1. Identify the Independent Apparatus and Method Claims

A patent's independent claims are those upon which usually one or more claims immediately following depend. A patent's broadest claims are those with the fewest words, and that therefore provide the broadest patent coverage. The patent's broadest claims are its independent claims. As a general rule, if you find infringement of one of the broadest claims, all the other patent's claims that depend on that claim are infringed. Conversely, if you don't find infringement by comparison with a broad claim, then you won't find infringement of claims which depend on it. Although infringement is declared on a claim-by-claim basis (for example, when Claim #4 of patent #5,999,999 is infringed), generally it will be declared that the patent itself is infringed.

2. Break the Independent Apparatus and Method Claims Into Their Elements

First you must understand how to identify the elements in both an apparatus (machine) claim and a method (process) claim—the two types of claims that are most common to software-based inventions.

a. Elements of an Apparatus Claim

In apparatus claims, the elements are usually conceptualized as the a), b), c), etc. parts of the apparatus that are listed, interrelated, and described in detail following the word "comprising" at the end of the preamble of the claim.

Example of the Elements in An Apparatus Claim for "Intelligent Help System":

15. *A help information system for aiding a user comprising:*

a computer having a processor and a memory;

a display device coupled to said computer;

an input device coupled to said computer;

monitoring means coupled to the input device for monitoring a sequence of user-directed events and for generating data indicating said events,

a knowledge base coupled to said monitoring means and stored in said memory, said knowledge base comprising said general data, a plurality of rules for analyzing said generated data to determine appropriate help information, and a help information database for storing said appropriate help information;

inference engine means, coupled to said knowledge base, for applying said rules to said data to generate an inference engine outputs and

display engine means, coupled to said help information database, for interpreting said inference engine output to select appropriate help information for display by said display device to the user.

The elements in this claim clearly include a computer with a processor and a memory, a display device, and monitoring means. Further elements of the invention may be subdivisions of these broader elements, such as the parts of the monitoring means: a plurality of rules, and an on-line help information database.

b. Elements in a Method Claim

Elements in method claims are the steps of the method, and sub-parts of those steps.

Example of a Method Claim for the Same Invention (an "Intelligent Help System"):

In a computer system, a method for aiding a user of a computer program, said method operating independent of said computer program, comprising the steps of:

storing a help information database;

storing a knowledge base for maintaining data;

identifying a series of user-directed events;

comparing said identified series with data stored in the knowledge base;

if said identified series is unknown to said knowledge base, asserting in said knowledge base data for indicating said unknown identified series;

if said identified series contradicts said knowledge base, retracting in said knowledge base data that contradicts said identified series;

if said identified series is already known to said knowledge base, reasserting in said knowledge base data for indicating said already known identified series;

storing a plurality of rules for analyzing said knowledge base to determine appropriate help information;

detecting a request for help information from the user;

testing said rules against said knowledge from the user;

testing said rules against said knowledge base using an inference engine, whereby rules that are satisfied by data stored in the knowledge base approved rules;

selecting in response to said testing step appropriate help information from said help information database; and

displaying said selected help information to the user.

The elements of this method claim include all the steps listed, such as the first three steps: storing a help information database, storing a knowledge base for maintaining data, and identifying a series of user-directed events. A few of the steps are conditional and refer to three different conditions about the identified series: whether it is unknown to the knowledge base, contradicts the knowledge base or is known to the knowledge base.

For each of these conditions, the next step required is different. When the series is unknown to the knowledge base, the series must be asserted in it. When the series contradicts the knowledge base, the part of the data in the knowledge base that contradicts the series must be retracted. And when the series is already known to the knowledge base, the series information should be reasserted into the base. Any one of these possible relations between the series and the knowledge bases could be an element of the claim.

INTERPRETING CLAIMS CONTAINING "MEANS PLUS FUNCTION" LANGUAGE

Sometimes an apparatus claim can have elements which are described in general "means plus function" language. For example, claim 15 of the Alappat case (see an abstract of the case in the Appendix) has as its first element a "means for determining the vertical distance between the endpoints of each of the vectors in the data list." How do we know what this element of the invention is about? We look to other parts of the patent specification—the detailed narrative description of the invention or additional claims—for examples of what the inventor had in mind. In the Alappat case, the description of the invention indicated that the means the inventor had in mind was "an arithmetic logic circuit configured to perform an absolute value function" This means, and equivalents to it, are what the patent in that case covers.

In sum, when you encounter a means plus function clause in a claim, you must proceed to read the rest of the claims and the rest of the specification (that is, the detailed description of the invention) to understand completely what the claim covers.)

3. Compare the Elements of the Broadest Claims to the Infringing Device or Process

If each and every element of the patent's broadest claims are in the infringing device, the patent is probably infringed. The reason you start by analyzing the broadest claim is that by definition that claim has the fewest elements and it is therefore easier to find infringement. For instance, if a claim has only two elements, you only need to find the same two elements in a device or process to prove infringement. But if the claim has 10 elements, then you need to find all 10 elements (or their equivalents—see Section H4, below) in the alleged infringing device or process.

4. Are the Device's Elements Equivalent to the Patent's Elements in Structure, Function and Result?

Even if infringement can't be found on the basis of the literal language in the claims, the courts may still find infringement if the alleged infringing device's elements are equivalent to the patent claims in structure, function and result. Known as the Doctrine of Equivalents, this rule is difficult to apply in practice, and explaining it further is beyond the scope of the book. (See Chapter 14 for suggestions about doing further research in this area.)

I. If You are Accused of Patent Infringement

As a software programmer you may find yourself in one of two positions relative to infringement. You could be the patent owner whose invention is infringed by another company or person, or you could be the person or company who infringes someone else's patent. Whether you are the infringer or the infringee, you will almost certainly have to consult with a patent attorney to intelligently understand your options.

If you are the patent owner, your options are sufficiently complex to warrant us not offering any advice as to how to proceed. But if you are accused of infringement, there are a few basic points you should consider. Above all, you should act fast to determine your rights. Continuing to infringe a patented invention after you learn of it can result in liability for triple the patent owner's actual damages.

If you are served with a lawsuit. If you are served with a lawsuit alleging infringement, you must act quickly to file an answer, which means contacting a patent attorney without delay.

1. Analyze the Patent Owner's Business

A patent attorney's strategy in an infringement situation will often depend on whether the company alleging infringement is large and powerful, or small enough that it is less likely to want a full-fledged patent fight. If you haven't been served with a lawsuit, before you visit an attorney research the company or person. Investigate whether they hold any patents, their reputation in the business for either fairness or aggression, their product lines and methods of production, marketing and doing business, and any other useful information you can find.

2. Do a Cost/Benefit Analysis

As a general rule, a company accused of patent infringement can solve the problem by stopping its use of the infringing device. Although you may be really proud of your invention, whether or not you received a patent on it, the invention's actual economic value may not warrant either the payment of royalties to the patent owner or a court battle.

3. Decide Whether You Can Design Around the Patent

Often it is feasible to modify an infringing invention so that it no longer infringes. Called "designing around a patent," this process may be your best response to an infringement claim. Also, the ability to design around a patent means that the patent owner may be willing to settle with you on extremely favorable terms, perhaps only charging you pennies per product as a royalty. But before you spend any money designing around a patent, consult with a patent attorney about your plans. ■

CHAPTER 6

Trademarks and Software

Trademarks help a software company carve out a distinct and recognizable identity in the highly competitive and rapidly changing software industry. Trademarks like *LOTUS* and *WORDPERFECT* have become well-established in the public's mind and help the companies that own them continually dominate their markets despite the introduction of competing products. A well-known trademark can be just as valuable as a copyright or patent, if not more so.

This chapter provides a brief overview of trademarks, with an emphasis on how to select a strong trademark. But for step-by-step guidance on all important aspects of selecting and protecting a trademark, you should read *Trademark: How to Name a Business and Product*, by Kate McGrath & Stephen Elias (Nolo Press).

A. What Is a Trademark?

A trademark is any visual mark that accompanies a particular tangible product, or line of goods, and serves to identify and distinguish it from products sold by others and to indicate its source. A trademark may consist of letters, words, names, phrases or slogans, numbers, colors, symbols, designs or shapes. As a general rule, to be protected from unauthorized use by others, a trademark must be distinctive in some way.

Example: *The word and numbers "LOTUS 1-2-3" constitute a trademark that identifies a particular electronic spreadsheet program as the product of the Lotus Development Corp. and distinguishes it from similar programs.*

The word "trademark" is also a generic term used to describe the entire broad body of state and federal law that covers how businesses distinguish their products and services from the competition. Each state has it own set of laws establishing when and how trademarks can be protected. There is also a federal trademark law called the Lanham Act (15 U.S.C. 1050 *et seq.*), which applies in all 50 states. Generally, state trademark laws are relied upon for marks used only within one particular state, while the Lanham Act is used to protect marks for products that are sold in more than one state or across territorial or national borders.

OTHER TYPES OF MARKS

Trademarks are the type of mark of most interest to software developers, since software is a product. However, there are other more specialized marks, including:

- *Service marks.* A mark that is used to identify services, rather than products, is called a service mark.

   Example: *The word CITIBANK is a service mark for banking services and MICROSOFT is a service mark for computer software services. The rules for determining when and how service marks qualify for protection are the same as for trademarks.*

- *Collective marks.* A symbol, label, word, phrase or other identifying mark used by members of a group or organization for goods they produce or services they render is called a collective mark.

   Example: *The symbol showing one person handing a floppy to another is used by members of the Association of Shareware Professionals. Only members of the organization are entitled to use the collective mark.*

- *Certification marks.* A mark used for the express purpose of certifying various characteristics or qualities of products and services manufactured by others is called a certification mark.

   Example: *The "Good Housekeeping Seal of Approval" is a certification mark.*

B. Selecting a Trademark

Not all trademarks are treated equally by the law. The best trademarks are "distinctive"—that is, they stand out in a customer's mind because they are inherently memorable. The more distinctive a trademark is, the "stronger" it will be and the more legal protection it will receive. Less distinctive marks are "weak" and may be entitled to little or no legal protection. Obviously, it is much better to have a strong trademark than a weak one.

For some reason, computer companies often do a very poor job in selecting their trademarks and end up using weak marks that will be difficult or impossible to enforce. Companies that use weak trademarks often throw away the chance to develop a very valuable asset.

Generally, selecting a mark begins with brainstorming for general ideas (possibly with the aid of a professional name consultant or a name-generating computer program). After several possible marks have been selected, the next step is often to use formal or informal market research techniques to see how the potential marks will be accepted by consumers. Next, a "trademark search" is conducted. This means that an attempt is made to discover whether the same or similar marks are already in use.

TRADE NAMES MAY BE USED AS TRADEMARKS

A trade name is the formal name of a business or other organization. For example, Apple Computer Inc. and Lotus Development Corp. are trade names. A trade name is used to identify a business for such purposes as opening bank accounts, paying taxes, ordering supplies, filing lawsuits and so on. However, a trade name may become a trademark (or service mark) when it is used to identify individual products (or services) sold in the marketplace. Businesses often use shortened versions of their trade names as all or part of a trademark; a good example is the trademark *LOTUS 1-2-3.*

Trade names, whether the name of a corporation, partnership or sole proprietorship, must be registered with appropriate state or local authorities. Each state has its own business license requirements requiring that trade names be registered with city, county or state offices. (For more information, see *Trademark: How to Name a Business and Product,* by Kate McGrath & Stephen Elias (Nolo Press), Chapter 3.)

1. What Is a Distinctive Trademark?

You should create a trademark that is distinctive rather than descriptive. A trademark is "distinctive" if it is capable of distinguishing the product to which it is attached from competing products. Certain types of marks are deemed to be inherently distinctive and are automatically entitled to maximum protection. Others are viewed as not inherently distinctive and can be protected only if they acquire "secondary meaning" through use.

a. Inherently Distinctive Marks

Arbitrary, fanciful or coined marks are deemed to be inherently distinctive and are therefore very strong marks. These are words and/or symbols that have absolutely no meaning in the particular trade or industry prior to their adoption by a particular manufacturer for use with its goods or services. After use and promotion, these marks are instantly identified with a particular company and product, and the exclusive right to use the mark is easily asserted against potential infringers.

Fanciful or arbitrary marks consist of common words used in an unexpected or arbitrary way so that their normal meaning has nothing to do with the nature of the product or service they identify. For example, the trademark *LOTUS 1-2-3* in no way describes a computer spreadsheet program. Other examples of arbitrary/fanciful marks include *PEACHTREE SOFTWARE* and *APPLE COMPUTER*. Coined words are words made up solely to serve as trademarks. Examples in the computer field include the marks *XEROX*, *ZEOS*, *INTEL* and *ZILOG*.

Suggestive marks are also inherently distinctive. A suggestive mark indirectly describes the product it identifies but stays away from literal descriptiveness. That is, the consumer must engage in a mental process to associate the mark with the product it identifies. For example, the trademark *WORDPERFECT* indirectly suggests word processing as does *WORDSTAR*. *SUPERCALC* and *VISICALC* indirectly suggest electronic spreadsheets. *CROSSTALK* suggests communication between different computers.

b. Descriptive Marks

Descriptive marks are not considered to be inherently distinctive. They are generally viewed by the courts as weak and thus not deserving of much, if any, judicial protection unless they acquire a "secondary meaning"—that is, become associated with a product in the public's mind through long and continuous use.

There are three types of descriptive marks:

- Marks that directly describe the nature or characteristics of the product they identify—for example, the mark *QUICK MAIL* used for an electronic mail program, *CALENDAR CREATOR* for a calendar program, or *CHESSMASTER* for a computer chess game.
- Marks that describe the geographic location from which the product emanates—for example, *OREGON SOFTWARE*.
- Marks consisting primarily of a person's last name—for example, *NORTON UTILITIES*.

A mark that is in continuous and exclusive use by its owner for a five year period is presumed to have acquired secondary meaning and qualifies for registration as a distinctive mark.

Example 1: *Pinnacle Software, Inc. develops and markets a desktop publishing program called "Self-Publisher." This name is clearly descriptive of the nature of the product. However, over time, and with the help of an advertising campaign the name loses its sole meaning as a description and instead becomes associated with the Pinnacle program.*

Example 2: *NORTON UTILITIES, which started out descriptive, by now has acquired a secondary meaning and is distinctive for that reason.*

c. Generic Marks

A generic mark is a word(s) or symbol that is commonly used to describe an entire category or class of products or services, rather than to distinguish one product or service from another. Generic marks are in the public domain and cannot be registered or enforced under the trademark laws. Words and phrases that are inherently generic in the software field undoubtedly include: "software," "computer," "mouse," "crt," "cpu," "floppy disk," "hard disk," "modem," "ROM," "RAM," "dot matrix," "menu," "pull-down menu," "footprint," "laptop" and "icon."

A term formerly protectible as a trademark may lose such protection if it becomes generic. This often occurs when a mark is assimilated into common use to such an extent that it becomes the general term describing an entire product category. For example, "escalator" was originally a protected trademark used to designate the moving stairs manufactured by a particular company. Eventually, however, the word became synonymous with the very idea of moving stairs and lost its protection. "Xerox" is another example of a mark that originally was understood to refer to one product line but which is now used to describe the photocopying process and product. Accordingly, "Xerox" is probably close to becoming generic.

WAYS TO PREVENT A TRADEMARK FROM BECOMING GENERIC

A trademark owner should take the following steps to help keep its mark from becoming generic:

- The mark should only be used as a proper adjective in connection with a noun—for example, "*GROK* brand software." A trademark should never be used as a verb ("to Grok") or as a noun ("the Grok"), or in the plural form ("Groks"). Also, don't modify a mark with prefixes, suffixes, deletions or additions.
- Make the trademark as distinctive as possible. For example, use it only with an initial capital letter, all capitals, in quotations marks, in italics or in some other distinctive style or typeface.
- Always use a trademark in the same form, or in a small number of similar forms.
- If the mark has been federally registered, use the "®" symbol with it. If it hasn't been registered, use the "™" superscript.
- Instruct employees, licensees, dealers, agents and suppliers only to use the trademark properly.

2. Trademark Searches

A mark you think will be good for your product could already be in use by someone else. If your mark is confusingly similar to one already in use, its owner may be able to sue you for trademark infringement and get you to change it and even pay damages. (See Section D, below.) Obviously, you do not want to spend time and money marketing and advertising a new mark, only to discover that it infringes on another preexisting mark and must be changed. To avoid this, state and federal trademark searches should be conducted to attempt to discover if there are any existing similar marks. You can conduct a trademark search yourself, either manually or with the aid of computer databases; or you may pay a professional search firm to do so. For more on trademark searches, refer to *Trademark: How to Name a Business and Product*, by Kate McGrath & Stephen Elias (Nolo Press), Chapters 5 and 6.

C. Trademark Registration

A trademark is registered by filing an application with the United States Patent and Trademark Office (PTO) in Washington, D.C. Registration is not mandatory; under both federal and state law, a company may obtain trademark rights in the states in which the mark is actually used. However, federal registration provides many important benefits. These include:

- The mark's owner is presumed to have the exclusive right to use the mark nationwide.
- Everyone in the country is presumed to know that the mark is already taken (even if they haven't actually heard of it).
- The trademark owner obtains the right to put an "®" after the mark (see sidebar, below).
- Anyone who begins using a confusingly similar mark after the mark has been registered will be deemed a willful infringer. This means that the trademark owner can collect large damages, thus afford to file an infringement lawsuit.

- The trademark owner obtains the right to make the mark "incontest-able" by keeping it in continuous use for five years. This substantially reduces others' ability to legally challenge the mark.

To qualify for federal trademark registration, a mark must meet several requirements. The mark must:

- actually be used in commerce (but not solely within one state's borders),
- be sufficiently distinctive to reasonably operate as a product identifier, and
- not be confusingly similar to an existing federally registered trademark.

TRADEMARK NOTICES

The owner of a registered trademark is entitled to use a special symbol along with the trademark, notifying the world of the fact of registration. Use of trademark notices is not mandatory, but makes it much easier for the trademark owner to collect meaningful damages in case of infringement. It is also a powerful deterrent against use of the mark by others.

The most commonly used notice for trademarks registered with the PTO is an "R" in a circle—®—but "Reg. U.S. Pat. & T.M. Off." may also be used. The "TM" superscript—™—may be used to denote marks that have been registered on a state basis only or marks that have not yet officially been registered by the PTO.

---

1. Intent to Use Registration

If you seriously intend to use a trademark on a product in the near future, you can reserve the right to use the mark by filing an intent to use registration. If the mark is approved, you have six months to actually use the mark on a product sold to the public. If necessary, this period may be increased by six-month intervals to up to 24 months if you have a good explanation for the delay. No one else may use the mark during this interim period. You should promptly file an intent to use registration as soon as you have definitely selected a trademark for a forthcoming product.

D.   Enforcing Trademark Rights

The owner of a valid trademark has the exclusive right to use the mark on its products. Depending on the strength of the mark and whether and where it has been registered, the trademark owner may be able to bring a court action to prevent others from using the same or similar marks on competing or related products.

Trademark infringement occurs when an alleged infringer uses a mark that is likely to cause consumers to confuse the infringer's products with the trademark owner's products. A mark need not be identical to one already in use to infringe upon the owner's rights. If the proposed mark is similar enough to the earlier mark to risk confusing the average consumer, its use will constitute infringement.

Determining whether an average consumer might be confused is the key to deciding whether infringement exists. The determination depends primarily on whether the products or services involved are related (that is, sold through the same marketing channels), and, if so, whether the marks are sufficiently similar to create a likelihood of consumer confusion.

If a trademark owner is able to convince a court that infringement has occurred, she may be able to get the court to order the infringer to stop using the infringing mark and to pay monetary damages. Depending on whether the mark was registered, such damages may consist of the amount of the trademark owner's losses caused by the infringement or the infringer's profits. In cases of willful infringement (infringement occurring where the infringer is aware of the existence of the infringed mark), the courts may double or triple the damages award.

Example: *AcmeSoft develops a computer program designed to automate the manufacture of widgets. AcmeSoft markets the program under the name "Widgeteer." AcmeSoft registers this descriptive mark with the U.S. Patent & Trademark Office. One year later, Badd Software, Inc. markets a widget manufacturing program under the name "Widgeter." AcmeSoft sues Badd for using a mark confusingly similar to its own on a similar product. AcmeSoft is able to convince a judge that a substantial number of consumers are being confused by Badd's use of the "Widgeter" mark. The judge orders Badd to stop using the mark on its widget manufacturing programs and awards AcmeSoft damages for willful infringement.*

A trademark owner must be assertive in enforcing its exclusive rights. Each time a mark is infringed upon it loses strength and distinctiveness and may eventually die by becoming generic. (See Section B1c, above.) ■

C H A P T E R 7

Workers in the Software Industry: Employees vs. Independent Contractors

This chapter is for both employers and workers in the software industry. It explains when workers qualify as independent contractors for tax and other purposes and when they must be treated as employees.

A. Introduction

The software industry places heavy reliance on self-employed workers. Whether they are called "independent computer consultants," "dailies," "vendors," or nothing at all, such workers routinely provide software companies with a variety of services, including programming and software development and design, technical advice, software maintenance, training and software-related technical writing. The general term for a self-employed individual who offers services to the public is "independent contractor."

Independent contractors are treated very differently from employees for tax, insurance and other purposes. They must also be treated very differently from employees by the businesses that hire them. Significant savings can be realized by treating a worker as an independent contractor rather than as an employee. However, as we'll discuss below, there are significant risks as well. If the IRS and/or a state taxing authority concludes that a worker is really an employee and not an independent contractor, substantial penalties may be imposed on that worker's employer. There may also be significant and surprising consequences if an independent contractor creates a copyrightable work.

Various government agencies—the IRS, Department of Labor, state taxing authorities and unemployment insurance agencies—may decide, independently of each other, whether a worker is an employee or independent contractor. Where disputes arise over the ownership of a work product—such as code, documentation or interface design—the courts may have to determine employment status for copyright purposes.

> **SOLE PROPRIETORS AND PARTNERS ARE NEITHER CONTRACTORS NOR EMPLOYEES**
>
> If you're a sole proprietor or partner in your own business, you're neither an independent contractor nor an employee. You're responsible for paying your own income tax and Social Security self-employment tax. If you're a shareholder and work in a corporation, you're generally an employee.

B. Benefits and Drawbacks of Using Independent Contractors

A hiring firm that classifies workers as independent contractors obtains many financial and other benefits, but may face serious risks and drawbacks as well. Let's look at these in detail.

1. Benefits of Using Independent Contractors

Perhaps the main reason any business uses independent contractors is that it can save a great deal of money. A business that hires an employee incurs a number of obligations in addition to paying that employee's salary, including:

- *Federal tax withholding.* The employer must withhold federal income tax from the wages paid to an employee and pay them to the IRS. Each year, the employer must send the employee a Form W-2 showing how much he or she earned and how much was withheld.
- *Social security and Medicare taxes.* Social security and Medicare taxes (FICA) are levied on both the employer and employee and must be paid together with the withheld federal income tax.
- *Federal unemployment taxes.* Employers must pay federal unemployment taxes (FUTA).

- *State taxes.* In many states, employers must also withhold state income taxes from employees' paychecks and pay state unemployment taxes.
- *Workers' compensation insurance.* Employers must provide workers' compensation insurance coverage for employees in case they become injured on the job.
- *Employment benefits.* If an employer has a health insurance and/or retirement plan, all employees must generally be covered. Employees are also normally given sick leave and paid holidays and vacations.
- *Office space and equipment.* An employer normally provides an employee with office space and whatever equipment he or she needs to do the job.

All of these items add enormously to the cost of hiring and keeping an employee. More than one-third of all employee payroll costs go for social security, unemployment insurance, health benefits and vacation.

By hiring an independent contractor instead of an employee, a business incurs none of these obligations. It need not withhold or pay any taxes. Perhaps most importantly, an independent contractor need not be provided with health insurance, workers' compensation coverage, a pension plan or any other employee benefits. The business need only report amounts paid to an independent contractor by filing a Form 1099-MISC with the IRS. (Even this form need not be filed if an independent contractor is paid less than $600 in a calendar year.)

There is another important reason businesses often prefer to use independent contractors: It avoids making a long-term commitment to the worker. An independent contractor can be hired solely to accomplish a specific task, enabling a business to obtain specialized expertise only for a short time. The hiring firm need not go through the trauma, severance costs and potential lawsuits brought on by laying off or firing an employee.

2. Drawbacks and Risks of Using Independent Contractors

If you're an employer, you might now be thinking, "I'll never hire an employee again; I'll just use independent contractors." Before doing this, you should know that there are some substantial risks involved in classifying workers as independent contractors.

a. Adverse Tax Consequences

The IRS and most states want to see as many workers as possible classified as employees, not independent contractors. This way, the IRS and states can immediately collect taxes based on payroll withholding. It also makes it far more difficult for workers to under-report their income or otherwise evade taxes. In recent years, the IRS has mounted an aggressive attack on employers who, in their view, misclassify employees as independent contractors. One of the industries the IRS appears to have targeted is the software business.

The IRS can learn about a business's hiring and classification practices in a number of ways. If the IRS audits your business, it will examine independent contractor relationships, regardless of the purpose of the audit. The IRS may look into the affairs of an independent contractor who hasn't been paying income taxes. Disgruntled workers (both current and past) may tip off the IRS that a company is misclassifying its employees as independent contractors. The IRS also examines the 1099 forms filed by hirers of independent contractors and will likely question the classification of any independent contractor who receives all income from a single source.

When the IRS audits a business, all persons performing services for that business are presumed to be employees. It is up to the business to prove to the IRS that those workers classified as independent contractors really are independent contractors. If the IRS concludes that an employer has misclassified an employee as an independent contractor, the agency usually demands that the business pay an amount equal to the employee's social security tax, federal income tax and federal unemployment insurance for the previous three years. The IRS can—and often does—add interest and substantial penalties.

An employer's woes do not necessarily end with the IRS. The state version of the IRS and/or state unemployment office may also audit the employer and order that it pay back taxes and/or unemployment insurance.

Such assessments can easily put a small company out of business. Also, keep in mind that the owners of the business will be held *personally liable* for such assessments and penalties, even if the business is a corporate entity. If the business owners cannot pay the taxes or fees, other responsible company officials such as the controller or treasurer may be held personally liable for them.

What happens to an employee who was misclassified as an independent contractor? He or she could end up getting audited by the IRS and may have to pay taxes on business deductions that were taken, along with penalties and interest.

b.   Potential Loss of Intellectual Property Rights

Another potential drawback that may arise from using independent contractors instead of employees is that the hiring firm faces a possible loss of copyright ownership. Unless the hiring firm obtains a written assignment (transfer) of the contractor's copyright rights, the contractor may end up owning the copyright in the software or other materials the contractor creates—even though the hiring firm paid the contractor to do the work. To avoid this, hiring firms must obtain written assignments from independent contractors. (See Chapter 8 for a detailed discussion.)

c.   Loss of Control Over Workers

By using independent contractors, the hiring firm gives up control of the worker. Independent contractors may not be treated like employees. The hiring firm may not supervise an independent contractor. He or she must more or less be left alone to perform the agreed-upon services without substantial help or interference. (See the discussion in Section D, below.) If you want to control how a worker performs, classify him or her as an employee.

C. Benefits and Drawbacks of Being an Independent Contractor

From the worker's point of view, the principal benefit of being an independent contractor is independence. You are your own boss, with all the risks and rewards that entails. This freedom from control is particularly appealing to many of the highly creative and independent people involved in the software industry.

Some independent contractors obtain higher gross compensation than employees doing the same work. In addition, they are better able than employees to deduct business expenses such as home offices, computers, cars and travel. Independent contractors need not have their taxes withheld; instead, they usually make quarterly estimated tax payments. Independent contractors don't pay state or federal unemployment taxes, but also can't collect unemployment.

On the down side, independent contractors must pay the entire amount of their social security and Medicare taxes themselves. Independent contractors also do not receive the fringe benefits to which most employees are entitled, such as health insurance, sick leave, paid vacations and pension plans.

D. Which Workers Qualify as Independent Contractors?

Given the substantial risks involved in misclassifying an employee as an independent contractor, it is important for those hiring in the software industry to clearly understand whether a worker qualifies as an independent contractor or should be treated as an employee. Unfortunately, deciding whether a worker qualifies as an independent contractor or is an employee is a little like defining beauty—it's all in the eye of the beholder. There are no hard-and-fast rules. A person you think qualifies as an independent contractor may look like an employee to an IRS auditor. The guidelines in this section should, however, help you troubleshoot.

Stated simply, an independent contractor is a person who is in business for herself. Independent contractors earn their living by selling their services to the public. Examples include professionals with their own practices, like doctors, lawyers, dentists and accountants. Although your dentist may occasionally work on your teeth, he is an independent businessman who offers his services to the public generally; he is not your employee. You don't have to be a "professional" to be an independent contractor. Anyone with an independent business qualifies.

How do you decide whether a worker is an independent businessperson or a mere employee? The IRS and courts look at the degree of control the hiring party has over the worker. An independent contractor has the *right to control* the way she works, including the details of when, where and how the work is done. The hiring party's control is limited to accepting or rejecting the final result of the independent contractor's work. An independent contractor is just that—independent.

If the person or company that hires a worker has the right to control the worker, that worker is an employee. This is so whether or not that right was actually exercised—that is, whether the worker was really controlled. If the right of control is present, the IRS will view her as an employee, even if you have a written agreement calling her an independent computer consultant, independent contractor, partner or co-venturer.

⚠️ **Part-time workers can be employees.** If the right to control the worker exists, it also makes no difference whether a person only works part-time. Even a part-time worker will be considered an employee if he or she is not operating an independent business.

1. IRS Factors for Measuring Control

To help determine whether a worker is an employee or independent contractor, the IRS has developed a set of factors it uses to measure how much control the hiring firm has over the worker. These factors are an attempt by the IRS to synthesize the results of court decisions on who is and is not an independent contractor. These factors are intended to serve as flexible guidelines for IRS auditors, not as a strict series of tests. Not all the factors may apply to a given worker, and some may be more important than others. Let's take a look at them.

a. Factors Tending to Show the Worker Is an Employee

A worker is likely to be categorized as an employee in instances such as these:

- The hiring firm requires—or can require—the worker to comply with its instructions about when, where and how to work.
- The hiring firm trains the worker to perform services in a particular manner.
- The hiring firm integrates the worker's services into its business operations.
- The hiring firm requires the worker to render services personally; the worker can't hire others to do some of the work.
- The hiring firm hires, supervises and pays assistants for the worker.
- The hiring firm has a continuing relationship with the worker, or work is performed at frequently recurring intervals.

- The hiring firm establishes set hours of work.
- The hiring firm requires the worker to devote substantially full time to its business.
- The hiring firm has the worker do the work on its premises.
- The hiring firm requires the worker to do the work in a sequence that it sets.
- The hiring firm requires the worker to submit regular oral or written reports.
- The hiring firm pays the worker by the hour, week or month, unless these are installment payments of a lump sum agreed to for a job.
- The hiring firm pays the worker's business or traveling expenses.
- The hiring firm furnishes significant tools, equipment and materials.
- The hiring firm has the right to discharge the worker at will, and the worker has the right to quit at will.

b.   Factors Tending to Show the Worker Is an Independent Contractor

A worker tends toward independent contractor status when:
- The worker hires, supervises and pays his or her assistants.
- The worker is free to work when and for whom he or she chooses.
- The worker does the work at his or her own office.
- The worker uses his or her own tools and equipment.
- The worker is paid by the job or receives a straight commission.
- The worker invests in facilities used in performing services, such as renting an office.
- The worker can realize a profit or suffer a loss from his or her services, such as a worker who's responsible for paying salaries to his or her own employees.
- The worker performs services for several businesses at one time (although sometimes a worker can be an employee of several businesses).
- The worker makes his or her services available to the general public.

- The worker can't be fired so long as he or she meets the contract specifications.

Because of the way the software business works, some of the factors the IRS views as tending to show employment status will be present in most software company-consultant relationships. For example, because of the difficulty in accurately estimating how long a software project will take, many independent contractors in the software field bill by the hour rather than charge a fixed fee for an entire project. The presence of such factors tending to show employment status will not necessarily result in the worker being classified as an employee.

As a general rule, a software consultant will be viewed as an independent contractor by the IRS so long as he or she:

- *Serves several clients simultaneously.* A consultant who works for three or four clients in course of a week, with no more than 20 hours for any one, will likely be considered an independent contractor. Working for several clients one at a time over the course of a year is much less helpful: Such a worker may be viewed as an employee of each "client."
- *Works outside the hiring firm's premises.* The bulk of the work should not be performed at the hiring firm's office. Rather, it should be performed at an identifiable work location—whether an outside or home office—used exclusively for computer-related services. Even mainframe consultants can work at home or at their own office via a remote dial-up to the client's mainframe.
- *Markets services directly to clients.* Consultants who obtain work through consulting firms or brokers have a greater chance of being classified as employees than those who market their services directly to clients. The IRS frequently finds that consultants who obtain work through brokers are employees of either the broker or client. To avoid this, some brokers will only deal with consultants who have their own clients.
- *Can show risk of loss.* Being able to show financial risk is a very strong

factor in favor of independent contractor status. One way would be to agree to flat fee contracts, since this creates a risk that the consultant will end up losing money on the deal. However, this is probably too risky for most consultants. The best way may be to have regular monthly expenses such as assistants' salaries, office rent and leased equipment, which could outweigh receipts in any given month.

Let's consider a few examples to see how these rules operate:

Example 1: *Connie is a systems analyst who markets her services directly to various client companies on a short-term project basis. Connie does the bulk of her work at her own office on her own computers and employs a part-time assistant. She bills her clients by the hour and is reimbursed for travel and other expenses. Connie is undoubtedly an independent contractor. The hourly billing and expense reimbursement are mild indicators of employee status. But these are heavily outweighed by the fact that Connie works for multiple clients on a short-term basis and has her own office and employees. These strongly show that she is running an independent business; in other words, employees don't do these things.*

Example 2: *Ace Technical Services is engaged in the business of providing temporary technical services to its clients. Ace maintains a roster from which it selects workers it expects will suit its clients' needs. Susan signs a contract with Ace to work as a programmer for one of its clients. Susan spends almost all her time working for the client, at the client's office. She accounts to Ace for the time spent. Ace bills the client and pays Susan. Ace has the right to terminate Susan if she fails to perform the agreed-upon services or is otherwise unacceptable to the client. Susan is Ace's employee. (This example is based on IRS Revenue Ruling 87-41.)*

SIX WAYS TO SHOW THE WORLD YOU'RE RUNNING AN INDEPENDENT BUSINESS

Here are six relatively easy steps you can take to help establish that your computer consulting practice is a separately-established business:

1. *Incorporate.* Incorporating will make you appear and function more like an independent business than working as a sole proprietor. However, corporate formalities must be adhered to, otherwise the corporation may be viewed as a sham. (For a detailed discussion, see *The Legal Guide for Starting & Running a Small Business*, by Fred Steingold (Nolo Press).)

2. *Invest in equipment.* The more expensive the equipment you purchase, the more it will look like you're an independent contractor.

3. *Advertise.* Make the public aware of your services by advertising with business cards and stationery and listing yourself in industry directories.

4. *Register a fictitious business name.* Register and use a trade name other than your surname, also known as a fictitious business name or "dba" (short for "doing business as").

5. *Join a trade association.* Join an independent computer consultant organization or trade association.

6. *Invest in training and publications.* Invest time and money in business-related training and publications.

2. Section 530—The Employer's "Safe Harbor"

Applying the factors discussed just above, in Section D1, is a highly subjective exercise, leading to a great deal of uncertainty. Moreover, many employers and tax experts believe that IRS examiners often arbitrarily interpret the facts in order to find an employment relationship.

In an attempt to make life a little easier for hiring firms, Congress added Section 530 to the Internal Revenue Code in 1978. Section 530 serves as a "safe harbor" for a firm that classifies a worker as an independent contractor. Section 530 prohibits the IRS from retroactively reclassifying a worker from independent contractor to employee if the hiring firm had a "reasonable basis" for treating the worker as an independent contractor. What constitutes a "reasonable basis" is supposed to be liberally construed by the IRS in the hiring firm's favor. The factors discussed above are not applied.

Among the ways a hiring firm can establish reasonable basis in an audit is to show at least one of the following:

- It is a recognized, long standing practice for a large segment of the industry to treat such workers as independent contractors. (This can be difficult; one way to show this is to conduct a survey of similar businesses or to present affidavits or witnesses who are familiar with industry practice.)
- In a past IRS audit, the firm was not charged fines for treating workers doing a similar type of work as independent contractors.
- The firm relied on judicial rulings, IRS rulings or IRS technical advice that the worker was an independent contractor.

In addition, to qualify for the safe harbor, the hiring firm must not have treated the worker as an employee anytime after 1977 and must have filed all the required Form 1099s reporting the independent contractor's income to the IRS. Also, the hiring firm must have consistently treated individuals doing similar work as independent contractors. This last requirement was apparently intended to prevent an employer from converting employees into independent contractors to take advantage of the safe harbor rule. It would not appear to prevent a software company from having some employee-programmers and others who were treated as independent contractors.

Unfortunately, although Section 530 was designed by Congress to help hiring firms, it often doesn't work out that way. Companies attempting to invoke Section 530 have usually found that the IRS fights against them tooth and nail. In some cases it may be easier to show that a particular worker is an independent contractor under the rules discussed in Section D1, above, rather than attempt to convince the IRS that Section 530 applies.

⚠️ **Safe harbor cannot be claimed by brokers or consulting firms.** The Section 530 safe harbor does not apply to consulting firms or brokers who provide computer consultants and other technical services workers to third parties (IRC Section 530(d)).

Example: *Ace Technical Services hires Burt, a freelance programmer, to perform programming services for Painless Software, Inc. Painless pays Ace, who in turn pays Burt, after deducting a broker's fee. Ace treats Burt as an independent contractor. However, because it is in the middle of a three-party relationship, Ace would not be entitled to claim the safe harbor if audited by the IRS. The IRS would employ the factors discussed in Section D1, above, to determine whether Burt was Ace's employee.*

DO'S AND DON'TS FOR SOFTWARE COMPANIES THAT USE INDEPENDENT CONTRACTORS

Software firms that classify workers as independent contractors need to remember that they must be treated like independent businesspeople, not like employees. Treat the worker the same way you would the accountant who does your company's taxes or the lawyer who handles your legal work. This means:

- *Sign a written contract with the independent contractor before the work begins.* The contract should specify the work to be performed and make it clear that the worker is an independent contractor. The contract should be for a term of no longer than three to six months. Even where extensive projects are involved, this can be accomplished by narrowly defining the work to be done and then drawing up new contracts to cover additional tasks. (See Chapter 10.)
- *Don't provide ongoing instructions or training.* If the independent contractor needs special training, she should procure and pay for necessary training herself.
- *Don't supervise the independent contractor or establish working hours.* It's up to the independent contractor to control when and how to accomplish the job.

(continued)

- *Don't require formal written reports.* An occasional phone call inquiring into the work's progress is acceptable, but requiring regular written status reports indicates the worker is an employee. However, contracts for specific projects can (and should) have benchmarks for show-and-tell demonstrations or reports.
- *Don't invite an independent contractor to employee functions.* The exception is where outside vendors will be there as well.
- *Don't ever fire an independent contractor.* Instead, terminate the contract if she fails to meet the specifications or standards set forth in it.
- *Don't ever refer to an independent contractor as an "employee."* This should not be done verbally or in writing.
- *Set up a separate vendor file for each independent contractor you hire.* Keep in this file the independent contractor's contract, invoices, copies of 1099 forms and any other information that shows the worker is operating an independent business. This may include the independent contractor's business card and stationery, and evidence that the independent contractor has workers' compensation insurance coverage for her employees. Don't keep independent contractor records with your employee personnel files.
- *Don't pay independent contractors on a weekly, bi-weekly, or monthly basis like you pay your employees.* Rather, require all independent contractors to submit invoices, which are paid the same time you pay other outside vendors, such as your office supply company. ■

CHAPTER 8

Ownership of Software Created by Employees and Independent Contractors

When you hire a person to create, or aid in the creation of, a computer program, documentation or similar work, you probably assume that you will own the work you pay for. Due to recent court decisions, nothing could be further from the truth. To protect their interests, software developers must be aware of the rules of intellectual property ownership and use written agreements with employees and independent contractors. This chapter examines the rules regarding ownership of copyrights, patents and trade secrets. For a detailed discussion of the nature of these forms of intellectual property, see Chapter 3 (copyrights), Chapter 4 (trade secrets) and Chapter 5 (patents).

A. Copyright Ownership

The moment an employee or independent contractor creates a computer program (or any other work of authorship), it is protected by copyright. At that same moment, someone acquires ownership of the copyright in the work. That someone will not necessarily be the person or company who pays the employee's salary or independent contractor's fee.

Consider this scenario: You hire Jane, a freelance programmer, to help write the code for a communications program you're developing. Jane works at home under her own direction, sets her own hours, and uses her own computer. You do not consider Jane to be your employee. Jane completes her work, delivers her code and you pay her. Who owns the copyright to the code Jane has written? Quite possibly, Jane! This means Jane can sell the code to someone else—and you can't.

Fortunately, it's really quite easy to avoid this type of result. You just need to understand the rules of copyright ownership and use properly drafted agreements with employees and independent contractors.

1. Ownership of Works Created by Employees ("Works Made for Hire")

Copyrightable works created by an employee *within the scope of employment* are owned by the employer. Such works are called "works made for hire." Not only is the employer the owner of the copyright of a work made for hire, it is considered to be the work's "author" for copyright purposes. This is so whether the owner is a human being or a business entity such as a partnership or corporation. As the author, the employer is entitled to register the work with the Copyright Office, exercise its copyright rights in the work (such as distributing it to the public), permit others to exercise these rights, or sell all or part of its rights. The employee—the actual creator of the work—has no copyright rights at all. All she receives is whatever compensation the employer gives her.

This result is considered to be an obvious and natural consequence of the employer-employee relationship. It's assumed that an employee understands and agrees to this when she takes a job. Thus, an employer doesn't have to tell an employee that it will own copyrightable works she creates on the employer's behalf; the employee is supposed to know this without being told. Likewise, the employer need not have the employee sign an agreement relinquishing her copyright rights—the employee doesn't have any.

This all sounds very simple and pleasant for employers of programmers and other persons who create copyrightable works. However, there are two big problems that can create havoc if not properly dealt with before work is commenced. These are:

- determining who is an "employee," and
- determining when a work is created within the scope of employment.
  Let's explore both of these in detail.

a. Problem One: Who Is an Employee?

We discussed who is an employee for IRS purposes in Chapter 7. The main distinguishing feature of an employment relationship is that the employer has the *right to control* both the manner and means by which the work is created. Pretty much the same criteria are considered by the courts in determining whether a person is an employee for copyright purposes. The sidebar below lists the factors considered by courts in determining whether such a right of control is present for copyright purposes. (These are very similar to the control factors used by the IRS, discussed in Chapter 7, Section D1.)

FACTORS CONSIDERED IN DETERMINING EMPLOYEE STATUS FOR COPYRIGHT PURPOSES

Here are some of the factors the Supreme Court says judges are supposed to consider in determining if a person is an "employee" for copyright purposes:

- the skill required to do the work;
- the source of tools and materials used to create the work;
- the duration of the relationship;
- whether the person who pays for the work has the right to assign additional projects to the creative party;
- who determines when and how long the creative party works;
- the method of payment;
- who decides what assistants will be hired, and who pays them;
- whether the work is in the ordinary line of business of the person who pays for the work;
- whether the creative party is in business for himself;
- whether the creative party receives employee benefits from the person who pays for the work; and
- the tax treatment of the creative party.

One recent case makes clear that two factors are of prime importance:

- whether the hiring firm pays the worker's social security taxes, and
- whether the hiring firm provides employee benefits.

The court held that a part-time programmer employed by a swimming pool retailer was not the company's employee for copyright purposes and the programmer was therefore entitled to ownership of a program he wrote for the company. The court stated that the company's failure to provide the programmer with health, unemployment or life insurance benefits, or to withhold social security, federal or state taxes from his pay, was a *"virtual admission"* that the programmer was an independent contractor. The court stressed that the company could not treat the programmer as an independent contractor for tax purposes and then turn around and claim he was an employee for software ownership purposes (*Aymes v. Bonelli*, 980 F.2d. 857 (2d Cir. 1992)). In no other case has a court determined that a worker was an employee for copyright purposes where the hiring firm treated him as an independent contractor for tax purposes. *The moral is this:* If you don't pay a worker's social security taxes and provide him with benefits available to other employees, you should assume he is an independent contractor for copyright ownership purposes.

Given the track record in the courts, you can probably safely assume that a formal salaried employee for whom you pay social security taxes and employee benefits would be considered an employee for copyright purposes. When anything short of a formal, salaried employment relationship is involved, there is always a risk it will not be deemed an employment relationship for copyright purposes.

b. Problem Two: Is a Work Created Within the Scope of Employment?

Even when it is clear that an employment relationship exists, serious disputes can arise as to whether an employee who creates a copyrightable work did so within the scope of employment. Works created by employees outside the scope of their job duties are subject to the same rules as those for works created by independent contractors discussed in Section A2, below. The result is that an employee (or disgruntled ex-employee) could end up owning the copyright in his contribution to a software project because he can convince a court he was neither hired nor paid to create that work. For example, an employee hired to help create database software who ends up creating an arcade game might claim that his creation did not come within the scope of his employment. As you might expect, such disputes can get messy and very expensive, particularly if valuable software is involved.

c. The Solution to Problems One and Two

There is an easy solution to these problems: Have creative (or potentially creative) employees sign employment agreements assigning (transferring) the employer their copyright rights in all the works they create within the scope of their job. (See our discussion of copyright ownership in Chapter 3.) Not only should new employees assign their copyright rights to their employers, but existing employees should do so as well, if they haven't already. To avoid future disputes, it is also a good idea to clearly define the employee's job duties in writing. (See Chapter 9 for a detailed discussion of employment agreements.)

2. Ownership of Works Created by Independent Contractors

Subject to the exceptions discussed in the sidebar below, works created by independent contractors are not works made for hire—that is, the independent contractor, *not the hiring party*, owns all or part of the copyright in the created work. To avoid such a situation, the hiring party should always require independent contractors to sign written agreements assigning their copyright ownership to the hiring party. Such an agreement should be signed *before* the independent contractor commences work on the project. (See Chapter 10 for sample independent contractor agreements containing this all-important language.)

What happens if an independent contractor fails to assign her copyright rights to the hiring party in writing? There are two possible results, neither of them pleasant for the hiring party: The best thing that can happen from the hiring party's point of view is that the hirer will be deemed to be a co-author of the work and jointly share copyright ownership in it. For this to occur, the hiring party (or its employees) must have actually contributed protectible work (minimally creative expression in tangible form) to the project. More-over, this contribution must be significant in both qualitative and quantita-tive terms. Thus, a person who merely describes to a programmer what a program should do or look like is not a joint author. If the requirements for joint ownership are met, each joint author is entitled to use and license the work without the approval of the other co-authors, but must account for the other authors' share of the profits generated by the work's exploitation. (See Chapter 3, Section G1c, for further information about joint copyright ownership.)

If the hiring party did not contribute sufficient copyrightable expression to be considered a joint author of the work, the independent contractor will be the sole copyright owner. However, the hiring party would have a nonexclusive right to use the work (the hiring party paid for it after all!). But the independent contractor could resell his work to others without the hiring party's permission and without sharing any profits with the hiring party.

WHEN WORKS CREATED BY INDEPENDENT CONTRACTORS MAY BE WORKS MADE FOR HIRE

Certain types of works created by independent contractors are consid-ered to be works made for hire to which the hiring party automatically owns all the copyright rights—provided that the parties sign an agree-ment stating that the work is made for hire. These works include:

- contributions to a collective work (a work created by more than one author),
- parts of an audiovisual work,
- translations,
- "supplementary works" such as forewords, afterwards, supplemental pictorial illustrations, maps, charts, editorial notes, bibliographies, appendixes and indexes,
- compilations, and
- instructional texts.

(continued)

However, it is unclear whether contributions by independent contractors to computer programs fall within any of these categories. A computer program might constitute a collective work, compilation or even an audiovisual work, but no court has so ruled. Moreover, in 1982, the Copyright Office officials stated that, in their opinion, none of the commissioned work for hire categories applied to software. For this reason, until the question is conclusively resolved by court or Congressional action, persons who hire independent contractors to work on software should *never* rely on the work made for hire rule. Instead, they should have the independent contractor assign all copyright rights to the hiring party.

B. Trade Secret and Patent Ownership

The rules for determining ownership of trade secrets and patentable inventions by workers (employees or independent contractors) are essentially the same. Unlike copyright ownership, the basic rule for patents and trade secrets is that if you pay someone to invent or develop something, you own any patents or trade secrets developed in the course of the work.

1. Employees and Independent Contractors Hired to Invent Specific Items

When an employee or independent contractor is hired to develop or invent a specific product, device or procedure, the employer owns the patent and trade secret rights to that item. In this situation, the employee or independent contractor is deemed to have sold whatever rights he may have had in the invention or trade secret to the employer in advance, in return for his salary or other compensation.

Example: *Abe, a programmer, is hired by TopSoft to develop a program that determines the genealogy of race horses. TopSoft owns the rights to any patentable inventions and trade secrets developed by Abe in the course of his assigned task.*

2. Generally Inventive Employees or Independent Contractors

If, instead of being hired to invent or develop a specific item, the employee or independent contractor is hired to do research in a general area and/or is generally employed to design something, the employer will own the rights to any patentable inventions and trade secrets developed by the worker so long as they were created:

- during working hours, and
- within the scope of employment.

   Example: *Assume that instead of being hired specifically to invent a race horse genealogy program, Abe in the example above is hired by TopSoft simply to create new and useful programs. Abe decides to develop the race horse program and designs it during working hours. TopSoft owns the rights to any patents and trade secrets created by Abe in developing the program.*

3. Noninventive Employees or Independent Contractors

An employee who is *not* hired to invent or develop new products or technology owns the rights to any patentable inventions or trade secrets she creates. However, the employer will be entitled use the invention and include it in the products it sells without the employee's permission and without paying the employee for the use if:

- the employee used the employer's resources in creating the invention (for example, did a substantial amount of the work during business hours or used the employer's equipment), or
- the employee allowed the employer to promote the invention with a reasonable expectation of royalty-free use by the employer.

   This type of license is called a "shop right." It is non-exclusive (it does not prevent an employee-inventor from transferring her patent rights to others) and nontransferable by the employer.

   Example 1: *Ada is employed by Phoenix Developers as an accountant. Her job duties do not include developing new software. Ada develops a tax accounting program containing patentable features and other features that she maintains as a* *trade secret. Ada owns these patent and trade secret rights because she is a non-inventive employee—she was hired by Phoenix solely to do accounting work.*

Example 2: *Assume that Ada developed her program during working hours on a Phoenix computer. Ada still owns the patentable inventions and trade secrets she developed, but Phoenix is entitled to use the program for free—it has a "shop right" in the program. But Phoenix cannot sell the program or use rights to others.*

Example 3: *Assume that Ada develops her program at home and then shows it to a Phoenix programmer. She permits him to use a portion of the program in a new tax accounting package he's developing for Phoenix. Ada does not ask to be compensated for the use. Phoenix subsequently sells the package to the public. Phoenix has a shop right in the code Ada let Phoenix use for free. By failing to ask for compensation, Ada led Phoenix reasonably to believe that they could use the code without paying her.*

C. Contracts Assigning Patentable Inventions and Trade Secrets to Hiring Party

Unless someone is clearly hired to develop a specific product, bitter and costly disputes can develop as to the ownership of patentable inventions and/or trade secrets developed by employees and independent contractors. The way virtually all high-technology companies avoid these types of disputes is to have all employees and independent contractors sign agreements transferring their ownership rights in advance to the hiring party.

Most states permit hiring parties to use employment contracts providing for the transfer of all inventions created by the employee or independent contractor in exchange for his or her salary or other compensation. However, seven states, notably including California, have statutory restrictions on invention assignments in employment contracts. We discuss employment contracts in detail in Chapter 9. Contracts with independent contractors are discussed in Chapter 10. ■

CHAPTER 9

Employment Agreements

T his chapter is about agreements with a software developer's employees. Typically, the employer drafts an employment agreement and presents it to the prospective employee when a job offer is made, or soon afterward. Accordingly, Part I, below, provides employers with guidance on drafting such agreements. In Part II, we discuss the prospective employee's concerns when presented with such an agreement.

PART I. EMPLOYER'S GUIDE TO DRAFTING EMPLOYMENT AGREEMENTS

It is essential that a software developer enter into written agreements with its employees. This should always be done *before* they commence work. Continuing employees who have not already done so should be asked to sign appropriate agreements, as discussed in Section D, below.

This chapter only covers agreements between employers and employees. If you're not sure whether a worker qualifies as an employee or an independent contractor, review Chapter 7. (Agreements with independent contractors are discussed in Chapter 10.)

A. Why Use Employment Agreements?

Employment agreements are used by software developers to help accomplish the following goals:
*   to make clear to employees that they are in a confidential relationship with the employer and have a duty not to disclose confidential information to outsiders without the employer's permission,

- to identify as specifically as possible what information the employer regards as confidential,
- to assign to the employer, in advance, all proprietary rights (copyright, trade secret and patent) the employee may have in his or her work product, and
- where appropriate and legal, to impose reasonable restrictions on the employee's right to compete with the employer after the employment relationship ends.

B. Who Should Sign

All employees who might have access to trade secrets should sign an employment agreement. In order of priority, this includes:

- employees (programmers, systems engineers and other technical personnel) who play the key role in developing your software; in some companies, this is only a handful of employees;
- other employees who help develop your software;
- marketing people; and
- administrative and clerical staff.

C. When Should New Employees Sign?

A developer should be sure to give a new employee the agreement before she starts work—preferably, at the same time a job offer is made. This way, the hiree can take the agreement home and study it and even have her lawyer look at it. Don't wait until the employee has actually started work. At this point, after quitting her old job (and perhaps even moving), the employee may feel she has no choice but to sign the agreement as written. If you later need to enforce the agreement, a court may conclude that it was not a freely-bargained contract and refuse to enforce it. This has happened.

D.   Agreements with Current Employees

As stated above, an employment agreement containing assignment, nondisclosure and/or noncompetition clauses should be signed by the employee before he or she begins the job or, at the latest, on the first day of work. This ensures that the employment agreement is supported by adequate consideration. "Consideration" is the legal term for the value or *quid pro quo* that each party is supposed to receive from the other in exchange for entering into a contract. Unless a contract provides some consideration for each party, the law will usually not recognize it as binding.

In the case of an employment agreement (which is simply one type of contract), the consideration the employee receives for agreeing to work for the employer under the terms and conditions contained in the agreement is usually a salary and various employee benefits. A salary is considered by most courts to be adequate consideration for a new employee's agreement to assign any rights she may have in work-related creations, and to abide by nondisclosure and/or noncompetition restrictions.

A problem with consideration arises, however, when an employer attempts to have a current employee sign an agreement containing assignment, nondisclosure and/or noncompetition clauses. Courts in many states view a veteran employee's agreement to abide by such provisions as a new contract that must be supported by new consideration. Thus, when an employer wishes to have a continuing employee sign such an agreement, it should give the employee something of value in return—for example, a small cash bonus, a pay raise, stock options, vacation time or some other remuneration. This costs the employer something, but it ensures that the agreement will be enforceable. (It will also encourage the employee to sign the agreement.) The consideration given to a continuing employee for signing an employment agreement doesn't have to be enormous. Courts seldom look at the nature or amount of consideration as long as some mutuality of benefit is present. But the greater the consideration, the clearer it will be that there was a benefit to the employee and a binding contract was thereby created.

Example: *Burt has been working as a staff programmer for Elite Software since its earliest days. When he was first hired, Elite did not have him sign any type of employment agreement. A few years later, Elite management realizes that Burt, a highly skilled programmer, has been exposed to valuable Elite trade secrets and has been intimately involved in the creation of some of Elite's most valuable products. Elite decides to ask Burt to sign an agreement containing nondisclosure and invention assignment clauses. To ensure that the agreement is supported by adequate consideration, Elite gives Burt a pay raise in return for signing.*

PROBLEMS GETTING EXISTING EMPLOYEES TO SIGN EMPLOYMENT AGREEMENTS

One big problem software developers have with employment agreements is that they are usually not popular with employees, and some will refuse to sign them. Your employees may tell you that they know they can't divulge company trade secrets and view being asked to sign an agreement to that effect as unnecessary and an insult. This can be particularly true for small companies where the company owners and employees are (or view themselves as) friends.

Be sure to stress to any potentially offended employee that the use of such an agreement is no reflection on his character or trustworthiness. It is simply a standard legal precaution used by virtually all hi-tech businesses. Also, you may need to make the agreement as palatable as possible to the employee—for example, not attempt to impose post-employment noncompetition restrictions on the employee, as discussed in Section E2, below. When dealing with a truly key employee, consider offering substantial monetary or other benefits in return for signing the agreement—that is, more than would be legally necessary to constitute valid consideration for signing the agreement.

E. Selecting Employment Agreements You Need

In the following two sections (and on the forms disk), we provide two employment agreements:

- Employment Agreement for Nontechnical Employee (EMPLOY1.TXT on disk), and
- Employment Agreement for Technical Employee (EMPLOY2.TXT on disk).

Be sure to read the instructions and discussion to draft the forms; not all the provisions in the agreements may be appropriate for your situation. For example, California employers should not include noncompetition restrictions in their employment agreements, because they are unenforceable in California.

F. Employment Agreement for Nontechnical Employee

This is an employment and nondisclosure agreement for use with nontechnical employees—that is, employees who are not expected to help develop software. This includes clerical staff, production workers, personnel managers, marketing staff, sales staff and so forth. This agreement does not contain a copyright and invention assignment clause, since such employees are not being paid to help develop copyrightable or patentable works.

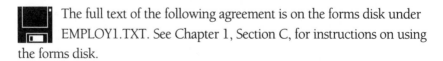 The full text of the following agreement is on the forms disk under EMPLOY1.TXT. See Chapter 1, Section C, for instructions on using the forms disk.

Introductory Paragraph

Select Alternative 1 if a new employee will be signing the agreement, and fill in the name of the company.

Select Alternative 2 if the agreement is with an existing employee. Fill in the name of the company. To be a legally binding contract, the agreement must be supported by consideration—that is, the employee must receive something of value for signing it. If the agreement is with a continuing employee, some additional consideration over and above her normal salary and benefits should be provided, such as cash or stock options. Specify the compensation to be provided.

1. Company's Trade Secrets

As discussed in Chapter 4, an employee who learns trade secrets as a result of a confidential relationship with his or her employer has a legal duty not to disclose them to others without the employer's permission. This clause defines the company's trade secrets; the next clause addresses the employee's nondisclosure obligations.

Like all provisions in an employment agreement (or any other contract), this clause must be reasonable. It should not cover everything in the employee's brain. A clause that attempts to do so will likely be unenforceable in court, because it is unreasonable. You don't need to add anything to this clause; it sets out the types of information and material that should be considered to be trade secrets.

2. Nondisclosure of Trade Secrets

This clause bars the employee from making unauthorized disclosures of the company's trade secrets. There are several good reasons for an employer to include a nondisclosure clause in its employment agreements. As we discussed in Chapter 4, software and other information qualifies as a trade secret only if reasonable precautions are taken to keep it secret. The use of nondisclosure clauses in employment agreements (or separate nondisclosure agreements; see Chapter 4, Section G) is perhaps the single most important reasonable precaution. Confidential information may not be deemed to be a trade secret where an employer does not use such agreements.

Including a nondisclosure clause in an employment agreement makes clear to the employee that he has a duty to protect the employer's trade secrets. It also shows that the employer is serious about keeping trade secrets secret.

This clause clearly defines employee obligations regarding trade secrets, which will also make it easier to obtain relief in court if an employee or ex-employee makes unauthorized disclosures.

However, as explained in this clause, the employee's nondisclosure obligation should not extend to information the employee knew before coming to work for the company, information he learns from sources outside the company and information that is not confidential because it is public knowledge (so long as the employee didn't make it public).

3. Confidential Information of Others

It's a good idea to remind new employees that they have a duty not to disclose to the employer trade secrets learned from prior employers or others. Employers who take advantage of such information can easily end up being sued.

4. Return of Materials

It's important that employees understand their obligation to return all materials containing trade secrets when they leave the company. They should be reminded of this obligation in their employment agreement and before they leave.

5. Confidentiality Obligation Survives Employment

It's important to make clear that the employee's duty not to disclose her employer's confidential information does not end when she leaves the company, but continues for as long as the material remains a trade secret.

6. Conflict of Interest

This clause is intended to make clear to the employee that he shouldn't compete with the company while employed by it or engage in any activity that may harm the company.

7. Enforcement

If the employee breaches, or threatens to breach the Agreement, this clause gives the employer the automatic right to an injunction to prevent such a breach. This clause does not preclude the employer's right to seek additional remedies.

8. General Provisions

These general provisions are standard in many types of legal documents:

- *Successors.* This clause obligates all successors and heirs to the contents of the Agreement.
- *Governing Law.* Here you specify which state law governs the contract—usually either the state of incorporation or the company's business home. It's generally more convenient to choose the state in which you live. That way, you can hire an attorney locally to handle any legal problems that might arise under the Agreement.
- *Severability.* In the event that some part of the Agreement is declared invalid by a court, this clause ensures that the rest of the document is still valid.
- *Entire Agreement.* This clause clarifies that the Agreement supersedes any prior signed agreements.
- *Modification.* This clause stipulates that future modifications must be in writing, signed both by the company and the employee.

Signatures

Although not absolutely necessary, it's a good idea to have the employee's signature witnessed by a company representative. This is intended to prevent the employee from later claiming her signature was forged.

 Skip to Chapter 1, Section D, for information about preparing the final agreement.

SAMPLE
EMPLOYMENT AGREEMENT FOR NONTECHNICAL EMPLOYEE

In consideration of my continued employment with SOFTWARE OF AMERICA, INC. (the "Company") and also in consideration of stock options to purchase One Hundred (100) shares of the Company's stock, the receipt and sufficiency of which I hereby acknowledge, I agree as follows:

1. Company's Trade Secrets: I understand that in performance of my job duties with the Company, I will be exposed to the Company's trade secrets. "Trade secrets" means information or material that is commercially valuable to the Company and not generally known in the industry. This includes, but is not limited to:

(a) any and all versions of the Company's proprietary computer software, hardware, firmware and documentation;

(b) technical information concerning the Company's products and services, including product data and specifications, know-how, formulae, diagrams, flow charts, drawings, source code, object code, program listings, test results, processes, inventions, research projects and product development;

(c) information concerning the Company's business, including cost information, profits, sales information, accounting and unpublished financial information, business plans, markets and marketing methods, customer lists and customer information, purchasing techniques, supplier lists and supplier information and advertising strategies;

(d) information concerning the Company's employees, including salaries, strengths, weaknesses and skills;

(e) information submitted by the Company's customers, suppliers, employees, consultants or co-venturers with the Company for study, evaluation or use; and

(f) any other information not generally known to the public which, if misused or disclosed, could reasonably be expected to adversely affect the Company's business.

2. Nondisclosure of Trade Secrets: I will keep the Company's trade secrets, whether or not prepared or developed by me, in the strictest confidence. I will not use or disclose such secrets to others without the Company's written consent, except when necessary to perform my job. However, I shall have no obligation to treat as confidential any information which:

(a) was in my possession or known to me, without an obligation to keep it confidential, before such information was disclosed to me by the Company;

(b) is or becomes public knowledge through a source other than me and through no fault of mine; or

(c) is or becomes lawfully available to me from a source other than the Company.

3. Confidential Information of Others: I will not disclose to the Company, use in the Company's business, or cause the Company to use, any information or material that is a trade secret of others.

4. Return of Materials: When my employment with the Company ends, for whatever reason, I will promptly deliver to the Company all originals and copies of all documents, records, software programs, media and other materials containing any of the Company's trade secrets. I will also return to the Company all equipment, files, software programs and other personal property belonging to the Company.

5. Confidentiality Obligation Survives Employment: I understand that my obligation to maintain the confidentiality and security of the Company's trade secrets remains with me even after my employment with the Company ends and continues for so long as such material remains a trade secret.

6. Conflict of Interest: During my employment by the Company, I will not engage in any business activity competitive with the Company's business activities. Nor will I engage in any other activities that conflict with the Company's best interests.

7. Enforcement: I agree that in the event of a breach or threatened breach of this Agreement, money damages would be an inadequate remedy and extremely difficult to measure. I agree, therefore, that the Company shall be entitled to an injunction to restrain me from such breach or threatened breach. Nothing in this Agreement shall be construed as preventing the Company from pursuing any remedy at law or in equity for any breach or threatened breach.

8. General Provisions:

(a) Successors: The rights and obligations under this Agreement shall survive the termination of my service to the Company in any capacity and shall inure to the benefit and shall be binding upon: (1) my heirs and personal representatives, and (2) the successors and assigns of the Company.

(b) Governing Law: This Agreement shall be construed and enforced in accordance with the laws of the State of New York.

(c) Severability: If any clause of this Agreement is determined to be invalid or unenforceable, the remainder shall be unaffected and shall be enforceable against both the Company and me.

(d) Entire Agreement: This Agreement supersedes and replaces all former agreements or understandings, oral or written, between the Company and me, except for prior confidentiality agreements I have signed relating to information not covered by this Agreement.

(e) Modification: This Agreement may not be modified except by a writing signed both by the Company and me.

I have carefully read and considered all clauses of this Agreement and agree that all of the restrictions set forth are fair and reasonably required to protect the Company's interests. I acknowledge that I have received a copy of this Agreement as signed by me.

_____   Date: _____
Employee's Signature

_____
Typed or Printed Name

Witness:

_____   Date: _____
Signature

_____
Typed or Printed Name

_____
Title

G. Employment Agreement for Technical Employee

This agreement is for use with technical employees—programmers, systems analysts, employees who create documentation, software engineers and others whose job is to help the company develop software.

The full text of the following agreement is on the forms disk under EMPLOY2.TXT. See Chapter 1, Section C, for instructions on using the forms disk.

Introductory Paragraph

Select Alternative 1 if a new employee will be signing the agreement, and fill in the name of the company.

Select Alternative 2 if the agreement is with an existing employee. Fill in the name of the company. To be a legally binding contract, the agreement must be supported by consideration—that is, the employee must receive something of value for signing it. If the agreement is with a continuing employee, some additional consideration over and above her normal salary and benefits should be provided, such as cash or stock options. Specify the compensation to be provided.

1. Company's Trade Secrets

As discussed in Chapter 4, an employee who learns trade secrets as a result of a confidential relationship with his or her employer has a legal duty not to disclose them to others without the employer's permission. This clause defines the company's trade secrets; the next clause addresses the employee's nondisclosure obligations.

Like all provisions in an employment agreement (or any other contract), this clause must be reasonable. It should not cover everything in the employee's brain. A clause that attempts to do so will likely be unenforceable in court, because it is unreasonable. You don't need to add anything to this clause; it sets out the types of information and material that should be considered to be trade secrets.

2. Nondisclosure of Trade Secrets

This clause bars the employee from making unauthorized disclosures of the company's trade secrets. There are several good reasons for an employer to include a nondisclosure clause in its employment agreements. As we discussed in Chapter 4, software and other information qualifies as a trade secret only if reasonable precautions are taken to keep it secret. The use of nondisclosure clauses (or separate nondisclosure agreements; see Chapter 4, Section G) is perhaps the single most important reasonable precaution. Confidential information may not be deemed to be a trade secret where an employer does not use such agreements.

Including a nondisclosure clause in an employment agreement makes clear to the employee that he has a duty to protect the employer's trade secrets. It also shows that the employer is serious about keeping trade secrets secret.

This clause clearly defines employee obligations regarding trade secrets, which will also make it easier to obtain relief in court if an employee or ex-employee makes unauthorized disclosures.

However, as explained in this clause, the employee's nondisclosure obligation should not extend to information the employee knew before coming to work for the company, information he learns from sources outside the company and information that is not confidential because it is public knowledge (so long as the employee didn't make it public).

3. Confidential Information of Others

It's a good idea to remind new employees that they have a duty not to disclose to the employer trade secrets learned from prior employers or others. Employers who take advantage of such information can easily end up being sued.

4. Return of Materials

It's important that employees understand their obligation to return all materials containing trade secrets when they leave the company. They should be reminded of this obligation in their employment agreement and before they leave.

5. Confidentiality Obligation Survives Employment

It's important to make clear that the employee's duty not to disclose her employer's confidential information does not end when she leaves the company, but continues for as long as the material remains a trade secret.

6. Computer Programs Are Works Made for Hire

Where technical employees are involved, clauses that assign (transfer rights of ownership) intellectual property rights to the employer are even more important than nondisclosure clauses. This clause covers assignment issues, as do these clauses discussed below:

- "Disclosure of Developments" clause,
- "Assignment of Developments" clause, and
- "Post-Employment Assignment" clause.

We explained in Chapter 8 that computer programs, documentation and other copyrightable works created by employees within the scope of their employment are "works made for hire" to which the employer is considered the "author" for copyright purposes. However, it is dangerous for employers to rely solely on the work made for hire rule. This is because of possible legal uncertainty regarding who is an "employee" for copyright purposes, and when copyrightable works are created within the scope of employment. Therefore, the employee should be required to assign, in advance, all copyright rights in job-related works to the employer.

This clause makes clear that the employee may create copyrightable works as part of his job and that such works will be works made for hire. But if for some reason the work for hire rule does not apply, the employee assigns all copyright rights in work-related works to the employer.

7. Disclosure of Developments

The employee must be required to disclose promptly to the employer any and all work-related inventions and other developments she creates. This clause complies with state restrictions on invention assignments discussed in the "Assignment of Developments" clause, below.

In Washington State, you must include the paragraph on disk that states that the Company will maintain a written record of all such disclosures for at least five years.

8. Assignment of Developments

As discussed in Chapter 8, absent an assignment of rights to an employee's work-related inventions and other developments, the employer may not own what the employee creates. Or, at the very least, the employer may be subject to a costly and bitter legal fight over ownership rights.

An assignment is simply a transfer of ownership. An employee may transfer his ownership rights in any copyrights, trade secrets, patentable inventions or "mask works" (semiconductor chip designs) he creates on the employer's behalf before he actually commences work. This is when an assignment ideally should be made—*before* an employee begins his job. As discussed in Section D, above, if an assignment is executed long after an employee is hired, the employer must give the continuing employee a raise or other compensation to ensure that the assignment is enforceable.

9. Post-Employment Assignment

Unfortunately, not all employees are honest when it comes to intellectual property rights. Some might try to steal materials they create that belong to their employer. Consider this scenario:

Example: *Josephine, a programmer employed by Miracle Systems, has signed an enforceable, reasonable assignment agreement. While employed by Miracle, she develops a potentially valuable program that should be assigned to Miracle under the terms of the agreement. However, Josephine conceals her new program from Miracle. She leaves Miracle and two months later registers her program with the Copyright Office, listing herself as the sole owner. Does Miracle have any ownership rights in the program? Maybe, if it can convince a court she developed it while employed by Miracle. But a lengthy and expensive court battle would be required.*

To help avoid these type of shenanigans, many hi-tech employers require inventive employees to agree to assign copyrightable or patentable works they create after the employment relationship ends. Such post-employment assignments are enforceable in most states if they are reasonable. To be reasonable, a post-employment assignment must:

• be for a limited time—probably no more than six months to one year after employment ends,

• apply only to works that relate to the inventor's former employment, and

• apply only to works actually in existence, not to mere ideas or concepts in the employee's brain.

10. Notice Pursuant to State Law

A prospective or continuing employee and his or her employer are usually in an unequal bargaining position—the employer generally has the upper hand. Some hi-tech employers have attempted to take advantage of their leverage by requiring their employees to agree to very broadly worded assignments that purport to transfer to the employer in advance ownership of everything the employee creates, whether related to the job or not. In the words of one court, these employers try to obtain "a mortgage on a man's brain" (*Aspinwall Mfg. Co. v. Gill*, 32 F. 697 (3d Cir. 1887)).

To protect employees, several states, including California, impose restrictions on the permissible scope of assignments of employee-created inventions. Note that these restrictions apply only to "inventions" an employee creates—that is, software or other items for which a patent is sought. The restrictions apply only to employees, not to independent contractors.

The California restrictions are typical, and probably of most importance to the software industry. Under California law, an employee cannot be required to assign any of her rights in an invention she develops "entirely on his or her own time without using the employer's equipment, supplies, facilities, or trade secret information" unless:

- when the invention was conceived or "reduced to practice" (actually created or a patent application filed) it *related to the employer's business* or actual or "demonstrably anticipated" research or development, or

- the invention resulted from any work performed by the employee for the employer (California Labor Code, Section 2870).

The following states impose similar restrictions:

- Delaware (Delaware Code Annotated, Title 19, Section 805).
- Illinois (Illinois Revised Statutes, Chapter 140, Sections 301-303).
- Kansas (Kansas Statutes Annotated, Section 44-130).
- Minnesota (Minnesota Statutes Annotated, Section 181.78).
- North Carolina (North Carolina General Statutes, Sections 66-57.1, 66-57.2).
- Utah (Utah Code Annotated, Sections 34-39-2, 34-39-3).
- Washington (Washington Revised Code Annotated, Sections 49.44.140, 49.44.150).

WHAT ABOUT THE OTHER STATES?

Employers doing business in states that do not have laws restricting invention assignments like the eight states discussed above should nevertheless not attempt to impose unreasonable invention assignments on their employees. Even in the absence of a state law like California's, a court could well refuse to enforce an assignment agreement that it deemed unreasonable—that is, that tried to obtain a "mortgage on a man's brain." Assignments complying with California law would probably be deemed reasonable in these states.

Here are examples that illustrates how these types of restrictions operate in practice.

Example 1: *Jim is a programmer employed by Orchid Development Co. Orchid is located in Northern California and is in the business of developing and marketing computer databases for business use. Before he began working for Orchid, Jim signed an employment agreement containing an invention assignment, complying with California law. An active computer game player, Jim creates a computer adventure game for children that uses revolutionary new methods to animate its characters in a very life-like way. Portions of this program could well constitute a patentable invention.*

Assume that Jim wrote his program at home, completely on his own time. Who owns Jim's invention, Orchid or Jim? Probably Jim. Since Orchid is not in the business of creating computer games, Jim's invention probably doesn't relate to its business or research and development; nor did Jim's game result from any work he performed for Orchid.

Example 2: *Assume the same facts above. But what if Jim created his game during working hours? In this event, Orchid's invention assignment would probably be effective—that is, it would own any inventions contained in the game.*

Example 3: *Again, assume the same facts. What if Jim created the game at home, but his new animation method was a spin-off from work he performed for Orchid? Orchid's invention assignment would probably be effective because Jim's invention resulted from work he performed for Orchid.*

If the employee will work in California, Illinois, Kansas, Minnesota or Washington State, state law requires that the employee be given written notice of state law restrictions on an employer's right to obtain an assignment of employee inventions. If this is not done, the assignment might be unenforceable. If the employee will work in any other state, delete this entire clause. Otherwise, include the appropriate state notice on disk that states that an Exhibit A is attached, which sets forth written notice of state assignment restrictions. The applicable Exhibit A, setting forth the text of the state law, must also be attached to the agreement. (This is covered below.)

11. Execution of Documents

This clause simply requires the employee to execute any documents necessary to effect the assignment of intellectual property rights.

12. Prior Developments

Unless the parties desire otherwise, the Agreement's assignment of intellectual property rights should not cover software, patents and other materials created and owned by the employee before commencing employment with the company. Since the employee wasn't working for the company when such items were created, the company shouldn't own them. This provision makes this clear and requires the employee to list all such prior developments.

13. Conflict of Interest

This clause is intended to make clear to the employee that he shouldn't compete with the company while employed by it or engage in any activity that may harm the company.

14. Post-Employment Noncompetition Agreement

A post-employment noncompetition agreement (also called a "covenant not to compete" or "noncompete clause") is designed to discourage a former employee from competing for a given period of time in the market in which the employer does business.

a. States That Prohibit Post-Employment Noncompetition Clauses

Post-employment noncompetition clauses are unenforceable under the laws of several states:

- Alabama (Alabama Code, Section 8-1-1 a).
- California (California Business & Professions Code, Section 16660).
- Colorado (Colorado Revised Statutes, Section 8-2-113- 3).
- Hawaii (Hawaii Revised Statutes Annotated, Section 480-4).
- Louisiana (Louisiana Revised Statutes Annotated, Section 23:921).
- Montana (Montana Code Annotated, Section 28-2-703 to 705).
- Nevada (Nevada Revised Statutes, Section 613.200).
- North Carolina (North Carolina General Statutes, Section 75-2).
- North Dakota (North Dakota Cent. Code, Title 9, Section 08-06).
- Oklahoma (Oklahoma Statutes Annotated, Title 15, Section 217-219).
- Oregon (Oregon Revised Statutes, Section 653.295).
- South Dakota (South Dakota Codified Laws Annotated, Section 53-9-8 to 11).
- Wisconsin (Wisconsin Statutes Annotated, Section 103.465).

Employers in these states must rely on nondisclosure clauses alone and/or employ the alternatives to noncompetition clauses discussed in the sidebar below.

If the employee will work in Alabama, California, Colorado, Hawaii, Louisiana, Montana, Nevada, North Carolina, North Dakota, Oklahoma, Oregon, South Dakota and Wisconsin, delete this clause and skip to the Section G16, "Noninterference with Company Employees," below.

ALTERNATIVES TO NONCOMPETITION RESTRICTIONS

To put it mildly, noncompetition clauses are not popular with employees. Some potential (or continuing) employees will simply refuse to sign them. There are other, less drastic ways, to accomplish the same goals:

- *Deferred compensation.* Instead of forcing employees to sign an agreement with a noncompetition clause, many hi-tech companies give their employees stock options, pension benefits or other benefits that fully vest only after several years of employment. This gives the employee a strong financial incentive to stay.

- *Employment contracts for a definite term.* Normally, employment is "at will"—meaning the employer can fire the employee for any reason or no reason at all. Likewise, the employee can quit at any time. However, this can be changed by either a written or oral contract. One way a developer can help assure a key employee will stay with the company is to have him or her sign an employment contract guaranteeing employment for a definite term—say two or three years. This means the employer can't fire the employee during that time and the employee can't quit. If he does, the employer can sue him for breach of contract.

  These types of agreements are common in some businesses, for example, the entertainment industry and professional sports; but they can have a real down side. If the employee doesn't work out, keeping her on can be a horrible burden for the company. Moreover, if an employee really wants to be somewhere else, the quality of her work will inevitably suffer. Obviously, both parties need to consider carefully before making such a long-term commitment.

- *Employee promissory notes.* Some hi-tech companies require employees to sign promissory notes for the monetary value of the training they receive. The note is forgiven—the employee doesn't have to pay it—if the employee stays with the company for a specified time period. But if the employee quits too soon, she will have to pay off the note, which gives the employee a financial incentive to stay. Whether these notes are enforceable is not clear; court challenges are currently underway.

b. Why Use Post-Employment Noncompetition Clauses

From an employer's point of view, a noncompetition clause in an employment agreement can serve several highly useful functions:

- By making it difficult, if not impossible, for a key employee to leave the company, it helps ensure that the employer will receive full return on its investment in training the employee.
- It may help an employer maintain a competitive advantage by preventing key employees from working for — and thereby aiding — competitors.
- It can help keep the employer's valuable trade secrets out of the hands of competitors.

Indeed, where enforceable, noncompetition clauses are far more effective in protecting trade secrets than nondisclosure clauses. It can be very difficult for an employer to know whether an ex-employee has disclosed trade secrets to a competitor. Moreover, even if the employer is sure trade secrets have been disclosed, it can be difficult to obtain court relief for violations of a nondisclosure clause. The ex-employer must prove that the employee actually disclosed confidential information or that there is an imminent threat of such an unauthorized disclosure. This can be an onerous task — especially where the ex-employee claims that the information allegedly disclosed didn't qualify as a trade secret.

These problems do not exist with noncompetition clauses. It's usually easy to discover whether an ex-employee has gone to work for a competitor. To enforce a noncompetition clause in court, the ex-employer need only show that the ex-employee went to work for a competitor in violation of the clause's terms.

The best part about a noncompetition clause from an employer's point of view is that it will deter both the employee from seeking employment with a competitor and the competitor from hiring him or her. This significantly reduces an employee's incentive and opportunity to divulge trade secrets.

Of course, noncompetition clauses can make it impossible for an employee to earn a living in her chosen line of work if he or she leaves her job. The right to earn a living is considered to be one of the most fundamental rights a person has. For this reason, courts generally look on such clauses with disfavor and will only enforce them if the terms are reasonable and enforcement serves a legitimate interest of the employer.

c. When to Use Post-Employment Noncompetition Clauses

Don't try to use a post-employment noncompetition clause simply to chain an employee to his job or obtain an unfair advantage over your competitors. A noncompetition clause should be used only in states where it's allowed, when there is a legitimate business need for it. For example:

- *Protection of trade secrets.* An employer has a legitimate interest in preventing its trade secrets from being disclosed to competitors. Thus, a noncompetition clause may be called for where the employee has access to trade secrets.

- *Return on substantial investment in employee.* Where an employer spends substantial time and money giving an employee special training, it has a legitimate interest in obtaining a fair return on its investment. Thus, an employer may legitimately insist that an employee sign an agreement with a noncompetition clause before making such an investment in him or her.

- *Key employees.* Particularly in the software industry, where highly valuable programs are often created by a few extremely talented individuals, an employer may have a legitimate interest in preventing employees with special, unique or extraordinary skills from working for competitors.

d. Reasonableness Requirement

To be enforceable in the states that permit them, a noncompetition clause must be *reasonable*. If such an clause is found to be unreasonable, courts in some states will refuse to enforce it at all; others will ignore the unreasonable provisions and apply what they deem to be reasonable restrictions.

To be reasonable, a noncompetition clause must be limited as to time, scope and geographic region:

- *Time.* A noncompetition clause cannot last forever; it must have a definite time limit—the shorter the better. Such clauses typically last for no more than six months to two years.
- *Scope.* A noncompetition clause should be no more restrictive than necessary to accomplish the employer's legitimate objectives. The clause should define as specifically as possible exactly what type of activities the employee cannot perform for a competitor. Generally, these activities ought to be similar to those currently being performed by the employee.
- *Geography.* A noncompetition clause must specify the geographic region in which it applies. It should be limited to the geographic area in which the company does business or in which it has made definite plans to do business in the immediate future. Of course, most software developers market their work to customers throughout the United States, so their noncompetition clauses can apply to the entire country.

e. Choosing a Noncompetition Clause

The more limited a noncompetition clause is in scope and time, the more likely it will be deemed reasonable and therefore enforceable in court. Presented on disk are a range of options, from a fairly "stiff" noncompetition clause to a relatively mild one. Choose one of the following for paragraph (a):

- *Alternative 1.* This is our strictest noncompete clause.
- *Alternative 2.* This clause bars an ex-employee from taking competi-

tive employment only if it requires him or her to disclose any of the company's confidential information. This is much weaker than Alternative 1, thus much more easily enforced.

- *Alternative 3.* This clause is limited to products and services the employee actually worked on for a specified time period before leaving the company. It's the weakest and therefore the most "reasonable" clause of all.

In addition to the particulars of paragraph (a), each noncompete clause, should contain:

(b) *Diversion of Company Business.* This prohibits the employee from soliciting or diverting company business. This provision should apply only to the period six to 12 months before the employee left the company and for no more than six to 12 months after termination. Fill in the desired time periods.

(c) *Geographic Restrictions.* Most software companies do business throughout the United States, so their noncompetition covenants should apply in every state as well. This provision makes this clear.

15. Additional Post-Employment Noncompetition Terms

If you completed the Post-Employment Noncompetition Agreement clause above, you have the option to add any or all of the following:

(a) *Written Consent.* This lets the employee off the hook if he can convince the company that no confidential information will be disclosed to his new employer. It will help make the noncompete clause appear reasonable to a judge. This would be most appropriate where the employee's new duties wouldn't tempt him or her to disclose the prior employer's trade secrets.

(b) *Inability to Secure Employment.* An excellent way for an employer to make a noncompetition clause appear reasonable in the eyes of a court is for the employer to agree to pay all or part of the ex-employee's salary if the employee is unable to find work because of the noncompetition clause. This can be expensive, but it may be worth it to prevent a key employee from working for the competition and possibly divulging trade secrets.

16. Noninterference With Company Employees

It's pretty much impossible for an employee to quit and start a competitive business by herself. She needs help and she'll usually try to find it among her co-workers. Indeed, it has been a common occurrence in the hi-tech field for groups of employees to leave a company to start a competitive company. This clause tries to prevent this by barring the employee from persuading other employees to leave the company.

This simple provision can be almost as effective as a covenant not to compete, while not presenting the difficult enforcement problems that noncompetition restrictions do. (But, of course, this clause will not prevent an employee from joining an already-established competitor.) This optional clause may be used in any state, including those that prohibit post-employment noncompetition clauses.

17. Enforcement

If the employee breaches, or threatens to breach the Agreement, this clause gives the employer the automatic right to an injunction to prevent such a breach. This clause does not preclude the employer's right to seek additional remedies.

18. General Provisions

These general provisions are standard in many types of legal documents:
- *Successors.* This clause obligates all successors and heirs to the contents of the Agreement.
- *Governing Law.* Here you specify which state law governs the contract — usually either the state of incorporation or the company's business home.

It's generally more convenient to choose the state in which you live. That way, you can hire an attorney locally to handle any legal problems that might arise under the Agreement.

• *Severability.* In the event that some part of the Agreement is declared invalid by a court, this clause ensures that the rest of the document is still valid.

• *Entire Agreement.* This clause clarifies that the Agreement supersedes any prior signed agreements.

• *Modification.* This clause stipulates that future modifications must be in writing, signed both by the company and the employee.

Signatures

Although not absolutely necessary, it's a good idea to have the employee's signature witnessed by a company representative. This is intended to prevent the employee from later claiming her signature was forged.

Exhibit A

To protect employees, several states impose restrictions on the permissible scope of assignments of employee-created inventions. If the employee will work in California, Illinois, Kansas, Minnesota or Washington State, include the appropriate notice of state law provided on disk. Delete all state law notices that don't apply.

 Skip to Chapter 1, Section D, for information about preparing the final agreement.

SAMPLE
EMPLOYMENT AGREEMENT FOR TECHNICAL EMPLOYEE

In consideration of the commencement of my employment with Elite Software, Inc. (the "Company") and the compensation hereafter paid to me, I agree as follows:

1. Company's Trade Secrets: I understand that in performance of my job duties with the Company, I will be exposed to the Company's trade secrets. "Trade secrets" means information or material that is commercially valuable to the Company and not generally known in the industry. This includes:

(a) any and all versions of the Company's proprietary computer software (including source code and object code), hardware, firmware and documentation;

(b) technical information concerning the Company's products and services, including product data and specifications, diagrams, flow charts, drawings, test results, know-how, processes, inventions, research projects and product development;

(c) information concerning the Company's business, including cost information, profits, sales information, accounting and unpublished financial information, business plans, markets and marketing methods, customer lists and customer information, purchasing techniques, supplier lists and supplier information and advertising strategies;

(d) information concerning the Company's employees, including their salaries, strengths, weaknesses and skills;

(e) information submitted by the Company's customers, suppliers, employees, consultants or co-venturers with the Company for study, evaluation or use; and

(f) any other information not generally known to the public which, if misused or disclosed, could reasonably be expected to adversely affect the Company's business.

2. Nondisclosure of Trade Secrets: I will keep the Company's trade secrets, whether or not prepared or developed by me, in the strictest confidence. I will not use or disclose such secrets to others without the Company's written consent, except when necessary to perform my job. However, I shall have no obligation to treat as confidential any information which:

(a) was in my possession or known to me, without an obligation to keep it confidential, before such information was disclosed to me by the Company;

(b) is or becomes public knowledge through a source other than me and through no fault of mine; or

(c) is or becomes lawfully available to me from a source other than the Company.

3. Confidential Information of Others: I will not disclose to the Company, use in the Company's business, or cause the Company to use, any information or material that is a trade secret of others.

4. Return of Materials: When my employment with the Company ends, for whatever reason, I will promptly deliver to the Company all originals and copies of all documents, records, software programs, media and other materials containing any of the Company's trade secrets. I will also return to the Company all equipment, files, software programs and other personal property belonging to the Company.

5. Confidentiality Obligation Survives Employment: I understand that my obligation to maintain the confidentiality and security of the Company's trade secrets remains with me even after my employment with the Company ends and continues for so long as such material remains a trade secret.

6. Computer Programs Are Works Made for Hire: I understand that as part of my job duties I may be asked to create, or contribute to the creation of, computer programs, documentation and other copyrightable works. I agree that any and all computer programs, documentation and other copyrightable materials that I am asked to prepare or work on as part of my employment with the Company shall be "works made for hire" and that the Company shall own all the copyright rights in such works. **IF AND TO THE EXTENT ANY SUCH MATERIAL DOES NOT SATISFY THE LEGAL REQUIREMENTS TO CONSTITUTE A WORK MADE FOR HIRE, I HEREBY ASSIGN ALL MY COPYRIGHT RIGHTS IN THE WORK TO THE COMPANY.**

7. Disclosure of Developments: While I am employed by the Company, I will promptly inform the Company of the full details of all my inventions, discoveries, improvements, innovations and ideas (collectively called "Developments")—whether or not patentable, copyrightable or otherwise protectible—that I conceive, complete or reduce to practice (whether jointly or with others) and which:

(a) relate to the Company's present or prospective business, or actual or demonstrably anticipated research and development; or

(b) result from any work I do using any equipment, facilities, materials, trade secrets or personnel of the Company; or

(c) result from or are suggested by any work that I may do for the Company.

The Company will maintain a written record of all such disclosures for at least five years.

8. Assignment of Developments: I hereby assign to the Company or the Company's designee, my entire right, title and interest in all of the following, that I conceive or make (whether alone or with others) while employed by the Company:

(a) all Developments;

(b) all copyrights, trade secrets, trademarks and mask work rights in Developments; and

(c) all patent applications filed and patents granted on any Developments, including those in foreign countries.

9. Post-Employment Assignment: I will disclose to the Company any and all computer programs, inventions, improvements or discoveries actually made, or copyright registration or patent applications filed, within six months after my employment with the Company ends. I hereby assign to the Company my entire right, title and interest in such programs, inventions, improvements and discoveries, whether made individually or jointly, which relate to the subject matter of my employment with the Company during the 12-month period immediately preceding the termination of my employment.

10. Notice Pursuant to State Law: I understand that this Agreement does not apply to any invention that qualifies fully under the provisions of Washington Revised Code Annotated Sections 49.44.140(1) and (2), the text of which is attached as Exhibit A. This section shall serve as written notice to me as required by Washington Revised Code Annotated Section 49.44.140(3).

11. Execution of Documents: Both while employed by the Company and afterwards, I agree to execute and aid in the preparation of any papers that the Company may consider necessary or helpful to obtain or maintain any patents, copyrights, trademarks or other proprietary rights at no charge to the Company, but at its expense.

12. Prior Developments: As a matter of record, I have identified below all prior developments ("Prior Developments") relevant to the subject matter of my employment by the Company that have been conceived or reduced to practice or learned by me, alone or jointly with others, before my employment with the Company, which I desire to remove from the operation of this Agreement. The Prior Developments consist of: None.

I represent and warrant that this list is complete. If there is no such list, I represent that I have made no such Prior Developments at the time of signing this Agreement.

13. Conflict of Interest: During my employment by the Company, I will not engage in any business activity competitive with the Company's business activities. Nor will I engage in any other activities that conflict with the Company's best interests.

14. Post-Employment Noncompetition Agreement: I understand that during my employment by the Company I may become familiar with confidential information of the Company. Therefore, it is possible that I could gravely harm the Company if I worked for a competitor. Accordingly, I agree for two years following the end of my employment with the Company not to compete, directly or indirectly, with the Company in any of its business if the duties of such competitive employment inherently require that I use or disclose any of the Company's confidential information. Competition includes the design, development, production, promotion or sale of products or services competitive with those of the Company.

(a) Diversion of Company Business: For a period of 12 months from the date my employment ends, I will not divert or attempt to divert from the Company any business the Company enjoyed or solicited from its customers during the six months prior to the termination of my employment.

(b) Geographic Restrictions: I acknowledge and agree that the software developed by the Company is, or is intended to be, distributed to customers nationally throughout the United States. According, I agree that these restrictions on my post-employment competitive activity shall apply throughout the entire United States.

15. Additional Post-Employment Noncompetition Terms: The following post-employment noncompetition term(s) shall apply:

(a) Written Consent: I understand that I will be permitted to engage in the work or activity described in this Agreement if I provide the Company with clear and convincing written evidence, including assurances from my new employer and me, that the contribution of my knowledge to that work or activity will not cause me to disclose, base judgment upon or use any of the Company's confidential information. The Company will furnish me a written consent to that effect if I provide the required written evidence. I agree not to engage in such work or activity until I receive the written consent from the Company.

(b) Inability to Secure Employment: If, solely as a result of this noncompetition agreement, I am unable to secure employment appropriate to my abilities and training despite my diligent efforts to do so, the Company shall either: (1) release me from my noncompetition obligations to the extent necessary to allow me to obtain such employment, or (2) pay me a periodic amount equal to my monthly base pay at termination for the balance of the term of this noncompetition agreement.

If and while the Company elects to pay me the amounts described above, I promise to diligently pursue other employment opportunities consistent with my general skills and interests. I understand that the Company's obligation to make or continue the payments specified above will end upon my obtaining employment, and I will promptly give the Company written notice of such employment.

16. Noninterference with Company Employees: While employed by the Company and for 12 months afterwards, I will not:

(a) induce, or attempt to induce, any Company employee to quit the Company's employ,

(b) recruit or hire away any Company employee, or

(c) hire or engage any Company employee or former employee whose employment with the Company ended less than one year before the date of such hiring or engagement.

17. Enforcement: I agree that in the event of a breach or threatened breach of this Agreement, money damages would be an inadequate remedy and extremely difficult to measure. I agree, therefore, that the Company shall be entitled to an injunction to restrain me from such breach or threatened breach. Nothing in this Agreement shall be construed as preventing the Company from pursuing any remedy at law or in equity for any breach or threatened breach.

18. General Provisions:

(a) Successors: The rights and obligations under this Agreement shall survive the termination of my service to the Company in any capacity and shall inure to the benefit and shall be binding upon: (1) my heirs and personal representatives, and (2) the successors and assigns of the Company.

(b) Governing Law: This Agreement shall be construed and enforced in accordance with the laws of the state of Washington.

(c) Severability: If any provision of this Agreement is determined to be invalid or unenforceable, the remainder shall be unaffected and shall be enforceable against both the Company and me.

(d) Entire Agreement: This Agreement supersedes and replaces all former agreements or understandings, oral or written, between the Company and me, except for prior confidentiality agreements I have signed relating to information not covered by this Agreement.

(e) Modification: This Agreement may not be modified except by a writing signed both by the Company and me.

I have carefully read and considered all provisions of this Agreement and agree that all of the restrictions set forth are fair and reasonably required to protect the Company's interests. I acknowledge that I have received a copy of this Agreement as signed by me.

_____   Date: _____
Employee's Signature

_____
Typed or Printed Name

Witness:

_____   Date: _____
Signature

_____
Typed or Printed Name

_____
Title

EXHIBIT A

Washington Revised Code Annotated Section 49.44.140 provides as follows:

(1) A provision in an employment agreement that provides that an employee shall assign or offer to assign any of the employee's rights in an invention to the employer does not apply to an invention for which no equipment, supplies, facilities, or trade secret information of the employer was used and that was developed entirely on the employee's own time, unless:

(a) the invention relates (i) directly to the business of the employer, or (ii) to the employer's actual or demonstrably anticipated research or development, or

(b) the invention results from any work performed by the employee for the employer.

Any provision that purports to apply to such an invention is to that extent against the public policy of this state and is to that extent unenforceable.

(2) An employer shall not require a provision made void and unenforceable by subsection (1) of this section as a condition of employment or continuing employment.

PART II. EMPLOYMENT AGREEMENTS FROM THE EMPLOYEE'S VIEWPOINT

In this section, we discuss employment agreements from the employee's point of view. Hi-tech employees are commonly asked to sign various agreements either before or after they begin work. They may be told that these merely are "standard forms" that everyone signs. These forms may be quite lengthy and filled with difficult to understand legalese. *Before you sign any agreement, read it carefully and make sure you both understand and are comfortable signing it!*

Of course, the extent to which the employer will be willing to alter any of the provisions in an employment agreement depends largely on how badly it wants you as an employee. And, the extent to which you may be willing to demand significant changes depends on how much you want the job.

ASK FOR COPY OF EMPLOYMENT AGREEMENT BEFORE YOU ACCEPT THE JOB

Be sure to ask any prospective employer if you will be required to sign an employment contract, and, if so, ask for a copy *before* you accept the job. You don't want to be presented with a harsh agreement after you've already started work. At this point, having quit your old job, you may feel you have no choice but to sign it as written; or, at the very least, you will be in a much worse bargaining position than you were before accepting the new job.

Following are some of the key items you should look for when reviewing an employment agreement:

- confidentiality of trade secrets,
- intellectual property ownership rights, and
- post-employment noncompetition restrictions.

Let's discuss each in more detail.

H. Confidentiality of Trade Secrets

The agreement may contain a clause requiring you to keep the company's trade secrets confidential. There is nothing to object to here. Even without such a clause, you have a legal duty not to disclose your employer's trade secrets if you're routinely exposed to them as a part of your job. (See Chapter 4, Section B1, for a detailed discussion.) This duty applies not only to your new employer, but to all past employers as well. In other words, do not bring to your new job or disclose to your new employer your old employer's trade secrets.

Be careful what you take from your prior employer. The best way to get your new employer and yourself involved in a trade secret suit is to take materials containing trade secrets belonging to your old employer when you leave for your new job. This includes not only documents but computer disks and even trade journal articles (you may have written valuable notes on these that belong to your old employer). The wisest policy is to ask your old employer's permission before taking any document, disk or other item that could conceivably contain the employer's trade secrets. It's best to get such permission in writing.

I. Intellectual Property Ownership

If the employer knows what it is doing, the agreement should contain a provision by which you transfer your intellectual property ownership rights in the software and other materials you create as part of your job duties. (See the discussion in Sections G6-8, above.) This is perfectly reasonable and unobjectionable. However, if you and your new employer are going to share ownership of any of your work product, make sure that the employment agreement (or perhaps another side agreement) spells out exactly what you've agreed to. The discussion of ownership of custom software in Chapter 11, Section D10, should be useful here as well. It discusses the various ways a software developer and customer can parcel out ownership rights. Rights in employee-created software can be handled in the same way.

1. Employee-Owned Materials

If you own any software, development tools (for example, pieces of code you've created and used in all your software), patents or other valuable materials and you want these items to remain your sole property, the agreement should make clear that your employer is not acquiring any ownership rights in them. Following is a sample clause for this; you'll need to type it yourself.

Example: *The following Developments [if many, add: "relevant to the subject matter of my employment by the Company"] have been conceived or reduced to practice or learned by me, alone or jointly with others, before my employment with the Company and I desire that they be removed from the operation of this Agreement: [list all employee-owned materials].*

2. Work Outside the Scope of Employment

You need to be very careful if you intend to create software or other potentially valuable products on your own time. As we discuss in detail in Chapter 8, an employer owns the intellectual property rights in software created by an employee within the scope of employment. Moreover, an employer may even have certain rights over works created outside the scope of employment if the employee used the employer's resources—for example, did a substantial amount of the work during business hours or used the employer's equipment. If an employee creates a valuable work on her own time, an unscrupulous employer might try to assert ownership over it by claiming that the work was within the scope of employment or the employee used its resources.

To avoid potential problems, if you plan to do work on your own, make sure you inform your new employer and obtain its written acknowledgment that it has no ownership interest in such work.

Example: *Art Acres is hired by TalkSoft to help develop communications software. On his own time, Art decides to develop a computer game. Art's work on the game is in no way connected with his work for TalkSoft, nor could the game be competitive with any of TalkSoft's products. However, just to make sure there will be no problems, Art informs his boss about his plans and gets TalkSoft to sign the following agreement:*

TalkSoft Corp. hereby acknowledges that:

(1) Art Acres is employed as a computer programmer for TalkSoft;

(2) Art Acres intends to create a computer game, tentatively entitled You Are What You Eat;

(3) You Are What You Eat will be created by Art Acres on his own time, outside the scope of his employment by TalkSoft and shall not constitute a work made for hire; and

(4) TalkSoft shall claim no ownership interest whatsoever in this computer game.

TalkSoft Corp., by _____

Date: _____

3. Post-Employment Invention Assignments

Some employers seek to include a provision by which the employee agrees to assign to the employer copyrightable or patentable work the employee creates after the employment relationship ends. Such post-employment assignments are enforceable only if they are reasonable. (See the discussion in Section G9, above.) From your point of view, a post-employment assignment provision is just as undesirable as a noncompetition clause. (See Section J, below.) It can make it very difficult for you to get a new job because your new employer may not be entitled to own anything you create during the period of the assignment provision.

Try to avoid signing agreements containing such provisions or at least seek to keep the length of the restriction as short as possible. Also, make sure the assignment applies only to works actually in existence, not to mere ideas or concepts in your brain.

J. Post-Employment Restrictions on Competition

Post-employment restrictions on competition (also called "covenants not to compete") are contractual provisions that attempt to prevent an employee from competing with the employer after the employment relationship ends. This is one area in which the interests of the employer and employee are diametrically opposed. Quite simply, you don't want to have any restrictions on your right to work for others if you leave the company. However, the more valuable your skills, the more likely it is that your employer will want to prevent you from working for the competition.

Fortunately for employees, post-employment noncompetition restrictions are highly disfavored by the courts. Moreover, several states, including California, have laws making employee covenants not to compete unenforceable. (See Section G14a, above, for a list.) If you're in a state that doesn't have such a law, this doesn't mean the employer may impose extremely harsh noncompetition restrictions on you. Covenants not to compete must be reasonable to be enforceable. A noncompetition clause that would prevent you from earning a living in your chosen occupation for a substantial time would likely be unenforceable in court. (See Section G14d, above, for detailed discussion.)

If your prospective employer absolutely insists on having a noncompetition clause, at least try to limit it as much as possible. Here are some pointers:

• *Time.* Seek to make the length of the restriction as short as possible. Try for six months or a year; anything over two years is probably unreasonable.

- *Scope.* Try to avoid promising not to work for any of the company's competitors or for certain named competitors. Rather, agree not to help develop products or services competitive with or similar to products you actually worked on for the company.
- *Geography.* The noncompete clause should apply only to the geographic areas in which the company does business or has definite plans to do business when you terminate your employment. However, if the company distributes its software throughout the United States (as most do), a noncompete clause can apply to the entire country.

See Section G14e, above, for sample language incorporating these restrictions into a noncompetition clause. ■

CHAPTER 10

Agreements With Independent Contractors

T his chapter covers agreements between software companies and workers hired to perform services as independent contractors. In this chapter, we'll refer to "independent contractors" and "consultants" interchangeably. (For agreements between employers and employees, see Chapter 9.)

A. Introduction

This chapter explains all aspects of independent contractor agreements. A complete independent contractor agreement is contained in the forms disk at the back of this book. It is advisable, however, that you read the following discussion in conjunction with using the forms disk. The disk contains a number of options you'll have to choose from, and the rest of this chapter explains these options in detail.

Before using any independent contractor agreement, the parties should be reasonably certain that the worker legally qualifies as an independent contractor rather than an employee. Review the discussion in Chapter 7. If you still have questions, consult an attorney.

SHOULD YOU USE AN INDEPENDENT CONTRACTOR AGREEMENT OR CUSTOM SOFTWARE AGREEMENT?

If a consultant is being hired to help create computer software, you may be uncertain whether to use the independent contractor agreement contained in this chapter or the much longer custom software agreement discussed in Chapter 11.

If an independent contractor is being hired to create an entire computer system, the custom software agreement should be used. The independent contractor agreement covered in this chapter is much simpler and is designed for more limited projects.

B. Key Provisions in Independent Contractor Agreements

In some cases, the hiring firm will prepare an agreement for a consultant to sign. In others, the consultant will have his or her own agreement for the hiring firm to agree to. In either event, this section discusses the main issues such an agreement should address.

The full text of the Independent Contractor Agreement is on the forms disk under INDPCONT.TXT. See Chapter 1, Section C, for instructions on using the forms disk.

The Independent Contractor Agreement is self-explanatory, with the following clarifications.

1. Introductory Paragraph

Fill in the date the agreement should take effect. This can be the date the agreement is signed, but it doesn't have to be. The agreement can take effect weeks before or after it's actually signed. Next, fill in the hiring company's name (the "Client"). Finally, fill in the name of the independent contractor (the "Consultant").

2. Definitions

This clause defines key terms used in the Agreement.
  (b) *Background Technology.* The consultant's background technology should be described in as much detail as possible.

3. Services Performed by Consultant

The agreement should describe, in as much detail as possible, what the consultant is expected to do. If a computer program is to be produced, describe it in as much detail as possible. Make sure to cover anything else the consultant should deliver, such as documentation.

It is often helpful to break down the project into discrete parts or stages—often called phases or "milestones." This makes it easier for the hiring firm to monitor the consultant's progress and may aid the consultant in budgeting her time. For example, the consultant's pay could be contingent upon the completion of each milestone. (Payment schedules are covered below, under "Consultant's Payment.")

4. Consultant's Payment

There are a number of ways a consultant may be paid; choose the alternative that suits your needs:

- *Alternative 1: Fixed Fee.* The simplest way for a consultant to be paid is by a fixed fee. The client agrees to pay an initial sum of money when the work is commenced and the remainder when it's finished.

- *Alternative 2: Installment Payments.* Paying a consultant a fixed fee for the entire job, rather than an hourly or daily rate, supports a finding of independent contractor status. However, this can pose problems for the consultant due to difficulties in accurately estimating how long the job will take. One way to deal with this problem is to break the job down into phases or "milestones" (discussed in "Services Performed by Consultant," above) and pay the consultant a fixed fee upon completion of each phase.

- *Alternative 3: Payment by the Hour/Day/Week/Month.* If a fixed fee for the job is impractical, it doesn't make much difference for IRS purposes whether the consultant is paid by the hour, day, week or month. The hiring firm may wish to include the "Optional" sentence provided on disk, which places a cap on the consultant's total compensation. This may be a good idea if the firm is unsure how reliable and/or efficient the consultant is. Obviously, the consultant would prefer that there be no cap.

5. Expenses

The IRS considers the payment of a worker's business or traveling expenses to be a mild indicator of an employment relationship. A consultant should not seek reimbursement of ordinary business expenses such as parking, telephone, photocopying and so forth. At most, he or she should be reimbursed for extraordinary expenses, such as nonlocal travel.

Select only one of the three alternatives. Alternative 1 is the most generous to the consultant, as it allows for reasonable travel expenses. Alternative 2 calls for specified travel expenses, which must be set out in the clause. Alternative 3 requires that the consultant pay all of his or her own travel expenses.

6. Invoices

An independent contractor should never be paid weekly, bi-weekly or monthly the way an employee is. Instead, he or she should submit invoices, which should be paid at the same time and manner as the client pays other vendors.

7. Consultant an Independent Contractor

One of the most important functions of an agreement between a hiring firm and consultant is to help establish that the consultant is not the hiring firm's employee. In an audit of the hiring firm, an IRS examiner or similar official will almost surely want to see the firm's agreements with all workers classified as independent contractors. If the agreement indicates that the hiring firm has the right to control the worker, he or she will undoubtedly be viewed as an employee by the IRS. This will cause problems not only for the hiring firm, but for the consultant as well. (See Chapter 7, Section B2, for a detailed discussion.)

On the other hand, an agreement that indicates a lack of control on the part of the hiring firm will contribute to a finding of independent contractor status. But such an agreement will not be determinative in and of itself. Simply signing a piece of paper will not make a worker an independent contractor. The agreement must reflect reality—that is, the hiring firm must actually not control the worker.

The language in this clause addresses most of the factors the IRS and other agencies consider in measuring the degree of control of the hiring firm. (These factors are discussed in Chapter 7, Section D.) All provisions show that the hiring firm lacks the right to control the manner and means by which the consultant will perform the agreed-upon services.

 If you draft your own agreement, include all of provisions a-j that apply to your particular situation. The more that apply, the more likely that the consultant will be viewed as an independent contractor.

8. Ownership of Consultant's Work Product

Usually, the client will want to obtain sole ownership of what the consultant creates, whether it be a computer program, documentation or other material. However, there is no rule that this has to be the case. Two different owner-ship alternatives are presented in the contract. Choose only one alternative and delete the other. Here's an explanation.

* *Alternative 1: Client Owns Consultant's Work Product.* If the parties agree that the client will own the consultant's work product, the client should obtain a written assignment of the independent contractor's intellectual property rights in such work. Alternative 1 effects such an assignment. As we discuss in detail in Chapter 8, a hiring firm can never be sure it owns what it pays an independent contractor to create unless it obtains such an assignment. The consultant should always assign all copyright rights to the hiring firm, otherwise the hiring firm may not have the right to create "derivative works" based on the original work product—for example, new versions of a program originally created by the consultant.

An assignment of all rights means that the consultant may not use the work performed for the hiring firm without permission—for example, he or she may not include it in a program written for someone else. If desired, such permission can be included in the independent contractor agreement. The optional sentence in this clause grants the consultant a nonexclusive license to use the work product. The license can be limited in any way—for example, as to term or area of use. If the client decides to grant the consultant such a license, it must decide if it will be "irrevocable"—that is, last forever; or be limited to a specified time period—for example, one or two years. The appropriate language in the optional clause should be used.

Tip for hiring firms: Before hiring a consultant, the hiring firm should ask whether the consultant has previously worked or is currently working for competitors in the same field. If so, the hiring firm should review any agreements the consultant has previously signed with competitors. The consultant might have trade secrets of the competitor and be contractually obligated to assign inventions made by him in the field to the competitor. Obviously, a hiring firm should not retain a consultant who has such conflicts.

- *Alternative 2: Consultant Owns Work Product.* In some cases, the consultant and client may agree that the consultant will retain her ownership rights in the work product (perhaps in return for receiving reduced monetary compensation). In this event, instead of assigning her rights to the client, the consultant will grant the client a nonexclusive license to use the work product.

  This clause grants the client a nonexclusive license to use the consultant's work product in any of its products, but prevents it from selling the consultant's work to others. Such a license could be more restrictive—for example, it could limit the use to a particular product. If this is desired, modify the last sentence of the clause to indicate the restrictions.

9. Ownership of Background Technology

A software consultant will often have various development tools, routines, subroutines and other programs, data and materials that she brings with her to the job and that might end up in the final product. One term for these type of items is "background technology." The "Definitions" section of our form agreement defines background technology and requires the consultant to identify her specific background technology.

Unless the consultant wants to transfer ownership of such background technology to the hiring firm, she should made sure the independent contractor agreement provides that she retains all her ownership rights in this material. But, in this event, the agreement must also give the hiring firm a nonexclusive license to use the background technology that the consultant includes in her work product.

There are two clauses to choose from:

- *Alternative 1: Client's License Extends to All Products.* The client would probably prefer to have the right to use the consultant's technology in any of its products. In this event, some sort of payment or royalty provision may be appropriate; if so, include the optional sentence and describe the compensation.

- *Alternative 2: Client's License Limited to Specific Products.* This clause permits the hiring firm to use the background technology only in a particular product or products. Make sure you describe any such products in detail.

Tip for consultants. If possible, identify your background technology in the source code copies of the programs you deliver to the client and in any printouts of code delivered to the client. You might include a notice like the following where such material appears: "*[Your Company Name]* CONFIDENTIAL AND PROPRIETARY."

10. Confidential Information

In the course of her work, the consultant may be exposed to the client's most valuable trade secrets. It is reasonable, therefore, for the client to seek to include a nondisclosure provision in the agreement. Such a provision states that the consultant may not disclose the client's trade secrets to others without the client's permission.

However, a consultant should not agree to a broad "blanket" nondisclosure provision barring the unauthorized disclosure or use of any technical, financial or business information obtained (directly or indirectly) from the client. Such provisions may be appropriate for employees, but they are not appropriate for non-employee consultants, because they can make it very difficult for a consultant ever to do similar work for others without fear of breaching the duty of confidentiality to the previous client.

Our agreement contains confidentiality provisions that are fair to the consultant, while giving the client adequate protection. These are of particular importance:

(a) This clause provides that the consultant has a duty not to disclose to others the work he or she creates for the hiring firm. This clause should be deleted from the agreement if the consultant retains ownership of her work product.

(b) This clause prevents the unauthorized disclosure by the consultant of any written material of the client marked "confidential" or information disclosed orally that the client later writes down, marks as confidential and delivers to the consultant. This enables the consultant to know for sure what material is, and is not, confidential. These restrictions should last no more than three years. The shorter the better, from the consultant's point of view.

The consultant's confidentiality obligation is limited to information that is marked confidential, or information orally disclosed that is later reduced to writing and appropriately marked. Whenever trade secrets are orally disclosed to a consultant, a follow-up letter or document must be sent stating that the information is confidential. If you're an employer, make sure that your employees understand this policy and confirm all oral disclosures to outside consultants in writing.

(c) A consultant should have no duty to keep material confidential if it does not qualify as a trade secret, is lawfully learned from persons other than the client, or is independently developed by the consultant.

(e) If the client doesn't want to permit the consultant to disclose their business relationship, include this clause.

11. Noncompetition

A firm that hires a consultant naturally doesn't want him or her to perform the same work for a competitor, allowing the competitor to benefit from work originally paid for by the hiring firm. A hiring firm is protected from this problem to some extent where it obtains an assignment of all the consultant's rights in the work product. (See "Ownership of Consultant's Work Product," above.) Theoretically, in this case the consultant can't use the work product on other projects because she doesn't own it. However, in practice it can be difficult to determine whether or not the consultant is using the client's work product on other projects. Moreover, such a competitive use may not even be intentional: The consultant may have difficulty in separating the work product bought and paid for by one client from another, or from his background technology.

A hiring firm obtains much greater protection by including a noncompetition clause in the independent contractor agreement. As discussed in Chapter 9, restrictions on competition are enforceable only if reasonable. To be viewed as reasonable by the courts, such restrictions must be drafted as narrowly as possible.

This optional clause only prevents the consultant from performing the exact same services for competitors that it performed for the hiring firm. This provision can be limited to the time the consultant is working for the client, or it can be extended for a limited period afterwards; no more than two years would be considered reasonable by most courts.

Obviously, the consultant should carefully consider the impact of such a noncompetition restriction on its future business. If such a restriction may have a severe negative impact, the consultant should either refuse to agree to it or demand additional money from the client to compensate for its potential loss of future business.

As a general rule, where a client contracts with a consultant because it specializes in a particular market niche—accounting programs for shoe stores, waterflow, stress on trees, for example—the consultant should resist agreeing to restrictions on its ability to work in its area of specialization. At most, such a consultant might agree not to perform the same services for others while working for the client.

12. Term of Agreement

Ideally, a independent contractor agreement should last no more than three to six months, and never more than one year. Anything longer makes the consultant look like an employee. Successive agreements can be used if the project can't be completed in the time frame set out in this agreement.

13. Termination of Agreement

Many consultants and hiring firms want to have the right to terminate their agreements for any reason on two weeks' notice. Unfortunately, the IRS considers such an unfettered termination right to be a very strong indicator of an employment relationship (an employee normally can quit or be fired at any time). This clause attempts to reach a compromise between the parties' desire to be able to get out of the agreement and at the same time satisfy the IRS and others that the consultant is an independent contractor. Of particular note are:

(a) This paragraph permits either party to terminate the agreement if the other has breached it and failed to remedy the breach within 30 days.

(b) Most software independent contractor agreements are basically contracts for personal services. If the client becomes dissatisfied with the service he's receiving and loses confidence in the consultant, he should have the right to terminate the agreement. This paragraph permits the client to terminate the agreement only if in his "reasonable judgment" the consultant's performance is inadequate or unnecessary. This stops short of giving the client a completely unfettered right to fire the consultant at will.

(c) If the agreement is terminated, the client is still obligated to pay the consultant for any work performed or time reserved for the client during the 30-day period after written notice of termination is received.

14. Warranties and Representations

A warranty is a promise or statement regarding the quality, quantity, performance or legal title of something being sold. Software independent contractor agreements typically contain a warranty provision by which the consultant guarantees that the services performed by the consultant, and the materials used by him, are free of any claim of legal impropriety or violation of the rights of others.

In this clause, the consultant promises that the client will obtain a "clean" license to the consultant's work product and background technology—that is, a license not subject to conflicting legal claims of others. The consultant also promises that he will not knowingly infringe on others' copyrights, patents, trade secrets or other intellectual property rights. However, the consultant makes no absolute warranty of noninfringement. This is because it is often difficult or impossible to know with any degree of certainty whether a program or other work infringes on others' intellectual property rights.

In return for granting these warranties, a consultant may reasonably seek a provision disclaiming (disavowing) any other warranties, whether made by the consultant himself before the agreement was signed or arising by operation of law. (For a detailed discussion, see Chapter 11, Section D13j.) To be effective, such a disclaimer should be written in *boldface capitals*. [The sample agreement contains an optional disclaimer that may be included after the warranty provisions. Remember to make the capital letters bold.]

a.　Warranties as to Quality of Consultant's Work Product

[The hiring firm may wish to include in the agreement additional warranties concerning the quality of the consultant's work. We discuss such warranties in detail in the chapter on custom software agreements (Chapter 11, Section D13) and provide sample clauses, which can be added to the end of the warranty clause.]

15. Limitation on Consultant's Liability to Client

Many consultants seek to include a provision in their agreements limiting their total liability to the client and/or third parties. Obviously, clients would prefer that there be no such clause, so we've included one only as an option. The clause contains four separate liability limiting provisions, any of which may be included or excluded from the agreement; this is a matter for negotiation.

Under paragraph (a), the consultant is relieved from liability for any lost profits of client, or special, incidental or consequential damages arising from defects in the work furnished by the consultant. These types of damages— lost profits in particular—can far exceed the consultant's total compensation and could even send the consultant into bankruptcy.

Paragraph (b), which is perhaps the most important, limits the consultant's total liability to the client to the amount of money actually received from the client, or, if desired, a specific dollar amount.

Paragraph (c) provides that the consultant will not be liable to the client for claims brought against client by third parties, except for claims of intellectual property infringement.

Paragraph (d) requires the client to indemnify the consultant against third party claims not relating to intellectual property infringement. This means the client must pay attorney fees and other costs of defending such claims and any damages ultimately awarded against the consultant.

16. Employment of Assistants

Because independent contractor agreements are basically personal services contracts, it's often appropriate for the client to have some control over who will do the work. Choose the alternative Paragraph (a) that best suits you:

- *Alternative 1: Consultant May Employ Assistants.* This clause leaves the issue up to the consultant.
- *Alternative 2: No Assistants Without Client's Consent.* This clause requires the client's prior approval.

As discussed in detail in Chapter 8, the copyright in software, documentation and similar works created by an employee will automatically be owned by the employer only if created within the scope of employment. Copyrightable works created by an independent contractor will be owned by the hiring party only if assigned to it by the independent contractor.

This means that unless the consultant obtains an assignment of intellectual property rights from its employees and subcontractors, there is no way for either the client or consultant to know for sure whether the consultant owns the copyright rights in software or other materials created by its employees or subcontractors. If the consultant does not own these rights, it can't transfer or license them to the client, so the client ends up owning little or nothing, or lacks a valid license to the software or other materials.

To avoid this potential nightmare, the consultant should:

- have independent contractors sign consulting agreements assigning all intellectual property rights to the consultant, and

- have all employees sign employment agreements assigning their intellectual property rights in the software and other materials they create as part of their job to the consultant. (See Chapter 9 for a detailed discussion.) If, for some reason, this is not possible (some employees may refuse to sign an employment agreement, for example), the consultant should have such workers sign an assignment agreement transferring their rights to the consultant.

To protect the client (and, in reality, the consultant as well), Paragraph (b), which should be included in all agreements, requires the consultant to either:

- provide the client with signed copies of employment or consulting agreements with all employees and independent contractors who will work on the project assigning their rights in their work to the consultant, or
- have employees or independent contractors sign an assignment agreement, which is attached as an exhibit to this agreement.

 A form for this purpose is included in the independent contractor agreement on the forms disk (INDPCONT.TXT). It is titled "Exhibit A: Acknowledgment of Independent Contractor Status and Assignment of Rights."

Paragraph (c) is optional. It should be used if the client has hired the consultant because the consultant has promised that certain key employees will be doing the work. If such employees quit working for the consultant, the client will want to have the option to terminate the agreement and hire someone else. Fill in the names of key employees and the amount of time the consultant will have to find acceptable replacements.

17. General Provisions

These general provisions are standard in many types of legal documents:

(a) This clause stipulates that future modifications must be in writing, signed both by the client and the consultant.

(b) This clause clarifies that the agreement supersedes any prior signed agreements. In the event that some part of the agreement is declared invalid by a court, this clause ensures that the rest of the document is still valid.

(c) This clause specifies which state law governs the contract. This should be the state in which the client does business or is incorporated.

(d) Fill in the name and mailing address for both the client and consultant.

18. Signatures

It is not necessary for the parties to sign the agreement in the same room or on the same day. At least two copies should be signed, with each party retaining one.

19. Exhibit A

Remember to include this exhibit (Acknowledgment of Independent Contractor Status and Assignment of Rights) if the consultant will be hiring anyone to assist in the work. (See discussion under "Employment of Assistants," above.)

SAMPLE
INDEPENDENT CONTRACTOR AGREEMENT

This Agreement is made as of March 4, 199X between Earthworks Software Research Lab ("Client") and Jack Aubrey ("Consultant").

1. Definitions: The following definitions shall apply for purposes of this Agreement:

(a) "Work Product" means all programs, systems, data and materials, in whatever form, first produced or created by or for Consultant as a result of, or related to, performance of work or services under this Agreement.

(b) "Background Technology" means all programs, systems, data and materials, in whatever form, that do not constitute Work Product and are: (1) included in, or necessary to, the Work Product; and (2) owned either solely by Consultant or licensed to Consultant with a right to sublicense.

Background Technology includes, but is not limited to, the following items: *[list specific items of background technology].*

2. Services Performed by Consultant: Consultant agrees to perform the following services for Client: *[describe services consultant will perform, including any agreed-upon work schedule]*

3. Consultant's Payment: Consultant shall be compensated at the rate of $_____ per hour. Unless otherwise agreed upon in writing by Client, Client's maximum liability for all services performed during the term of this Agreement shall not exceed $_____.

4. Expenses: Client shall reimburse Consultant for all reasonable travel and living expenses necessarily incurred by Consultant while away from Consultant's regular place of business and engaged in the performance of services under this Agreement. Consultant agrees to maintain appropriate records and to submit copies of all receipts necessary to verify such expenses at the time and in the manner prescribed by Client.

5. Invoices: Consultant shall submit invoices for all services rendered. Client shall pay the amounts agreed to herein upon receipt of such invoices.

6. Consultant an Independent Contractor: Consultant is an independent contractor and neither Consultant nor Consultant's staff is, or shall be deemed, Client's employees. In its capacity as an independent contractor, Consultant agrees and represents, and Client agrees, as follows:

(include all of provisions 6a-j that apply:)

(a) Consultant has the right to perform services for others during the term of this Agreement subject to noncompetition provisions set out in this Agreement, if any.

(b) Consultant has the sole right to control and direct the means, manner and method by which the services required by this Agreement will be performed.

(c) Consultant has the right to perform the services required by this Agreement at any place or location and at such times as Consultant may determine.

(d) Consultant will furnish all equipment and materials used to provide the services required by this Agreement, except to the extent that Consultant's work must be performed on or with Client's computer or existing software.

(e) The services required by this Agreement shall be performed by Consultant, or Consultant's staff, and Client shall not be required to hire, supervise or pay any assistants to help Consultant.

(f) Consultant is responsible for paying all ordinary and necessary expenses of its staff.

(g) Neither Consultant nor Consultant's staff shall receive any training from Client in the professional skills necessary to perform the services required by this Agreement.

(h) Neither Consultant nor Consultant's staff shall be required to devote full-time to the performance of the services required by this Agreement.

(i) Client shall not provide any insurance coverage of any kind for Consultant or Consultant's staff.

(j) Client shall not withhold from Consultant's compensation any amount that would normally be withheld from an employee's pay.

7. Ownership of Consultant's Work Product: Subject to full payment of the consulting fees due hereunder, Consultant hereby assigns to Client its entire right, title and interest in the Work Product including all patents, copyrights, trade secrets and other proprietary rights in or based on the Work Product.

Consultant shall execute and aid in the preparation of any papers that Client may consider necessary or helpful to obtain or maintain any patents, copyrights, trademarks or other proprietary rights at no charge to Client, but at Client's expense. Client shall reimburse Consultant for reasonable out-of-pocket expenses incurred.

Client grants to Consultant a nonexclusive, irrevocable license to use the Work Product subject to noncompetition provisions set out in this Agreement, if any.

8. Ownership of Background Technology: Client agrees that Consultant shall retain any and all rights Consultant may have in the Background Technology. Subject to full payment of the consulting fees due hereunder, Consultant hereby grants Client an unrestricted, nonexclusive, perpetual, fully paid-up worldwide license to use and sublicense the use of the Background Technology for the purpose of developing and marketing its products, but not for the purpose of marketing Background Technology separate from its products.

9. Confidential Information:

(a) During the term of this Agreement and for two years afterwards, Consultant will not use or disclose to others without Client's written consent Client's confidential information, except when reasonably necessary to perform the services under this Agreement. "Confidential information" is limited to:

    (1) any written or tangible information stamped "confidential," "proprietary" or with a similar legend, and

    (2) any written or tangible information not marked with a confidentiality legend, or information disclosed orally to Consultant, that is treated as confidential when disclosed and later summarized sufficiently for identification purposes in a written memorandum marked "confidential" and delivered to Consultant within 30 days after the disclosure.

(b) Consultant shall have no obligation not to disclose or use any information that:

    (1) was in Consultant's possession or known to Consultant, without an obligation to keep it confidential, before such information was disclosed to Consultant by Client,

(2) is or becomes public knowledge through a source other than Consultant and through no fault of Consultant,

(3) is independently developed by or for Consultant,

(4) is disclosed by Client to others without any restriction on use and disclosure, or

(5) is or becomes lawfully available to Consultant from a source other than Client.

(c) Client acknowledges and agrees that the confidentiality restrictions contained in this Agreement shall not apply to the general knowledge, skills and experience gained by Consultant or Consultant's employees while engaged by Client.

(d) All information concerning the existence of this Agreement and the existence of any business relationship between Consultant and Client shall be kept in confidence.

(e) Consultant will not disclose to Client information or material that is a trade secret of any third party.

(f) The provisions of this clause shall survive any termination of this Agreement.

10. Noncompetition: Consultant agrees that during performance of the services required by this Agreement and for six months after completion, Consultant will not perform the same services for any competitor of Client in the specific field in which Consultant is performing services for Client.

11. Term of Agreement: This Agreement will become effective on the date indicated in the introductory paragraph of this Agreement, and will remain in effect for six months from such date or until terminated as set forth in the section of this Agreement entitled "Termination of Agreement."

12. Termination of Agreement:

(a) Each party has the right to terminate this Agreement if the other party has materially breached any obligation herein and such breach remains uncured for a period of 30 days after notice thereof is sent to the other party.

(b) If at any time after commencement of the services required by this Agreement, Client shall, in its sole reasonable judgment, determine that such services are inadequate, unsatisfactory, no longer needed or substantially not conforming to the descriptions, warranties or representations contained in this Agreement, Client may terminate this Agreement upon 30 days' written notice to Consultant.

(c) Upon termination of this Agreement for any reason, each party shall be released from all obligations and liabilities to the other occurring or arising after the date of termination. However, any termination of this Agreement shall not relieve Client from the obligation to pay Consultant for services rendered prior to receipt of the notice of termination and for work performed or hours reserved for Client during the 30-day termination notice period.

13. Return of Materials: Upon termination of this Agreement, each party shall promptly return to the other all data, materials and other property of the other held by it.

14. Warranties and Representations: Consultant warrants and represents that:

(a) Consultant will not knowingly infringe upon any copyright, patent, trade secret or other property right of any former client, employer or third party in the performance of the services required by this Agreement.

(b) Consultant has the authority to enter into this Agreement and to perform all obligations hereunder, including, but not limited to, the grant of rights and licenses to the Work Product and Background Technology and all proprietary rights therein or based thereon.

(c) Consultant has not granted any rights or licenses to any intellectual property or technology that would conflict with Consultant's obligations under this Agreement.

THE WARRANTIES AND REPRESENTATIONS SET FORTH IN THIS CLAUSE ARE THE ONLY WARRANTIES GRANTED BY CONSULTANT WITH RESPECT TO THE SOFTWARE OR SERVICES FURNISHED HEREUNDER. CONSULTANT DISCLAIMS ALL OTHER WARRANTIES, EXPRESS OR IMPLIED, INCLUDING, WITHOUT LIMITATION, ANY IMPLIED WARRANTIES OF MERCHANTIBILITY OR FITNESS FOR A PARTICULAR PURPOSE, AND ANY ORAL OR WRITTEN REPRESENTATIONS, PROPOSALS OR STATEMENTS MADE PRIOR TO THIS AGREEMENT.

15. Indemnities: Consultant agrees to indemnify and hold harmless Client against all losses and liabilities arising out of or resulting from all injuries or death or damage to property, including theft, on account of performance of work or services by Consultant or Consultant's employees or subcontractors pursuant to this Agreement. Consultant shall maintain liability insurance sufficient to fulfill its obligations under this paragraph, in amounts acceptable to Client, and shall submit proof of such insurance to Client upon request. Such insurance may not be changed by Consultant during the term of this Agreement without Client's prior written consent.

16. Limitation on Consultant's Liability to Client:

(a) In no event shall Consultant be liable to Client for lost profits of Client, or special, incidental or consequential damages (even if Consultant has been advised of the possibility of such damages).

(b) Consultant's total liability under this Agreement for damages, costs and expenses, regardless of cause, shall not exceed the total amount of fees paid to Consultant by Client under this Agreement.

(c) Consultant shall not be liable for any claim or demand made against Client by any third party except to the extent such claim or demand relates to copyright, patent, trade secret or other proprietary rights, and then only as provided in the section of this Agreement entitled "Warranties and Representations."

(d) Client shall indemnify Consultant against all claims, liabilities and costs, including reasonable attorney fees, of defending any third party claim or suit, other than for infringement of intellectual property rights, arising out of or in connection with Client's performance under this Agreement. Consultant shall promptly notify Client in writing of such claim or suit and Client shall have the right to fully control the defense and any settlement of the claim or suit.

17. Employment of Assistants:

(a) Consultant may, at Consultant's own expense, employ such assistants or subcontractors as Consultant deems necessary to perform the services required by this Agreement. However, Client shall have the right to reject any of Consultant's assistants or subcontractors whose qualifications in Client's good faith and reasonable judgment are insufficient for the satisfactory performance of the services required by this Agreement.

(b) Consultant represents that before an employee or subcontractor of Consultant performs any services required by this Agreement, Consultant shall either:

(1) provide Client with a signed copy of an employment or independent contractor/consulting agreement effecting the assignment to Consultant of such employee's or subcontractor's rights in all copyrightable or patentable software or other materials he or she creates as a result of the performance of work or services under this Agreement; or

(2) deliver to Client an Assignment of Rights ("the Assignment") in substantially the form attached hereto as Exhibit A signed by such employee or subcontractor. Consultant shall orally inform each employee or subcontractor of the substance of the Assignment before he or she executes such form.

18. Mediation and Arbitration: Except for the right of Consultant to bring suit on an open account for simple monies due Consultant, any dispute arising under this Agreement shall be resolved through a mediation—arbitration approach. The parties agree to select a mutually agreeable, neutral third party to help them mediate any dispute that arises under the terms of this Agreement. If the mediation is unsuccessful, the parties agree that the dispute shall be decided by binding arbitration under the rules of the American Arbitration Association. The decision of the arbitrators shall be final and binding on the parties and may be entered and enforced in any court of competent jurisdiction by either party. Costs and fees associated with the mediation shall be shared equally by the parties. The prevailing party in the arbitration proceedings shall be awarded reasonable attorney fees, expert witness costs and expenses, and all other costs and expenses incurred directly or indirectly in connection with the proceedings, unless the arbitrators shall for good cause determine otherwise.

19. General Provisions:

(a) This Agreement is the sole and entire Agreement between the parties relating to the subject matter hereof, and supersedes all prior understandings, agreements and documentation relating to such subject matter. Any modifications to this Agreement must be in writing and signed by both parties.

(b) If any provision in this Agreement is held by a court of competent jurisdiction to be invalid, void or unenforceable, the remaining provisions will continue in full force without being impaired or invalidated in any way.

(c) This Agreement will be governed by the laws of the state of New York.

(d) All notices and other communications required or permitted under this Agreement shall be in writing and shall be deemed given when delivered personally, or five days after being deposited in the United States mails, postage prepaid and addressed as follows, or to such other address as each party may designate in writing:

Client: Earthworks Software Research Lab

(client's address)

Consultant: Jack Aubrey

(consultant's address)

(e) This Agreement does not create any agency or partnership relationship.

(f) This Agreement is not assignable by either party without the prior written consent of the other.

CLIENT: Earthworks Software Research Lab

By: _____
                    (Signature)

_____
                (Typed or Printed Name)

Title: _____

CONSULTANT: Jack Aubrey

By: _____
                    (Signature)

_____
                (Typed or Printed Name)

Title: _____

Social Security Number: _____

EXHIBIT A
ACKNOWLEDGMENT OF INDEPENDENT CONTRACTOR STATUS AND ASSIGNMENT OF RIGHTS

1. Independent Contractor Status: I am an employee or subcontractor of Jack Aubrey ("Consultant"). I acknowledge and agree that Consultant and its employees and subcontractors are performing the services required by this Agreement as independent contractors of Earthworks Software Research Lab ("Client"), and not as Client's employees.

2. Assignment of Rights: I assign to Consultant my entire right, title and interest (including all copyright and patent rights) in all copyrightable or patentable inventions, discoveries, improvements, innovations, ideas, designs, drawings, computer programs, computer code or writings produced or created by me for Consultant as a result of, or related to, performance of work or services under this Agreement. This assignment is effective as of the date of the creation of any protectible works created under this Agreement.

I will cooperate with all lawful efforts of Consultant to register and enforce this assignment. I shall execute and aid in the preparation of any papers that Consultant may consider necessary or helpful to obtain or maintain any patents, copyrights, trademarks or other proprietary rights at no charge to Consultant, but at its expense. Consultant shall reimburse me for reasonable out-of-pocket expenses incurred.

3. Confidentiality: I acknowledge that all information and materials I may acquire about Client's business is Client's confidential and proprietary information. I agree during and after the term of this Agreement to hold such confidential information in strict confidence. I will not disclose Client's confidential information to anyone other than employees or agents of Consultant working on this project who must have such information to perform Consultant's obligations under this Agreement unless I obtain Client's prior written authorization. Upon Client's request, I will promptly return to Client all originals and copies of all documents, records, software programs, media and other materials containing any confidential information of Client.

Employees/Subcontractors:

Name (typed or printed)   Signature

_____   _____

Date: _____

_____   _____

Date: _____

_____   _____

Date: _____

Accepted by Client

By: _____

Date: _____
■

C HAPTER 11

Agreements for Development of Custom Software

This chapter covers contracts for the development of custom software. It is designed to be used by both custom software developers and their clients, whom we'll refer to as "customers." Of course, the interests of the developer and customer often differ—what is good for the developer may be bad for the customer and vice versa. Accordingly, portions of this chapter address the particular concerns of the developer or customer. If these don't apply to you, you can skip them; but reading them may give you valuable insight into the other side's needs and concerns and aid you in the drafting and negotiating process.

There is no standard definition of "custom" software. In this chapter, we'll use the term to mean software—usually an entire system—created especially for a particular customer. But custom software need not be created entirely from scratch. Many of the components of the system may have been used by the developer before (and may be used again for other customers), but as long as the system as a whole is unique, it fits the custom software definition.

A. Overview of the Custom Software Development Process

To understand what a contract for the development of custom software should contain, you'll need a good idea of how such software is normally created. The steps outlined below will not necessary occur in the order indicated; some may even occur simultaneously or many times throughout the life of the project.

- *Problem Recognition.* Custom software development begins with a customer's recognition that a problem exists that might be solved by obtaining new software or modifying existing software.
- *System Requirements Analysis.* The next step is to define the customer's needs as clearly as possible, determine how these needs can be met

and estimate how much it will cost. The customer will often obtain expert help from a software developer or computer consultant, who analyzes the customer's problems and needs.

- *Specifications.* During this stage, a precise description is made of the software's function, environment in which it is to operate and constraints on its performance. This description serves as the heart of the contract between the developer and customer.

- *System design.* Next, the developer actually designs the software, in much the way an architect draws a building. This is usually the most difficult and time-consuming part of the development process. The developer may create flow charts showing each program's structure— that is, how each discrete portion of the program (module) functions and interacts with the rest of the program. The user interface, including the appearance of screens, definition of command languages, structure of permanent files and range of acceptable input, are all described; they may be actually laid out using a prototyping tool like *HYPERCARD* or *DIRECTOR*.

- *Coding.* After the detailed design is completed, the system is actually written—"coded"—by one or more programmers. The computer code consists of a number of programming statements in a high-level computer language such as C++ or *COBOL*, which can be read and understood by other programmers. This programming code, together with the programmer's written comments explaining why the code is structured like it is, constitutes the program's "source code."

- *Documentation.* Two different types of instructions on how to maintain and operate the software must be produced:
  1. *system/program documentation* contains a detailed description of the technical structure of the system, which is necessary for a programmer to maintain or modify the software, and
  2. *user documentation* shows potential customers how to use the software—that is, load and run it and deal with anticipated problems.

- *Testing.* Newly-created software will normally contain at least some "bugs"—errors in the code that may cause the software to "crash" or malfunction. During the testing stage, the software is put through its paces in an attempt to discover and eliminate as many errors as possible. Thoroughly testing a complex program can take months. There are often two stages of testing:
    1. *in-house testing,* which is done by the developer's personnel, and
    2. *user testing,* which is done by the customer and/or an independent third party (usually called "beta testing").
- *Maintenance.* After a system is delivered to the customer and is up and running, new bugs are usually discovered that were not uncovered during testing. "Software maintenance" consists of ongoing bug elimination and making minor changes or improvements to a system.

B. Defining the Custom Software Project

By far the greatest difficulty in drafting a contract to develop new software— and indeed, in creating the software itself—is deciding exactly what to create. Producing a new computer program is a little like constructing a building. To get good results, advance planning is essential.

Initially, someone must make a study of the customer's needs and prepare a functional specification—a document generally defining what the software is supposed to do (see Section B1, below). Unless a customer has a computer expert on staff, it will need outside assistance.

Typically, the best approach is for the user to hire an independent computer consultant to undertake a systematic study of its needs. The consultant then drafts a professional quality functional specification and can serve as an independent expert to help the user select a developer, draft detailed specifications (see Section D3a), and oversee the developer's work. (See Chapter 10 for a sample contract that may be used with an independent computer consultant.)

Alternatively, a customer can simply hire a developer to perform all the development steps outlined in Section A, above—everything from analyzing the user's needs to writing and testing the program. However, relying on a developer to do all the work from the start is usually a mistake. The customer loses the benefit of getting advice from an independent expert who doesn't benefit by adding expensive bells and whistles to the software. Having someone other than the developer do the initial analysis and specification work can be advantageous for the developer as well. The developer won't have to spend as much time working on the specifications (a task few developers enjoy). Moreover, the developer will get the benefit of an expert's analysis and advice—all paid for by the customer.

HOW A CUSTOMER CAN FIND A GOOD COMPUTER CONSULTANT

Probably the best way to find a good computer consultant is through colleagues or friends in the customer's business or industry who have used consultants in the past. If this doesn't work, the customer should try contacting the Independent Computer Consultant's Association (ICCA). The ICCA is a non-profit organization of over 1700 independent computer consultant firms, with chapters in most major cities, and can assist the customer in finding a qualified consultant. The customer can call the ICCA at 800-GET-ICCA, or write the national office at 933 Gardenview Office Parkway, St. Louis, MO 63141; the CompuServe ID is 70007,1407.

1. Drafting Functional Specifications

Functional specifications (sometimes called "requirements specifications") describe the software from the customer's point of view. Functional specifications can be thought of as the equivalent of a preliminary builder's blueprint or architect's drawing. They show what the customer wants, and the developer will later use them as its guide in drafting far more technical detailed specifications, the equivalent of a final builder's blueprint.

The functional specifications should be written in natural language the customer can understand, not in indecipherable computer jargon.

One way to draft a functional specification is to divide it into six parts, as follows:

1. *Functional requirements* describe exactly what the software will do.

2. *Technical requirements* contain information on hardware platforms, communication software, necessary memory for files, type of programming code to be used, interface requirements, preliminary screen designs, backup and recovery procedures, documentation to be provided and so forth.

3. *Database requirements* include which database to use, memory requirements on database tables, data definitions and field lengths of data attributes to be used.

4. *Constraints* are factors that will influence how the software will be created—for example, available resources (personnel, time, money and memory), response times and the like.

5. *Testing procedures* should state as explicitly as possible how the software will be tested. For example, will both the developer and customer conduct testing? Where will it be conducted? How long will the testing last? What testing methodology will be used—for example, what test data will be used and how will the tests be evaluated? What testing documentation will the developer provide the customer? (See Section D7, below, for a detailed discussion of software testing.)

6. *Guidelines* provide the developer with guidance on how to create the system.

The completed functional specifications will later be attached to the development agreement as an exhibit. Together with the detailed specifications to be created later as part of the project development plan, they establish exactly what the developer is supposed to create and form the basis for judging its performance.

C. Introduction to Custom Software Development Agreements

Once the custom software project is defined, as described in Section B, above, and a developer selected, the customer and developer are ready to draft a development agreement.

1. Why the Agreement Is Important

Creating a brand new piece of software (even one that contains much existing code) is a difficult and risky process. Without careful planning reflected in a thorough contract (written agreement), the parties may end up dissatisfied. Consider these examples:

Example 1: *Gemini, Inc., a biotechnology firm, contracts with AA Software for the development of a program to automate its laboratory. The program was to be completed in six months for a fixed price of $50,000. Six months later, AA informs Gemini that it hasn't finished the program and needs more money. Gemini, facing the unhappy possibility that the work will simply not get done, reluctantly pays AA another $20,000. The program is finally delivered five months late. Gemini discovers that the program has significant bugs, poor documentation and is difficult to use. By this time, Gemini is so sick of AA that it decides to cut its losses by discarding the program and starting over with another developer. Gemini considers suing AA for breach of contract, but its lawyer estimates that this could cost $100,000 with no guarantee that Gemini will be able to collect any judgment against AA. So Gemini concludes it must write the whole deal off to experience.*

Example 2: *AcmeSoft, a small software developer, signs a contract with WidgetCo to develop a multimedia sales presentation for WidgetCo's annual convention. AcmeSoft delivers the program on time and within budget, expecting that it will be paid the full contract price. No payment is forthcoming. Three months later, WidgetCo's lawyer writes AcmeSoft, claiming that the program was totally unsuitable and that as a result WidgetCo had no multimedia presentation at its convention. The letter states that the company not won't pay AcmeSoft, but will file suit for breach of contract seeking damages far in excess of the contract price.*

A well-written contract anticipates the problems that commonly arise in developing new software and provides solutions in advance. A carefully drafted and realistic contract benefits both the customer and the developer. For the customer, it avoids disputes about whether the customer is getting what it agreed to pay for, by clearly defining the standard of performance.

2. Importance of a Contract From the Customer's Point of View

The worst way for a customer to negotiate a software development contract is to select a developer and have it immediately commence work—and then begin to think about drafting a development contract. After work has already started, the customer has the least amount of leverage and the developer the most. The customer may agree to unduly harsh contractual terms rather than risk having the developer leave a partially completed job.

Customers should avoid making oral agreements or signing any interim agreements or "agreements to agree later," such as letters of intent. The customer should insist that a final contract be signed *before* work commences. This means that the contract should be among the first items the customer and developer think about, not the last.

3. Importance of a Contract From the Developer's Point of View

Contrary to conventional wisdom, a developer does not benefit by starting work immediately on the basis of a handshake or a brief letter that sets forth the contract price and a vague description of the project.

Unfortunately, many development projects are handled in just this way. However, this approach is a recipe for disaster. If problems later develop—particularly if the customer had unrealistic expectations or failed to understand exactly what the developer agreed to do—the developer will have no contract to fall back on for help. That piece of paper—the development contract—is the developer's lifeline. If properly drafted, it will prevent disputes by making it clear exactly what's been agreed to. If problems develop, it will provide ways to solve them. If the parties end up in court, it will establish their legal duties to each other.

Negotiating a contract can take some time and effort, but by using the phased approach we advocate in Section C2, below, the delay should be minimized. Under this approach, the contract can be signed without final detailed specifications and a delivery and payment schedule (often the most time-consuming parts of a development agreement). These are created by you later as the first phase of the project.

4. Phased Agreements Work Best for Both Parties

A customer's worst nightmare is to pay a developer to create software and then to hear nothing until months later when the developer delivers an unsatisfactory product. The best way to avoid this scenario is to break down the project into discrete parts or stages, often called phases or "milestones." At the end of each stage, the developer must deliver an acceptable product. This makes it easier for both parties to monitor the developer's progress and resolve problems early on in the project (or even terminate the project).

This type of phased development is also advantageous for the developer. Having the customer sign off on each phase of the project avoids unwarranted claims of nonperformance or unsatisfactory performance by the customer when the project is concluded.

This approach also allows opportunity to deal with the customer's changing needs and wants. Few software projects ever completely follow the original specifications. The project usually grows as the work is done and the developer and customer get ideas for a better (and usually more complex) project. Developing in phases is a convenient way for the parties to meet and discuss changes and how much they will cost. The developer must make sure, however, that the delivery schedule is reasonable and provides some flexibility.

At the very least, a custom software development project should consist of two phases:

- *Specification phase.* The developer prepares a detailed design specification and proposes a completion schedule. In our model development agreements, the developer includes these items as part of a development plan to be provided to the customer. (See Section D3, below.)
- *Development phase.* If the customer is satisfied with the detailed specifications, the customer typically pays a specified sum and the developer commences to create the software.

If the customer is not satisfied with the detailed specifications, the developer either revises them or the contract is canceled. It's usually best for the parties to go their separate ways if they can't reach some sort of agreement up-front on detailed project specifications.

Most custom software projects are too lengthy and complex to be divided into only two phases. After the initial specifications phase is completed, the customer will want the developer to deliver specified portions of the system as they are completed. In some cases, these system portions (often called "modules") can run independently of each other so they can be tested as soon as they are completed.

Example: *A contract for the development of an accounting and inventory system for a business might be divided into six phases as follows: (1) specifications; (2) accounts receivable module; (3) accounts payable module; (4) order processing module; (5) invoicing module; and (6) inventory control module.*

5.   Who Writes the Contract?

Either the developer or customer may create a first draft of a contract for the other party to review. The initial draft may undergo many changes, but it serves as the basis for the final contract. The most important rule of all contractual negotiations is that the party that creates the first draft usually obtains the best deal. Typically, the developer will present the customer with a form agreement to sign, but there is no rule against the customer insisting that its form be used instead.

D. Contents of Custom Software Development Contracts

We hope, we've convinced you by now that writing a detailed custom software development contract is essential. You may be thinking "great, give me a contract I can use." Unfortunately, there is no single off-the-shelf software development contract, or even a single way to approach writing one. What is right for one situation, may not be right for another. It all depends on the nature of the project, how much the customer is willing to spend and many other factors.

That's why, instead of giving you a "one-size-fits-all" custom software development contract, we are going to discuss in detail below all the issues a custom software development agreement must address, as well as some optional issues.

After our discussion of each issue, we'll provide sample contract provisions, which are reproduced on the disk as file CLSCUST.TXT. For many issues, we provide a range of options—sample provisions that are customer-oriented, developer-oriented and more or less neutral.

At first, you may want to use only those clauses that favor you. But it's quite possible you'll find that the other party will object if your contract is totally one-sided. In the real world, a contract that is grossly unfair to one side often ends up being a disaster for both. That's why you may find the neutral provisions especially useful, both when you create the first draft of your contract and when you negotiate changes with the other side.

The forms disk contains three complete sample contracts, in addition to a file that contains all of the clauses presented in this chapter. You may use these model contracts as written, or pick and choose among them to create your own contract. Each contract has a different emphasis, the details of which are set out in the accompanying chart:

- The first model contract (CUSTSFT1.TXT on the disk) is designed to favor the developer. Under this "no frills" agreement, the developer promises to create software for hourly payment, but assumes absolutely no liabilities, and provides few or no warranties.

- The second model contract (CUSTSFT2.TXT on the disk) strongly favors the customer. The developer provides extensive warranties and promises to indemnify the customer against any intellectual property infringement claims. A developer might demand substantially greater compensation in return for undertaking these potential liabilities.
- The third model contract (CUSTSFT3.TXT on the disk) attempts to reach a balance between the parties' interests. It may be easier and wiser to get the other side to agree to this middle course than to a contract that solely favors you.

If none of the model contracts meet your needs, you can create your own contract by picking and choosing among the sample clauses contained on the sample clause file CLSCUST.TXT.

See Chapter 1, Sections C and D, for instructions on using the forms disk and preparing documents. However, before using any of the clauses or contracts on the forms disk, be sure to read the detailed discussion below. This will help you understand what is in each clause and contract and thereby aid you in the drafting and negotiating process.

The sample clauses and the contracts on the forms disk are by no means the only ways to write a custom software contract and some of them may not be suitable for you. For example, the model contracts may be far too detailed for extremely simple development projects, or not detailed enough for some extremely large and complex projects. You may, of course, alter the language of any of these provisions or draft entirely new ones. If you do so, make sure the resulting contract is clear and internally consistent. You need not use convoluted legal language replete with words such as "whereas" and "heretofore." Simple, easy-to-understand wording is just as legal—and more practical. Also, it is highly advisable to have someone review your contract when you're finished. This could be an attorney, but it doesn't have to be. A knowledgeable nonattorney with experience in software contracting could also perform this function.

COMPARISON OF SAMPLE CUSTOM SOFTWARE DEVELOPMENT AGREEMENTS

The following chart provides a comparison of the major features of the three model contracts. All of the legal issues and terms are explained in the remainder of the chapter.

Issue	Model Contract 1: Favorable to Developer (CUSTSFT1.TXT)	Model Contract 2: Favorable to Customer (CUSTSFT2.TXT)	Model Contract 3: Neutral Toward Both Parties (CUSTSFT3.TXT)
How Developer is paid	Hourly basis (See Clause 4)	Flat fee for entire project (See Clause 4)	Parties choose between a flat fee or hourly basis (See Clause 4)
Who owns the software	Developer owns and grants Customer license, or software jointly owned (See Clause 11)	Customer sole owner (See Clause 10)	Parties choose between sole ownership by Customer, ownership by Developer with license to Customer or joint ownership (See Clause 11)
Source code access	Optional provision for a source code escrow; Developer keeps source code (See Clause 13)	Customer receives source code (no provision for a source code escrow)	Optional source code escrow provision should be included if Customer will not receive source code (See Clause 13)
General warranties by Developer	Developer furnishes software "as is" (no warranties) or provides only a performance warranty (See Clause 14)	Developer provides provides warranties of performance, title, compatibility and against disablement (See Clause 12)	Developer provides provides warranties of performance, title, compatibility and against disablement and disclaims all other warranties (See Clause 14)

(continued)

Intellectual property infringement warranties by Developer	None; Developer will not indemify Customer for such claims (See Clause 15)	Broad warranty that software will not infringe third party copyright, patent or trade secret; Developer will fully indemnify Customer against infringement (See Clause 13)	Two options: Developer may warrant no copyright or trade secret infringement and provide "no knowledge" representation as to patent infringement; or Developer may provide no warranties and extend "no knowledge" representation to copyright and trade secret infringement as well as patent (See Clause 15(a))
Developer's liability	An outside limit is given (See Clause 16)	Unlimited	Developer not liable for Customer's consequential damages. Optional provision limits Developer's total liability to Customer to amount paid Developer or a specified sum (See Clause 17)
Confidentiality	Narrow confidentiality restrictions favor Developer (See Clause 18)	Broad confidentiality restrictions favor Customer (See Clause 16)	Narrow confidentiality restrictions favor Developer; this seems fair because broad restrictions may unduly burden Developer (See Clause 20)
Noncompetition clause	None; Developer may do the same or simliar work for others while working for Customer	Developer barred from doing the same or similar work for others (See Clause 17)	Developer barred from working for named competitors of Customer (See Clause 21)

1. Identification of the Parties

Contracts normally begin by identifying the parties—that is, the people and/ or companies making the contract. Your contract should begin with the following language:

> This Agreement is made between *(name of customer)* (the "Customer") and *(name of software developer)* (the "Developer").

Note: If either of the parties is a corporation, it should be identified by its corporate name.

2. Purpose of Agreement

It is customary to briefly state at the beginning the reason for the contract. This helps establish the parties' intent to create a legally binding contract, and may be helpful if the contract has to be interpreted and enforced by a judge or arbitrator, perhaps years after it was written. Note that the functional specifications, which describe the software in detail, should be attached to the agreement as an exhibit. (Functional specifications are discussed in Section B1, above.)

> Customer desires to retain Developer as an independent contractor to develop the computer software (the "Software") described in the Functional Specifications attached to this Agreement as Exhibit ___ and incorporated herein by reference. Developer is ready, willing and able to undertake the development of the Software and agrees to do so under the terms and conditions set forth in this Agreement. Accordingly, the parties agree as follows:

3. Preparation of Development Plan

The first phase of the project is the developer's preparation of a software development plan. The development plan should show the customer what the developer intends to do and how long it will take. In our clause, the customer's commitment to proceed with the project is contingent upon its acceptance of the development plan. This protects both the customer and developer. The customer's financial exposure is minimized: If the design fails to meet its original expectation, it can terminate the contract and seek a new developer without much loss. The developer is protected by having the customer agree in writing to the detailed specifications and delivery schedule before it actually starts to create the software. This prevents later claims that the finished product doesn't meet the customer's requirements.

We also include an optional provision requiring the customer to pay the developer for creating the development plan if the customer finds it unacceptable and terminates the contract.

The development plan should contain:

- detailed system specifications,
- a list of all items to be provided to the customer (often called "deliverables"),
- a delivery schedule stating when each deliverable will be completed and furnished to the customer, and
- if the developer is being paid a fixed price, a payment schedule.

Let's look at these in detail.

a. Specifications

As discussed in Section B1, above, before the development agreement is signed, the customer (often with the aid of a computer consultant), or the developer, should create a functional specification describing the software in general terms. The developer will use the functional specifications as a guide in creating a far more technical detailed specification. The detailed specifications serve as the final project blueprint. They describe the project in a very precise technical manner and should provide the developer with all the information it needs to actually create the software.

Detailed specifications typically include flowcharts, input and output formats and screen descriptions; file and data layouts, program descriptions, communications capabilities, software security procedures, a description of system limits, accuracy and reliability as well as detailed testing procedures.

Drafting detailed specifications is beyond the scope of this book; see the sidebar below for further information.

GUIDES TO DRAFTING SOFTWARE SPECIFICATIONS

Some sources on how to draft specifications include:

- *An Introduction to Formal Specification and Z*, by Sinclair & Till (Prentice Hall)
- *Information Systems Development: Methodologies, Techniques and Tools*, by Avison and Fitzgerald (Blackwell Scientific Publications)
- *Software Engineering*, by Jones (John Wiley & Sons)
- *Software Requirements Analysis and Specification*, by Davis (Prentice Hall)
- *The Specification of Complex Systems*, by Harwood and Jackson (Addison-Wesley)

CREATING A PROTOTYPE

It can be difficult or impossible for a technically unsophisticated customer to get a feel for how the proposed software will function from written specifications. For this reason, the developer may be asked to create a prototype of the actual system.

The prototype should include a complete set of proposed report formats, screen displays and menus so that the customer can review the program's customer interface. The prototype can be done either by hand on "storyboards" or on computer, using a tool like *HYPERCARD* or *MACROMIND DIRECTOR* for the Macintosh or *DESIGNER* for MS-DOS computers.

b. Deliverables

The development plan should list all deliverables—that is, every item the customer wants the developer to provide. This includes not only the software itself, but the program and customer documentation as well.

 The development plan lists everything to be provided to the customer. If the customer cannot judge the adequacy of the development plan, it should seek guidance from a reliable computer expert or software lawyer.

Following is a checklist of deliverables for a typical software project.

CHECKLIST OF DELIVERABLES

Software projects usually include the following deliverables:
* final specifications for the completed Software showing any changes from the specifications contained in the Development Plan,
* complete customer documentation, including a description of how to access and use each application, screen prints of menus and input/output screens, data input descriptions, sample output/report forms, error code descriptions and solutions where appropriate and explanations of all necessary disks and data used by the Software,
* complete program/technical documentation, including technical information about files and their locations, file names, file/database structure, record structure and layout and data elements,
* if the customer will receive a copy of the source code, program source code listings with comments,
* description of backup and recovery procedures, including process, medium for backup and number of diskettes or tapes to do a complete backup, and
* master copy of Software on magnetic media, including all programs, on-line documentation and any documentation developed on computer.

---

c. Delivery Schedule

The development plan should include a schedule showing when each deliverable will be completed. The developer must take care that the delivery schedule provides sufficient time to complete the project. Developers tend to be incorrigible optimists, so they constantly underestimate how long development projects will take. It's best for the developer to be realistic up-front, and not promise the customer what it can't deliver. Since delays are so common, the development agreement should state how delays will be dealt with (See Section D6, below).

IMPORTANCE OF SOFTWARE DOCUMENTATION

"Software documentation" refers to the user and technical manuals the developer provides with the completed software. The importance of software documentation cannot be overemphasized; it is vital for training the customer's employees and to help them keep the software running smoothly without having to constantly call on the developer for assistance. There are two types of documentation:

*   *User or customer documentation* shows the customer how to use the software and deal with anticipated problems—in other words, a "user manual," and
*   *System/program documentation* contains a detailed description of the technical structure of the software; this information is needed to maintain and/or modify the software. If source code is provided the customer, it should be documented as well so that a programmer will be able to understand it.

It can take longer to write system documentation than to create the software itself. The specifications should state how long the documentation must be, what it should contain, and provide quality standards (see the deliverables checklist in Section D3b, below).

d. Sample Contract Provision

Below is a sample contract provision requiring the developer to deliver a detailed development plan and allowing the customer to terminate the contract if the plan is deemed unsatisfactory. This provision also gives the developer time to cure any deficiencies in the plan before the customer may terminate the contract. This seems only fair given the substantial investment of time and effort the developer will usually expend to create a development plan.

> Developer shall prepare a development plan ("Development Plan") for the Software, satisfying the requirements set forth in the Functional Specifications. The Development Plan shall include:
> (a) detailed specifications for the Software;
> (b) a listing of all items to be delivered to Customer under this Agreement ("Deliverables");
> (c) a delivery schedule containing a delivery date for each Deliverable; and
> (d) *(optional; include if developer is paid fixed price:)* a payment schedule setting forth the amount and time of Developer's compensation.

> Developer shall deliver the Development Plan to Customer by *(date)*. Customer shall have ____ days to review the Development Plan. Upon approval of the Development Plan by Customer, it will be marked as Exhibit __ and will be deemed by both parties to have become a part of this Agreement and will be incorporated by reference. Developer shall thereupon commence development of Software that will substantially conform to the requirements set forth in the Development Plan.

> If the Development Plan is in Customer's reasonable judgment unsatisfactory in any material respect, Customer shall prepare a detailed written description of the objections. Customer shall deliver such objections to Developer within ____ days of receipt of the Development Plan. Developer shall then have ____ days to modify the Development Plan to

respond to Customer's objections. Customer shall have _____ days to review the modified Development Plan. If Customer deems the modified Development Plan to be unacceptable, Customer has the option of terminating this Agreement upon written notice to Developer or permitting Developer to modify the Development Plan again under the procedure outlined in this paragraph. If this Agreement is terminated, the obligations of both parties under it shall end except for Customer's obligation to pay Developer all sums due for preparing the Development Plan and the ongoing obligations of confidentiality set forth in the provision of this Agreement entitled "Confidentiality."

e. Payment for Development Plan

Drafting a development plan—particularly the specifications—is difficult and time-consuming. Thus, the developer should be fairly compensated for its efforts. Where the developer is being paid a fixed price, it normally receives a portion as a down payment upon execution of the contract. If the plan is not accepted and the contract canceled, the down payment may provide the developer with too little or too much money for the work it did on the plan.

The following clause deals with this problem by providing that the developer will be paid on a "time and materials" basis for the development plan if the plan is not accepted and the contract is canceled. ("Time and materials" means the developer is paid for its time and actual costs.) If this amount is less than the down payment, the developer must return the excess to the customer.

The following paragraph need not be included in contracts in which the developer is to be paid on an ongoing hourly basis (see Section D4a, below). It would merely be redundant.

If the Development Plan is not accepted by Customer and Customer terminates this Agreement, Developer shall be entitled to compensation on a time and materials basis at an hourly rate of $_____ plus expenses to the date of termination. Developer shall submit an invoice detailing its time and expenses preparing the Development Plan. If the invoice amount is less than the amounts paid to Developer prior to termination, Developer shall promptly return the excess to Customer. If the invoice amount exceeds the amounts paid to Developer prior to termination, Customer shall promptly pay Developer the difference. *(optional: "However, Developer's total compensation for preparing the Development Plan shall not exceed $_____.")*

f. Ownership of Development Plan

Having paid for the development plan, it's only fair that the customer should own it. Even if the customer finds the plan unacceptable, or the project is otherwise terminated before the software is completed, the plan may contain valuable information and serve as the basis for negotiation with other developers. The following clause transfers ownership of the plan to the customer.

> If this Agreement is terminated because Customer rejects the Development Plan, Customer shall be entitled to exclusive ownership of the Development Plan. Upon payment to Developer of all sums due hereunder, Developer shall assign to Customer its entire right, title and interest in the Development Plan.

4. Payment

There are two basic ways to pay a developer for creating custom software:
- a pay per hour ("time and materials") agreement, or
- a fixed price agreement.

Let's take a look at each payment scheme and some sample contractual provisions.

a.　"Time and Materials" Agreements

Under a "time and materials" agreement, the developer charges the customer by the hour, day or month at a flat hourly cost.

Time and materials agreements have several drawbacks for the customer. First and foremost, they give the developer a strong incentive to provide cheap programmers, since the developer's profit is based on the difference between its hourly cost and what it pays its programmers. Second, because the developer makes more money the longer the project takes, the financial incentives are 180 degrees wrong and almost guarantee that the project will take too long. To give the developer some incentive to finish the project in a timely manner, the customer may wish to place a cap on the developer's total compensation for the project and possibly pay a bonus for early or timely completion.

Following is an hourly payment provision, including an optional cap on the developer's total compensation:

> Developer shall be compensated at the rate of $_____ per hour (or "day," "week," "month").Payment will be made within _____ days of Developer's submission of an itemized statement for work completed. (optional: "Unless otherwise agreed upon in writing by Customer, Customer's maximum liability for all services performed during the term of this Agreement shall not exceed $_____.")

Another way to encourage the developer to finish the work as quickly as possible, is to pay a bonus based on the number of hours billed. The fewer the hours, the higher the bonus. This may end up saving the customer money in the long run, as well as getting the job done faster. The developer's bonuses should be phased. This way, if an unscrupulous developer under-states its hours to collect a bonus, the total amount paid will not be substantially more than if the correct number of hours were reported. Here's an example:

As an incentive to efficient performance, Developer shall be paid a bonus as follows:

(a) The total number of hours billed by Developer under this Agreement shall be multiplied by $_____ if the total number of hours billed is _____ or less.

(b) The total number of hours billed by developer under this Agreement shall be multiplied by $_____ if the total number of hours billed is _____.

(c) The total number of hours billed by developer under this Agreement shall be multiplied by $_____ if the total number of hours billed is _____.

There shall be no bonus if the total number of hours billed by Developer under this Agreement exceeds _____.

b. Fixed Price Agreements

The other payment option is for the customer to pay the developer a fixed price for the entire project. In theory, this payment scheme favors the customer by giving the customer certainty as to what the project will cost. Moreover, if payments are tied to the progress of the developer's work, it gives the customer substantial leverage to insist on timely and successful completion of the project.

At first glance, fixed price agreements would seem to be risky for developers: If the project takes much longer than originally anticipated, the developer could end up losing money. However, as a practical matter, fixed price agreements usually do not end up favoring the customer as much as one would think. If it turns out that the fixed price originally agreed upon will not provide the developer with fair compensation, because the project ends up taking too long, the customer will probably end up agreeing to pay the developer more money. Otherwise the developer may quit or end up delivering a hastily-completed and shoddy product.

Remember, a deal that ends up being awful for one side often ends up being a disaster for both. Both parties have an interest in seeing that both feel fairly treated.

The developer's fixed price quote should be included in the Development Plan, which will also contain the detailed specifications, deliverables list and delivery schedule. Obviously, the developer should complete these last three items, particularly the detailed specification, before deciding how much to charge for the entire project. Only at this point can the developer have a reasonably accurate idea of how much time the project will require.

Fixed price contracts are normally paid in installments, with payment of each installment tied to completion and acceptance of a phase of the project. In addition, an initial down payment is usually made when the contract is signed. The following provision requires that a payment schedule be included as part of the development plan, which will be attached to the contract as an exhibit. The developer should make sure that the schedule requires the customer to make regular periodic payments so that the developer can meet its own financial obligations.

> The total contract price shall be set forth in the Development Plan. Customer shall pay the Developer the sum of $_____ upon execution of this Agreement and the sum of $_____ upon Customer's approval of the Development Plan. The remainder of the contract price shall be payable in installments according to the payment schedule to be included in the Development Plan.
>
> Each installment shall be payable upon completion of each project phase by Developer and acceptance by Customer in accordance with the provision of this Agreement entitled "Acceptance Testing of Software."

The amount of the down payment is often a point of contention in fixed price contracts. Naturally, the developer wants as large a down payment as possible; ideally, equal to its anticipated profit on the project. However, customers prefer to minimize any down payment to no more than 10-20% of the total price. The more the customer pays the developer up front as a down payment, the less leverage it will have to insist upon prompt and satisfactory performance by the developer. It is in the customer's best interest to withhold at least 10-30% of the total payment price until final acceptance of the software. This is usually the minimum amount the customer must withhold to retain its bargaining position.

Example: *An accounting system is being developed for a business. The software will be developed in five separate modules—accounts receivable, accounts payable and so forth—and a payment made upon delivery of each module. The total projected fixed price for the project is $100,000. Here is the payment schedule:*

PHASE	ESTIMATED PAYMENT
1. Execution of Agreement	$10,000
2. Acceptance of Development Plan	$20,000
3. Acceptance of accounts receivable module	$10,000
4. Acceptance of accounts payable module	$10,000
5. Acceptance of order processing module	$10,000
6. Acceptance of invoicing module	$10,000
7. Acceptance of completed system	$30,000

In some fixed price contracts, the customer withholds a portion of the payment until after the software has been up and running for a specified time period. This is because a customer is often unable to determine whether new software is functioning properly until it starts running in a live operating environment. Withholding partial payment until a period of live operation has been completed gives the developer incentive to respond promptly to any problems that may occur. In contrast, if the developer is paid off when the software is first installed, it may lose interest in the customer's needs. Three months of live operation is usually sufficient time to determine if the software is functioning properly. Here's a sample provision:

Customer shall withhold _____% from each payment until 90 days after final acceptance of the completed Software, at which time such withheld sums shall be due and payable.

5. Payment of Developer's Costs

Whether a fixed price or time and materials payment arrangement is used, the developer is usually reimbursed by the customer for at least some out-of-pocket expenses incurred in performing its duties under the contract. The extent of such reimbursement is a matter for negotiation. Following are two sample expense reimbursement provisions. The first provision below calls for payment of all the developer's out-of-pocket expenses; this may include items like communications charges (telephone, fax, postage, etc.).

Alternative 1 (all out-of-pocket expenses paid): Customer shall reimburse Developer for all out-of-pocket expenses incurred by Developer in performing its responsibilities under this Agreement. Such expenses include, but are not limited to:

(a) all communications charges;

(b) costs for providing conversion services for converting Customer's data base;

(c) media costs (tapes and disks); and

(d) non-local travel and living expenses incurred by Developer in fulfilling its obligations under this Agreement.

One problem with the above provision, aside from the cost to the customer, is that the IRS considers payment of a worker's ordinary business expenses to be a mild indicator of an employment relationship. (See Chapter 7 for a detailed discussion of why this may be a problem.)

The following provision limits reimbursement to extraordinary expenses, such as nonlocal travel, and will not be viewed as indicative of an employee-employer relationship.

Alternative 2 (extraordinary expenses paid): Customer shall reimburse developer for all reasonable travel and living expenses necessarily incurred by Developer while away from Developer's regular place of business and engaged in the performance of services under this Agreement.

6. Changes in Project Scope

It's quite common in the course of software development for the customer to wish to make changes—adding new features and/or deleting others. Of course, any changes to the specifications or any other provision of the contract should be in writing and signed by both parties to be effective. (This is required by Section D28b, below.)

Major changes in the scope of the project may greatly increase—or decrease—the amount of work the developer has to do. If the developer is paid a fixed fee, it is only fair that its compensation should be increased or decreased to reflect the change in the workload. This usually is not an issue where the developer is paid by the hour; but if there is a cap on the total hourly compensation to be paid, it may have to be increased.

Changes in the scope of the project may also require changes in proposed delivery dates, and perhaps in the contract's warranty and/or indemnification provisions. (Warranties are discussed below, in Section D13; see Section D14, concerning indemnification.)

The following provision sets forth a procedure for the parties to follow if the customer wants to change the specifications or other parts of the development plan. First, the customer must submit a written proposal to the developer showing the desired changes. The developer then responds to this proposal in writing, stating, among other things, what impact the desired changes will have on the contract price and delivery schedule. If the customer wants to go ahead with the changes, it submits a "Development Plan Modification Agreement" specifying all the agreed-upon changes and their effect on the provisions of the Agreement (see sidebar below). The developer has 10 days to accept or reject the Development Plan Modification Agreement.

CHANGES REQUESTED BY DEVELOPER

In many instances, the developer, not the customer, will wish to alter the specifications. This may be because the specifications contain an error, do not accurately reflect the customer's true needs, or the project as originally agreed upon proves commercially unfeasible for a developer being paid a fixed fee. All such changes should be in writing and signed by both parties as required by the clause dealing with modifications to the agreement. (See Section D28b, below.)

If at any time following acceptance of the Development Plan by Customer, Customer should desire a change in Developer's performance under this Agreement that will alter or amend the Specifications or other elements of the Development Plan, Customer shall submit to Developer a written proposal specifying the desired changes.

Developer will evaluate each such proposal at its standard rates and charges. Developer shall submit to Customer a written response to each such proposal within 10 working days following receipt thereof. Developer's written response shall include a statement of the availability of Developer's personnel and resources, as well as any impact the proposed changes will have on the contract price, delivery dates or warranty provisions of this Agreement.

Changes to the Development Plan shall be evidenced by a "Development Plan Modification Agreement." The Development Plan Modification Agreement shall amend the Development Plan appropriately to incorporate the desired changes and acknowledge any effect of such changes on the provisions of this Agreement. The Development Plan Modification Agreement shall be signed by authorized representatives of Customer and Developer, whereupon Developer shall commence performance in accordance with it.

Should Developer not approve the Development Plan Modification Agreement as written, Developer will so notify Customer within 10 working days of Developer's receipt of the Development Plan Modification Agreement. Developer shall not be obligated to perform any additional services prior to its approval of the Development Plan Modification Agreement.

For purposes of this Agreement, each Development Plan Modification Agreement duly authorized in writing by Customer and Developer shall be deemed incorporated into and made part of this Agreement. Each such Development Plan Modification Agreement shall constitute a formal change to this Agreement adjusting fees and completion dates as finally agreed upon.

Here's an example of an agreement modifying the portion of a development plan dealing with delivery of the program:

Example of Development Plan Modification Agreement: *This is a modification to Section 2 of the Development Plan agreed to by the parties in their Agreement dated January 15, 199X. Section 2 of the Development Plan shall be deleted and superseded by the following section:*

2. Delivery of Software

The completed system shall be delivered by Developer to Customer by September 15, 199X.

Name of Developer	Name of Customer
By: _____	By: _____
Title: _____	Title: _____
Date: _____	Date: _____

7. Delays

It is rare for custom software to be completed and delivered by the developer exactly on schedule. There are several explanations for this:

* Estimating how long it will take to create new software is an uncertain art at best (exacerbated by the fact that most programmers are incorrigible optimists and many customers are terminally impatient).

- Changes in the specifications may cause delays.
- The developer may have staffing changes or increased demands on existing staff.

It is wise for the agreement to lay out how the inevitable delays will be handled. A delivery schedule is contained in the Development Plan. (See Section D3b, above.)

The developer would naturally prefer that the delivery schedule be viewed merely as a guide for when the project should be completed, not as a firm, binding contractual commitment. The customer, on the other hand, usually wants the developer to take the delivery deadlines very seriously. Some customers even insist that the developer pay monetary penalties if deadlines are missed. (This probably does not set a very good tone at the outset of a development project!)

The following provision attempts to follow a middle course. It makes clear to the developer that it should do all in its power to deliver the software on schedule. However, recognizing the developer's inherent difficulties, it allows the developer up to 60 days' slippage on any deadline. This 60-day figure is not written in stone; for example, if the customer can't live with it, the time can be adjusted downward.

After more than 60 days (or whatever time frame's been set), the customer will have the option of terminating the agreement. But this does not necessarily mean that the customer will do so. It may well be cheaper and quicker for the customer to agree to an extension of the delivery schedule rather than try to find a new developer to start from scratch.

Developer acknowledges that its failure to deliver the Software according to the Development Plan's delivery schedule will result in expense and damage to Customer. Developer shall use all reasonable efforts to deliver the Software on schedule. Developer shall inform Customer at its earliest opportunity of any anticipated delays in the delivery schedule and of the actions being taken to assure completion of the Software within a time period acceptable to Customer.

Developer shall not allow any delivery date to slip by more than sixty (60) calendar days. If any delivery date is missed by more than 60 days (excluding excusable delays), Customer may, at its option, consider the delay an irreparable delay and a default of the Developer under this Agreement. Should Customer elect to excuse the delay, it shall do so in writing, which shall include the new delivery date(s).

The delivery schedule shall be adjusted for mutually agreed-upon delays, or for delays solely attributable to Customer.

a. Excusable Delays

Sometimes a project is delayed due to circumstances beyond the developer's control—for example, where an earthquake, fire or other act of God destroys or severely damages the developer's office and equipment. In this event, it is only fair that the developer's delay be excused. A special provision (often called a "force majeure" clause) is commonly included in development contracts to excuse a party's nonperformance due to circumstances beyond its control. The clause below is fairly simple:

Any delay or nonperformance of any provision of this Agreement caused by conditions beyond the reasonable control of the performing party shall not constitute a breach of this Agreement, provided that the delayed party has taken reasonable measures to notify the other of the delay in writing. The delayed party's time for performance shall be deemed to be extended for a period equal to the duration of the conditions beyond its control.

Conditions beyond a party's reasonable control include, but are not limited to, natural disasters, acts of government after the date of the Agreement, power failure, fire, flood, acts of God, labor disputes, riots, acts of war and epidemics. Failure of subcontractors and inability to obtain materials shall not be considered a condition beyond a party's reasonable control.

8. Acceptance Testing of Software

"Acceptance testing" is a procedure by which the software is tested to see if it satisfies the detailed specifications set forth in the Development Plan. Acceptance testing is one of the most important phases of the software development process. The purpose is to determine whether the software does what it is supposed to do and is reliable. Particularly where safety is involved (for example, software implemented in a "911" service or designed to run an elevator), the software should be tested as thoroughly as possible.

Of course, the developer should test the software before it is delivered to the customer, but the customer should not rely solely on such testing. Before accepting and paying for the software, the customer should either:

- test the software itself (assuming it has personnel qualified to do so),
- have the developer test the software under the customer's supervision on the customer's hardware at its place of business, or
- have the software tested by an independent testing lab.

The acceptance testing should force the software to perform repeatedly, without failure, on a variety of the customer's actual data, with speed and accuracy to match the specifications. It is also a good idea to stress test a system—that is, try to break it—to see how it recovers. Each section of the software should be tested independently and in combination with other sections.

The nature of the tests to be performed, the data to be used and the procedure to be followed should be defined by the parties before the testing begins. In many cases, the acceptance tests cannot be well defined until the final specifications are agreed upon or even until the software is completed. The specifications for acceptance testing should be included as part of the development plan. (See Section B1, above.) Of course, these specifications may be subsequently modified by the parties.

Unfortunately, many bugs will not be discovered during acceptance testing. Some bugs appear only after many hundreds or thousands of customer hours. For this reason, it's common for the developer to agree to fix bugs free of charge for a stated period after the software is accepted—usually 90 days to a year. (See Section D13e, below, for a detailed discussion.)

TRIVIAL BUGS

No software is absolutely perfect. It is virtually impossible for a developer to create software that is completely bug-free. However, there is a big difference between true bugs—defects that prevent the software from performing the customer's required tasks satisfactorily—and interface and peripheral glitches and other minor irritants that don't materially affect the software's performance. A developer should never promise that its software will be completely bug-free. (See the discussion in Section D13j, below.) Moreover, the acceptance criteria should be designed so as to overlook trivial bugs that can simply be ignored.

---

a. Acceptance Testing Provision for Multi-Phase Projects

Complex software systems often consist of a number of independent units or "modules" that can be tested when completed. This way, the customer doesn't have to wait until the entire project is finished to test the software and see how the work is progressing. Of course, the schedule for delivery of each portion of the system should be set forth in detail in the development plan's delivery schedule.

If the software does not satisfy the acceptance criteria, the customer should explain the problems to the developer and then give it an opportunity to correct them. Developers are typically given 30 days to make corrections, but more time may be required if the software is extremely complex. If the developer cannot make the corrections, or re-delivers software that is still nonconforming, the customer should have the option of giving the developer more time or terminating the contract.

In fixed price contracts, upon acceptance, the customer will be obligated to pay the developer in accordance with the payment schedule. When the developer is paid on a hourly basis, it will be paid every two weeks or monthly regardless of the progress, but the customer can terminate the contract if the developer's work product is unacceptable.

The following acceptance testing provision is designed to be used with a phased project:

Alternative 1: Immediately upon completion of each development phase set forth in the Development Plan's delivery schedule, Developer shall deliver and install the Software and shall deliver all documentation and other materials required to be provided in accordance with the delivery schedule. Customer shall have _____ days from the delivery of the Software to inspect, test and evaluate it to determine whether the Software satisfies the acceptance criteria in accordance with procedures set forth in the Development Plan, or as established by Developer and approved by Customer prior to testing.

If the Software does not satisfy the acceptance criteria, Customer shall give Developer written notice stating why the Software is unacceptable. Developer shall have 30 days from the receipt of such notice to correct the deficiencies. Customer shall then have 30 days to inspect, test and reevaluate the Software. If the Software still does not satisfy the acceptance criteria, Customer shall have the option of either: (1) repeating the procedure set forth above, or (2) terminating this Agreement pursuant to the section of this Agreement entitled "Termination." If Customer does not give written notice to Developer within the initial 30-day inspection, testing and evaluation period or any extension of that period, that the Software does not satisfy the acceptance criteria, Customer shall be deemed to have accepted the Software upon expiration of such period.

Upon completion of the final development phase set out in the development plan, acceptance testing shall be performed on the Software in its entirety to determine whether the Software satisfies the acceptance criteria and operates with internal consistency. Customer shall have _____ days to perform such tests. If the completed Software does not satisfy the acceptance criteria, the parties shall follow the notification and perfection standards described in the preceding paragraph.

(include in fixed price contracts: "If and when the acceptance tests establish the Software delivered upon completion of any phase of development complies with the acceptance criteria, Customer shall promptly notify Developer that it accepts the delivered Software. The date of such notification shall be the date on which Customer shall be obligated to make the applicable payment specified in the payment schedule set forth in the development plan.")

b. Alternate Acceptance Testing Provision

Some types of software really can't be tested until the entire system is completed and running, except perhaps the print and display functions. Following is a simpler acceptance testing provision designed to be used where serious testing won't be conducted until the software is delivered in final form. This provision should also be used for projects where the entire program will be delivered at one time, rather than in phases.

Alternative 2: Customer shall have 30 days from the date of delivery of the Software in final form to inspect, test and evaluate it to determine whether the Software satisfies the acceptance criteria in accordance with procedures set forth in the Development Plan, or as established by Developer and approved by Customer prior to testing.

If the Software does not satisfy the acceptance criteria, Customer shall give Developer written notice stating why the Software is unacceptable. Developer shall have 30 days from the receipt of such notice to correct the deficiencies. Customer shall then have 30 days to inspect, test and evaluate the Software. If the Software still does not satisfy the acceptance criteria, Customer shall have the option of either (1) repeating the procedure set forth above, or (2) terminating this Agreement pursuant to the section of this Agreement entitled "Termination." If Customer does not give written notice to Developer within the initial 30-

day inspection, testing and evaluation period or any extension of that period, that the Software does not satisfy the acceptance criteria, Customer shall be deemed to have accepted the Software upon expiration of such period.

9. Training

The customer and/or its employees will usually have to be trained how to use the software. Following is a provision requiring the developer to conduct training. Where the developer is paid a fixed fee, the cost of training can be included in the overall fee. However, where the developer is paid on an hourly basis, it will have to be paid extra for training. In either event, the customer should be responsible for its own costs associated with such training.

Developer shall provide _____ days of training in the use of the Software by at least one (but not more than _____) qualified Developer personnel ("trainers"). The training will be conducted on such dates and locations as the parties may agree.

Customer will be responsible for all costs and expenses of all Customer's trainees, including room, board, transportation, salary, insurance and other benefits, and other expenses while attending the training.

Option 1: Customer shall pay the travel expenses of the trainers, but the training will otherwise be at no additional charge to Customer.

Option 2: Customer shall pay Developer the sum of $_____ for each *(hour/day)* of training by each trainer, plus each trainer's travel expenses.

10. Maintenance of Software

"Maintenance" is a term used for upkeep of software after it has been put into operation. There are two types of maintenance:

- fixing bugs (sometimes called "remedial maintenance"), and
- modifying and/or enhancing software because the customer's needs have changed (sometimes called "adaptive maintenance").

It can cost far more to maintain software than to develop it in the first place. Many developers consider maintenance to be a nuisance and would prefer to use their resources on other new development projects. Such developers want to terminate their work for the customer upon delivery and acceptance of the software. The customer, on the other hand, needs someone to maintain the software. It is often most efficient for the persons who originally create a piece of software to maintain it. Their familiarity with the original software's design should enable them to do a better job than someone who is completely new to the software. Thus, particularly where the customer has no programming capability of its own, it may want to rely on the developer to maintain the software.

Tip for customers. Probably the best way to provide for ease of maintenance is to require documentation that can be used by any third party ordinarily skilled in the art. Only accept delivery of the project after a third party (your independent computer consultant, for example) inspects the documentation. With good documentation, the cost of bringing in someone else won't be prohibitive if the developer is unavailable or unwilling to maintain your software.

Typically, custom software development agreements contain a warranty in which the developer promises to fix any bugs for free for a limited time—usually 90 days to a year. (See Section D13d, below, for a detailed discussion.) The following provision addresses post-warranty remedial maintenance (bug correction) only. Adaptive maintenance (enhancements and modifications) should be handled in a separate agreement.

This provision requires the developer to perform remedial maintenance and provide telephone hot line support after the warranty expires. The customer pays the developer an annual fee for this service. Note that the provision applies only to "reproducible errors...so that the Software is brought into substantial conformance with the Specifications." This protects the developer from committing to fix trivial errors or errors that may occur only once in many thousands of hours of operation and that cannot be readily reproduced.

If the developer retains the source code (see Section D12, below), the customer should make sure the developer agrees to maintain the software or gives a copy of the source code to someone who will. The software cannot be maintained without access to the source code. (See Section D12 for a detailed discussion.)

Beginning on the first day of the first month following expiration of the warranty period set forth in the section of this Agreement entitled "Warranties," Developer shall provide the following error-correction and support services:

(a) telephone hot-line support during Developer's normal days and hours of business operation. Such support shall include consultation on the operation and utilization of the Software. Customer shall be responsible for all telephone equipment and communication charges related to such support; and

(b) error correction services, consisting of Developer using all reasonable efforts to design, code and implement programming changes to the Software, and modifications to the documentation, to correct reproducible errors therein so that the Software is brought into substantial conformance with the Specifications.

Payment for Maintenance: Customer shall pay Developer for error-correction and support services the annual sum of $_____, payable in quarterly installments beginning on the first day of the first month following expiration of the warranty period set forth in the section of this

Agreement entitled "Warranties." Three years after the date of Customer's final acceptance of the Software, Developer shall be entitled to increases in the maintenance fee upon at least 10 days' prior written notice to Customer.

Customer's Role in Maintenance: The provision of the error-correction and support services described above shall be expressly contingent upon Customer promptly reporting any errors in the Software or related documentation to Developer in writing and not modifying the Software without Developer's written consent.

Term of Support: Subject to timely payment by Customer of the maintenance fees, Developer shall offer the maintenance described above for a minimum of five years after completion of the development work under this Agreement.

Customer Termination of Maintenance: Customer may discontinue the maintenance services described above upon not less than 90 days' written notice to Developer.

11. Ownership of Software

The moment computer code is written, it is protected by copyright and someone becomes the owner of that copyright. Similarly, patent and trade secret ownership rights may come into existence. Many customers of software developers harbor the misapprehension that, since they are paying for the creation of the software by the developer, they will automatically own all rights to it. This is not the case. Absent a written contract transferring ownership from the developer to the customer, the developer will own the copyright in the software, unless the developer is considered the customer's employee or, perhaps, if it was part of a larger work and was prepared under a written work for hire agreement. (See Chapter 8, Section A.)

One of the most important functions of a software development agreement is to establish exactly who will own the intellectual property rights to the software to be created. This is often one of the most hotly contested issues between the developer and customer, and can easily become a "dealbreaker." We discuss ownership rules for intellectual property in detail in Chapter 8. We'll focus here how to handle these issues in a custom software development agreement.

FLOPPY DISK OWNERSHIP ISN'T INTELLECTUAL PROPERTY OWNERSHIP

Owning the material object in which software is embodied—whether a floppy disk, tape, hard disk or ROM—is separate and distinct from intellectual property ownership. When a customer is given a floppy disk containing a software program written by the developer, the customer owns that disk—no one can legally take it away from him—but the customer cannot exercise any of the developer's exclusive copyright rights in the software contained on that disk absent a transfer (license or sale) of such rights from the developer to the customer.

This means that the customer could not legally make more than one archival copy of the software, could not distribute it to the public, and could not create derivative works based upon it—modified versions, for example. This is what we're talking about when we discuss software ownership—ownership of intangible intellectual property rights—not ownership of floppy disks.

There are many ownership options available. We provide four ownership alternatives:
- sole ownership by the customer,
- ownership by developer with an exclusive license to customer,
- ownership by developer with a nonexclusive license to customer, and
- joint ownership

Before delving into particular ownership provisions, let's look at why certain forms of ownership would be preferable, respectively, to the customer and the developer.

a. Advantages of Software Ownership for the Customer

If the customer owns the software, including the source code and technical documentation, the developer will not be able to sell or license the software to the customer's competitors. The customer would have the right to sell or license the software to others, thereby providing additional income.

b. Advantages of Software Ownership for the Developer

Ownership issues are far more important for the developer. If a developer signs a contract with a customer transferring its ownership of the intellectual property rights in the software, the developer can never use, sell or license that software again. A developer who signs such a contract may end up giving up far more than it actually realized or intended—it *may* lose the ability to do similar work for other customers in the future.

We emphasized the "may" above because no one knows exactly to what extent computer software is protected by the law. We do know that copyright protects source code, so a developer who relinquishes copyright ownership in a program may not use that same source code again. But we also know that copyright protection goes beyond a program's literal source code. It is here that things get iffy. Depending on a number of factors, copyright may also protect a program's "structure, sequence and organization," the "user interface," and even its "look and feel." (See Chapter 3 for a detailed discussion.) This *could* mean that, in an extreme case, a developer who has transferred copyright ownership to a customer would violate the customer's copyright rights if the developer creates a program for somebody else with similar menus, an otherwise similar customer interface, or even a similar overall design or structure.

But potential problems do not end here. Copyright does not protect ideas, concepts, know-how, techniques, formulae or algorithms. However, these items may be protected by trade secrecy or, in some instances, patents. Thus, a developer that relinquishes all its intellectual property rights in the software it creates for a customer could conceivably be barred by trade secrecy or patent law from using similar ideas, techniques and so forth in other programs.

The moral is this: A developer should make sure that it retains enough ownership rights so that it can continue to do similar development work for other customers or obtain enough money from the customer to compensate it for the possible lost future business.

One way a developer can protect its future business is to obtain a nonexclusive license to use the software. Another is to retain ownership of the software and provide the customer with a license to use the software. Both these options are discussed below. In addition, the developer should be careful to retain ownership of its "background technology." That includes the programs and materials that the developer uses over and over again in most or all of its projects—such as routines for displaying menus, document assembly and printing. (See Section D11, below, for a detailed discussion.)

c.   Alternative 1: Ownership by Customer

Because they are paying the developer to create the software, some customers insist on receiving sole ownership. The following clause grants all ownership rights in the software to the customer, with no restrictions. Typically, a developer that relinquishes all its ownership rights will demand more payment than if it were allowed to retain at least some ownership and profit from the software by licensing it to others.

> **Alternative 1:** Subject to payment of all compensation due under this Agreement and all other terms and conditions herein, Developer hereby assigns its entire right, title and interest (including trade secret, patent and copyright interest) in the Software and associated documentation to Customer. Developer agrees to cooperate with and assist Customer to apply for and execute any applications and/or assignments reasonably necessary to obtain any copyright, patent, trademark or other statutory protection for the Software and associated documentation. All such applications shall be made at Customer's expense.

As mentioned above, an assignment of all of the developer's rights means that the developer may not use the software created for the customer, for example, by including part of it in a program created for someone else. This can work a substantial hardship on the developer, especially one that regularly works on similar types of software.

One way to make such an ownership transfer more palatable to the developer, and probably reduce the developer's price, involves the customer granting the developer back a nonexclusive license to use the software. A nonexclusive license gives someone the right to use software or other copyrighted work, but does not prevent the copyright owners from granting others the same rights at the same time.

The license can be limited in any way—such as in duration or the type of software in which it can be used. For example, the developer can be barred from using the software to help the customer's named competitors or from developing similar types of products. The following optional provision granting a license to the developer would be used in addition to the assignment from developer to customer above.

> *(Optional:)* Customer hereby grants to Developer a nonexclusive, *("irrevocable license" or "license for the term of _____ years")* to use the Software subject to the following restrictions: *(Add any noncompetition provisions, payment provisions or other restrictions—for example: "Developer shall not, without Customer's prior written consent, license or use the software for any firm engaged in [specify competitor's field] for a period of two years after Customer accepts the Software.")*

d. Alternative 2: Ownership by Developer with Exclusive License to Customer

Another option is for the developer to retain ownership of the software and give the customer an exclusive license to use it. (Nonexclusive licenses are covered below, in Alternative 3.)

With an exclusive license, only the customer has the right to use it—within the scope of the license. If an exclusive license gives the customer the right to use the software in every possible context at every possible location, it would be the functional equivalent of ownership. In practice, however, the parties usually agree to limit the customer's use rights. For example, the customer's right to use the software may be limited as to duration, area (worldwide or domestic), market or hardware (the customer could be permitted to use the software only on a particular platform). The developer has the exclusive right to modify the software and may sell or license it to others outside the customer's area of exclusivity.

This arrangement often benefits both the customer and developer: The customer is assured that the developer will not sell or license the software to competitors during the term of the exclusive license. At the same time, the developer retains control over the software and will have the opportunity to earn income by licensing to others outside the area of the customer's exclusivity and/or after the exclusive license expires.

The following provision grants an exclusive license that is limited as to time. When the exclusive license expires, the customer receives a perpetual *nonexclusive* license, meaning that the developer is free to license the software to others. This license is nontransferable—it does not permit the customer to sub-license the software to others, but this can be permitted if the parties desire. The license permits the customer to use the software on any number of computers for internal purposes and to make as many back-up copies as it needs.

Alternative 2: Subject to payment of all compensation due under this Agreement and all other terms and conditions herein, Developer hereby grants Customer a nontransferable royalty-free license to the Software in object code form. The license granted hereunder shall be exclusive in *(name territories, such as "the United States")* for a period of _____ following acceptance by Customer of the Software as set forth in this Agreement. The license shall automatically revert to a perpetual nonexclusive license following the period of exclusivity granted herein.

The license granted herein shall authorize Customer to:

(a) install the Software on computer systems owned, leased or otherwise controlled by Customer,

(b) utilize the Software for its internal data-processing purposes (but not for time-sharing or service bureau purposes), and

(c) copy the Software only as necessary to exercise the rights granted herein.

e. Alternative 3: Ownership by Developer with Nonexclusive License to Customer

The most favorable ownership arrangement for the developer may be for the customer to be given only a nonexclusive license to use the software. This means that the developer is free to license the software to anyone else, including the developer's competitors. This type of ownership arrangement should result in the lowest possible price to the customer, because the developer may earn additional income by licensing the software to others.

Alternative 3: Subject to payment of all compensation due under this Agreement and all other terms and conditions herein, Developer hereby grants Customer a nonexclusive, nontransferable, royalty-free license to use the Software furnished to Customer by Developer under this Agreement.

The license granted herein shall authorize Customer to:

(a) install the Software on computer systems owned, leased or otherwise controlled by Customer,

(b) utilize the Software for its internal data-processing purposes (but not for time-sharing or service bureau purposes), and

(c) copy the Software only as necessary to exercise the rights granted herein.

One objection a customer might have to such an arrangement is that it permits the developer to sell the software to the customer's competitors. The parties might agree to add a provision like the following restricting the developer's right to license the software to the customer's competitors for a specified time.

(Optional:) Subject to payment of all compensation due under this Agreement and all other terms and conditions herein, Developer agrees that for a period of _____ years following completion of the Software developed under this Agreement, it shall not sell or license the Software to the following competitors of Customer without Customer's written permission: *(list competitors)*.

In nonexclusive license arrangements, it is not uncommon for the developer to agree to pay the customer a royalty for each license it sells to third parties. This often seems fair because the customer paid to have the software created in the first place. The total cumulative royalty is usually limited to the total price the customer paid the developer for the software. The royalty can be a percentage of the total price paid for each license or a set dollar amount.

(Optional:) Developer shall pay Customer a royalty of $_____ *(or specify percentage of the total purchase price)* for each license to the Software Developer grants to third parties. The total royalties paid to Customer shall not exceed $_____.

f.   Alternative 4: Joint Ownership

Yet another option is for the customer and developer to jointly own the software. Under a joint ownership arrangement, each party is free to use the software or grant nonexclusive licenses to third parties without the other's permission (unless they agree to restrict this right). Normally, joint owners must account for and share with each other any monies they earn from granting such licenses. This is probably not desirable in the developer-customer situation, so the sample provision below specifically provides that neither party need account to the other—in other words, they need not share any money they earn from the software.

> **Alternative 4:** Developer hereby grants Customer an undivided one-half interest in the Software and associated documentation. The Software may be freely used by either party without accounting to the other party. Customer and Developer agree to execute all documents reasonably necessary to legally establish their joint ownership of the Software.

12. Ownership of Background Technology

A software developer will normally bring to the project various development tools, routines, subroutines and other programs, data and materials. One term for these items is "background technology." It's quite possible that background technology may end up in the final product. For example, this may include code used for installation, window manipulation, displaying menus, data searching, data storing and printing.

If the developer transfers complete ownership of the software to the customer, the customer also may end up owning this background technology. Such an arrangement would prohibit the developer from using the background technology in other projects without obtaining the customer's permission (and perhaps paying a fee). A developer is usually well advised to avoid this problem by making sure the agreement provides that the developer retain all ownership rights in background technology. In this event, the agreement also should give the customer a nonexclusive license to use the background technology that's included in the customer's software.

The provision below permits the customer to use the background technology as included in the software, but keeps ownership in the hands of the developer. The developer should prepare a separate exhibit that identifies in as much detail as possible the background technology to be included in the software. It may not be possible to know before the software is created all the items of background technology that will be used, so the agreement should allow for additional items to be added later.

Note: The following provision need not be included in a contract in which the developer retains ownership of the software.

> Customer acknowledges that Developer owns or holds a license to use and sublicense various preexisting development tools, routines, subroutines and other programs, data and materials that Developer may include in the Software developed under this Agreement. This material shall be referred to hereafter as "Background Technology." Developer's Background Technology includes, but is not limited to, those items identified in Exhibit __, attached hereto, and made a part of this Agreement.
>
> Both parties acknowledge that as of the date of this Agreement, it is not possible for Developer to anticipate and list all Background Technology that may be included in the Software when finally completed. At the time the completed Software is delivered to Customer, Developer shall update Exhibit __ so that it may reflect as accurately as possible what Background Technology the Software contains. A copy of the updated Exhibit __ shall be provided to Customer and made a part of this Agreement.
>
> Customer agrees that Developer shall retain any and all rights Developer may have in the Background Technology. Developer grants Customer an unrestricted, nonexclusive, perpetual, fully paid-up worldwide license to use the Background Technology in the Software developed and delivered to Customer under this Agreement, and all updates and revisions thereto. However, Customer shall make no other commercial use of the Background Technology without Developer's written consent.

Tip for developers. If possible, identify your background technology in the source code copies of the programs in any printouts of code you deliver to the customer. You might include a notice like the following where such material appears: "*[Your Company Name] CONFIDENTIAL AND PROPRIETARY.*"

13. Source Code Access

Most computer software is never really finished. Whether it's being de-bugged, upgraded, modified and/or enhanced, software is constantly evolving. This fact of life presents a serious problem for customers because you can't even correct minor bugs in a computer program, much less make other changes, without access to the source code.

A program's "source code" is the version of the program actually written by human computer programmers in high level English-like computing languages such as C++, COBOL and many others.

Anyone who wants to debug, update or modify a computer program must have access to the program's source code. A customer who pays a developer to create custom software must either:

• obtain a copy of the source code and technical documentation (see Section D3b), or

• rely solely on the developer to make any desired or necessary modifications or maintenance of the software.

If the customer obtains ownership of the software, it should receive the source code and system/program documentation created by the developer. But if the developer retains ownership and merely grants the customer a license to use the software, source code access becomes an important issue. Software developers are often reluctant to give anybody a copy of their proprietary source code. This reluctance is understandable. A software developer's most important asset is usually its source code, which may contain highly valuable trade secrets. Moreover, some developers may wish to make their customers dependent upon them for all software maintenance and/or modifications. This can be accomplished quite nicely by retaining the source code.

A customer with no programming capability of its own may be happy to rely on the developer to maintain the software. (See Section D9 for sample maintenance provisions.) In this event, the customer has no real use for the source code and should have no objection to the developer not revealing it. However, there are some potential problems that a customer in this situation should consider and deal with in the development contract:

- *What happens if the developer goes out of business?* This happens all too often in the highly competitive software industry. The original developer may no longer be able or willing to give the customer the support it needs. The customer may find it difficult or impossible to obtain the source code from a defunct or bankrupt developer and will therefore be unable to modify or maintain the software. If important software is involved, this could cause the customer significant business disruption and/or financial loss.

- *What happens if the developer fails to satisfactorily maintain the software or jacks up the price to an unacceptable level?* A customer without access to the source code will be unable to look elsewhere for software maintenance and modifications.

Over the years, software developers and customers have come up with several different solutions to these potential problems; some have worked better than others. One approach is to include a provision in the development contract requiring the developer to release the source code to the customer upon the occurrence of certain events (such as the developer's bankruptcy). But if the developer refuses to live up to this agreement, the developer may have to spend substantial time and money going to court to enforce it. And if the developer goes bankrupt, the agreement may not be enforceable at all.

The most common solution to the source code access problem is the use of source code escrows. Escrows are by no means a perfect solution, but they currently seem to be the best option available. We discuss these in detail just below.

a. Source Code Escrows

Under a source code escrow agreement, the developer gives a copy of the source code and documentation to a neutral third party for safekeeping. The third party will release the source code to the customer only upon the occurrence of specified conditions, such as the developer's bankruptcy or failure to maintain the software. This keeps the developer's source code confidential while, in theory, assuring the customer access to it should it become necessary.

So long as the customer pays for the escrow and the conditions for its release are reasonable, this arrangement works well for the developer. However, source code escrows can sometimes fail to adequately protect the customer. One problem is ensuring that the escrow contains the latest version of the software. Software developers, particularly those on the verge of going out of business, may fail to deposit the most current version of the source code with the escrow agent. If the developer then goes bankrupt, the customer may find that the escrowed source code is out-of-date and perhaps useless.

There can also be problems deciding just when the customer is entitled to the source code under the terms of the escrow agreement. Such agreements often provide that the customer is entitled to access to the source code if the developer fails to adequately maintain the software. How is the escrow agent to decide whether the developer's performance has been adequate? The developer may have to resort to arbitration and/or litigation and obtain a favorable ruling before the escrow agent will release the code.

Finally, software escrows can be expensive when a professional software escrow agent is used. An initial fee must be paid as well as annual fees. These fees vary widely, but can easily run into several thousand dollars over a five-year period.

Despite these problems, source code escrows have become the most common means of resolving the developer's need to keep its source code secret and the customer's need to gain access to it in time of need.

Tip for customers. If the customer's business will be severely disrupted or ruined if it can't use the software, the customer should insist on obtaining a copy of the source code from the developer as well as copies of all updates. This is the only sure way the customer can be sure it will be able to maintain the software if the developer is unable or unwilling to do so. If the developer won't agree to a contract providing that the customer will receive a copy of the source code, the customer should look for another developer who will.

Literally anybody can serve as the escrow agent. In the past, attorneys, accountants and bank escrow departments have frequently been used. In recent years, though, a number of escrow houses specializing in software have been established. (See the sidebar below.)

Using an escrow firm that specializes in software affords several advantages. First, these companies provide a carefully controlled environment for storage of magnetic media, assuring that the deposited material is undamaged. In addition, some software escrow houses also provide a verification service. This may consist of simply making sure the materials deposited match the requirements of the escrow agreement. However, for an additional charge, some escrows will take the source code provided by the developer and compile it (turn it into object code) to see if it is identical to the object code given to the customer. Software escrow companies normally supply detailed form escrow agreements for the parties to sign. These agreements attempt to evenly balance the interests of both parties.

PROFESSIONAL SOFTWARE ESCROW COMPANIES

The following is professional software escrow houses provide nation-wide service. There may be other software escrow houses near your local area. It pays to shop around, since fees vary widely.

Data Securities International
6165 Greenwich Drive #220
San Diego, CA 92122
619-457-5199

Fort Knox Safe Deposit Inc.
235 DeKalb Industrial Way
Decatur, GA 30030
404-292-0700; 800-875-5669

National Escrow Corporation
P.O. Box 190810
Dallas, TX 75219
214-526-8383; 800-383-1800

National Safe Depository
2109 Bering Drive
San Jose, CA 95131
408-453-2753; Fax 408-441-6826

Zurich Depository Corporation
1165 Northern Blvd.
Manhasset, NY 11030
516-365-4756

Since there is no guarantee when a development project is commenced that the software will be satisfactorily completed, it makes sense to delay spending the time and money involved in setting up a source code escrow until the software is actually written. Below is a clause obliging the parties to set up an escrow with a software escrow house to be determined later. The escrow agreement is also to be negotiated later. This clause makes clear that the customer will pay for the escrow. This is fair because the escrow is really for the customer's benefit. It also sets forth the circumstances under which the escrowed materials will be released to the customer by the escrow company; this should also, of course, be spelled out in detail in the escrow agreement.

Customer agrees that the Software developed under this Agreement shall be delivered to Customer in object code form only. Developer agrees that one copy of the source code version of the Software and associated documentation shall be deposited with an escrow agent specializing in software escrows to be mutually agreed upon in writing by Developer and Customer after good faith negotiation. Customer and Developer shall enter into a supplementary escrow agreement with the escrow agent.

The source code shall be delivered to the escrow agent within _____ days after delivery of the object code to Customer. Thereafter, the source code version of all updates, enhancements and modifications of the Software created by Developer on Customer's behalf, as well as associated documentation, shall be deposited by Developer with the escrow agent. Customer shall pay all fees necessary to establish and maintain the escrow.

Developer hereby grants to Customer a contingent license to receive the source code from the escrow agent and to use the source code to support its use of the Software in machine-readable form if one or more of the following conditions occurs:

(a) Developer, whether directly or through a successor or affiliate, ceases to be in the software business.

(b) Developer fails to fulfill its obligations to maintain the Software as provided in this Agreement.

(c) Developer becomes insolvent or admits insolvency or a general inability to pay its debts as they become due.

(d) Developer files a petition for protection under the U.S. Bankruptcy Code, or an involuntary petition is filed against it and is not dismissed within 60 days.

(Optional:)

(e) Developer comes under the control of a competitor of Customer.

The source code shall be used solely by Customer to maintain the Software and shall be subject to every restriction on use set forth in this Agreement. Customer agrees not to disclose the source code to third parties except on a need-to-know basis under an appropriate duty of confidentiality.

14. Warranties

A warranty is a promise or statement regarding the quality, quantity, performance or legal title of something being sold. We all have some familiarity with warranties. Whenever we buy an expensive product from a car, to a television to a computer, the seller normally warrants that the product will do what it is supposed to do for a specific or reasonable time period, otherwise the seller will fix or replace it.

When goods are sold in the course of business, they generally are warranted. If the goods later prove defective and the seller fails to repair or replace them in accordance with the warranty, it is called a "breach of warranty" and the buyer can seek relief in the courts. In many states, hefty damages can be obtained against sellers who fail to live up to their warranties. These may include not only the cost of replacing the defective software, but any economic losses suffered by the customer as a result of the defect, such as lost profits.

Custom software developers are naturally hesitant about giving a warranty for something that is not yet in existence when the warranty is made. However, for good reason, some customers usually demand assurance that the product will work.

Because this is an area of active bargaining between the developer and customer, warranty provisions vary widely. Before we discuss sample warranty provisions for custom software development contracts, let's take a quick look at the various types of warranties.

a. Express Warranties

When a developer makes an actual promise about how the software will work, whether orally or in writing, it is making an "express warranty." An express warranty can be created by using formal words such as "guarantee," "affirm," or "warrant." However, it is important to understand that no magic words are necessary to create a warranty. Representations make by salespeople, sales literature, statements at product demonstrations, proposals, manuals or contractual specifications can all constitute express warranties. And this can even be true where the developer did not intend to create a warranty. Express warranties can last for any period of time, ranging from a few months to the lifetime of the software.

Customers often seek an express warranty from software developers guaranteeing that the software is free from defects and will meet the functional and design specifications set forth in the development plan. (See Section D13e, below.) Another common express warranty is a guarantee that the software will not infringe any third party's copyright, patent or trade secret rights.

b. Implied Warranties

In every commercial transaction involving the sale of movable goods, certain representations by the seller are assumed to be made, even if no words are written or spoken. These representations are implied by state laws based on the Uniform Commercial Code ("UCC"), a set of model laws designed by legal scholars that have been adopted by every state but Louisiana. The UCC establishes uniform rules governing the sale of goods and other commercial transactions. In the past, a number of courts have disagreed on whether custom software qualifies as a "good" governed by these state UCC laws, but today the trend appears to be that these laws apply to custom software sales transactions. (There is no question that the UCC applies when software is bundled with hardware, or when standard off-the-shelf software is customized.)

We can't give you a whole course on the UCC here, but you should be aware that there are four implied warranties that automatically exist in contracts for the sale of goods unless they are expressly disclaimed (disavowed). These are:

- *Implied warranty of title.* All sellers warrant that they are transferring good legal title to the goods; that they have the right to make the transfer; and, as far as they know, the goods are not subject to any liens, encumbrances or security interests. This warranty is particularly important for software development agreements because the software often contains elements that have been licensed from or to third parties.

- *Implied warranty against infringement.* The seller warrants that the product will be delivered free of any rightful claim by any third party that the product infringes such person's patent, copyright, trade secret or other proprietary rights.

- *Implied warranty of fitness for a specific purpose.* If a customer is relying on the seller's expertise to select suitable goods, and the seller is aware that the customer intends to use the goods for a particular purpose, the product becomes impliedly guaranteed for that purpose. For example, if a developer knows that the customer needs software to operate an assembly line at a particular speed, and agrees to develop software for that purpose, there is an implied warranty that the software will operate the line at the proper speed even if this specification isn't made a part of the contract. This warranty virtually always applies in custom software transactions.

- *Implied warranty of merchantability.* The seller promises that the goods are fit for their commonly intended use—in other words, they are of at least average quality. This means that software must perform so as to satisfy most customers' expectations. The software need only perform in a minimally acceptable manner to satisfy this warranty; it need not satisfy the highest function, speed or other performance criteria.

c. Disclaimer of All Warranties

There is no requirement in most states that the seller of goods provide any warranties at all. The implied warranties discussed above (and any express warranties) may be expressly disclaimed by the seller. This means that the goods are sold "as is." While an "as is" statement will protect a seller from many types of claims, it won't protect it from charges of outright fraud (if it lied about the goods in question). To be effective, "as is" statements must be "conspicuous"—for instance, printed in boldface capitals and large type—so they won't be overlooked by the customer (no proverbial "fine print"). Here's an example:

THE SOFTWARE FURNISHED UNDER THIS AGREEMENT IS PROVIDED ON AN "AS IS" BASIS, WITHOUT ANY WARRANTIES OR REPRESENTATIONS EXPRESS OR IMPLIED, INCLUDING, BUT NOT LIMITED TO, ANY IMPLIED WARRANTIES OF MERCHANTABILITY OR FITNESS FOR A PARTICULAR PURPOSE.

If the developer disclaims all warranties, make sure the "as is" statement is in capital letters. If possible, it should also be bold or underlined.

d. What Warranties Should a Custom Software Development Contract Contain?

Although creating custom software is a difficult and often uncertain process, it is reasonable for the customer to expect the developer to stand behind its product. In a custom software development agreement, the developer typically gives the customer certain express warranties and disclaims any and all implied warranties. The parties need to negotiate exactly what type of express warranties the developer will make. Naturally, the customer wants the developer's warranties to be as expansive as possible, while the developer wishes them to be narrowly drawn. A compromise must be reached.

The express warranties commonly found in custom development agreements include all or some of the following:

- warranty of software performance,
- warranty of title,
- warranty against infringement,
- warranty against disablement, and
- warranty of compatibility.

We'll discuss each type of warranty in the following sections and provide sample contractual warranty provisions.

 Tip for developers. If you really don't want to provide the customer with all the warranties discussed below, the customer might be willing to accept only a warranty of software performance or even take the software "as is" (that is, with no warranties at all) if you offer a lower price for the software.

e. Warranty of Software Performance

Under a warranty of software performance, the developer guarantees that the software will function properly. The developer promises that the software is free from material defects (but not absolutely perfect) and will perform in substantial conformance with the specifications.

This warranty is usually limited in time, to anywhere from 90 days to one year. During the warranty term, the developer is required to correct any defects and modify the software as necessary, free of charge. Normally excluded from coverage are any defects caused by the customer's misuse of the software or from causes beyond the developer's control, such as power failure.

Developer warrants that for *(warranty period)* following acceptance of the Software by Customer, the Software will be free from material reproducible programming errors and defects in workmanship and materials, and will substantially conform to the specifications in the development plan when maintained and operated in accordance with Developer's instructions. If material reproducible programming errors are discovered during the warranty period, Developer shall promptly remedy them at no additional expense to Customer. This warranty to Customer shall be null and void if Customer is in default under this Agreement or if the nonconformance is due to:

(a) hardware failures due to defects, power problems, environmental problems or any cause other than the Software itself,

(b) modification of the Software operating systems or computer hardware by any party other than Developer, or

(c) misuse, errors or negligence of Customer, its employees or agents in operating the Software.

Developer shall not be obligated to cure any defect unless Customer notifies it of the existence and nature of such defect promptly upon discovery.

f. Warranty of Title

The developer warrants that it has the legal right to grant the customer all rights specified in the contract. This normally means that no intellectual property rights to the software have been licensed to others on an exclusive basis. In addition, if the developer has used any code covered by another's copyright, patent or trade secret protections, it has the legal right to do so.

Developer owns and has the right to license or convey title to the Software and documentation covered by this Agreement. Developer will not grant any rights or licenses to any intellectual property or technology that would conflict with Developer's obligations under this Agreement.

g. Warranty Against Infringement

This warranty provides that the materials produced under the agreement will not violate any third party's copyright, patent, trade secret or other intellectual property rights. We've included this warranty in a catch-all section dealing with intellectual property infringement claims. (See the discussion in Section D14a, below.)

h. Warranty Against Disablement

Developers who are concerned that they might not be paid fully or that the customer may breach the terms of the development contract have been known to include "computer viruses" and disabling devices in their software. These devices are intended to disable the software, either automatically with the passage of time or under the developer's control. The purpose, obviously, is to prevent the customer from using the software if it fails to uphold its end of the agreement.

Is this legal? One court has indicated it might be, but only if the developer tells the customer in advance that disabling devices will be included in the software and the customer agrees (*Frank & Sons v. Information Solutions* (N.D. Okla. No. 88C1474E), Computer Indus. Lit. Rep., Jan. 23, 1989, at 8927-35). In the absence of such notice and consent, a developer who disables a customer's software could be liable for all the customer's resulting damages. These could be substantial, especially if the customer's entire computer system is affected. In one well-known case, a developer included a disabling device in an inventory control system it created for cosmetics manufacture for Revlon, Inc.

When Revlon stopped paying the developer because it was dissatisfied with the system's performance, the developer sent Revlon a letter warning that it would disable the software if payment was not forthcoming. The developer then activated the disabling device by dialing into Revlon's computer system. As a result, two of Revlon's distribution centers were completely shut down for several days. Revlon estimated its losses at $20 million. Revlon sued the developer, who settled for an undisclosed amount (*Revlon, Inc. v. Logisticon, Inc.* No. 705933 (Cal. Super. Ct., Santa Clara Cty., complaint filed Oct. 22, 1990)). The lesson is clear: A developer should absolutely never include any disabling device in software without informing the customer and obtaining its consent in advance. Even then, the developer should think twice if a customer does consent—it might sue the developer anyway if activation of a disablement device causes it substantial losses.

Not only will most customers refuse to allow inclusion of a disabling device in their software, they will often demand that the developer expressly guarantee that none has or will be included. Here's an example of such a guarantee:

> Developer expressly warrants that no portion of the Software contains or will contain any protection feature designed to prevent its use. This includes, without limitation, any computer virus, worm, software lock, drop dead device, Trojan-horse routine, trap door, time bomb or any other codes or instructions that may be used to access, modify, delete, damage or disable Customer's Software or computer system. Developer further warrants that it will not impair the operation of the Software in any way other than by order of a court of law.

i. Warranty of Compatibility

The warranty of compatibility provides that the software will be compatible with the hardware on which it will run and with any non-custom software included in the customer's system. This warranty is particularly important where a customer is acquiring a system from multiple vendors—that is, hardware from one or more vendors, and software from others.

> Developer warrants that the Software shall be compatible with the Customer's hardware and software as set forth in the development plan Specifications.

Note that this guarantee of compatibility applies only to software and hardware described in the specifications. This is designed to protect the developer, since there can be substantial problems getting custom software to work in conjunction with other standard software. The developer needs to know up-front exactly what software and hardware the customer software must work with.

 The specifications may need to be modified to include details about the customer's hardware and software. (See Section D5, above.)

j. Disclaiming Warranties Not in Agreement

In return for the express warranties included in the contract, the customer typically agrees to allow the developer to disclaim any and all other warranties, whether express or implied. Such a disclaimer should be typed in capitals, preferably bold face, to be enforceable.

THE WARRANTIES SET FORTH IN THIS AGREEMENT ARE THE ONLY WARRANTIES GRANTED BY DEVELOPER. DEVELOPER DISCLAIMS ALL OTHER WARRANTIES EXPRESS OR IMPLIED, INCLUDING, BUT NOT LIMITED TO, ANY IMPLIED WARRANTIES OF MERCHANTABILITY OR FITNESS FOR A PARTICULAR PURPOSE.

 If you include this disclaimer, make sure it is in capital letters. If possible, it should also be bold or underlined.

WARRANTIES A DEVELOPER SHOULD NOT MAKE

A developer should only provide a warranty as to those matters *within its control*. This is a matter of fairness and common sense. Matters beyond a developers control include:

- *Error free software.* A developer cannot realistically warrant that the software will be completely bug-free. All software, particularly custom software, inevitably contains some bugs. But there is a big difference between true bugs—defects that prevent the software from performing the customer's required tasks satisfactorily—and interface and peripheral glitches and other minor irritants that don't materially affect the software's performance. The most a developer should promise is that the software will not contain "material" defects. A developer should never promise to fix trivial bugs free of charge. Fixing minor bugs can be just as difficult and expensive as fixing major ones. Moreover, the customer really doesn't need to have trivial bugs fixed at all. All the customer needs is stable software that performs satisfactorily. Trivial bugs that don't prevent the software from performing satisfactorily can simply be ignored.
- *Software will be free from defects in materials and workmanship.* This type of warranty is commonly found in contracts for machinery, including computer hardware. However, it does not belong in software development contracts. Again, no developer can safely guarantee that custom software will be perfect.
- *Software will perform in exact conformance with specifications.* Developers shouldn't promise this unless they're absolutely sure it will be true. It's far better for the developer to warrant that the software will perform "in substantial conformance" with the specifications, meaning that trivial variations will not violate the warranty.

15. Intellectual Property Infringement Claims

If you're a custom software customer, here's one of your worst nightmares: You enter into a contract with a developer to create custom software vital to your business. The developer completes the software on time and does a superb job. You're ecstatic. Six months later, you're served with a lawsuit for copyright infringement. It turns out that the developer's ace programmer allegedly pirated major portions of "your" software from a prior employer. Said employer immediately obtains a court order enjoining you from using the software. Your business is totally disrupted; meanwhile, your company is a defendant in an infringement suit along with the developer.

Just how concerned should a customer be about intellectual property infringement claims? Very concerned. Becoming embroiled in an infringement lawsuit is costly, stressful and time-consuming.

If a customer is sued, it may be of little comfort to know that it may be liable for the developer's copyright or trade secret infringement only if it:

* should have known of the infringement, or
* continues to use the software after being notified of the infringement.

The fact that a customer ultimately may not be liable for copyright or trade secret infringement doesn't mean that it won't be joined in an infringement suit along with the developer, particularly if the customer is a large, solvent business and the developer is not.

Obviously, the customer should seek to insulate itself as much as possible from liability for intellectual property infringement and from the disruption such claims may cause. Just as obviously, it is in the developer's best interests to try to limit the extent of the protection it will provide the customer in the event of an infringement claim. We'll discuss below three types of provisions commonly included in software development contracts concerning intellectual property infringement:

* express warranty provisions by the developer guaranteeing that the software will not violate third party intellectual property rights,
* indemnification provisions in which the developer promises to defend the customer if it is sued for intellectual property infringement; a number of alternative provisions are provided, and
* a repair or replacement provision in which the developer promises to fix infringing software to make it noninfringing, replace it with other noninfringing software or give back the customer's money.

All, some or none of these provisions may be included in a development agreement.

Tip for customers. The customer should be aware that the warranty and indemnity provisions discussed here may not be worth much if the developer doesn't have the financial resources to honor them and has inadequate or no insurance. If a customer is deeply concerned about possible infringement claims, it may prefer to pay a higher development fee to a developer that has adequate insurance to cover such claims or obtain its own insurance. Proof of insurance coverage should always be provided.

INSURANCE COVERAGE FOR INFRINGEMENT CLAIMS

Whether you're a developer or its customer, your business may be insured for intellectual property infringement claims and you may not even know it. The Comprehensive General Liability Insurance ("CGL") policies typically obtained by businesses may provide such coverage. Several courts have held that the "advertising injury" provision included in many CGL policies covers infringement claims. However, not all CGL policies provide such coverage, particularly those written after 1986.

Ask your insurance broker whether your policy covers infringement claims. If the broker doesn't know, you may need to consult with an insurance attorney who represents policyholders. If your CGL policy doesn't cover infringement claims, you may be able to obtain such coverage by purchasing umbrella or excess policy coverage from your insurer.

---

a. Express Warranty Against Intellectual Property Infringement

"Intellectual property" is a catch-all terms that includes copyrights, patents, trade secrets and trademarks. (See Chapter 2 for a detailed discussion.) Most software development agreements contain some kind of express warranty against intellectual property infringement. The extent of such a warranty is subject to negotiation. In this section, we look at several versions of such warranties, ranging from the most favorable to the customer to the most favorable to the developer.

Tip for developers. In this highly litigious world, intellectual property infringement is an issue the developer must think about carefully. In some cases, the developer may even choose to lower its price or make other concessions to the customer to avoid making a broad warranty of noninfringement.

Under the most favorable warranty for the customer, the developer guarantees that the materials produced under the agreement will not violate any third party's copyright, trade secret, patent or other rights. Here's an example of such a warranty:

> **Alternative 1:** Developer warrants that the Software and documentation delivered to Customer under this Agreement shall not infringe on the copyright, patent or trade secrets of any third party. To the extent this material contains matter proprietary to a third party, Developer shall obtain a license from the owner permitting the use of such matter and granting Developer the right to sub-license its use.

Although such a provision has been considered standard in the past, developers are becoming increasingly wary about providing a broad warranty of noninfringement. As discussed in detail in Chapter 5, it is very difficult for a developer to know for sure whether its software might violate a patent, primarily because pending patent applications are kept secret. At most, a developer should warrant that the software does not violate any United States patents that have issued as of the date the software is delivered. This clause addresses such agreement:

Alternative 2: Developer warrants that the Software and documentation delivered to Customer under this Agreement shall not infringe on any existing United States patent, copyright, or trade secret of any third party. To the extent this material contains matter proprietary to a third party, Developer shall obtain a license from the owner permitting the use of such matter and granting Developer the right to sub-license its use.

However, even limiting warranties to existing patents is problematic because patent searches of existing software patents are far from foolproof. Far better from the developer's point of view is to simply promise that to the best of the developer's knowledge the software will not infringe any existing patent, but not to provide any warranty as to noninfringement. The following language accomplishes this:

Alternative 3: Developer warrants that the Software and documentation delivered to Customer under this Agreement shall not infringe on the copyright or trade secrets of any third party. To the extent this material contains matter proprietary to a third party, Developer shall obtain a license from the owner permitting the use of such matter and granting Developer the right to sub-license its use. Developer will not knowingly infringe upon any existing patents of third parties in the performance of services required by this Agreement, but Developer MAKES NO WARRANTY OF NONINFRINGEMENT of any United States or foreign patent.

Even better for the developer is to provide no warranty of noninfringement at all, and instead extend the "no-knowledge representation" to copyrights and trade secrets as well as patents. Because there are no uniform national rules, it remains far from clear exactly how far copyright protection for software extends. (See Chapter 3.) As a result, it can be difficult or impossible to know for sure if custom software violates the copyright in any similar preexisting programs. In fact, there have been many instances in which a developer's employees have included in software elements belonging to a prior employer; as a practical matter, it can be impossible for a developer to know about or prevent this.

> **Alternative 4:** Developer represents, BUT DOES NOT WARRANT, that to the best of its knowledge the Software delivered to Customer under this Agreement will not infringe any valid and existing intellectual property right of any third party.

Best of all, from the developer's point of view, is a provision like the following, in which the developer states that it makes no warranties or representations of any kind regarding intellectual property infringement and will not indemnify the customer if an infringement claim is made (see discussion of indemnification below).

> **Alternative 5:** THE SOFTWARE FURNISHED UNDER THIS AGREEMENT IS PROVIDED WITHOUT ANY EXPRESS OR IMPLIED WARRANTIES OR REPRESENTATIONS AGAINST INFRINGEMENT. DEVELOPER SHALL NOT INDEMNIFY CUSTOMER AGAINST CLAIMS OF INFRINGEMENT OF ANY PATENTS, COPYRIGHTS, TRADE SECRETS OR OTHER PROPRIETARY RIGHTS.

 If you use this clause, it should be printed in bold-faced, capital letters.

b. Indemnification Against Liability for Infringement

Under an indemnification provision, one party agrees to defend the other (pay for the costs) if it is sued for various specified reasons and to pay any damages if the suit proves successful. In effect, one party is acting as an insurer. Naturally, the customer would like the developer to indemnify it against all infringement claims arising from use of the software, while the developer would prefer not to indemnify the customer at all. Below are two different intellectual property indemnification provisions. The first is more favorable to the customer than the second.

Neither of the indemnification provisions below is mandatory. And the developer would certainly prefer that neither appear in the contract. (See the end of Section D13c, above, for sample language making clear that developer will not indemnify customer for intellectual property infringement claims.) However, customers of software developers may reasonably refuse to do business with a developer who is not prepared to defend it against infringement claims.

Alternative 1: Indemnification Provision Favorable to Customer

The following provision indemnifies the customer against all intellectual property claims arising from creation and use of the software:

> **Alternative 1:** Developer shall indemnify Customer and any of its employees or agents against all liabilities, claims and legal costs (including reasonable attorney fees) arising from any claim or suit alleging infringement by the Software of any United States patent or copyright, or the trade secret or trademark rights of any third party. Developer's obligations hereunder will survive any expiration or termination of this Agreement. Customer shall promptly notify Developer in writing of any third party claim or suit and Developer shall have sole control of the defense of any such action and all negotiations for its settlement or compromise. Customer may participate at its own expense in the defense of any such action if such claim is against Customer. The foregoing represents Developer's entire liability to Customer in connection with claims alleging intellectual property infringement by the Software.

This provision can easily result in the developer's bankruptcy if an infringement claim is brought! "Defense" means paying the fees of an attorney hired to oppose the claim. Such fees can easily run into tens or hundreds of thousands of dollars, even if a third party infringement claim has absolutely no merit. If the claim does have merit, the developer can end up paying damages in addition to attorney fees. A developer that accepts such a broad indemnification provision as that above should raise its price enough to purchase a very good insurance policy or put aside a sinking fund to cover potential legal costs.

Alternative 2: Indemnification Provision More Favorable to Developer

As discussed in the sidebar in Section D13j, above, a developer should assume liability only for those things it has control over. A developer does have some ability to prevent copyright and trade secret infringement claims. Thus, it is reasonable for the customer to require the developer to indemnify it—at least to some extent—for copyright and trade secret claims. However, as discussed in Chapter 5, there is no way a developer can know for sure whether its software violates any third party patents. It seems far less reasonable, therefore, for the customer to expect the developer to indemnify it for all patent infringement claims. A far more reasonable indemnification provision from the developer's point of view would either eliminate indemnification for patent claims altogether or at the most cover only patents in existence when the software was created.

In addition, the developer should try to exclude from its indemnity obligation claims that arise from the customer's actions, not the developer's. For example, the customer could modify the software in a way that results in an infringement claim.

Finally, and most importantly, the developer will want to limit its total liability to a specified dollar amount or no more than the total contract price. This is often one of the most hotly contested areas between the parties. Since the customer may have to pay any sums in excess of this amount if an infringement claim is brought, it should have the right to approve any settlement of a claim by the developer and to hire its own attorney to participate in the defense. Here's what such a provision would look like:

> **Alternative 2:** Developer shall indemnify Customer and any of its employees or agents against all liabilities, claims and legal costs (including reasonable attorney fees) arising from any claim or suit alleging that the Software infringes:

(a) any United States copyright,

(b) the trade secret or trademark rights of any third party

(Optional:) (c) any United States patent existing on the date the Software developed under this Agreement is delivered to Customer.

Developer's obligations hereunder will survive any expiration or termination of this Agreement. Customer shall promptly notify Developer of any third party claim and Developer may, at its option, conduct the defense of any such third party action and Customer promises to fully cooperate with such defense. Customer may appear in any such infringement action through counsel of its choice at its own expense. In no event shall Developer settle any infringement action without Customer's prior written approval.

Developer shall have no liability for, and shall not indemnify Customer for, any infringement claim resulting from Customer's:

(a) modification of the Software,

(b) combination of the Software with hardware, software or other items provided by anyone other than Developer, or

(c) use of the Software in any manner not specified in the specifications or documentation provided by Developer.

In no event shall Developer's liability under this Section exceed the total amount paid to Developer by Customer under this Agreement *("or $_____, whichever is greater")*. The foregoing represents Developer's entire liability to Customer in connection with claims alleging intellectual property infringement by the Software.

c. Repair or Replacement of Infringing Software

If a court issues an injunction preventing the customer from using the software, the customer will want the developer to replace it, fix it or give back its money. This is particularly important to the customer where the software is a key part of its operation. A provision like the following is commonly included in custom software development agreements. This clause favors the customer.

If a third party infringement claim is sustained in a final judgment from which no further appeal is taken or possible, and such final judgment includes an injunction prohibiting Customer from continued use of the Software or portions thereof, Developer shall, at its sole election and expense:

(a) procure for Customer the right to continue to use the Software pursuant to this Agreement, or

(b) replace or modify the Software to make it noninfringing, provided that the modifications or substitutions will not materially and adversely affect the Software's performance or lessen its utility to Customer, or

(c) if none of the above options is reasonably available, refund the purchase price paid by Customer for the Software, minus depreciation based on a five-year useful life, upon Customer's return of the Software.

16. Indemnification of Customer Against Personal Injury and Property Damage

The following provision should cause little controversy. It insulates the customer from liability for any personal injury or property damage resulting from the developer's work—for example, if one of the developer's employees slipped and broke a leg while working on the software at the customer's place of business.

Developer shall indemnify Customer against any and all liability for personal injuries and property damage arising out of the performance of this Agreement by Developer or its employees, agents or representatives.

17. Limitation of Developer's Liability to Customer

Although it may be rather frightening and depressing to think about, custom software developers face potentially enormous liabilities. Improperly designed or bug-ridden software can cause the customer serious financial losses for which the customer may look to the developer to make good.

Example: *BioWorkware creates a custom software system designed to automate a biotechnology laboratory. A few weeks after installation, the system crashes. While BioWorkware tries to find out went wrong, the lab is forced to purchase software from another vendor to get the lab up and running. As a result of all this, the lab is shut down for a week and loses several experiments potentially worth hundreds of thousands of dollars. The lab demands that BioWorkware repay the losses caused by the crash. To pay this amount, BioWorkware would have to liquidate its business. BioWorkware refuses to pay, and the lab sues.*

To prevent a nightmarish scenario of this type from driving them out of business, developers often insist on a provision limiting their liability to the customer.

a. No Liability for Consequential Damages

The consequential damages arising out of even a modest problem can easily bankrupt a developer. At the very least, the developer should insist that it be excluded from any liability for incidental or consequential damages arising out of the agreement. Such damages include lost profits or other economic damages arising from a malfunction where the developer had reason to know that such losses could occur if the software malfunctioned. This could include, for example, the value of the experiments lost by the biotech lab in the example above. Here's a sample provision:

> In no event shall Developer be liable to Customer for lost profits of Customer, or special or consequential damages, even if Developer has been advised of the possibility of such damages.

b. Limit on Developer's Liability to Customer

Another way to handle the developer's potential liability limits the developer's total liability to the customer to a specified amount. A typical liability limit is the amount paid by the customer for the software. This amounts to a money-back guarantee for the customer, while getting the developer off the hook for a potentially much larger liability. If desired, a liability standard not based on the contract price can be set. Obviously, such a provision highly favors the developer.

> Developer's total liability under this Agreement for damages, costs and expenses, regardless of cause, shall not exceed the total amount of fees paid to Developer by Customer under this Agreement *("or $_____, whichever is greater")*.

Tip for developers. One way to limit your liability in case you're sued is to incorporate your business. Legally, a corporation is a separate entity from the individuals who own or operate it. If a court judgment is entered against the corporation, you stand to lose only the money you've invested. Generally, as long as you observe the necessary corporate formalities and acted solely in a corporate capacity (as an employee, officer or director of your corporation) and without the intent to defraud creditors, your home, personal bank accounts and other personal property can't be touched by someone who wins a lawsuit against the corporation. Bear in mind, however, that your investment in your corporation is at risk. In many cases, this could constitute your entire net worth. Accordingly, the protection afforded by incorporating is often more theoretical than real. For a detailed discussion, see *The Legal Guide for Starting & Running a Small Business,* by Fred Steingold (Nolo Press).

18. Developer's Liability for Third Party Claims

The harm caused by malfunctioning software is not necessarily limited to the customer; it may economically or even physically damage third parties as well.

Example: *SafeSoft writes a custom software package designed to operate a chemical factory. The software crashes and so does the factory, resulting in a chemical spill costing hundreds of thousands of dollars to clean up. Dozens of suits are brought against the chemical company by property owners affected by the spill. The chemical company demands that SafeSoft pay off these claims.*

To avoid this type of scenario, the developer may seek to include in the development agreement a clause providing that it is not liable for any claim made against the customer by any third party (other than for intellectual property infringement if it is providing a warranty against infringement). Of course, such a clause is highly favorable to the developer.

> Developer shall not be liable for any claim or demand made against Customer by any third party except to the extent such claim or demand relates to copyright, patent, trade secret or other proprietary rights, and then only as provided in the section of this Agreement entitled Intellectual Property Infringement Claims.

TESTING "DANGEROUS" SOFTWARE IS A MUST

The best way to avoid third party claims is to test the software as thoroughly as possible before it is actually used. Particularly where inherently "dangerous" software is involved, the customer should do as much of its own testing as possible. This is especially wise where the software could detrimentally affect others' health and safety and the developer is small and has few resources.

If a claim is brought, evidence that the software was well tested will help in court. Most software testing is done in a random, intuitive way that gives little or no protection if a subsequent lawsuit claims damages from software failure. However, when health and safety is involved, testing protocols are increasingly followed that are documented and repeatable. Often this is done by independent labs that are prepared to testify in court as to the testing methodology.

a.   Indemnification of Developer for Third Party Claims

If third parties are harmed by malfunctioning software, they'll likely sue everyone involved, including the developer. Both the customer and the developer may be liable for the full amount of such claims. Indemnification provisions are used to require one party to pay the other's attorney fees and damages arising from such claims. Indemnification provisions don't affect the third party claimant. They simply straighten liability between the developer and the customer.

In our example above, property owners affected by the chemical spill would undoubtedly sue not only the chemical factory, but SafeSoft as well, claiming that it negligently designed the software. A developer in this situation could find itself faced with defending itself against suits brought persons and entities it never heard of. Its attorney fees alone could far exceed what it was paid to create the software.

Ideally, the developer would like the customer to agree to indemnify the developer against such third party claims. Realizing that their software may adversely affect many people they never contracted with, more and more developers are seeking provisions like this which, of course, highly favor the developer. A developer of software that poses an obvious risk of potential financial and/or physical damage to third parties—for example, software implemented in banking hardware or airline radar—should seriously consider seeking a provision like the following in the development agreement:

> Customer shall indemnify Developer against all claims, liabilities and costs, including reasonable attorney fees, of defending any third party claim or suit arising out of the use of the Software provided under this Agreement, other than for infringement of intellectual property rights, and then only as provided in the section of this Agreement entitled "Intellectual Property Infringement Claims." Developer shall promptly notify Customer in writing of any third party claim or suit and Customer shall have the right to fully control the defense and any settlement of such claim or suit.

Note that the above provision does not include third party claims of intellectual property infringement. The developer often agrees to indemnify the customer for such claims as discussed in Section D14b, above. But if the developer does not indemnify the customer for such claims, you can delete the phrase "other than for infringement of intellectual property rights," and then only as provided in the section of this agreement entitled "Intellectual Property Infringement Claims."

19. Insurance

The developer should have insurance coverage for injuries to its employees, for property damage, automobile liability and for any claims or suits arising out of the performance of the agreement. The following language requires the developer to obtain a comprehensive general liability policy, naming the customer as an additional insured. As mentioned in Section D14, above, some comprehensive general liability (CGL) policies provide coverage for intellectual property infringement.

> During the term of this Agreement, Developer shall maintain at its own expense comprehensive general liability insurance with limits not less than $1 million combined single limit if Developer has eight or more employees, or not less than $500,000 combined single limit if Developer has fewer than eight employees. Before beginning work under this Agreement, Developer will deliver to Customer a certificate of insurance showing the coverage specified above, which names Customer as an additional insured, and which provides a 30-day notice period for cancellation or reduction in coverage or limits.

20. Confidentiality

In the course of developing the software, the developer probably will learn a good deal about the customer's business, including many of the customer's most vital trade secrets. Likewise, the customer may be exposed to or learn many of the developer's trade secrets, methods and know-how. It is important to both parties, therefore, that the agreement contain a confidentiality provision restricting both parties from disclosing the other's confidential information to third persons.

However, because the developer may wish to do similar work for similar businesses in the future, it is usually in its best interests to seek a narrowly drawn confidentiality provision. In contrast, precisely because the developer may later be in close contact with the customer's competitors, the customer should prefer as broad a confidentiality restriction as possible, barring the unauthorized disclosure or use of any technical, financial or business information the developer obtained (directly or indirectly) from the customer. The customer would also like the nondisclosure restrictions to be open-ended.

Let's take a look at confidentiality provisions favorable to the customer and developer, respectively.

a. Alternative 1: Broad Confidentiality Provision Favoring Customer

This broadly written confidentiality provision bars either party from disclosing or using the other's trade secrets without the other's consent (except for employees and agents who need to know trade secrets to perform the services required by the agreement). The only good thing about this provision from the developer's point of view is that the confidentiality requirements are mutual.

> **Alternative 1:** Developer acknowledges that it will acquire information and materials about Customer, including, but not limited to, its business plan, data processing techniques, computer programs, experimental works and lists of its customers and suppliers. Customer acknowledges that it may acquire information and materials about Developer, including, but not limited to, its methods, systems, technology and know-how.
>
> Both parties acknowledge that all such knowledge, information and material so acquired are the trade secrets and confidential and proprietary information of the other party (hereafter "Confidential Information"). Both parties agree, during and after the term of this Agreement, to hold such Confidential Information in strict confidence and not to disclose it to others or use it in any way without the other party's prior written authorization.
>
> The parties further agree to take all reasonable precautions to protect the confidentiality of the Confidential Information, including, without limitation, implementing and enforcing operating procedures to minimize the possibility of unauthorized use or copying of the Confidential Information. However, a party may disclose Confidential Information without such authorization to an employee or agent of the party who must have such information to perform its obligations under this Agreement, provided that the employee or agent has been advised of the confidential

nature of such information and is under an express written obligation to maintain such confidentiality.

Agreements requiring the developer's employees or other agents to adhere to such confidentiality are covered in Chapter 4, Section G.

b. Alternative 2: Narrow Confidentiality Provision Favoring Developer

Broad confidentiality restrictions like those in the previous section may make it very difficult for a developer ever to do similar work for others without fear of breaching his or her duty of confidentiality to the previous customer. This is particularly true because it can be far from clear exactly what constitutes a confidential trade secret. To avoid this problem as much as possible, the developer should sensibly prefer a confidentiality provision that is limited in scope, applies only to written materials marked "confidential" and lasts for a limited time.

The following clause prevents the unauthorized disclosure by the developer of any written material of the customer marked "confidential" or information disclosed orally that the customer later writes down, marks as confidential and delivers to the developer. This enables the developer to know for sure what material is, and is not, confidential. This clause may not appeal to the customer because it imposes the burden of reducing to writing all trade secrets disclosed to the developer. On the plus side for the customer is the fact that no confidentiality restrictions are imposed on it.

> **Alternative 2:** During the term of this Agreement and for _____ years afterwards, Developer will not use or disclose to others without Customer's written consent Customer's Confidential Information, except when reasonably necessary to perform the services under this Agreement. "Confidential Information" is limited to:
> (a) any written or tangible information stamped "confidential," "proprietary" or with a similar legend, and

(b) any written or tangible information not marked with a confidentiality legend, or information disclosed orally to Consultant, that is treated as confidential when disclosed and later summarized sufficiently for identification purposes in a written memorandum marked "confidential" and delivered to Consultant within thirty (30) days after the disclosure.

Developer shall disclose such Confidential Information only to those of its employees and sub-contractors who need to know it for the performance of this Agreement, and shall ensure that each of those employees and sub-contractors has signed an agreement to keep such information confidential.

Agreements requiring the developer's employees or other agents to adhere to such confidentiality are covered in Chapter 4, Section G.

c. Software Treated as Confidential (Optional)

Where the customer acquires ownership of the software, the clause below should be included in agreements, in addition to the confidentiality clause above. It provides that the developer has a duty not to disclose to others the software created for the customer.

Alternative 1: Developer agrees that the Software is Customer's sole and exclusive property. Developer shall treat the Software on a confidential basis and not disclose it to any third party without Customer's written consent, except when reasonably necessary to perform the services under this Agreement. Developer shall be relieved of this confidentiality obligation if and when Customer discloses the Software without any restriction on further disclosure.

If the developer retains ownership of the software, it wants to make sure that the customer treats it as confidential. The following language should be included in the development agreement:

Alternative 2: Customer acknowledges that the Software is Developer's sole and exclusive property. Customer shall treat the Software on a confidential basis and shall not, at any time, disclose the trade secrets embodied in the Software or supporting documentation to any other person, firm, organization or employee who does not need to obtain access thereto consistent with Customer's rights under this Agreement. Under no circumstances may Customer modify, reverse compile or reverse assemble the object code contained in the Software. Customer shall devote its reasonable best efforts to ensure that all persons afforded access to the Software and supporting documentation protect Developer's trade secrets against unauthorized use, dissemination or disclosure.

Agreements requiring the developer's employees or other agents to adhere to such confidentiality are covered in Chapter 4, Section G.

d. Excluded Materials

Neither party should have any duty to keep confidential material that does not qualify as a trade secret, is legitimately learned from persons other than the client or is independently developed. The following provision should be included in all development contracts:

Developer and Customer shall have no obligation to keep confidential or refrain from using any information which:
(a) was in its possession or known to it, without an obligation to keep it confidential, before such information was disclosed to it by the other party,
(b) is or becomes public knowledge through no fault of its own,
(c) is independently developed by or for it,
(d) is disclosed by the other party to others without any restriction on use and disclosure, or
(e) is or becomes lawfully available to it from a source other than the other party.

21. Noncompetition

A customer naturally doesn't want the software developer it's hired to perform the same or similar work for a competitor, allowing the competitor to benefit from work originally paid for by the customer (and potentially divulging the customer's trade secrets as well).

A customer is protected from this problem to some extent in cases where it obtains ownership of the software. Theoretically, the developer can't use the work product on other projects because it doesn't own it. However, in practice it can be difficult to determine whether or not the developer is using the customer's software on other projects. Moreover, such a competitive use may not even be intentional: The developer may have difficulty separating the work bought and paid for by one customer from another, or from its own background technology.

Where the customer obtains an exclusive license to use the software, the developer has the right to use and/or distribute the software outside the area of the developer's exclusivity. And, of course, if the customer merely has a non-exclusive license, the developer has an unfettered right to use and/or resell the software to others. In either situation, the only way the customer can prevent the software from ending up in competitors' hands is through a noncompetition provision in the development agreement that prohibits the developer from working for competitors.

To be acceptable to the developer and enforceable in court, such a restriction must be drafted very narrowly. The sample clause below only prevents the developer from performing the exact same services that it performed for the customer for certain named competitors of the customer. This provision can be limited to the time the developer is working for the customer or it can be extended for a limited period afterwards (no more than two years would be considered acceptable by most courts).

> Developer agrees that during performance of the services required by this Agreement *("and for _____ after completion,")* Developer will not perform the same services for the following competitors of Customer: *(list competitors).*

Tip for developers. A developer should carefully consider the impact of a noncompetition agreement on its future business. If such a restriction may have a severe negative impact, the developer should either refuse to agree to it or demand additional money from the customer as compensation for its loss of future business. As a general rule, where a customer contracts with a developer because it specializes in a particular market niche—accounting programs for shoe stores, waterflow, stress on trees, for example—the developer should resist agreeing to future restrictions on its ability to work in its area of specialization. At most, such a developer might agree not to perform the same services for others while it's working for the customer.

22. Term of Agreement

The term of a software development should run from the date it is executed (signed by both parties) until full performance or earlier termination or cancellation.

> This Agreement commences on the date it is executed and shall continue until full performance by both parties, or until earlier terminated by one party under the terms of this Agreement.

23. Termination of Agreement

The language governing how the contract may end is very important to both parties. The provision set out below is fairly standard. It permits either party to terminate the agreement if the other materially breaches any of its contractual obligations and fails to remedy the breach within 30 days. A "material" breach means a breach that is serious, rather than minor or trivial. Missing a deadline by one day is not "material"; missing it by three months is.

For developers, the material breach most likely to result in termination is the customer's failure to pay the developer in a timely fashion. For customers, however, there are four likely material breaches that may result in termination of the contract:

1. The developer fails to deliver the system at the agreed-upon price.
2. The system will not perform in accordance with the specifications.
3. Delivery of the system is delayed past the deadline slippage period (usually 60 days).
4. The developer declares bankruptcy or becomes insolvent.

As a practical matter, that the customer has the right to terminate the contract upon the occurrence of any of these events does not necessarily mean it will do so. If the project is far along, it may be cheaper for the customer to pay the developer more, extend the delivery deadline and/or accept nonconforming software than to find another developer and start from scratch.

The following standard termination provision should be included in all agreements. Note that just because the agreement is terminated doesn't mean all obligations cease. Certain obligations are ongoing and survive even after termination. These should include the developer's obligation to indemnify the customer if it's sued for intellectual property infringement, as well as both parties' duty of confidentiality.

> Each party shall have the right to terminate this Agreement by written notice to the other if a party has materially breached any obligation herein and such breach remains uncured for a period of thirty (30) days after written notice of such breach is sent to the other party.
>
> The rights and obligations under the sections entitled "Intellectual Property Infringement Claims," "Confidentiality" and "General Provisions" shall continue to bind the parties after termination of the Agreement as provided herein.

The customer may want the option to terminate the agreement at its convenience if it decides for some reason it doesn't want to go through with the project. In this event, the customer should have to pay the developer all amounts due for accepted work and relinquish any rights in the software.

(Optional:) This Agreement may be terminated by Customer for its convenience upon thirty 30 days' prior written notice to Developer. Upon such termination, all amounts owed to Developer under this Agreement for accepted work shall immediately become due and payable and all rights and licenses granted by Developer to Customer under this Agreement shall immediately terminate.

The termination provision should specify who takes title to the software (assuming all or part of it has been completed) and how the monies previously paid to developer will be allocated. If the customer terminates the agreement because of the developer's default, it will want to do whatever makes the most economic sense. This may mean that the customer:

- keeps whatever work the developer has completed and lets the developer keep whatever it's owed for such work, or
- returns the software and gets all its money back (less the value of any services actually received and used by the customer).

Alternative 1 (customer terminates agreement): If this Agreement is terminated by Customer because of the Developer's default, Customer shall have the option to either:

(a) return to Developer all copies and portions of the Software and related materials and documentation in its possession furnished by Developer under this Agreement, whereupon Developer shall promptly return all monies received from Customer under this Agreement, less the reasonable value of those services actually received and used by Customer; if the parties are unable to agree upon the reasonable value of such services, they shall appoint an arbitrator to do so pursuant to the section of this Agreement entitled "Mediation and Arbitration"; or

(b) pay Developer all amounts owed or accrued for the work performed under this Agreement, whereupon all rights and licenses granted to Customer by Developer under this Agreement shall continue and survive royalty free and fully paid-up.

If the developer terminates the agreement because of the customer's default (usually because the customer has failed to pay the developer), the customer should return any software or other materials received from the developer and should pay the developer for the work it has done.

> **Alternative 2 (developer terminates agreement):** If Developer terminates this Agreement because of Customer's default, all of the following shall apply:
> (a) Customer shall immediately cease use of the Software.
> (b) Customer shall, within 10 days of such termination, deliver to Developer all copies and portions of the Software and related materials and documentation in its possession furnished by Developer under this Agreement.
> (c) All amounts payable or accrued to Developer under this Agreement shall become immediately due and payable.
> (d) All rights and licenses granted to Customer under this Agreement shall immediately terminate.

24. Insolvency

If a party goes bankrupt or becomes insolvent, its ability to carry out its contractual obligations is left in serious doubt. Therefore, it is standard in development agreements for a party's bankruptcy or insolvency to be considered an act of default giving the other party the option of terminating the agreement as provided above.

> If either party becomes insolvent, files a bankruptcy petition, becomes the subject of an involuntary bankruptcy petition, makes a general assignment for the benefit of creditors, has a receiver appointed for its assets, or ceases to conduct business, it shall be considered in default of this Agreement. If any of these events happen to a party, it shall immediately notify the other party.

TERMINATION AND BANKRUPTCY

An insolvency clause is customarily included in virtually all business contracts. However, you should be aware that it may not be enforceable if a bankruptcy proceeding is filed. When an insolvent debtor files for bankruptcy, all its assets and any contracts or licenses it has made come under the control of the official (trustee) appointed by the federal bankruptcy court to handle the case. To help give the debtor a fresh start and to avoid loss of the estate's resources, the debtor or bankruptcy trustee (an official appointed by the bankruptcy court to administer the debtor's affairs) has the power under the Bankruptcy Code to reject (terminate), with court approval, any executory (outstanding) contracts. In most cases where this occurs, the injured party is left with an unsecured claim against the bankruptcy estate. Depending upon the financial condition of the debtor, such a claim may be valuable; but in many cases it is worthless.

Virtually all uncompleted software development agreements would be considered "executory" and thus subject to rejection by a debtor or bankruptcy trustee. However, any license of intellectual property rights from the debtor to you can still remain effective. A special provision of the Bankruptcy Code (Section 365(n)) gives licensees of intellectual property (including software) certain rights that most other bankruptcy creditors don't have. If the debtor or trustee elect to reject a software license, the licensee has the option of either:

- treating the license as terminated by the rejection and pursuing any legal remedies the licensee may have—that is, filing a claim for damages against the bankruptcy estate, or
- retaining its rights under the license for the term of the license (and any contractually permitted extensions of the term).

If the licensee elects to retain its rights under the license, the debtor or bankruptcy trustee must allow it to exercise those rights. But the licensee must continue to pay any royalty amounts due under the license agreement. This is so even though the bankruptcy filing relieves the licensor from any obligation to perform maintenance services under the license agreement. However, if the parties entered into a source code escrow agreement, the licensee is entitled to obtain a copy of the program source code from the source code escrow holder so it can perform maintenance on its own (or hire someone else to do it).

25. Taxes

It is customary in custom software development agreements for the customer to pay any required state and local sales, use or property taxes.

> Customer shall be responsible for payment of all taxes based on work performed or products delivered under this Agreement except for all of Developer's income taxes and employment taxes.

26. Assignment

In the absence of a prohibition in the contract, either party generally may assign its rights and obligations under the contract. This means the developer may get a third party to perform some of the work, or even assign the entire contract to another developer. Such an unfettered right of assignment is usually not in the customer's best interests. A customer engages a particular software developer because of its expertise, reputation for performance and financial stability. As a result, the customer does not want the developer to subcontract work out to third parties without its knowledge and approval. Similarly, the developer may lose confidence if the customer assigns its duty to pay the developer to some third party.

The following provision bars either party from assigning its rights and duties under the agreement without the other's consent. However, it excepts assignments to a successor in interest of the customer if the customer is merged with or acquired by another company or reorganized. Absent such an exception, the customer may be in default of the agreement if any of these events occurs.

> Neither party may assign or subcontract its rights or obligations under this Agreement, either in whole or in part, without the prior written consent of the other party, which shall not be unreasonably withheld. Any attempt to do so shall be void and of no effect. However, Customer may assign without prior written consent its rights and obligations under this Agreement to a successor in interest due to Customer's acquisition, merger or reorganization.

Bankruptcy note. This assignment provision may not be enforceable against a party who files for bankruptcy. (See discussion of the impact of a bankruptcy filing at Section D23, above.)

27. Developer's Employees and Subcontractors

Following are several provisions concerning the developer's employees and subcontractors.

a.   Assignment of Rights by Employees or Subcontractors

As discussed in detail in Chapter 8, the copyright in software, documentation and similar works created by a developer's employee will automatically be owned by the developer only if created within the scope of employment. Copyrightable works created by an independent contractor will be owned by the developer only if assigned to it by the independent contractor.

This means that unless the developer obtains an assignment of intellectual property rights from its contractors, there is no way for either the customer or developer to know for sure whether the developer owns the copyright rights in software or other materials created by its employees or subcontractors. If the developer does not own these rights, it can't transfer or license them to the customer, so the customer ends up owning little or nothing, or lacks a valid license to the software.

To avoid this potential nightmare, the developer should:

- Have independent contractors sign consulting agreements assigning all intellectual property rights to the developer. (See Chapter 10 for a detailed discussion.)
- Have all employees sign employment agreements assigning their intellectual property rights in the software and other materials they create as part of their job to the developer. (See Chapter 9 for a detailed discussion.) If, for some reason, this is not possible (some

employees may refuse to sign an employment agreement, for example), the developer should have such workers sign an assignment agreement transferring their rights to the developer.

To protect the customer (and, in reality, the developer as well), the following provision requires the developer to either:

- provide the customer with signed copies of employment or consulting agreements with all employees and independent contractors who will work on the project assigning their rights in their work to the developer, or
- have employees or independent contractors sign an assignment agreement, which is attached as an exhibit to this agreement.

Here's a provision that covers these issues:

> Developer represents that before an employee or subcontractor of Developer performs any services required by this Agreement, Developer shall either:
>
> (a) provide Customer with a signed copy of an employment or independent contractor/consulting agreement effecting the assignment of such employee's or subcontractor's rights in all copyrightable or patentable software or other materials he or she creates as a result of the performance of work or services under this Agreement; or
>
> (b) deliver to Customer an Assignment of Rights ("the Assignment") in substantially the form attached hereto as Exhibit __ signed by such employee or subcontractor. Developer shall orally inform each employee or subcontractor of the substance of the Assignment before he or she executes such form.

An assignment form should be included as an exhibit to the agreement. A separate assignment form is included on the forms disk as ASSIGN.TXT. Here's what the assignment form should look like:

ASSIGNMENT OF INTELLECTUAL
PROPERTY RIGHTS

I am an employee or subcontractor of *(developer's name)*, hereafter referred to as "Developer." For good and valuable consideration, the sufficiency of which is hereby acknowledged, I assign my entire right, title and interest in all copyrightable or patentable writings, drawings, inventions, machines, designs, computer programs or process of my original creation first produced or created by me for Developer as a result of, or related to, performance of work or services under this Agreement.

This assignment is effective as of the date of the creation of any protectible works created under this Agreement. I will cooperate with any lawful efforts of Developer to register and enforce this assignment. I shall execute and aid in the preparation of any papers that Developer may consider necessary or helpful to obtain or maintain any copyrights, patents, or other proprietary rights at no charge to Developer, but at its expense. Developer shall reimburse me for reasonable out-of-pocket expenses incurred.

Employees/Subcontractors:

Name (typed or printed)   Signature

_____   _____

Date: _____

_____   _____

Date: _____

_____   _____

Date: _____

_____

Developer

By: _____

Date: _____

Accepted by: _____

By: _____

Date: _____

b. Key Employees

The customer may have engaged the developer primarily because of promises that certain highly able programmers and/or other key employees will be assigned to the project. In this event, the customer may want the right to terminate the agreement if such employees cease to be involved with the project and substitutes acceptable to the customer are not obtained.

> The parties agree that the services of *(name key employees)* are essential to the satisfactory performance by Developer of the services required by this Agreement. If such individual(s) leave the employ of Developer during the term of this Agreement for any reason or are unavailable to continue full-time the work called for in this Agreement, and if substitute individuals acceptable to Customer are not available to continue the work within _____ days, Customer shall have the right to terminate this Agreement upon thirty (30) days' written notice.

c. Nonsolicitation of Developer's Employees

One of a software developer's fears is that a customer will hire away a star programmer or other key employee and do future work on program enhancements and modifications in-house. The following provision is designed to give the developer some peace of mind.

> Customer agrees not to knowingly hire or solicit Developer's employees during performance of this Agreement and for a period of _____ after termination of this Agreement without Developer's written consent.

28. Mediation and Arbitration

Mediation and arbitration are two forms of "alternative dispute resolution"—means for settling disputes without resorting to expensive court litigation. Mediation is relatively informal, and by its nature is never binding. Typically, the mediator either sits the parties down together and tries to provide an objective view of their disputes, or shuttles between the parties as a cool conduit of what may be red-hot opinions. Where the real problem is a personality conflict or simple lack of communication, a good mediator can keep a minor controversy from shattering the relationship between software developer and customer. Where the argument is more serious, a mediator may be able to lead the parties to a mutually satisfactory resolution that will obviate time-consuming and expensive litigation.

In arbitration, an informal hearing is held before one or more arbitrators (usually attorneys or retired judges) who decide the merits of the issues and render a decision, which may or not be binding depending on the arbitration agreement. There are a number of professional arbitrators' organizations which conduct arbitrations, notably the American Arbitration Association which has offices in most major cities.

No one can be forced into mediation or arbitration; one must agree to it, either in the contract or later when a dispute arises. Commercial contracts often include binding arbitration provisions. However, this is not a matter to be agreed to lightly. By submitting to binding arbitration, you're basically giving up your constitutional right of access to the courts.

Arbitration has many good points. It is usually faster and cheaper than court litigation. Also, because the parties choose the arbitrator, they can select someone who is familiar with computer and software law. Such a person might be expected to render a better decision than a judge or jury with no familiarity with the software business.

However, arbitration can also have a down side. Litigants have often found that arbitrators seek to reach a compromise between the parties' positions rather than ruling squarely in favor of one or the other. Under the rules of the American Arbitration Association (which are most commonly used in arbitrations), no questioning of the parties or witnesses is allowed before the hearing (a process lawyers call discovery). This can lead to unfair results. Moreover, conducting an arbitration will not necessarily keep the parties out of court. If a party receives a bad result in an arbitration, it will often seek to have a court vacate (void) it. A court can do this if it finds the arbitrator guilty of misconduct, bias, fraud or corrupt (but proving this is extremely difficult). Finally, an arbitrator's decision is not self-enforcing; it must be entered with a court. In some cases (obtaining a quick restraining order, for example), you're better off going to court in the first place.

An arbitration clause can and should be drafted to avoid the kind of problems described above. The following clause attempts to do this.

 If the other side won't agree to the safeguards provided in this clause, you're better off without an arbitration clause.

Except for the right of either party to apply to a court of competent jurisdiction for a temporary restraining order or preliminary injunction to preserve the status quo or prevent irreparable harm pending the selection and confirmation of a panel of arbitrators, and for the right of Developer to bring suit on an open account for simple monies due Developer, any dispute arising under this Agreement shall be resolved through a mediation-arbitration approach. The parties agree to first try to resolve the dispute informally with the help of a mutually agreed-upon mediator. If it proves impossible to arrive at a mutually satisfactory solution through mediation, the parties agree to submit their dispute to binding arbitration in accordance with the Commercial Arbitration Rules of the American Arbitration Association.

The arbitration may be conducted by one impartial arbitrator by mutual agreement or by three arbitrators if the parties are unable to agree on a single arbitrator within 30 days of first demand for arbitration. All arbitrators are to be selected from a panel provided by the

American Arbitration Association. The chair shall be an attorney at law, and the other arbitrators shall have a background or training either in computer law, computer software technology or marketing of computer software products.

Upon request of a party, the arbitrators shall have the authority to permit discovery to the extent they deem appropriate. A court reporter shall record the arbitration hearing and the reporter's transcript shall be the official transcript of the proceeding. The arbitrators shall have no power to add or detract from the agreements of the parties and may not make any ruling or award that does not conform to the terms and conditions of this Agreement. The arbitrators shall have the authority to grant injunctive relief in a form substantially similar to that which would otherwise be granted by a court of law. The arbitrators shall have no authority to award punitive damages or any other damages not measured by the prevailing party's actual damages. The arbitrators shall specify the basis for any damage award and the types of damages awarded. The decision of the arbitrators shall be final and binding on the parties and may be entered and enforced in any court of competent jurisdiction by either party.

The prevailing party in the arbitration proceedings shall be awarded reasonable attorney fees, expert witness costs and expenses, and all other costs and expenses incurred directly or indirectly in connection with the proceedings, unless the arbitrators shall for good cause determine otherwise.

29. General Provisions

Following are several provisions that are customarily lumped together at the end of a software development agreement. This does not mean they are unimportant.

a. Complete Agreement

Computer software agreements normally contain a provision stating that the agreement constitutes the complete and exclusive agreement between the parties and supersedes all prior agreements made by the parties that are not expressly stated or incorporated in the agreement. This is also known as a "merger and integration" clause.

> This Agreement together with all exhibits, appendices or other attachments, which are incorporated herein by reference, is the sole and entire Agreement between the parties relating to the subject matter hereof. This Agreement supersedes all prior understandings, agreements and documentation relating to such subject matter. In the event of a conflict between the provisions of the main body of the Agreement and any attached exhibits, appendices or other materials, the Agreement shall take precedence.

Because of this clause, the customer must make sure that all documents containing any representations upon which the customer is relying are attached to the agreement as exhibits. This may include the developer's sales literature, side letters and so forth. If they aren't attached, they won't be considered to be part of the agreement. However, the customer's sales literature and specifications may contain provisions conflicting with other terms of the agreement or with each other. The parties should be sure to review such documents and delete any outdated or inappropriate statements before they are attached to the agreement. The clause does, however, provide that the main agreement has precedence if there is a conflict.

b. Modifications to Agreement

The following provision, which is very important, states that any changes to the agreement must be in writing and agreed to by both parties to be effective. This provision protects both parties; reducing all modifications to writing lessens the possibility of misunderstandings. In addition, oral modifications may not be legally binding.

> Modifications and amendments to this Agreement, including any exhibit or appendix hereto, shall be enforceable only if they are in writing and are signed by authorized representatives of both parties.

For an example of how to format a contract modification, see Section D5, above. The format for the Development Plan Modification Agreement in that section can be used for any contract modification; simply change the title of the document to "Contract Modification."

CONTRACT CHANGES IN THE REAL WORLD

In the real world, people make changes to their contracts all the time and never write them down. If the changes are very minor, this might not pose a problem. But be aware that a contract alteration might not be legally binding if it is not written down. And, of course, if a dispute develops, the lack of a writing will make it difficult to prove what you actually agreed to.

If you agree to a minor contract change (over the phone, for example) and don't want to go to the trouble of dealing with a formal signed contract modification, at least send a confirming letter to the other party setting forth the gist of what you've agreed to. This isn't as good as a signed contract modification, but it will be helpful if a dispute later develops.

c.   Waiver

The following clause requires that any waiver by a party of any of its rights under the Agreement must be in writing to be effective. Again, this prevents possible misunderstandings caused by oral agreements.

> No term or provision of this Agreement shall be deemed waived and no breach excused unless such waiver or consent is in writing and signed by the party claimed to have waived or consented.

d.   No Agency

The parties want to make sure they are viewed as separate entities, not partners or co-venturers liable for each other's debts and with the power to bind each other to third parties.

> Nothing contained herein will be construed as creating any agency, partnership, joint venture or other form of joint enterprise between the parties.

e.   Developer an Independent Contractor

The customer does not want the developer to be considered its employee and therefore be liable for withholding income taxes, social security taxes and even for providing the developer with health insurance and other employee benefits. The following paragraph is designed to make clear the developer is an independent contractor.

⚠ Simply including this paragraph in the Agreement will not automatically make the developer an independent contractor. To qualify as an independent contractor, the customer must not have the right to control the developer. See Chapter 7 for a detailed discussion of who qualifies as an independent contractor.

> The parties acknowledge that Developer will perform its obligations hereunder as an independent contractor. The manner and method of performing such obligations will be under Developer's sole control and discretion; Customer's sole interest is in the result of such services. It is also expressly understood that Developer's employees and agents, if any, are not Customer's employees or agents, and have no authority to bind Customer by contract or otherwise.

f. Notices

The following provision is self-explanatory:

> All notices and other communications required or permitted under this Agreement shall be in writing and shall be deemed given when delivered personally, or five days after being deposited in the United States mail, postage prepaid and addressed as follows, or to such other address as each party may designate in writing:
>
> Customer: *(name and mailing address)*
>
> Developer: *(name and mailing address)*

g. Attorney Fees

A provision such as the following is found in many contracts. If either party has to sue the other in court to enforce the agreement and wins (is the "prevailing party") the loser is required to pay the prevailing party's attorney fees and expenses. Be aware, however, that not all courts will enforce such a provision.

> If any action at law or in equity is necessary to enforce the terms of this Agreement, the prevailing party shall be entitled to reasonable attorney fees, costs and expenses, in addition to any other relief to which it may be entitled.

h. Applicable Law

The choice of law provision is usually not an issue. The contract laws of the various states are almost identical, so there is usually no legal advantage obtained from applying one state's law. But there is some advantage to having the law of your own state govern, since your local attorney will likely be more familiar with that law.

> This Agreement will be governed by the laws of the State of
> _____ .

i. Severability

The following is a standard provision that permits the agreement as a whole to continue even if portions of it are found invalid by a court or arbitrator.

> If any provision of this Agreement is held invalid, void or unenforceable under any applicable statute or rule of law, it shall to that extent be deemed omitted, and the balance of this Agreement shall be enforceable in accordance with its terms.

i. Headings Not Controlling

The following standard clause is self-explanatory:

> The headings in this Agreement are for reference purposes only and shall not be construed as a part of this Agreement.

30. Signatures

The end of the main body of the agreement should contain spaces for the parties to sign.

> Each party represents and warrants that on this date they are duly authorized to bind their respective principals by their signatures below.

_____

(Name of Developer)

By: _____

Title: _____

Date: _____

_____

(Name of Customer)

By: _____

Title: _____

Date: _____

31. Exhibits

The parties should make sure that all exhibits are attached to all copies of the agreement. Each exhibit should be consecutively numbered or letters ("A,B,C" or "1,2,3"). Also, the references to the exhibits in the main body of the agreement should match the actual exhibits. The exhibits to the agreement will include:

- the Functional Specification (see Section B1, above);
- the Development Plan (see Section D3, above);
- the developer's list of Background Technology (see Section D11, above); and
- the form for the assignment of intellectual property rights by the developer's employees and contractors (see Section D25a, above).

 Skip to Chapter 1, Section D, for information about how to put the agreement together. ■

CHAPTER 12

Software Author's Guide to Publishing Agreements

Here we discuss contracts for software that will be distributed to the general public, as opposed to custom software that is created to meet the needs of a particular customer (covered in Chapter 11). Because the focus of this chapter is to help the programmer/software writer understand and negotiate a publishing agreement with a software publisher, advice and sample contracts are presented from the author's point of view.

Note: *From time to time, you may need to refer to Chapter 11 for more detailed information.*

A. Introduction

In the early days of the personal computer, popular programs were often created by individual programmers (sometimes in the proverbial garage or basement), who then often sold the programs themselves. Marketing could be done fairly effectively and cheaply through mail order and trade shows.

Things have obviously changed. In today's competitive marketplace, few commercially successful programs are created single-handedly by individual programmers, and fewer still are marketed by their creators. Creating the more sophisticated software of the 1990s is usually a collaborative process, often requiring the work of dozens, or even hundreds, of people. Once a program is completed, it can cost tens of thousands—and sometimes millions—of dollars to effectively market it. For these reasons, the field is now dominated by established software publishers, not by the basement programmer.

Some publishers create their software mostly in-house and have little or no interest in publishing work by nonemployees. Many others, however, are at least somewhat receptive to outside ideas and are willing to publish innovative software supplied by outsiders. This chapter is designed to help the independent software author understand and negotiate a software publishing agreement with such a publisher.

The type of agreement covered in this chapter is one in which a programmer (we'll use the word "author" here) agrees to perform all or a substantial amount of the work necessary to develop a new program, or agrees to sell an existing program to a publisher in return for a royalty.

⚠ Independent contractors are not authors. Software publishers often hire outside programmers and others on an hourly or fixed fee basis to help them develop specific products. Such individuals are not independent software "authors" within the legal definition of this term. Rather, they are independent contractors performing specific tasks on a publisher's behalf. An independent contractor's relationship with the publisher should be governed by an independent contractor agreement, not by the type of author's contract covered here. (See Chapter 10.)

B. Key Provisions in Software Publishing Agreements

When a software author enters negotiations with a software publisher, he or she will likely be presented with a form publishing agreement drawn up by the publisher's lawyers, or perhaps a form agreement obtained from the Software Publisher's Association ("SPA")—the software publishers' trade association. Needless to say, this agreement will have been written with the publisher's interests in uppermost mind, not the author's.

Some authors sign the publisher's form agreement without studying and understanding it, an act they often come to regret. First, you should go over each clause of the contract and make sure you understand it. Then you should be ready to negotiate to improve all provisions you conclude are unacceptable or inadequate. To help you do this, we discuss below the key provisions that are typically included in such agreements.

In this chapter, we've included a number of sample contract clauses that you may wish to modify and include in your publishing contract. Unlike those you'll likely find in a publisher's form agreement, these provisions tend to be more favorable (and, of course, fairer) to the author than the publisher. Whether a publisher will agree to include a significant number of author-fair provisions in its contract with you is impossible to predict. In some instances, your only option will be to sign the publisher's agreement as written, or find another publisher. But, more typically, if the publisher is anxious to publish your software, it will be willing to negotiate at least some significant changes. At the very least, the discussion that follows should demonstrate to you that you are perfectly reasonable if you insist that the publisher's way is not the only approach to write a software publishing contract.

The full text of the clauses in this chapter are all on the forms disk, under CLSPUB.TXT. See Chapter 1, Sections C and D, for instructions on using the forms disk and preparing your documents.

1. Royalties

Obviously, the question of how, and how much, the publisher will pay you is of primary concern. Despite what a publisher may tell you, royalty amounts are almost always negotiable—at least within reasonable limits. This tends to be true even where a publisher has a take-it-or-leave-it attitude toward the rest of the terms in the contract.

There are a variety of ways a publisher may compensate a software author, each with its good and bad points. Let's look at the most commonly used compensation schemes.

FIXED ROYALTY AGREEMENTS

The simplest royalty arrangement is for the publisher to pay you a fixed sum, either at one time or in installments. For example, a publisher might offer you $50,000 paid in three installments—to be paid regardless of how well or how poorly the software actually sells. Clearly, this sort of cash buy-out of your ownership rights reduces both your risk and potential gain.

The big problem with a fixed royalty is determining a fair amount. It's very difficult to accurately estimate how well a new software product will do in the marketplace. Publishers usually make conservative estimates and offer to pay royalties accordingly. As a result, a fixed royalty may end up being substantially less than an author would have received under a per copy or percentage royalty scheme. So, as a general rule, unless the publisher offers a truly munificent sum, a fixed royalty is best rejected.

But what if you badly need an up-front cash infusion? Isn't a fixed royalty with a good sized chunk up front a good choice? Probably not. Because most publishers pay cash advances on percentage royalty contracts, you should be able to get the up-front cash you need without having to accept a fixed royalty. (See Section B1b, below.)

a. Percentage Royalties

By far the most common (and flexible) royalty arrangement is a percentage royalty—that is, a royalty based on a percentage of money the publisher earns from selling your software. Percentage royalties for software are almost always figured on the basis of "net receipts"—that is, dollars actually received by the publisher—not on gross sales, which typically refers to the suggested retail price. It is crucial that you clearly understand this difference.

Software publishers normally sell consumer software (and often business productivity software) at a steep discount to resellers (wholesalers and retailers). Often the publisher nets only 40%-50% of the retail sales dollar.

Thus, on a program priced at $100, a publisher may only end up with $45, and a royalty based on 10% of the net receipts dollar will result in a royalty of $4.50 per copy sold.

Example: *Nick and Nora develop a new personal productivity software package. Scribe Software Systems, Inc. agrees to publish and distribute it. Scribe agrees to pay Nick and Nora a 10% royalty based on net receipts. The listed retail price on the package will be $200, but Scribe sells it to wholesalers and retailers at a 50-60% discount off the list price. Because the 10% royalty is based on net receipts, Nick and Nora will not receive 10% of $200; instead, they are going to get 10% of the dollars Scribe actually receives—10% of $80-$100 netted for each sale.*

Depending on how savvy Nick and Nora are in negotiating software contracts, Scribe may try to subtract other expenses from the "net" figure. For example, Scribe may want to deduct some promotional costs. (For more on this, see "How are 'Net Receipts' Defined?" below.) In addition, Scribe's net will be reduced by the amount of refunds it will have to make when copies of the product are returned by distributors because they do not sell. So Nick and Nora will at best receive $8-$10 per unit sold (10% of Scribe's $80-$100 net return on each sale).

WHY ROYALTIES AREN'T BASED ON RETAIL PRICE

In theory, it is possible to base royalties on the retail price of software. (This is how authors of general audience books have traditionally been paid.) For example, the author could be paid 10% of $79.95—the price listed on the box. But just about all software publishers insist on basing authors' percentage royalties on the dollars they receive, not on full retail price. This is because:

- much consumer, business productivity and educational software is sold through mass retailing channels at a deep discount (it's a mark-it-up to mark-it-down business),
- software marketing costs are often high, and
- there is often a high rate of returns.

There are two main issues concerning percentage royalties that you should consider when negotiating a percentage royalty: the amount of the royalty and how "net receipts" are defined.

• *How big is the royalty?* Software royalty rates normally range from 5% to 20% of net receipts, with an average of about 12%-15%. Royalties are often based on a sliding scale, with the percentage going up as total sales increase. For example, a royalty of 5% of net might be paid on the first 5,000 copies sold or licensed, 7% on the next 5,000, 9% on the next five thousand, and 12% thereafter.

Obviously, if you expect sales to be substantial, you can obtain a much greater total return by agreeing to a low initial royalty in return for a much higher royalty as sales grow. But don't get carried away— very few programs sell huge numbers, and many publishers make a good living by romancing authors into accepting large royalty payments for big sales numbers they are unlikely ever to see, in exchange for accepting smaller than normal royalties for initial sales that are almost sure to happen.

Royalty rates may vary according to geographic area or market segment. For example, proposed royalties for domestic sales are typically higher than royalties for foreign sales, where a publisher's costs may be higher. Special (often lower) royalty rates may also be set for sales made directly through the mail to consumers, where costs typically gobble up more of net receipts than is true for sales to retail channels.

In addition, different royalty rates may apply to software bundled (grouped) with other programs, software licensed to hardware manufacturers for distribution with their machines and other special markets.

Here's an example of a sliding scale royalty provision that also contains several special royalty rates:

Royalties: The Author shall receive the following royalties:

(a) A percentage of Publisher's net receipts from each copy of the Software, or any portion of it, distributed by Publisher for use in the United States (except as otherwise provided below) as follows:

5% of the first 5,000 copies,

7% of the next 5,000 copies,

10% of the next 5,000 copies,

12% on all copies over 15,000,

(b) 5% of net receipts from each copy of the Software or any portion of it distributed directly through the mail to consumers, and

(c) 5% of net receipts from each copy of the Software or portion of it distributed by Publisher to third parties for use outside the United States.

• *How are "net receipts" defined?* You might think that net receipts simply means the actual amount the publisher receives from a distributor for your software—typically, 55% to 65% of the price on the box. Not so. Many publishers include all sorts of allowances and deductions in contract clauses defining net receipts for royalty purposes. From their point of view, there's an excellent reason for this; it reduces the amount the publisher has to pay you. So from your point of view, it's very important that the contract clearly define "net receipts." Obviously, the fewer items deducted from the amount the publisher receives for the software, the more money you, the author, will earn. Although this "fine print" may seem technical and boring, it's important that you seek to limit deductions from the money the publisher receives to only discounts, returns and refunds. For example, if the publisher proposes deducting packaging, marketing, advertising or trade show costs as well, you should just say no or, at the very least, bargain to set a maximum dollar limit on these costs.

Another important issue is whether the royalties are calculated based on shipment of the software from the publisher's warehouse or only when payment is actually received. It is far preferable for the author's royalties to be based on the amount shipped by the publisher, since some customers will never pay their bills. Bad debts and credit risks are traditional risks of the publishing business that the publisher should assume, not the author.

Here is an example of a net receipts definition favorable to the author:

> **Net Receipts Defined:** "Net receipts" is defined as all monies payable to Publisher from the licensing, sale or other commercial exploitation of the Software, minus quantity and cash discounts actually allowed and credits allowed for returned goods.

b. Royalty Advances

It is reasonable for you to ask the publisher for an up-front cash payment or payments, particularly if you will have to spend substantial time and effort designing, programming and otherwise putting the software into publishable form. From an author's point of view, negotiating a cash advance against future royalties is often a better approach than bargaining for an up-front payment that isn't tied to royalties. This is because, as noted in "Fixed Royalty Agreements," Section B1, above, the latter approach will almost always mean that a publisher will offer a much smaller ongoing royalty.

An advance normally takes the form of one or more cash payments, made before a program is published, which will be deducted against the author's royalties when the software is sold. Even if the software is nearly or completely finished when you approach a publisher, an advance payment will help tide you over until the software is published and royalties start coming in.

Advances can either be "refundable" or "nonrefundable." An advance is "refundable" when the author is supposed to repay it if the software is never published—for example, because the author is unable to finish it or the finished product is deemed unacceptable by the publisher. An advance is "nonrefundable" if the author is entitled to keep it no matter what.

Obviously then, if you provide the publisher with a finished product that the publisher accepts, the advance should be nonrefundable, since the publisher has already decided to market the product. However, it's more reasonable for a publisher to bargain for a refundable or partially refundable advance where you have yet to finish the product.

Authors sometimes ask what happens if a publisher demands that a refundable advance be returned, perhaps because the program was never finished. As a practical matter, authors typically spend the advance soon after it is received, so it can be very difficult or impossible for the publisher to obtain a refund. The publisher could always sue the author for the advance, but this can be expensive and won't do much good if the author doesn't have sufficient assets to pay any court judgment the publisher obtains. However, if the author has good income from other projects and the refundable advance was large, a publisher may go to court to seek its return.

A major issue of any contract providing for an author's advance is when the advance will be paid. Of course, it's better for the author to receive the entire advance in a single payment, or at least to receive a substantial first payment. But realizing that no matter what a contract says about refundability, a publisher is unlikely to recoup money paid out in the form of an advance, publishers often seek to pay advances in installments. Often, the publisher proposes that each payment be based on the author's achieving certain programming benchmarks (also called "milestones"). This way, the publisher's financial exposure is reduced if very little of the software is ever delivered and the project is canceled.

As mentioned above, the advance is normally repaid by the author by deducting it from the author's royalties. This means that if the advance is substantial, you may receive few or no royalties for some time, even if the program is selling well. To help with your cash flow, some publishers will agree to deduct the advance only against 50% of each royalty payment. This means the advance will take twice as long to repay, but you will have some income in the interim.

Many publishers are willing to increase their initial advance offer if you make it a key negotiating point. Never be afraid to ask. All the publisher can do is say no—it is very unlikely to cause the publisher to withdraw from the project.

Here's a contract provision for an author's advance that is favorable to the author: the advance is paid at one time (no installments), is nonrefundable and is recouped against only 50% of the author's royalty payments:

Author's Advance: Publisher shall pay to Author, upon execution of this Agreement, the amount of $15,000 as a nonrefundable advance royalty. Such advance royalty shall be recouped by Publisher by applying credits in the amount of 50% of earned royalties otherwise payable to Author under this Agreement to reduce the amounts otherwise so payable.

HOW BIG AN ADVANCE?

You should always try to get as large an advance as possible; an advance is money in hand right away. Also, publishers are often more likely to actively promote a program they have spent a lot for, if for no other reason than to try and prove themselves savvy businesspeople. There is no formula for determining the amount of an advance. The amount will be influenced by:

- how badly the publisher wants your program and how well it thinks the software will sell,
- what rights you're willing to give up (you should get a larger advance if you give up all your property ownership rights in the program, and a smaller advance if you keep some; see Section B2, below),
- your track record with previous software you've published, if any,
- the publisher's experience selling similar software, and
- the publisher's financial health.

c. No Royalty Due on Free Copies

Catalogs and 800 number software sellers that advertise in computer magazines often will not advertise and sell a publisher's product unless that publisher gives them numerous free copies. When orders are received, this "free" software is sold first and the publisher receives nothing for these sales. Only if more software is ordered than the publisher exchanged for the ad will the publisher make any money. Free software is often exchanged for other promotional considerations, sometimes even to put the software on the shelf.

Not surprisingly, most publishers include in their contracts provisions relieving them from the responsibility of paying the author a royalty for software traded for ads, promotions and shelf space. Here's a sample provision, which is reasonable for you to agree to:

> **Royalties and Software Traded for Promotion:** Publisher may trade copies of the Software for print advertising and catalog allowances free of the requirement to pay royalties to Author on such Software.

d. Reserve for Returns

Most mass-marketed software is normally returnable by the distributor—that is, the distributor may return unsold product to the publisher and get its money back. Some retail outlets often return a large percentage of what they order. Most publishers permit such returns to be made six months or even one year after the software is shipped to the distributor. Since royalties are only owed for software that is really sold (not returned), a publisher who pays royalties based on the original shipment of software could end up overpaying an author for a given royalty period if it doesn't make any up-front deduction for potential future returns. To avoid this, many publishing contracts permit the publisher to retain a portion of the monies due the author on the royalty statement as a hedge against the fact that some software is likely to be returned. This is called a "reserve for returns."

This practice is not unreasonable so long as the reserve—that is, the amount deducted from your royalties—is reasonable. As an author, you should avoid a contract that allows a "reasonable reserve" to be withheld from your royalties, since this is an invitation to the publisher to withhold far too much. Instead, negotiate for a specific percentage of royalties to be withheld. Depending on the type of software, a 10% to 25% reserve against returns should be reasonable. Also, the time period during that a reserve is withheld should be limited, since publishers permit distributors to return software only for a limited period. The publisher should credit you for all accumulated, unused reserves no later than three royalty accounting periods after the reserved royalties originally were earned.

> **Reserve for Returns:** In making accountings, Publisher shall have the right to allow for a reasonable reserve for returns from the amounts due Author, not to exceed 20%. Publisher shall pay Author any royalties reserved but not applied to returns with the payment due for the third royalty period after the reserved royalties have accrued. If a reserve is withheld for an accounting period, the royalty statement for that period shall set forth: (1) the amount being withheld, and (2) how any amounts previously withheld have been applied to Author's royalty account.

Example: *Nick and Nora's personal productivity software package is published by Scribe Software Systems. The publishing contract contains a reserve for a returns clause like that set forth above. Nick and Nora's royalties are paid quarterly. Scribe sells 1,000 units of the software the first quarter it is published and earns $100,000 in net receipts. Nick and Nora receive a 10% royalty based on Scribe's net receipts; thus they earned $10,000 in first quarter royalties. However, Scribe only pays Nick and Nora $8,000, retaining $2,000 (20%) as a reserve against returns. Over the next nine months, 100 units originally sold in the first quarter are returned, and Scribe must refund the money it received for these sales, amounting to $10,000. Scribe also deducts $1,000 from Nick and Nora's reserve account; this is the amount of royalties Scribe paid Nick and Nora for the returned software. At the end of the third royalty period (nine months after publication), Scribe pays Nick and Nora $1,000, the unused amount withheld from the first quarter royalties.*

e. Time of Payment

Publishers typically pay royalties quarterly (every three months) or twice a year. A publishing agreement calling for royalty payments less than twice a year is unreasonable—why should the publisher be able to use the author's money for such an extended period? Quarterly payments are obviously much more desirable for the author.

Publishers usually pay their authors two or three months after a royalty period ends. It would be better for you, of course, to be paid more quickly. You can ask to be paid no later than 30 days after each royalty period ends, but it is unlikely a publisher would agree to vary its accounting mechanism for one author.

Here is an example of a provision requiring quarterly payments within 30 days after each quarter ends:

> **Time of Royalty Payments:** Publisher shall make royalty payments to Author within 30 days after the end of the calendar quarter in which such royalties become due. Thus, royalties will be paid by April 30 for the quarter January 1 through March 31, and so on.

f. Protection Against Nonpayment of Royalties

Publishers have been known to pay authors less than they really owe, either because of accounting errors or because they're dishonest. One way to guard against poor publisher accounting practices and help ensure that you are properly compensated under the agreed-upon royalty arrangement is to ask that your royalties be accompanied by a statement giving sufficient information to enable you see whether the royalty was calculated correctly. For example, if your royalty is a percentage of "net receipts," and net receipts are defined to allow the publisher to subtract some costs from the actual dollars it receives, you should ask that the publisher's royalty statements report dollar amounts for all the factors that define "net receipts." Here's a provision requiring this:

Royalty Statements: Publisher shall submit to Author within 30-90 days after the end of each royalty period a clearly itemized statement separately setting forth the quantity and price of Software shipped, sublicensed and/or transferred, the total receipts amount received by the Publisher, all deductions made from gross receipts to arrive at the "net receipts" amount upon which royalties are paid, and the Author's royalty.

Unfortunately, some publishers do not provide all this information in their royalty statements, and if they don't, they will likely refuse your request to change their accounting practices, claiming it's too much trouble to satisfy a single author. Leaving aside the point that, of course, this is something all authors would like, you should at least insist that the publisher agree to a clause that allows you to obtain royalty and net receipts information upon your written request:

Author's Right to Information: Upon written request by Author, Publisher shall promptly furnish the following information as to any specific royalty period: the quantity and price of Software shipped, sublicensed and/or transferred, the total receipts amount received by the Publisher, and all deductions made from gross receipts to arrive at the "net receipts" amount upon which royalties were paid.

You should also have the right to audit (examine) the publisher's records to determine whether proper royalties have been paid. If the agreement does not contain such a provision, you may have to file a lawsuit for an accounting—an expensive proposition. It's customary for the author to pay for any requested audit unless major discrepancies are found, in which event the publisher should reimburse the author. The following provision gives the author an unfettered right to conduct accountings and requires the publisher to pay for them if errors of 5% or more are found.

Author's Right to Examine Records: Author and/or Author's agent shall have the right, upon five days notice, to examine all of Publisher's records relating to the production and distribution of the Software and the receipt of payment with respect thereto. Such examination shall take place at the place where they are regularly maintained during usual business hours. If such examination discloses an error of 5% or more with respect to any royalty statement, Publisher shall reimburse Author for Author's costs of the examination; otherwise, such costs shall be borne by Author.

Publisher's form agreements often attempt to impose a time limit on the author's right to sue for short payments. For example, a form agreement prepared by the Software Publisher's Association provides that unless the author challenges the information on a royalty report within one year, such information is conclusively deemed to be correct and legally binding on the author. In most states, a lawsuit alleging a breach of a publishing agreement can be filed anytime within four years. Thus, a clause with time limits substantially waives your legal rights and should be strongly resisted. It's best that the agreement state no time limit on your right to file suit.

2. Ownership of the Published Software

Another crucial issue that the publishing agreement must address is ownership of the software. Because of the nature of the legal protection afforded software authors, we talk here primarily about ownership of the copyright in the software. This is because most software does not qualify for patent protection (see Chapter 5). In addition, trade secret protection for mass-marketed software is limited to the time that it is being developed; once software is distributed to the public at large, its trade secret protection normally ceases to exist. (See the discussion in Chapter 4.)

As we discuss in detail in Chapter 3, the creator of a piece of software automatically acquires a bundle of exclusive copyright rights in that software.

These include:

- the exclusive right to make copies of the software,
- the right to distribute it to the public (publish it),
- the right to create derivative works based upon it (see the sidebar below), and
- the right to perform it in public (for example, demonstrate the software at computer shows).

DERIVATIVE WORKS

"Derivative works" refers to types of future works based upon (derived from) your software. This includes updates and enhancements of your original software, versions of the software designed to run on different operating systems (Macintosh, DOS, UNIX, Windows, Next-Step), and even new programs incorporating all or part of your program (unless the agreement restricts this right).

In return for the promise of a royalty and/or other compensation, you will transfer some or all of your rights to a publisher. Software publishers usually want to acquire all your rights. However, it should be emphasized that there is no legal or practical reason, aside from a publisher's insistence, for you to transfer your entire bundle of copyright rights.

Two basic types of ownership transfer are common:

- an assignment of all rights, or
- a granting of a license.

a. All Rights Assignments

If the publishing agreement contains language stating that you transfer to the publisher "all right, title and interest" to your software and supporting materials throughout the world, it means that you're giving the publisher all your copyright rights. The publisher obtains exclusive ownership of the code, the screens, the manuals and everything else. Not only does this mean the publisher has the exclusive right to sell the existing program in all markets, it also gives the publisher the exclusive right to create derivative works based upon the software. This means you can't, without the publisher's permission, use a substantial portion of the code in other software you create.

In addition, when you agree to an all rights transfer, you give up more than your copyright rights in the program code. This is because copyright protection goes beyond a program's literal source code. Depending on a number of factors, copyright *may* also protect a program's "structure, sequence and organization," the "user interface," and even, in some circumstances, its "look and feel." (See Chapter 3 for a detailed discussion.) This *could* mean that an author who has transferred copyright ownership to a publisher would violate the publisher's copyright rights if he or she developed a program for somebody else with similar menus or an otherwise similar user interface, or even with a similar overall design or structure. If the later program was successful, it could be well worth the publisher's time and money to sue you to get a piece of the profit.

Obviously, you should obtain a large royalty and/or lump sum payment for giving up all your rights in your creation. In addition, you may typically want to reserve the right to create similar programs in the future, so long as the resulting program doesn't directly compete with the publisher's product. You should also definitely retain control over those developmental tools included in the software that you'll want to use again. (See Section B2c, below, for a detailed discussion.)

b. Licenses

Instead of giving up all your exclusive copyright rights, you can retain them and grant the publisher permission to exercise one or more on a limited basis. Such a grant is called a "license." A license can be either "exclusive" or "nonexclusive." As the term implies, when you grant a publisher an exclusive license to exercise one or more of your copyright rights, no one else in world can exercise that right for the term of the license without the publisher's permission—not even you.

On the other hand, you can license your rights on a nonexclusive basis to any number of publishers and also exercise them yourself. Thus, for example, if you give Publisher X an exclusive license to copy and distribute your programs, that means that no one else can do so. But if you give it only a nonexclusive license, it means you can grant nonexclusive licenses to other publishers as well.

As mentioned, whether exclusive or nonexclusive, you may limit a license in any one of dozens of ways. Common limitations include:

- *Operating system limitations.* A license may be, and often is, limited to a particular operating system—*WINDOWS,* for example.
- *Hardware limitations.* A license may be limited to a particular type of hardware—PCs or Macintoshes, for example.
- *Time limitations.* The copyright in your software will last for over 50 years (see Chapter 3), but this does not mean that your transfer of rights must last for the entire life of the copyright. You may limit it to any time period you desire. For example, you could grant a three-year license to market your program, renewable for an additional three years if the publisher exercises an option to publish an updated version within that period.
- *Geographic limitations.* Your license may be limited to a particular geographic area—for example, North America.
- *Marketing limitations.* Your license may be limited to a particular market segment—for example, a sophisticated personnel management program could be licensed only for use by Fortune 1000 companies.

As noted, your whole bundle of copyright rights need not be licensed. The rights a publisher is interested in are primarily your right to:

- copy the software and distribute it to the public,
- create derivative works based upon it, and, to a lesser extent,
- perform it in public—for example, at computer shows.

These rights may be licensed on an exclusive or nonexclusive basis in any combination. For example, if you design a hot new game, you could give your publisher an exclusive license to copy and distribute your software, but no right (license) to create derivative works based on it. This way, you have retained the right to make and market a new version of the game. Or you can divide the market for the software. For example, you might give your publisher an exclusive license to copy and distribute your software in the United States, but only a nonexclusive license overseas; you could grant an exclusive license for the Mac but only a nonexclusive license for PCs; or you could grant an exclusive license for two years and a nonexclusive license thereafter.

Here's an example of a license limited as to geography, time and hardware:

License: Author hereby grants Publisher an exclusive license to use, reproduce, market and sublicense the Software and supporting documentation for use only in connection with Apple Macintosh computers. This license is limited to the United States. This license shall commence on the date of execution of this Agreement and terminate five years thereafter.

Avoid giving an unlimited license to a limited publisher. Limited licensing schemes such as that above may make sense where the publisher you're dealing with has experience and expertise in certain markets, but not in others. For example, if Publisher X has never sold a program outside the United States, you might prefer to retain your foreign rights and grant them to another publisher with foreign sales experience.

However, you'll find that many publishers will demand a very broad license—that is, one not containing many of the limitations outlined above—as a condition of publishing your software. Although some bargaining may be possible, publishers will be reluctant to limit their market for your software. Also, weigh in the fact that a publisher that is willing to accept a limited exclusive license or a nonexclusive license may not be willing to invest substantial resources marketing your product and will likely pay a lower royalty than for an exclusive license.

c. Background Technology

Most independent software developers (authors) create or acquire development tools to perform certain tasks and use them over and over again in different programs. A simple example might be a routine used to display a menu. Our term for such development tools, routines, subroutines, and other programs, data and materials is "background technology."

If you assign your rights in such materials to your publisher as part of authorizing the publisher to publish your software, or do the same thing by granting it an exclusive license to a program, you have given up your legal right to use your background technology again unless you get the publisher's permission. Although some publishers may not make an issue of this, if yours turns out to be a highly valuable program, the risk is very real that they will. To avoid this possibility, you should grant the publisher only a *nonexclusive* license to your background technology. This way you can use it in future projects and license your background technology on a nonexclusive basis to any number of other publishers.

The sample clause below permits the publisher to use the background technology as included in the published software, but keeps ownership in the hands of the author. This takes care of your need to use the technology in other projects. To be sure all parties are clear on what "background technology" is involved, you should identify it in as much detail as possible. Your list can be attached to the agreement in the form of a separate exhibit. Because it may not be possible to know before the software is created all the items of background technology that will be used, the agreement should allow for additional items to be added later.

Background Technology: Publisher acknowledges that Author owns or holds a license to use and sublicense various pre-existing development tools, routines, subroutines and other programs, data and materials that Author may include in the Software covered by this Agreement. This material shall be referred to hereafter as "Background Technology." Author's Background Technology includes, but is not limited to, those items identified in Exhibit __ attached to and made a part of this Agreement.

Both parties acknowledge that as of the date of this Agreement, it is not possible for Author to anticipate and list all the Background Technology that may appear in the Software when finally completed. At the time the completed Software is delivered to Publisher, Author shall update Exhibit __ so that it may reflect as accurately as possible all Background Technology contained in the Software, and shall provide a copy of the updated Exhibit __ to Publisher. Such updated Exhibit __ shall be made a part of this Agreement.

Publisher agrees that Author shall retain any and all rights Author may have in the Background Technology. Author hereby grants Publisher an unrestricted, nonexclusive, perpetual, fully paid-up worldwide license to use the Background Technology in the Software covered by this Agreement, and all updates and revisions thereto. However, Publisher shall make no other commercial use of the Background Technology without Author's written consent.

d. Trademark Ownership

Although your software itself will be protected primarily by copyright, the name your software is sold under will be protected by state and federal laws affecting trademarks. We discuss trademarks in Chapter 6. Suffice it to say that trademark ownership can be a critical issue. As with other mass-marketed products, brand name recognition is an extremely important factor affecting sales. The best software in terms of functionality, ease of use and other performance criteria may not sell nearly as well as a better known software package. In short, the name of a program can sometimes be more valuable than its code.

Publishers usually insist on owning the trademark to the software they sell. However, if you've already begun marketing a program under a certain name and have expended substantial time and money to establish your trademark, a publisher might be willing to leave the trademark ownership with you and just license its use. Here's a provision for this:

Ownership of Trademark Rights: Any and all trademarks and trade names that Author uses in connection with the items licensed hereunder are and remain Author's exclusive property. Author hereby gives Publisher a nonexclusive license to reproduce Author's trademarks and trade names as necessary for Publisher to fully promote and market the items set forth in this Agreement.

3. Future Versions of the Software

Most consumer software and many business application programs have a very short shelf-life, often no more than 18 months. To remain competitive in the marketplace, it then will usually be necessary to update the software, perhaps drastically. The publishing agreement should address how updates will be handled. There are several issues to be dealt with:
- how often the software will be updated,
- who will update the software,
- how you'll be compensated if you update the software,
- what will happen if you fail to update the software as promised, and
- how royalties on updated software will be calculated.

a. How Often Is the Software Updated?

Since your royalties are normally based on sales, it is in your best interest that the software product be updated as often as necessary to keep selling well. Therefore, it is generally in your interest that the publishing agreement state that an upgrade be done reasonably promptly and within a specified time. (But see Section B3b, "Who Does the Update?" below. Often there will be a conflict between your desire to receive maximum royalties and your reluctance to obligate yourself to program endless updates.)

Here's a sample clause:

> **Update of Software:** Publisher shall use its best efforts to ensure that an updated/revised version of the Software shall be published no later than every __ months/years after the Software's initial publication.

b. Who Does the Update?

There are three options available as to who will do the updates:

- *You can have no responsibility at all for new versions.* In this event, the publisher would have the responsibility for upgrading the software and, as a result, would surely insist on scaling back your royalties for each new version that is produced. After the third or fourth version, it's likely that all your original code would have been replaced and you'll receive little or nothing.
- *You can agree to do the work on each new version.* If you agree in advance to do the updates, you might want to include in the publishing agreement provisions limiting the amount of work you'll have to do and when you'll have to do it. For example, the agreement could specify that you'll only have to:
  (1) create a certain number of lines of code for each update;
  (2) do updates only at stated intervals; or
  (3) do an update only if your royalties fall below a stated amount.
- *The publisher could give you a right of first refusal.* Instead of committing yourself to doing new versions, the publisher would ask you first if you want to create (or hire someone to create) the new version. If you say no, the publisher could then hire others to create the new version and make a deduction from your royalties.

In some instances, the publisher will require you to agree to develop new versions of the software. This is most likely where the publisher lacks the in-house expertise to do so itself and does not want to have to find someone else to do the work down the line. From your point of view, the best arrangement is for you to have a right of first refusal to do the updates yourself or hire someone else to do so under your supervision. This gives you the option of doing them if you want to or refusing if you'd rather not.

Here is a sample provision giving the author a right of first refusal for future updates:

> **Author's Right to Update Software:** Publisher shall first offer Author the right to create any desired or necessary modifications or enhancements to the Software or to hire a third party to do so under Author's supervision. Author shall have 30 days to accept or decline publisher's offer to update the Software.

c. How Are You Compensated for Doing Updates?

If you agree to do the updating, at the least you should receive your full royalty when the updated version of the software is sold. However, if an enormous amount of work will be involved, this may not be enough to fairly compensate you. In some cases, it will be appropriate for you to receive an increased royalty. Also, if you're going to have to spend substantial time working on the update, you may want the publisher to give you a new advance. And if you'll have to buy new equipment or hire assistants to complete the update, you may want the publisher to reimburse you for some or all of these expenses.

When the publishing contract is originally drafted, it may not be possible to know what will be the appropriate level of compensation for future updates. The following provision requires the publisher to negotiate with you in good faith if you agree to do the update, while protecting you by setting a floor beneath which your compensation cannot go. "Good faith" means that the publisher will not seek an unfair advantage and will observe reasonable standards of fair dealing.

> **Compensation for Updates:** If Author agrees to do any update/ revision, the parties shall renegotiate in good faith Author's royalty percentages under this Agreement and discuss providing Author with an additional advance. However, in no event shall Author's royalty percentages on updates fall below the percentages received by Author under this Agreement for the original version of the Software.

d. What Happens If You Don't Do the Update?

If you decide not to do the updating (or later refuse to exercise your option to update), the publisher will want to deduct the cost of the update from your royalties or simply reduce your royalties for the updated version. It's reasonable for the publisher to reduce your cut (sales would drop without the update). Nevertheless, you still want to receive a fair amount for the work you did originally. The publisher will have no incentive to keep down the cost of the update, since you are, in effect, paying for it. If the publisher spends a lot of money on the update, you may receive no royalties at all for some time.

One way to give the publisher an incentive to keep the updating costs down and ensure that you will continually receive at least some royalties is to include a provision setting a limit on the amount of royalties that can be used by the publisher to pay for the update. For example, you might try to get the publisher to agree to apply no more than one-half of your royalties on each future version to the costs of the update.

Here's a sample provision:

Author's Costs of Updates: If Author is unable or unwilling to do an update/revision of the Software as set forth in this Agreement, Publisher shall have the right to have such work performed by third parties at a commercially reasonable fee and deduct these charges from Author's royalties on the enhanced version. However, in no event shall Author's compensation be reduced below one-half of what Author would otherwise have been entitled to under this Agreement.

e. Calculating Royalties on Updated Versions

If your royalties are based on a sliding scale, the issuance of a revised/updated version of the software should not set the sales total back to zero. For example, if the contract gives you a 5% royalty on the first 5,000 copies sold and 7% thereafter, and 6000 copies have already been sold when an updated version is issued, you should still receive a 7% royalty on sales of the new version, unless you have agreed to receive a lower royalty in the event that you didn't work on the update.

Here is a provision requiring this:

Royalties on Updated Versions: Sales of updated/revised versions of the Software shall be cumulative for purposes of royalty calculations and payment under this Agreement.

4. Author's Future Work

One of the most important questions you need to ask is: What happens after you sign the agreement and complete your work on the initial version of the software? Will you be free to work on other projects and even have them distributed by other publishers?

a.   Noncompetition Clauses

Many publishers will want to include in the publishing agreement some sort of noncompetition clause limiting your right to create competitive products for others in the future. Noncompetition provisions are not favored by the courts. To be enforceable in court, such restrictions must be narrowly drawn both as to time and scope. Most courts will refuse to enforce a noncompetition restriction that is so broad that it prevents or seriously limits you from ever working in your chosen field for an extended period. (See Chapter 9 for a detailed discussion.)

You should always try to delete or narrow competition restrictions from a publishing contract. While it may be reasonable to agree not to create very similar software for sale in the same market (an accounting program for retail stores, for example), anything beyond this clearly isn't. Point out to the publisher that it is in its own best interest to draft a noncompete provision that a court would enforce. This means that:

• the provision should be for a limited time—probably no more than two years, and

• the type of software to which the clause applies should be specifically identified.

Example: *Jane specializes in creating billing and office management software for doctors and dentists. MediSoft Management agrees to publish a dental office package Jane creates. MediSoft's form publishing agreement includes the following noncompetition clause: "During the term of this Agreement, Author will not, without Publisher's prior written consent, publish or furnish to any other party any computer program that might in the Publisher's opinion, interfere with or diminish the sale of the Software furnished under this Agreement."*

Such a broadly written provision might prevent Jane from ever creating and having published any type of software in the field of medical office management software. And if the publisher adapted the program for sale into other accounting markets, this might even prohibit Jane from authoring programs in these areas.

It is likely that a court would refuse to enforce such a broadly-worded noncompetition clause. However, Jane does not want the publishing agreement to include any provision she might have to go to court to invalidate. It would be far better for the agreement to limit this clause to software that is "substantially similar" to the software published by MediSoft. As an alternative, the agreement could actually list the particular features of the product that would be deemed to be unfairly competitive if Jane used them in future products. This at least provides some test against which to measure subsequent work, rather than leaving the judgment entirely to MediSoft.

Here's an example of a clause that limits the author's noncompetition to substantially similar software.

> **Noncompetition by Author:** Author will not, without Publisher's prior written consent, publish or furnish to any other party software substantially similar to that furnished under this Agreement if it would interfere with or diminish the sale of the Software furnished under this Agreement.

Even better from an author's point of view would be a clause limited to a specific term and containing language expressly allowing the author to create and publish software that would not compete with the publisher's product.

Example: *Jane wants to be able to create office management software for doctors that will be marketed separately from the dental package. She modifies the noncompetition clause as follows: "For a period of two years after acceptance by Publisher of the Software furnished by Author under this Agreement, Author will not, without Publisher's prior written consent, publish or furnish to any other party dental office management software if it would interfere with or diminish the sale such of Publishers dental management office software. However, Author reserves the right to develop and publish similar office management software products for the medical market."*

Negotiating tip. If the publisher insists on a noncompetition promise from you, ask that it promise not to publish any new products in the future competing with or supplanting the software covered by the agreement. It seems only fair for the publisher to make the same commitment not to compete as you do. Here's a sample clause: "Noncompetition by Publisher: Publisher will not, without Author's prior written consent, publish or cause to be published software substantially similar to the Software furnished by Author under this Agreement if it would interfere with or diminish the sale of such Software."

b. Options and Rights of First Refusal

Some publishers may want the right to publish new software you create in the future. Thus, the publisher's standard agreement may contain:

- *an "option" provision.* This gives the publisher the exclusive right to publish any software created by you in the future under the same terms and conditions as before; or
- *a "right of first refusal" provision.* This gives the publisher the right to match any offer you obtain from a third party to publish future work.

   If it turns out that the publisher does a good job marketing your software, you may be happy for it to publish your future creations, assuming they are in the same field. But if the publisher does not do a good job, or is a niche publisher with limited marketing ability, you may never want to deal with it again. Also, if your initial program is a big success and establishes your reputation as a programmer, it may be reasonable for you to receive a larger royalty for subsequent works. What all this means is that it's best from your point of view that the agreement contain no option or first refusal provisions. But, if the publisher insists, you should agree to a first refusal right rather than an option. Under an option, you are tied to the terms of the previous contract, while at the same time the publisher has no obligation to publish the new program. A first refusal right means that the publisher merely has the right to match the deal you've obtained elsewhere.

Negotiating tip. If a publisher insists on an option, ask for a hefty amount of cash up-front in the form of an option fee. This is appropriate because you are giving up a valuable right—the right to sell your subsequent program to the highest bidder—while the publisher is giving up nothing because it under no obligation to publish your next work.

Here's an example of an acceptable right of first refusal provision. It limits the publisher's first refusal right to the author's next work in the same area as that published previously.

> **Publisher's Right of First Refusal:** Author shall notify Publisher of Author's next work in the field of _____ and of any bona fide offers Author receives from third parties to publish such work. Publisher shall have the right to publish such work on terms equivalent to the best offer Author receives from a third party. This right of first refusal shall expire 30 days after Publisher is notified of Author's next work.

5. Author's Duties

It is not necessary—and is often impossible—for you to deliver a final finished product to the publisher before signing a publishing agreement. Such agreements are often signed on the basis of a partly-finished product or prototype, or even a mere idea alone. This means that a lot of work will have to be done to get the software ready for market.

Make sure the publishing agreement spells out exactly what you are supposed to do. Where the software is yet to be developed or is only partially completed, your agreement will need to include many of the detailed specifications and time lines common in a custom software development contract (discussed in Chapter 11). This should include:

- A specification detailing as thoroughly as possible what the software is supposed to do. (See Chapter 11, Section D3a, for a discussion of specifications.)

- A list of everything you're supposed to deliver to the publisher ("deliverables"). For example, will you provide user and technical documentation, artwork or other materials? Will you provide the developer with source code? If the publisher will own the software, you will; but if you retain ownership it may be preferable to deliver only object code and perhaps deposit the source code in escrow. (See Chapter 11, Section D12, for a detailed discussion of source code access.)
- A delivery schedule stating exactly when everything you are to provide the publisher is due and what, if anything, will happen if you miss a delivery deadline. (See Chapter 11, Section D3c.)

MAKE SURE YOU OWN WHAT YOU'RE SELLING

Before you can legally transfer the rights in completed software to a publisher, you obviously must own them. Follow this general rule: If you use any code you didn't write yourself, obtain written permission to use it, unless you're absolutely sure it's in the public domain. For example, if you use code or other materials created by a nonemployee, that person must assign his rights to you or your company in writing. (See Chapter 8 for a detailed discussion.) And be particularly careful if you use materials downloaded from computer bulletin boards (freeware or shareware programs)—such material is often made available to the public on bulletin boards for personal, but not commercial, use. Don't trust what the bulletin board or its operator says; contact the program's author and clearly establish in writing your right to use it. Such material can usually be licensed for very nominal fees. If you can't afford such fees, your publisher would probably be willing to pay them or advance you the money rather than risk a future lawsuit.

6. Publisher's Duties

The agreement should also define the publisher's responsibilities. A software publisher will usually play a substantial role in getting a product ready for market. This may include, for example, helping you complete the program itself, writing user and technical documentation, creating artwork and graphics, beta testing the software, creating the packaging, and finally manufacturing copies of the software package. After the product is shipped, the publisher usually provides end-user technical support.

7. Publisher's Advertising and Marketing Efforts

The main reason you are signing an agreement with a publisher, rather than distributing the software yourself, is probably because you expect the publisher to be able to do a far better job marketing your software then you could yourself. Unfortunately, a common lament of many authors—whether of books or software—is that their publishers fail to expend a reasonable amount of time and money advertising and otherwise marketing their work. What can you do to make sure the publisher puts in a creditable marketing effort? Here are a few ideas.

a. "Best Efforts" Clause

At the very least, seek to include in the agreement (if it's not already present) a provision requiring the publisher to use its "best efforts" to market and promote your software. Such language in a publishing agreement obligates the publisher to actively market the program.

Here's a sample best efforts provision:

Publisher's Marketing Efforts: Publisher shall use its best efforts to advertise, market, promote, sell and sublicense the Software.

But a clause like this is no panacea. What constitutes a publisher's "best efforts" is inherently ambiguous. Your publisher may decide that its best efforts means sending out a few promotional copies of your program and letting it sit on the shelf. It is far preferable for the agreement to spell out in some detail exactly what the publisher's "best efforts" will be. We provide some suggestions below.

BE LEERY OF ROYALTY DEDUCTIONS FOR MARKETING COSTS

The publisher might suggest that you allow some or all money spent by the publisher on marketing to be subtracted from net receipts for purposes of paying your percentage royalties. But this can be a big mistake—some publishers will try to bring all sorts of normal overhead and promotion costs into your marketing budget, thereby unfairly reducing your royalties.

---

b. Minimum Amount Spent on Marketing

Try to include in the contract a clause that requires the publisher to spend a minimum amount on promotion and marketing activities without any deductions from net receipts for purposes of calculating royalties. The minimum can be a dollar amount or a percentage of the net revenues received; 5% to 15% is often a reasonable amount, depending on the type of software.

Here's an example of such a provision:

Minimum Amount Spent on Marketing: Publisher shall invest, during the term of this Agreement, no less than 10% of the net revenue received from the Software in demonstration, promotion and advertising activities directed to expand and develop the market for the Software. This expenditure shall not affect the calculation of Author's royalties due under this Agreement.

c. Specific Marketing Activities

You could also try to obligate the publisher to engage in specific types of marketing activities. These may include, for example, requiring the publisher to arrange presentations of your software for magazines and other reviewers, feature it at trade shows, advertise in major magazines and do in-store or users' demonstrations and promotions. Some publishers are fairly open to this type of marketing fine-tuning. However, in general, you normally need to have a significant amount of bargaining power as a successful author to get a publisher to agree to such detailed marketing obligations.

8. Acceptance of Software by Publisher

In the case of yet to be developed or unfinished software, the agreement will contain a provision regarding acceptance by the publisher. Publishing agreements typically give the publisher the right to reject an author's software if it deems it "unacceptable" or "unsatisfactory." Unfortunately, some unscrupulous publishers, who may conclude that your program will be difficult to market profitably, may claim that your program is unacceptable, and decline to accept it, even though you deliver a perfectly good program. A publisher can use a broadly written acceptance provision as an excuse for not publishing a program it believes will not be a success in the marketplace, or for any other reason. This type of one-sided provision in effect gives the publisher a free exclusive option on your software.

To counter this, you will want to bargain for some limits on the publisher's right to reject your work. Common ones include requirements that:

1. The publisher may reject the software only if it fails to meet agreed-upon design specifications or if bugs or other problems mean it does not meet reasonable commercial standards for that type of software.
2. The publisher must act in good faith.
3. Before rejecting your work, the publisher must explain in writing what is wrong with it and give you the opportunity to correct the deficiencies.

Here's a good example of a fair acceptance provision:

Acceptance of Software by Publisher:

(a) The Software delivered by Author under this Agreement shall substantially conform to the documentation and operate on the computer provided by Publisher in such a manner as to demonstrate the functions described in the design specifications.

(b) Publisher shall have ___ days from the date of delivery of the Software in final form to inspect, test and evaluate it. Publisher shall have the responsibility to conduct all testing in good faith.

(c) Publisher shall be deemed to have agreed that the Software satisfies the conditions of Paragraph (a) above unless, within ___ days after receipt of the Software, Publisher sends Author a written statement of the ways in which Publisher maintains the Software does not satisfy these conditions. Author shall have ___ days from the receipt of such statement to correct the deficiencies. Publisher may terminate this Agreement by written notice to Author if Author does not deliver the corrected Software within the ___-day period.

(d) If Author corrects the Software and timely delivers it to Publisher, the corrected Software shall be deemed accepted by Publisher unless Publisher informs Author otherwise in writing within ___ days. If the corrected Software is deemed unacceptable by Publisher, Publisher shall have the option of either (1) repeating the procedure set forth in Paragraph (c) above, or (2) terminating this Agreement.

a. Return of Refundable Advances

If the publisher is giving you a refundable advance (that is, you must give it back if the program isn't published; see Section B1b, above), seek to require the publisher to defer your repayment of the advance upon rejection of your software until after you find another publisher and receive an advance or other monies from it. Here's a sample provision:

Alternative 1: Return of Refundable Advances: In the event the Software is rejected by Publisher, Author shall not be required to repay Publisher's advance until the receipt by Author of the first proceeds from a subsequent contract for publication of the Software by another publisher.

The publisher may not want to accept the above provision as written because it is so open-ended (it could take you forever to find a new publisher). You may have to agree to a time limit after which you have to repay the advance yourself. Here's an example:

Alternative 2: Return of Refundable Advances: In the event the Software is rejected by Publisher, Author shall use his/her best efforts to obtain another publisher. If Author is unable to do so within one year after Publisher's rejection of the Software, Author shall repay Publisher's advance in full.

9. Software Maintenance

The extent to which you will provide the publisher with maintenance and support is always a critical issue. Typically, software publishing agreements contain a warranty provision by which the author promises to fix any bugs for free for a limited time—usually between 90 days and a year. Clearly it is in your best interest to help ensure that the software is error free. Even so, it's reasonable for the publisher to pay you for bug corrections after the warranty period expires. Such work requires substantial time and effort and there is no assurance that any later increase in sales will be sufficient to fairly compensate you. In addition, there are commonly disagreements between author and publisher as to whether a proposed change amounts to "fixing a bug" or "enhancing the program."

Below is a provision requiring the publisher to pay you on a time and materials basis for bug correction services after the warranty expires:

Author's Correction of Software Errors: If Publisher so requests, Author shall correct any significant programming errors or anomalies in the Software that are discovered after expiration of the warranty period. Publisher shall pay Author a reasonable fee, based on Author's then current time and materials charges, for such services.

10. Intellectual Property Infringement Claims

Software publishers typically include provisions in their contracts in which authors warrant (guarantee) that the software will not infringe upon the intellectual property rights of third parties, including copyright, trade secret and patent rights of others. You should try to limit such warranties as much as possible. In particular, try to avoid providing a warranty against patent infringement, since it can be impossible for you to know or find out whether your software may infringe any patent. (See Chapter 5 for a detailed discussion.)

> ## OTHER WARRANTIES
>
> In addition to a warranty of noninfringement, the publisher may require you to provide various warranties regarding the quality of your work. These are discussed in detail in the chapter on custom software contracts. (See Chapter 11, Section D13.) Note that in Chapter 11, the "author" of the software is termed the "developer," and the "customer" performs the same role as the "publisher" in this chapter.

Software publishers also usually require the author to "indemnify" them if an infringement claim is brought because the author breaches a warranty.

This means the author must pay the attorney fees incurred defending such claims and pay any damages obtained by claimants. Most publishers' contracts require the author to indemnify the publisher for any claim, even if it proves to be groundless. You should seek to limit your indemnification duty only to:

- damages actually recovered in a suit against the publisher resulting from a breach of warranty, or
- the amount of a settlement agreed to by both the publisher and you.

Thus, for example, you would be required to pay the publisher's attorney fees and costs if a judgment were obtained against the publisher in a suit for copyright infringement. Similarly, if you and the publisher agreed to settle such a claim, you would have to pay the amount of the settlement. But the publisher would be responsible for all the costs involved in defending unfounded claims that are not settled and/or result in a judgment in the publisher's favor.

You should also try to limit the total amount you must pay under such an indemnification provision. Try to get the publisher to agree to a set dollar figure, or, at the most, to no more than the amount of royalties you will have received as of the date the indemnification amount is paid.

Here is a sample indemnification provision:

Indemnification by Author Against Infringement Claims: Author agrees to indemnify and hold harmless Publisher against any claim the Software infringes any copyright, trade secret or trademark if such claim is finally determined or settled with Author's consent. Author shall cooperate fully in the defense of any such claim and may retain counsel of his/her own choice at Author's own expense. In no event shall Author's liability under this Paragraph exceed the total amount paid to Author by Publisher under this Agreement [OPTIONAL: "or $_____, whichever is greater"]. The foregoing represents Author's entire liability to Publisher in connection with claims alleging intellectual property infringement by the Software.

11. Limits on Author's Liability to Publisher

In addition to limiting your liability to the publisher for intellectual property infringement claims, you should seek to limit your liability for any other losses the publisher might suffer because you fail to perform all your duties under the agreement, the software malfunctions, or for any other reason.

At the very least, ask for a provision excluding you from any liability at all for incidental or consequential damages arising out of the agreement. Such damages include the publisher's lost profits or other economic damages caused by your nonperformance. Here's a sample provision:

> **Limits on Author's Liability to Publisher:** In no event shall Author be liable to Publisher for lost profits of Publisher, or special, incidental or consequential damages, even if Author has been advised of the possibility of such damages.

You might also add a provision limiting your total liability to the publisher to the amount of royalties you've received or a specified amount. Obviously, such a provision is highly in your favor, and many publishers will refuse to accept it. In any event, here's a sample clause:

> **(Optional):** Author's total liability to Publisher under this Agreement for damages, costs and expenses, regardless of cause, shall not exceed the total amount of royalties paid to Author by Publisher under this Agreement [OPTIONAL: "or $_____, whichever is greater"].

12. Limits on Author's Liability to Third Parties

The people and businesses who buy and use some types of software could suffer financial or even personal harm if it malfunctions. For example, a business that uses a database program to keep track of its inventory could lose thousands of dollars if the program crashes. A malfunction in a program designed to analyze the results of medical tests could conceivably cost someone her life. If these sorts of problems occur, the people involved will likely not only sue your publisher, but sue you personally as well. The best way to guard against this is to insist on rigorous testing of the software before it is put on the market. Independent testing companies market these services, and if a malfunction in your software might cause real harm, it would be wise for you and the publisher to agree to have it rigorously tested. In addition, if there is a possibility that your software could cause customers harm or damage, you should definitely seek to limit your liability for such third party claims.

First, the agreement should require the publisher to include on the product a disclaimer (disavowal) of all warranties. This somewhat limits the liability of both you and your publisher and is obviously in the best interests of both. Here's a sample clause:

Limits on Author's Liability to Third Parties:

(a) Publisher is required to place a conspicuous disclaimer on each copy of the Software and supporting materials sold or otherwise distributed stating that the Software and supporting materials are sold "AS IS" and that neither the Author nor Publisher are making any warranties of any kind.

Second, try to get the publisher to provide you with insurance coverage against third party claims. This type of insurance is called "errors and omissions" insurance. It is expensive and available only through a few companies. Such insurance typically has a high deductible and numerous exclusions, so even with such a policy, you may have substantial out-of-pocket costs if you're sued. But it's far better than nothing.

Alternative 1: (b) During the lifetime of this Agreement, and for five years thereafter, Publisher shall purchase an insurance policy for $_____ *[at least $1 million]* listing Author as the insured. The policy will cover any and all claims that might be made against Author for use of the Software, except for those claims alleging violation of a third party's copyright, trade secret or patent rights.

A publisher might not be willing to provide you with insurance coverage because it is too expensive. As an alternative to insurance coverage, you could try to get the publisher to agree to a provision like the following that:

- makes clear that you are not responsible for any harm or damages incurred by customers, and
- requires the publisher to indemnify you if you are sued.

This means the publisher must pay your attorney fees and all damages. However, if you're dealing with a publisher without substantial assets, there's no assurance the company will be around when a third party claim is made. Even a company that's solvent now later might not have the money to live up to its promise to defend you.

> **Alternative 2:** (b) Author shall not be responsible for losses, damages, costs or expenses of any kind resulting from the use of the Software by any customer, including, without limitation, any business expenses, machine downtime or damages caused any third party by any defect, error or malfunction. Publisher at its own expense shall fully indemnify and defend Author against any third party claim alleging such losses, damages, costs or expenses.

13. Termination of Agreement

The agreement should address when it can be terminated by the parties. Such termination clauses are very important.

a. Publisher's Default or Bankruptcy

You should have the right to terminate the agreement if the publisher materially breaches any of its terms. A "material" breach means a breach that is serious, rather than minor or trivial. Missing a royalty payment by one day is not "material"; not paying royalties for months is.

The provision below is fairly standard. It permits you to terminate the agreement if the publisher fails to cure (remedy) a material breach within 30 days. The clause also provides that the publisher's bankruptcy is a material breach giving you the right to terminate the agreement. However, although this is a standard contract provision, it may not be enforceable. If the publisher files for bankruptcy, the federal bankruptcy laws will override the contract and prevent automatic reversion of the publisher's rights in the software to you. (See Chapter 11, Section D24, for a detailed discussion.) There may be some exceptions to this though, so it's useful to include this language.

Termination of Agreement:

(a) Author shall have the right to terminate this Agreement by written notice to Publisher if Publisher has materially breached any obligation herein and such breach remains uncured for a period of 30 days after written notice is sent by Author to Publisher. Publisher shall be deemed to be in material breach of this Agreement if it is adjudicated a bankrupt, files a voluntary bankruptcy petition or makes an assignment for the benefit of creditors.

b. Publisher's Nonpayment of Royalties

You should also seek to include a clause that gives you the right to terminate the agreement if the publisher fails to pay you your advance or royalties. Here's a sample:

(b) If Publisher defaults in the timely delivery of the advance, or of royalty statements and payments, and fails to deliver them after 30 days' written notice from Author, the Agreement will terminate without further procedure and without prejudice to Author's claim for monies due.

c. What Happens After Termination

If you terminate the agreement because of the publisher's default, bankruptcy or nonpayment, you should get back all your rights in the software, be able to keep your advance and get any monies the publisher owes you at the time of termination. Here's a sample clause.

> (c) In the event of such termination:
>   (1) all right, title and interest in the Software and supporting materials shall revert to Author and become Author's exclusive property; Publisher shall execute any documents necessary to accomplish such reversion of rights,
>   (2) Author shall have the right to immediately enjoin Publisher from any further copying, use, marketing or sublicensing of the Software and supporting materials, and
>   (3) Author shall be entitled to retain any advances paid to him/her under this Agreement and to receive immediate payment of all amounts payable under this Agreement at the time of termination.

d. Optional Termination Clauses

Following are some optional termination clauses granting you other termination rights that will put additional pressure on the publisher to do a good job selling your product.

First, if possible, obtain the right to terminate the agreement if the publisher does not actually publish your software by a certain date. Software publishers have been known to take an inordinate amount of time to bring products to market—particularly when they are unsure about a product's sales potential. You should not have to wait forever for the publisher to make up its mind whether to publish your software or not. Here's a sample clause:

> (d) Author may terminate this Agreement if Publisher has not published the Software within ___ months after Publisher's acceptance of the Software, in which case Author may retain all advances paid by Publisher.

Another termination provision that is in your favor gives you the right to terminate the agreement if stated sales targets are not met. Many publishers will agree to such a provision because, in their view, software that doesn't sell well is not a valuable asset they want to keep. However, the software may still be valuable to you, and another publisher may do a better job marketing it. Here is an example of such a provision:

(e) If the royalty payment due Author under this Agreement is less than $_____ for two consecutive royalty periods, Author may terminate this Agreement by giving Publisher three months written notice of the intent to terminate. At the end of the three-month period, all right, title and interest in the Software and supporting materials shall revert to Author and become Author's exclusive property, except that Publisher shall have the right to continue to advertise, market and sell any remaining inventory.

14. Mediation and Arbitration

Mediation and arbitration are two forms of "alternative dispute resolution"— means for settling disputes without resorting to expensive court litigation. Mediation is relatively informal, and by its nature is never binding. Typically, the mediator either sits the parties down together and tries to provide an objective view of their disputes, or shuttles between the parties as a cool conduit of what may be red-hot opinions. Where the real problem is a personality conflict or simple lack of communication, a good mediator can keep a minor controversy from shattering the relationship between a software author and publisher. Where the argument is more serious, a mediator may be able to lead the parties to a mutually satisfactory resolution that will obviate time-consuming and expensive litigation.

In arbitration, an informal hearing is held before one or more arbitrators (usually attorneys or retired judges) who decide the merits of the issues and render a decision, which may or not be binding depending on the arbitration agreement. There are a number of professional arbitrators' organizations which conduct arbitrations, notably the American Arbitration Association which has offices in most major cities.

No one can be forced into mediation or arbitration; one must agree to it, either in the contract or later when a dispute arises. Commercial contracts often include binding arbitration provisions. However, this is not a matter to be agreed to lightly. By submitting to binding arbitration, you're basically giving up your constitutional right of access to the courts.

Arbitration has many good points. It is usually faster and cheaper than court litigation. Also, because the parties choose the arbitrator, they can select someone who is familiar with computer and software law. Such a person might be expected to render a better decision than a judge or jury with no familiarity with the software business.

However, arbitration can also have a down side. Litigants have often found that arbitrators seek to reach a compromise between the parties' positions rather than ruling squarely in favor of one or the other. Under the rules of the American Arbitration Association (which are most commonly used in arbitrations), no questioning of the parties or witnesses is allowed before the hearing (a process lawyers call discovery). This can lead to unfair results. Moreover, conducting an arbitration will not necessarily keep the parties out of court. If a party receives a bad result in an arbitration, it will often seek to have a court vacate (void) it. A court can do this if it finds the arbitrator guilty of misconduct, bias, fraud or corrupt (but proving this is extremely difficult). Finally, an arbitrator's decision is not self-enforcing; it must be entered with a court. In some cases (obtaining a quick restraining order, for example), you're better off going to court in the first place.

An arbitration clause can and should be drafted to avoid the kind of problems described above. The following clause attempts to do this.

 If the other side won't agree to the safeguards provided in this clause, you're better off without an arbitration clause.

Mediation and Arbitration: Except for the right of either party to apply to a court of competent jurisdiction for a temporary restraining order or preliminary injunction to preserve the status quo or prevent irreparable harm pending the selection and confirmation of a panel of arbitrators, and Author's right to bring suit for royalties or other monies due Author or for an accounting, any dispute arising under this Agreement shall be resolved through a mediation—arbitration approach.

The parties agree to first try to resolve the dispute informally with the help of a mutually agreed-upon mediator. If it proves impossible to arrive at a mutually satisfactory solution through mediation, the parties agree to submit their dispute to binding arbitration in accordance with the Commercial Arbitration Rules of the American Arbitration Association.

The arbitration may be conducted by one impartial arbitrator by mutual agreement or three arbitrators if the parties are unable to agree on a single arbitrator within 30 days of first demand for arbitration. All arbitrators are to be selected from a panel provided by the American Arbitration Association. The chairman shall be an attorney at law, and the other arbitrators shall have a background or training either in computer law, computer software technology or marketing of computer software products.

Upon request of a party, the arbitrators shall have the authority to permit pre-hearing depositions, requests for production of documents and other discovery procedures, to the extent they deem appropriate. A court reporter shall record the arbitration hearing and the reporter's transcript shall be the official transcript of the proceeding. The arbitrators shall have no power to add or detract from the agreements of the parties and may not make any ruling or award that does not conform to the terms and conditions of this Agreement. The arbitrators shall have the authority to grant injunctive relief in a form substantially similar to that which would otherwise be granted by a court of law. The arbitrators shall have no authority to award punitive damages or any other damages not measured by the prevailing party's actual damages. The arbitrators shall specify the basis for any damage award and the types of damages awarded. The decision of the arbitrators shall be final and binding on the parties and may be entered and enforced in any court of competent jurisdiction by either party.

The prevailing party in the arbitration proceedings shall be awarded reasonable attorney fees, expert witness costs and expenses, and all other costs and expenses incurred directly or indirectly in connection with the proceedings, unless the arbitrators shall for good cause determine otherwise.

15. Attorney Fees

Under the following provision, if either party has to sue the other in court to enforce the agreement and wins (is the "prevailing party") the loser is required to pay the prevailing party's attorney fees and expenses. A clause like this is found in many contracts, and there is a good chance it is in the publisher's form; if not, ask that it be added since it may make it economically feasible for you to sue the publisher.

> **Attorney Fees:** If any action at law or in equity is necessary to enforce the terms of this Agreement, the prevailing party shall be entitled to reasonable attorney fees, costs and expenses, in addition to any other relief to which it may be entitled. ■

CHAPTER 13

Multimedia Projects

T his chapter is for anyone who is developing, or is thinking about developing, a multimedia program. Sections A through E discuss the special copyright problems that multimedia projects present. Section F covers the publicity and privacy concerns associated with multimedia. You should read all of Sections A through F before using the multimedia license agreements contained in Section G.

A. Introduction

Multimedia programs—software that combines text, graphics and sounds, typically on CD-ROM disks—are some of today's "hottest" software products. Multimedia educational programs are being sold to schools and parents, while more and more entertainment and business applications are being developed. Multimedia is expected to explode in the near future as new technologies become available, combining computers, video monitors, speakers and laser-read disks. IBM, Apple, Microsoft, Sun, Sony and many other big guns in the software and computer hardware industries are investing heavily in multimedia. However, before you or your company jump on the multimedia bandwagon, you need to be aware that multimedia projects can present difficult and expensive legal problems. These fall into two main categories:

- *The copyright permissions problem.* You may need to obtain permission to use all text, photos, video and film clips, software and music owned by third parties that is protected by copyright. Obtaining permissions for a project can involve tracking down many different copyright owners and negotiating licenses to use their material. (This is discussed in detail in Section E, below.)

- *Publicity/privacy problems.* Use of photos, film or video footage or audio recordings can constitute a breach of the privacy and/or publicity rights of the people whose likenesses are used. You'll need to consider whether you must obtain privacy releases from persons whose images or voices are used. (This is discussed in detail in Section F, below.)

Obtaining copyright permissions and publicity/privacy releases can be a weighty task.

Example: *MultiSolutions Software, a small software developer, decides to create an interactive multimedia CD-ROM package about Columbus's "discovery" of America. MultiSolutions wants its package to contain Macintosh operating system software, HyperCard programming software, and many other third party application software programs to support graphics, sound and animation. MultiSolutions also wants to incorporate into the program a variety of pre-existing materials about Columbus, including:*

- *text from various articles and books,*
- *photos from books, magazines and other sources,*
- *video clips from several television programs,*
- *film clips from two theatrical movies about Columbus, and*
- *music to be used as background to the images and text, and excerpts from a Broadway musical and Italian opera based on Columbus's life.*

All in all, MultiSolutions intends to incorporate hundreds of separate items into its software package. This sounds like a fine idea for a multimedia package. However, MultiSolutions needs to address and resolve the copyright permissions problem and publicity/privacy problems before it can legally distribute its product.

Clearly, MultiSolutions has its work cut out for it. The more third party material it uses, the more time and money it must spend to obtain the necessary permissions and releases.

Some developers have discovered that certain multimedia projects are not economically feasible in today's marketplace because the legal and licensing costs are too high. For example, one developer abandoned a project to copy baseball cards on CD-ROM disks when it discovered that to obtain the necessary rights, it would have to go through separate negotiations with more than 500 individual players (or their lawyers). The developer concluded that the profits that could reasonably be expected from the sales of the CD-ROM would be far too small to justify such an undertaking.

OTHER INTELLECTUAL PROPERTY CONCERNS

A multimedia developer's main concerns are with copyright and publicity/privacy problems. However, other intellectual property laws may come into play as well. For example:

- Third party software may be patented; photographic special effects may also be protected by patents. A license must be obtained to use any material protected by a patent.

  On August 31, 1993 the PTO issued a stunningly broad patent on the basic search and retrieval technology used in virtually all interactive multimedia products (Reed et al., patent number 5,241,671). The patent took the software development world by surprise, primarily because few thought that this type of technology could be patented at all.

  As a result of a concerted effort by other multimedia developers, the Patent and Trademark Office re-examined and subsequently ruled unpatentable the patent's main claim. However, the patent owners will be pursuing patent protection for at least part of the technology previously covered by that main claim.

- The federal and state trademark laws may protect character names, physical appearance and costumes; some titles; as well as product names, logos, slogans and packaging. A developer may have to obtain permission to use a trademark in a multimedia work. (See Chapter 6 for an overview of trademarks.)

- Finally, trade secret problems may occur whenever a multimedia developer uses or is exposed to any material or information (even a mere idea) that is covered by a confidentiality agreement. A developer must be particularly vigilant about avoiding use of confidential information any employee obtained from a prior employer. (See Chapter 4 for a detailed discussion of trade secrets.)

There are ways to get around, or at least alleviate, permissions problems. First we'll discuss when a software developer does and does not need to obtain permissions, and second, where and how to get them if they are needed. We'll then review the privacy and publicity issues that arise in multimedia projects.

OTHER MULTIMEDIA LAW RESOURCES

The legal problems associated with multimedia projects are varied and complex. We can't discuss all of them in detail in this chapter. For further information refer to:

- *Multimedia: Law & Practice*, by Michael D. Scott, published by Prentice Hall Law & Business; 270 Sylvan Ave, Englewood Cliffs, NJ 07632, 800-223-0231; and
- *Multimedia Law Handbook*, by J. Dianne Brinson and Mark F. Radcliffe, published by Ladera Press; 3130 Alpine Road, Suite 9002-200, Menlo Park, CA 94025, 800-523-3721.

In addition, a legal guide for multimedia developers by attorney Donna Demac was set for publication in the Spring of 1994 by the Interactive Multimedia Association (the multimedia developers' trade association) 3 Church Circle, Ste. 800, Annapolis, MD 21404, 410-626-1380, Fax: 410-263-0590.

B. When to Obtain Permission to Use Material in a Multimedia Project

Whether or not a software developer needs permission to include any given item in a multimedia project depends on:

- whether or not the material is created especially for the multimedia project,
- who created it (employee, independent contractor or third party), and
- the extent and nature of the intended use.

1. New Material Created for a Multimedia Project

No copyright permissions problems are normally presented when material is created especially for a multimedia project, whether by the developer's employees or independent contractors. For this reason, many multimedia programs today consist primarily of original material.

Under the copyright laws, a developer will automatically own the copyright in materials created in-house by its own employees. (See Chapter 8 for a detailed discussion.) As a result, the developer need not obtain permission from its employees to use copyrighted works—the developer already owns those rights. For example, MultiSolutions Software would not need to obtain permission to use drawings created by a staff artist in its multimedia program on Columbus.

When a developer hires an independent contractor to contribute to a multimedia project, it should require the contractor to assign copyright rights to the developer. For example, if MultiSolutions hires a freelance artist to create drawings for its Columbus project, it should have the artist sign an independent contractor agreement assigning her rights in the drawings to MultiSolutions before commencing work. (See Chapter 10 for a detailed discussion and sample forms.)

2. Preexisting Materials Created by Third Parties

When a developer wishes to use preexisting materials created by non-employees (or by employees before they became employees), the developer must determine whether permission for the use must be obtained from the copyright owner(s). The copyright owner(s) may be the original creator of the work or a person or entity to whom ownership has been transferred.

If you don't own copyright rights to material, you'll need to determine whether permission is required to use any given item. You can figure this out by answering the following two questions:

• Is the material in the public domain?

• Does your intended use of the material constitute a "fair use?"

If your answer to *both* questions is "no," you need permission; otherwise you don't. To help you answer these questions, Section C discusses what is in the public domain and Section D examines the fair use rule. (For a far more detailed discussion of both topics, see *The Copyright Handbook*, by Stephen Fishman (Nolo Press).)

3. Using Copyrighted Material Without Permission

You might be tempted to use copyrighted material without permission if you are unable to locate the copyright owner(s) or simply don't have the time, money or staff to obtain numerous permissions. If the copyright owner later discovers what you've done, at the very least you will be liable for the reasonable value of your use. If the material is not terribly valuable, this won't amount to much, and the owner will probably accept a small permission fee.

Example: *MultiSolutions Software wants to quote two pages from an old magazine article about Columbus. The magazine is out of business and neither the author nor her heirs can be located. MultiSolutions decides to use the quotation anyway. One year later, MultiSolutions is contacted by the article's copyright owner. The owner agrees to accept $250 from MultiSolutions for retroactive permission to use the quotation.*

On the other hand, if the material is valuable, you could find yourself in big trouble. At the very least, you'll be liable for a substantial permission fee, perhaps more than you'd be able or willing to pay. Instead of settling for a permission fee, the copyright owner might sue you for copyright infringement. In this event, you could face substantial damages. The copyright owner you've stolen from could ask the court for the reasonable value of your use and the amount of any economic loss caused by your theft; or, it could ask for special statutory damages, which can range up to $100,000 (it's up to the judge to decide how much). In some cases, you could even be subject to criminal prosecution. And don't forget, you'll be paying your attorney handsomely, regardless of how the case turns out.

Example: *MultiSolutions Software "borrows" several minutes from the video version of a recent theatrical movie about Columbus and uses it in its multimedia program. The film's copyright owners discover the theft and sue MultiSolutions for copyright infringement. They obtain an injunction prohibiting MultiSolutions from distributing the program with the pirated footage and ultimately obtain a court judgment against MultiSolutions. They ask the judge to award statutory damages, and, because the judge finds that the infringement was willful and blatant, she awards $50,000 in damages against MultiSolutions.*

See *The Copyright Handbook*, by Stephen Fishman (Nolo Press), for a detailed discussion of copyright infringement.

C. Works That Are in the Public Domain

We discussed the general nature of copyright protection in Chapter 3, Sections B, C and D. If you haven't read that material, do so now. Copyright protects all original works of authorship. This includes, but is not limited to, writings of all kinds, music, sound recordings, paintings, sculptures and other works of art, photographs, film and video. Of course, computer software is protected as well.

Luckily for multimedia developers, however, not every work of authorship ever created is currently protected by copyright—not by a long shot. A work that is not protected by copyright is said to be in the "public domain"; in effect, it belongs to everybody. Anyone is free to use it without asking permission, but no one can ever own the work again. By using public domain materials, a multimedia software developer can avoid going through the time, trouble and expense involved in getting permission to use copyrighted materials.

There are two main reasons why a work or other item may be in the public domain:

• the copyright in the work has expired, or
• the work was never protected by copyright in the first place.

Foreign distribution. This discussion only covers works in the public domain in the United States. A work in the public domain in the United States may still be protected by the copyright laws of foreign countries. One reason is that, before 1978, most foreign countries granted a longer period of copyright protection than did the United States. If you intend to distribute a multimedia work outside the United States, seek expert advice as to whether any public domain material included in the work must be licensed for use abroad.

1. Works In Which Copyright Protection Has Expired

Copyright protection does not last forever. When a work's copyright protection expires, it automatically enters the public domain. The copyright has expired on a truly vast body of literature, art, music, photographs and even early films. Two categories of works are now in the public domain because the copyright has expired:

- works published at least 75 years ago, and
- works published before 1964 that weren't copyright renewed.

a. Works Published More Than 75 Years Ago

All works *first published* in the United States (see sidebar below) more than 75 years before January 1 of the current year are in the public domain because the copyright has expired.

All copyright durations run until the end of the calendar year in which they would otherwise expire. For example, the copyright in a work that was first published in 1900 expired on December 31, 1975, regardless of what month and day during 1900 it was published. To determine whether a book or other work was first published more than 75 years ago, simply look at the year-date in the work's copyright notice. This should be the year of first publication.

WHAT CONSTITUTES PUBLICATION

A work is "published" for copyright purposes when copies are sold, rented, lent, given away or otherwise distributed to the public by the copyright owner or by others acting with the owner's permission—for example, a publisher. It is not necessary to sell thousands of copies of a work for it to be "published." So long as copies of a work are made available to the public, the work is published for copyright purposes, even if no copies are actually sold or otherwise distributed.

What matters for copyright duration purposes is when a work is first published. When a new edition or new version of a work is published, the new material's copyright duration is based on the publication date of the new edition or version, but the old material's copyright duration is based on the date of publication of the original edition or version.

Determining whether a work of visual art, such as a painting or sculpture, has been published can be difficult. A work of art is published if it is offered for sale to the public or if copies—photographs, for example—are publicly distributed. Simply displaying artwork in a gallery or museum does not constitute publication under current law. However, displays that occurred over 75 years ago could have constituted a publication under the law then in effect, particularly if the public was allowed to copy the displayed work. This is an unsettled area of the law.

b. Works Published Before 1964 That Were Not Renewed in Time

Some works that were first published before 1964, but less than 75 years ago, have also entered the public domain. This is because a work published before 1964 had an initial copyright term of 28 years and an additional 47-year renewal term if a renewal application was filed with the Copyright Office during the 28th year. This means that pre-1964 works that were renewed in time are protected by copyright for a total of 75 years (28 + 47 = 75). All pre-1964 works that were not renewed during the 28th year entered the pubic domain on the 29th year after publication.

Example: *Lisa, an outdoor photographer, published a book of photographs in 1960. The work had an initial copyright term of 28 years. For some reason, Lisa and her publisher failed to renew the copyright in the book by filing of a renewal application with the Copyright Office during 1988, the 28th year after publication. As a result, the work entered the public domain on January 1, 1989. Had a renewal been filed, the book would have received an additional renewal term of 47 years. But once it entered the public domain, there was no way for Lisa to get it back. The book is freely available for anyone to use.*

Most pre-1964 works with any value were renewed. However, mistakes occasionally were made and some noteworthy works were never renewed. When a book or other written work is reprinted after renewal, the copyright notice usually provides this information. Otherwise you'll probably need to research the Copyright Office's records to find out if a renewal was filed in time. (See the sidebar below.)

HOW TO RESEARCH COPYRIGHT RENEWALS

There are three ways to find out if a renewal was filed in time for a work:

1. Have the Copyright Office search its records for you. They charge $20 an hour for this service. Call the Reference & Bibliography Section at 202-707-6850 and ask for an estimate of how long they think your particular search will take. Then, send a letter requesting the search, along with a check in the estimated amount, payable to the Register of Copyrights. Your letter should state that you are requesting a search for a copyright renewal and indicate the type of work involved—for instance, a book, periodical, drama, music, motion picture, photograph, artwork, sound recording or map. Give the title and author of the work and copyright claimant, if known. Also state the year the work was published and the registration number, if known. Be sure to include your name, address and phone number and indicate if you want to receive the results of the search by phone. The letter should be sent to:

Reference & Bibliography Section, LM-451
Copyright Office
Library of Congress
Washington, DC 20559

2. Have a professional search firm conduct the search for you. This will probably cost much more than having the Copyright Office do the search (fees start at about $100), but you will get much faster service. Search firms usually report back in two to 10 working days, while it often takes the Copyright Office one or two months to conduct a search. There are five copyright search firms, located primarily in the Washington, DC area:

Copyright Council
2121 Crystal Dr., Ste. 704
Arlington, VA 22202
703-521-1669

Government Liaison Services, Inc.
3030 Clarendon Blvd., Ste.209
Arlington, VA 22201
800-642-6564 or 703-524-8200

Robert G. Roomian
P.O. Box 7111
Alexandria, VA 22307
703-549-7010

Thomson & Thomson
Copyright Research Group
500 E St., S.W., Ste. 970
Washington, DC 20024
800-356-8630
(This is the largest and best-known search firm.)

XL Corporate Services
62 White St.
New York, NY 10013
800-221-2972 or 212-431-5000

3. Search the Copyright Office records yourself. This entails looking up the work in the *Catalog of Copyright Entries (CCE)*. The CCE is a monumental series of annual catalogs listing and cross-referencing every work registered and renewed by the Copyright Office. The *CCE* is available to the public at the Copyright Office, located in the James Madison Memorial Building, 101 Independence Ave. S.E., Washington, DC. The Office is open from 8:30 a.m. to 5:00 p.m., Monday through Friday. Alternatively, the *CCE* can be found in government depository libraries throughout the country.

Before researching a copyright renewal yourself, obtain a copy of *Researching Copyright Renewal,* by Iris J. Wildman and Rhonda Carlson (Fred B. Rothman & Co., 10368 West Centennial Rd., Littleton, CO 80127, 800-457-1986). This 85-page paperback, written by two law librarians, clearly explains exactly how to go about determining whether a renewal was timely filed, including how to decipher the often cryptic entries in the *CCE.*

2. Pre-1989 Works Published Without a Valid Copyright Notice

There is one more class of works less than 75 years old that are in the public domain. These are works that were published before March 1, 1989 without a valid copyright notice. For written and most other works, that's the "c" in a circle © followed by a publication date (the date isn't mandatory on pictorial, graphic and sculptural works) and the copyright owner's name. A "p" in a circle is used for sound recordings.

Prior to 1989, all published works had to have a valid copyright notice to be protected by copyright. This is not the law anymore; copyright notices are now optional.

Few works, particularly valuable ones, have been published without a copyright notice. But on rare occasions, mistakes have been made. Any work published before 1978 (the date the current copyright law took effect) without a valid notice is now in the public domain, unless the notice was inadvertently left off a mere handful of copies. That may not be the case with unnoticed works published between January 1, 1978 and March 1, 1989, however. Such works did not enter the public domain if the copyright owner cured the omission by registering the work and making a reasonable effort to add a copyright notice to all copies distributed after the omission was discovered. If you want to use a work published between 1978 and March 1, 1989 without a copyright notice, contact the copyright owner to see if it cured the omission.

Again, it is not likely you'll ever find a work published without a copyright notice. Note that individual contributions to a collective work, like a magazine or anthology, don't need to have their own copyright notice; a single notice at the front of the work is sufficient. Also, bear in mind that a notice is only required for *published* works. Unpublished works have never had to have a copyright notice to be protected; they have automatic copyright protection. (For a detailed discussion of everything you would ever want to know about copyright notices and more, see *The Copyright Handbook*, by Stephen Fishman (Nolo Press).)

SPECIAL RULES FOR PRE-1972 SOUND RECORDINGS

None of the rules covered in this discussion of the public domain applies to sound recordings made before 1972. That's because recordings—phonograph records, for example—were not protected by the federal copyright laws until February 15, 1972. The underlying musical composition was protected by copyright, but not the recording itself. Before 1972, sound recordings were protected by state anti-piracy laws and common law (judge-made law). You probably won't find any copyright notice on a pre-1972 recording, but this does not mean it is not legally protected. These state law protections will not all expire until 2047.

3. Post-1963 Works Are Protected by Copyright Far Into the 21st Century

All works first published after 1963 will be protected by copyright until well into the 21st Century. Works published during the years 1964 through 1977 will be under copyright for 75 years after publication.

In 1978, the current copyright law took effect, and new copyright terms apply. Individually authored works created after 1977 usually are protected for the life of the author plus 50 years. Note that the copyright term begins when the work is created, not when it's published (which may be some time later). Post-1977 works made for hire are protected for 75 years after publication.

You don't have to memorize all these rules. Just remember that any work published after 1963 will be under copyright for many decades to come. Permission must be obtained to use such works in a multimedia project unless the use constitutes a fair used as discussed in Section D, below.

4. Unpublished Works

An unpublished manuscript, artwork or other work of authorship created by an individual author is under copyright for the life of the author plus 50 years. An unpublished work for hire is protected for 100 years after creation.

A special rule applies to unpublished works created by individual authors who have been dead over 50 years and unpublished works for hire created over 100 years ago. Under the rules outlined above, such works should now be in the public domain—but they're not. A special provision of the copyright law protects such works through December 31, 2002. But if such works are published before 2003, they will remain under copyright until the end of 2027.

Again, you don't have to memorize all of these rules. Just remember that, at least until 2003 (and far longer in most cases), you'll need permission to use any unpublished work.

5. Derivative Works

Special problems often arise determining the copyright status of derivative works—that is, works created by transforming or adapting preexisting works. Examples of derivative works include translations of foreign language works into English and transformation of a work into a new medium, such as a photograph of a painting or sculpture.

A derivative work is considered to be a brand new work for copyright purposes and is entitled to its own term of copyright protection, independent of the protection given to the underlying work. This means that many works you might think are in the public domain really aren't. Consider these examples:

- The original Greek version of Homer's *The Iliad* is in the public domain, but a 1980 English translation of *The Iliad* is a derivative work protected by copyright until well into the next century.

- Shakespeare's *Hamlet* is in the public domain, but a 1960 film of *Hamlet* is a protected derivative work. Likewise, a 1980 printed student edition of *Hamlet* is in the public domain, but footnotes and other explanatory material included in the edition are protected by copyright.

- Gainsborough's famous eighteenth century painting *Blueboy* is in the public domain, but a 1970 photograph of *Blueboy* is a copyrighted derivative work.

- The traditional song *Greensleeves* is in the public domain, but a 1950 arrangement of the song is protected by copyright.
- Beethoven's Fifth Symphony is in the public domain, but a 1990 recording of it by the New York Philharmonic is under copyright.

A multimedia developer must obtain permission to use the derivative works described above, or, alternatively, must go back to the original public domain source for the derivative work and use that instead. For example, a developer that didn't want to pay for permission to use the New York Philharmonic's recording of Beethoven's Fifth could hire musicians to make its own recording without getting permission from anybody.

It can be difficult to determine which parts of a derivative work are in the public domain and which are protected by copyright. You may wish to retain the services of a copyright search firm to investigate the work's copyright status. By searching Copyright Office and other records, these firms can tell you when each element of a work was created and/or published. (See the sidebar in Section C1b, above, for a list of search firms.)

6. Things That Are Never Protected by Copyright

Certain works of authorship and other items are never protected by copyright. These consist of:

- *Ideas and facts.* Because copyright only protects an author's expression, ideas and facts themselves are not protected. (See Chapter 3, Section D1, for a detailed discussion.)
- *Words, names, titles, slogans and other short phrases.* Individual words are always in the public domain, even if they are invented by a particular person. Names (whether of individuals, products or business organizations or groups), titles, slogans and other short phrases are also not copyrightable. However, these items may be protected under state and federal trademark laws if they are used to identify a product or service. (See Chapter 6.)

- *United States government works.* All works created by U.S. government employees as part of their jobs are in the public domain. This includes, for example, everything printed by the U.S. Printing Office, NASA photographs, the President's speeches and publications and other works by federal agencies. But this rule does not apply to U.S. postage stamps, which *are* protected by copyright. Also, this rule does not apply to works by state and local government employees; those works may be protected by copyright.

  Works created for the federal government by independent contractors—that is, persons who are neither U.S. government officers nor employees—can be protected by copyright. However, the government may require these persons to sign "work made for hire" agreements as a condition to receiving federal money. In this event, the U.S. government, not the individual who actually created the work, would be considered the "author" of the work; this would mean that the work would be in the public domain.

7. Works Dedicated to the Public Domain

The owners of some works have decided they don't want them to be protected by copyright and dedicate them to the public domain. For example, some software has been dedicated to the public domain; such software is sometimes referred to as "freeware." There are no formal procedures for dedicating a work to the public domain. The author just has to indicate on the work that no copyright is claimed. The Copyright Office will not register such a work.

8. Public Domain Works Are Not Always Freely Available

The fact that a work is in the public domain does not necessarily mean that it is freely available for use by a multimedia developer. Although the copyright in a work may have expired, the work itself may still be owned by someone, who may restrict or charge for access to it.

This is usually not a problem for written works, which can be found in bookstores and libraries, but it is a problem for other types of works. For example, all artworks published over 75 years old are in the public domain, but recent photographs of them are not. Museums and individual collectors usually control access to valuable works of art that are in the public domain and often own all available photographs of such works. Getting permission to use such photographs or to take new ones can be difficult and expensive. Some large software developers, such as Microsoft, are reportedly buying the exclusive right to use the photographs of many important artworks in multimedia programs.

Fees may also have to be paid to obtain access to and make use of public domain photographs, film and music from collectors, private archives and other sources. (See discussion in Section E, below.)

D. The "Fair Use" Exception to Copyrighted Works

Even if the material you want to use is protected by copyright, you will not need permission if your intended use constitutes a "fair use." Under the fair use rule, an author is permitted to make limited use of preexisting protected works without asking permission. All copyright owners are deemed to give their automatic consent to the fair use of their work by others. The fair use rule is an important exception to a copyright owner's exclusive rights.

The fair use rule is designed to aid the advancement of knowledge, which is the reason for having a copyright law in the first place. If scholars, educators and others were required to obtain permission every time they quoted or otherwise used brief portions of other authors' works, the progress of knowledge would be greatly impeded.

Determining whether the fair use privilege applies in any given situation is not an exact scientific process. Rather, it requires a delicate balancing of all the factors discussed below. Probably the best rule for fair use is the following variant of the Golden Rule: "*Take not from others to such an extent and in such a manner that you would be resentful if they so took from you"* (McDonald, *Non-infringing Uses*, 9 Bull. Copyright Society 466 (1962)).

The following four factors must be considered to determine whether an intended use of an item constitutes a fair use:

- the purpose and character of the use,
- the nature of the copyrighted work,
- the effect of the use upon the potential market for or value of the copyrighted work, and
- the amount and substantiality of the portion used in relation to the copyrighted work as a whole (17 U.S.C. 107).

Not all these factors are equally important in every case, but all are considered by the courts in deciding whether a use is "fair." You should consider them all in making your own fair use analysis.

 If you're not sure whether an intended use is a fair use, seek legal advice or get permission.

1. The Purpose and Character of the Use

First, the purpose and character of your intended use must be considered in determining whether it is a fair use. The test here is to see whether the subsequent work merely serves as a substitute for the original or "instead adds something new, with a further purpose or different character, altering the first with new expression, meaning, or message." *Campbell v. Acuff-Rose Music, Inc.* 114 S.Ct. 1164 (1994). The Supreme Court calls such a new work "transformative."

This is a very significant factor. The more transformative a work, the less important are the other fair use factors, such as commercialism, that may weigh against a finding of fair use. Why should this be? It is because the goal of copyright to promote human knowledge is furthered by the creation of transformative works. "Such works thus lie at the heart of the fair use doctrine's guarantee of a breathing space within the confines of copyright." *Campbell v. Acuff-Rose Music, Inc.*

Following are very typical examples of "transformative" uses where preexisting expression is used to help create new and different works. These types of uses are most likely to be fair uses:

- *Criticism and comment*—*for example, quoting or excerpting a work in a review or criticism for purposes of illustration or comment.*
- *News reporting*—*for example, summarizing an address or article, with quotations, in a news report.*
- *Research and scholarship*—*for example, quoting a passage in a scholarly, scientific or technical work for illustration or clarification of the author's observations.*

Although not really "transformative," photocopying by teachers for classroom use may also be a fair use since teaching also furthers the knowledge-enriching goals of the copyright laws.

Note that the uses listed above, with the possible exception of news reporting, are primarily for nonprofit educational purposes. Although some money may be earned from writing a review or scholarly work, financial gain is not usually the primary motivation—disseminating information or otherwise advancing human knowledge is. The fact that a work is published primarily for private commercial gain weighs against a finding of fair use.

2. The Nature of the Copyrighted Work

Since the purpose of the fair use privilege is to advance knowledge, you have more leeway in taking material from factual works (for example, scientific treatises, histories, newspapers) than you do from original creative works like novels, plays, artworks or musical compositions.

a. Unpublished Works

As a general rule, you need to get permission to use an unpublished work—that is, a work that has not been made available to the public on an unrestricted basis. Publishing someone's work before she has authorized it infringes upon the creator's right to decide when and whether her work will be made public.

Example: *Multisolutions Software discovers an unpublished Ph.D. thesis on Columbus. It would probably not be a fair use for Multisolutions to publish portions of the thesis in its multimedia program. The work's author should have the right to decide when and how to first publish her work. For example, she may want to incorporate it into a book.*

3. Effect of Use on Market for Work

You must also consider the effect of the use upon the potential market for or value of the copyrighted work. You must contemplate not only the harm caused by your act of copying, but whether similar copying by others would have a substantial adverse impact on the potential market for the original work.

Since fair use is an affirmative defense to copyright infringement, it is up to the defendant—the copier—in an infringement case to show there is no harm to the potential market for the original work. This can be difficult. The more "transformative" the subsequent work—the more it differs from the original and is aimed at a different market—the less likely will it be deemed to adversely affect the potential market for the original.

But, if you want to use an author's protected expression in a work of your own that is similar to the prior work and aimed at the same market, your intended use will probably be deemed to adversely affect the potential market for the prior work. This weighs against a finding of fair use.

For example, it would likely not be a fair use for MultiSolutions Software to take material from a competitor's multimedia work about Columbus, since this could impair the market for the competitor's program. Indeed, it may not even be a fair use for MultiSolutions to take material from a book about Columbus if the book's publisher intended to create a multimedia program of its own using the book as part of the contents.

**GIVING CREDIT DOES NOT MAKE A USE "FAIR"
(BUT SHOULD ALWAYS BE PROVIDED)**

Some people have the mistaken idea that they can use any amount of material so long as they give the creator or copyright owner credit. This is simply not true. Providing credit will not in and of itself make a use "fair." Nevertheless, attribution should *always* be provided for any material obtained or copied from third parties. Passing yourself off as the creator of other people's work is a good way to get sued for copyright infringement, and is likely to make a judge or jury angry if you are sued. Quoting with attribution is a very good hedge against getting sued, or losing big if you are sued. Thus, you should always provide a credit line for any material you make fair use of.

4. The Amount of Material Used

The more material you take, the more likely it is that your use will adversely affect the ability of the copyright owner to commercially exploit the work, which in turn makes it less likely that the use can be a fair use. There are no set limits on how much material can be taken under the fair use doctrine; it is not always "okay" to take one paragraph or fewer than 200 words of a written work. For instance, copying 12 words from a 14-word haiku poem wouldn't be a fair use. Nor would copying 200 words from a work of 300 words likely qualify as a fair use. However, copying 2,000 words from a work of 500,000 words might be "fair."

The *quality* of the material you want to use must be considered as well as the quantity. The more important it is to the original work, the less likely is your use a fair use. For example, in one famous case, *The Nation* magazine obtained a copy of Gerald Ford's memoirs prior to their publication. The magazine published an article about the memoirs in which only 300 words from Ford's 200,000-word manuscript were quoted verbatim. The Supreme Court held that this was not a fair use because the material quoted, dealing with the Nixon pardon, was the "heart of the book...the most interesting and moving parts of the entire manuscript" (*Harper & Row Publishers, Inc. v. Nation Enterprises*, 471 U.S. 539 (1985)).

E. Obtaining Permission to Use Copyrighted Materials

If you want to use material that is not in the public domain and your use doesn't qualify as a fair use, you need to get permission. With the notable exception of the music industry, which has had a system of rights collectives in place for many decades, obtaining permission to use copyrighted materials in a multimedia project is a difficult, time-consuming and often chaotic process.

Obtaining multimedia permissions can be especially hard because, for a variety of reasons, many copyright owners are reluctant to grant any multimedia permissions. Many owners have decided not to grant multimedia permissions for the time being because the market is so new they're unsure how much such rights are worth. Others are reluctant to permit their work to be reduced to digitized form for fear they will lose control over unauthorized copying. Still others intend to launch their own multimedia ventures and don't want to help potential competitors. Some owners will grant permission, but only for exorbitant amounts of money (there are no standard rates for such permissions).

Securing a multimedia permission, then, can require a good deal of persistence, salesmanship and creative negotiating on a developer's part. You should follow a two-step process:

- find out who owns the rights you need permission to exercise (license), then
- negotiate and have the rights owner sign a written Multimedia Publicity/Privacy Release or Multimedia License Agreement (see Sections F and G, below, for further information and sample forms).

We'll first provide an overview of copyright rights and ownership and then take a look at how to go about obtaining permission to use text, images, music and third-party software.

1. Who Owns the Rights You Need to License?

Finding out who owns the multimedia rights to the material you want to use can be your biggest headache of all. Let's first look at the different type of copyright rights then examine how to find who owns the rights you need to license.

a. Which Rights You May Need to License

When a copyrightable work is created, the creator or his or her employer or hirer automatically becomes the owner of a bundle of the following exclusive rights:

- *Reproduction rights.* The right to make copies of a protected work;
- *Distribution rights.* The right to sell or otherwise distribute copies to the public;
- *Rights to create adaptations (or "derivative works").* The right to prepare new works based on the protected work; and
- *Performance and display rights.* The right to perform or display in public a protected literary, musical, dramatic, choreographic, pantomime, motional picture or audiovisual work, whether in person or by means of a device like a television.

Which rights do you need to license? You'll always need permission to exercise the reproduction and distribution rights. If you plan to alter the original work in any way, you'll also need to license the right to creative adaptations (usually called "derivative works").

Performance and display rights will also be needed if the multimedia work will be performed or displayed to the public or at any place where a substantial number of persons outside the normal circle of a family and its social acquaintances are gathered. For example, performance rights would have to be licensed to use a clip from a motion picture in a multimedia sales presentation for a sales convention or in bars. Performance and display rights are not needed where a multimedia work is intended for personal use in the home or office.

b. Unitary vs. Multiple Ownership of Copyright Rights

Each of the copyright rights a work contains may be separately sold or licensed to others. For example, the author of a novel can grant the right to publish (reproduce and distribute) it to a publisher and sell the right to create adaptions (movies, for example) to another person or entity. Things don't stop there, however. Each copyright right may be subdivided and sold or licensed in an almost infinite number of ways; a copyright is infinitely divisible. For example, a book author may divide her reproduction and distribution rights by territory, time, and/or type of publication (an author may grant a publisher the right to publish her work in book form, but retain the right to use it in an electronic publication). Moreover, any of these rights can be granted on an exclusive or nonexclusive basis.

In many cases, a single person or entity will own all the rights in a work. In this event, it is clear who has the multimedia rights and you need only have the copyright owner sign a single license agreement.

But where the rights in a work have been transferred to multiple people or entities (or where an author has transferred some rights and retained others), you may need to obtain permission from several sources. Some investigation will often be necessary to determine who has the rights you need to license.

c. Investigating the Copyright Status of a Work

It is always a good idea to investigate a work's copyright status to make sure that you obtain permission from all the people or entities who control the rights you need. All transfer agreements (publishing and licensing agreements) should be reviewed and Copyright Office records searched. You can do a copyright search yourself at the Copyright Office in Washington, D.C., have the Copyright Office to do it or hire a search firm. The last option is often the best, even though it is the most expensive. Copyright search firms such as Thomson & Thomson Copyright Research Group (the best known search firm) can search not only the Copyright Office records to see if a work's copyright rights have been transferred or assigned, but can look through the extensive databases they maintain as well. Thomson & Thomson can research the status of an individual work, as well as all works by a given author. Depending on the extent of the search you request, search firms charge anywhere between $250-$500 or more. (See the sidebar, "How To Research

Copyright Renewals," in Section C1b, above, for a list of these firms and the address of the Copyright Office.)

d. Obtaining Warranties and Indemnifications from the Copyright Owner

It will not always be economically feasible to do a copyright search for every item to be included in a multimedia work. In addition, even if a search is done, it may not always be conclusive. This means there will often be some uncertainty as to whether the person or entity you're dealing with really has the rights you need. For this reason, you should try to get the copyright owner to warrant (guarantee) that your use of the work will not infringe upon the proprietary rights of any third party and agree to indemnify you (pay any attorney fees and damages) if a third party later claims that your use of the material violates her ownership rights. (See Section G1g, below, for detailed discussion.)

e. Insurance Coverage for Copyright, Publicity and Privacy Disputes

If a developer makes a mistake and fails to get the necessary permissions and/or releases to use a work, it can become embroiled in expensive litigation. The costs of defending lawsuits and perhaps paying damages could conceivably bankrupt a multimedia developer. It is possible—and often advisable—to obtain insurance to cover potential claims arising from alleged copyright infringement, invasions of privacy, violation of publicity rights and defamation. This kind of insurance is called "Errors and Omissions" coverage or "E&O" insurance. Producers of theatrical film and television shows commonly obtain this type of insurance; it is available for multimedia products as well. E&O insurance is expensive, however, and deductibles are often high. Also, an E&O insurer will demand that you make a diligent effort to obtain all necessary licenses and releases for the material you use, as well as conduct copyright searches. E&O policies typically exclude coverage for any work for which you failed to obtain the necessary licenses and releases. In other words, you can't use a work without permission just because you have E&O insurance.

Lenders and venture capitalists may require that you obtain such insurance. Some copyright owners may demand that you do so as well and name them as an additional insured on the policy. E&O coverage is offered by several companies; rates vary, so it pays to shop around. Contact an insurance broker familiar with these type of policies for help.

CLEARANCE FIRMS

If you need to obtain many permissions, or simply don't want to bother getting them yourself, there are private companies and individuals who obtain permissions on an author or publisher's behalf. These permission specialists may have contacts with some publishers that enable them to get better and faster results than you can yourself. Clearance firms usually charge by the hour.

Some of the best known clearance firms are:

- Jill Arofs, Total Clearance, P.O. Box 836, Mill Valley, CA 94942, 415-445-5800
- BZ Rights and Permissions, Inc., 125 West 72nd St., New York, NY 10023, 212-580-0615, Fax: 212-769-9224
- Clearing House, Ltd., 6605 Hollywood Blvd., Hollywood, CA 90028 213-469-3186, Fax: 213-469-1213
- The Content Company, 171 E. 74th Street, 2nd Floor, New York, NY 10021, 212-772-7363
- DeForest Research, 1645 Vine St., Suite 532, Hollywood, CA 90028, 212-469-2271.
- Betsy Strode, 1109 Southdown Rd., Hillsborough, CA 94010, 415-340-1370
- Suzy Vaughn Clip Clearance Services, 2029 Century Park East, #420, Los Angeles, CA 90067, 310-566-1409, Fax: 310-556-1861

Others are listed in the *Literary Market Place* (*LMP*), a directory for the publishing business, under "Permissions." The *LMP* can be found in the reference section of many libraries.

---

2. Written Materials (Text)

Obtaining permission to use any type of copyrighted written materials—excerpts from books, magazines, journals and so forth—can be merely difficult or simply impossible. There is no single, centralized group or organization granting such permissions and there are no standard fees. You—or someone you hire—must track down the copyright owner of the material you want to use, or his or her representative (usually publisher or agent), and cut your own deal.

a. Contact the Publisher

Your first step should be to contact the "permissions department" of the publisher of the material you want to use. The publisher may own the right to reproduce the material as part of a multimedia program or may have been given authority by the author or other copyright owner to grant permissions. If not, the publisher may forward your request to the author or other copyright owner.

If the publisher proves uncooperative, is out of business or can't be located, you'll need to contact the work's author or other copyright owner directly. A search of the Copyright Office's records will yield an address for the author or other copyright owner, which may or may not be current. (See discussion in Section E1c, above.)

Use the Multimedia License Permission Form set forth in Section G2, below, and be prepared to wait. It can take weeks or months for a publisher to process your request; some may never respond.

b. Verify Ownership of Multimedia Rights

When an author sells a book to a publisher, the publishing contract will define which rights the publisher gets and which the author keeps, if any. Normally, the publisher will acquire the exclusive right to publish the book in the U.S.; this is sometimes called the "primary right." All the other rights are called "subsidiary rights." These include, for example, film, television, radio and live-stage adaptation rights, as well as the right to create and distribute nondramatic audio recordings. The right to license a work for use in a multimedia program or other electronic publication is also a subsidiary right.

Typically a book author will transfer some or all of her subsidiary rights to the publisher and the publisher will agree to give the author a percentage of any monies it makes from them. (A 50-50 split is common.) Established authors with agents who can sell their subsidiary rights for them typically insist on retaining many of their more valuable subsidiary rights—film rights, for example. Such authors often retain the electronic rights to their work. Authors who do not have agents typically transfer all their subsidiary rights to their publisher.

When you're dealing with a publisher or agent, it will normally review the publishing contract to determine whether it has the rights you're seeking. If you're dealing directly with the author or other individual, you should ask for a copy of the publishing agreement and review it to see whether the author actually has the rights you need.

What should you look for? Newer publishing agreements usually contain provisions regarding ownership of "electronic rights," "motion picture and audiovisual rights" and/or "videocassette rights." Unfortunately, there are no standard definitions of these terms. Thus, in some contracts the holder of the electronic rights may have the multimedia rights, while in others they may belong to the owner of the motion picture and audiovisual rights. Older publishing contracts will not have any provisions directly mentioning computer software or electronic rights. Such contracts often contain a provision granting the publisher the right to sell all or part of the work for "mechanical reproduction and transmission" by any then known or later devised method for information storage, reproduction and retrieval. This may include multimedia rights, but it's not entirely clear.

Authors who are employees. Determining ownership of multimedia rights is usually straightforward for works created by authors employed by the publisher—for example, articles written by magazine or newspaper staff writers. These are works made for hire to which the publisher owns all the rights.

3. Photographs

If you need photographs, several sources are available. You can try to get the rights to use photos that have appeared in magazines, books and other publications; you can directly contact photographers and try to get permission to use their work; you can use commercially available clipmedia; or you can deal with stock photo agencies.

a. Clipmedia

A wide variety of photographs (as well as drawings and other graphics and sounds) is commercially available in the form of clipmedia. These materials are typically published on CD-ROM disks specifically for users to incorporate into multimedia and other works. Clipmedia is usually owned by someone, although some is in the public domain. Before you buy any clipmedia, review the license agreement to make sure you can publicly distribute the material for commercial purposes. Some clipmedia is available for personal use only.

b. Photos in Magazines, Books and Newspapers

Start by contacting the publication's permissions department. As with text, there may be difficulty determining who owns the right to reproduce a photo. Photos taken by employee-photographers (staff photographers for newspapers and magazines) are works made for hire, to which the employer owns all rights. However, photos taken by freelance photographers may or may not be owned by the publication in which they appear.

Some publications acquire all the copyright rights to the photos they publish, but this is generally not the case. This means the contract between the photographer and publication in which the photo first appeared must be tracked down and reviewed.

Simply locating the contract can be difficult and time-consuming. If it is found, you should read the contract yourself to make sure you're getting what you pay for. The contract may not directly address re-use in a multimedia product, so it can be hard to tell who has the right to permit such use. In addition, some contracts may require that an additional fee be paid to the photographer when a photo is reused, and may even impose restrictions on how it may be used.

c. Stock Photo Agencies

One alternative to going through the hassle of seeking permission to use photos from publications or photographers is to obtain photos from stock photo agencies. These are companies that acquire the rights to thousands or, in some cases, millions, of photos and license them over and over again to magazines, advertising agencies, book publishers and others. Some stock houses specialize in particular types of photographs—for example, sports photos or historical pictures. Stock houses typically charge a flat fee for each photo, usually at least $100-$200. However, it may be possible for a software developer to obtain a "blanket license" to use any of the photos in a stock agency's collection at a reduced rate.

There are hundreds of stock photo agencies in the U.S. Below is a list of directories that list stock photo agencies. No one directory lists all of them.

The ASMP Stock Photo Handbook
ASMP—National
419 Park Avenue S., #1407E
New York, NY 10016

ASPP—Member Directory
P.O. Box 594
Church Street Station
New York, NY 10008

Photo Marketing Handbook
Images Press
22 East 17th Street, 4th Floor
New York, NY 10003

Photographer's Market
Writer's Digest Books
1507 Dana Avenue
Cincinnati, OH 45207

Picture Sources
Special Libraries Association
1700 Eighteenth St. NW, Ste. 5
Washington, DC 20009

Stock Photo Deskbook
The Photographic Arts Center
163 Amsterdam Ave., #201
New York, NY 10023

OBTAINING STOCK PHOTOS ON-LINE

Several companies have started or are planning to start on-line stock photography services. The user connects via modem to a searchable central database containing thousands of images and then downloads high-resolution copies of the images she wants. These on-line services include:

- Comstock's On-Line Access, 800-225-2727
- Kodak Picture Exchange, 800-579-8737
- Picture Network International, 703-558-7860
- PressLink, 703-758-1740How To Research Copyright Renewals

4. Film and Video

A variety of film and video footage is available from stock houses— companies that acquire the right to license films and videos. Available footage may include historical and newsreel footage, commercials, documentaries and other material. Normally a flat fee is charged, depending on the number of seconds or frames of film being used and the nature of the use. Stock footage typically costs about $1,000 per minute, but you may be able to find some footage for much less. For example, Media-Pedia Video Clips offers a 50 minute library of clips on video or CD-ROM for just a few hundred dollars; their address is:

Media-Pedia Video Clips
22 Fisher Ave.
Wellesley, MA 02181
617-237-3440

An excellent directory of stock photo, film and video houses, which is available either in book form or CD-ROM (for Mac only), is:

Footage 91: Film and Video Sources
Prelinger Associates, Inc.
430 W. 14th St., Rm. 403
New York, NY 10014
800-243-2252

A directory that may be more easily found in libraries is:

Video Sourcebook, by Furtaw (R.R. Bowker)

Other excellent sources of information about video footage are these video trade magazines:

AV Video	*Videography*
Montage Publishing	United Business Publications
25550 Hawthorne Blvd., Ste. 314	475 Park Ave. South
Torrance, CA 90505	New York, NY 10016

Obtaining clips from theatrical films and TV shows is difficult and extremely expensive. In addition to obtaining the rights you need from the work's copyright owner, you may need permission from the work's creators—actors, writers, directors, choreographers and musicians. Re-use fees may have to be paid to some or all of these, pursuant to entertainment union contracts.

 If you want to use theatrical film or TV footage, it's advisable to hire a professional clearance firm or entertainment lawyer to negotiate the rights for you.

IMAGE SAMPLING

With modern digital technology, it is very easy for a multimedia developer to take a photo or film or video footage and alter it to such an extent that it is no longer recognizable by its original creator. Is this copyright infringement? If the end result is not recognizable as coming from the original, it may not be. In the words of one court, "copying... so disguised as to be unrecognizable is not copying" (*See v. Durang*, 711 F.2d 141 (9th Cir. 1983)). However, before the final result is reached, it may be necessary to create intermediate copies of the original work that are clearly recognizable. It is unclear whether this would constitute copyright infringement. The conservative approach is to obtain permission before using any copyrighted photo or footage.

---

5. Drawings and Other Artwork

Many drawings and other artwork can be obtained in the form of clipmedia. Permission to use and reproduce other drawings, paintings and other works of art must be obtained from the owner, or sometimes the artist. Artists sometimes retain the reproduction rights to a particular piece while selling the piece itself and the right to display it. The person or entity controlling the reproduction rights must be tracked down—whether a museum, individual collector, artist or artist's estate. Fees and terms for such rights vary widely.

a. Artists' Moral Rights

In many countries, creative people are granted "moral rights" in addition to and separate from their copyright rights in their creations. Briefly, moral rights consist of the right to proper credit or attribution whenever a work is published, to disclaim authorship of unauthorized copies, to prevent or call back distribution of a work if it no longer represents the author's views, and to object to any distortion, mutilation or other modification of the creator's work injurious to her reputation. The right to prevent colorization of a black and white film or photograph is one example of a "moral right."

In many countries, an author retains her moral rights even after she transfers her copyright rights in a work. In some countries, moral rights may be waived by contract; in others, they cannot. This means that an artist or author may have moral rights in some countries even after she has contractually granted a multimedia developer the right to edit or otherwise alter her work. Moral rights are particularly strong in France and other countries that follow the French civil law tradition.

Historically, moral rights have not been recognized in the United States. However, in 1991 Congress enacted the Visual Artists Rights Act ("VARA"; 17 U.S.C. 106A) to extend some of the moral rights discussed above to visual artists. The VARA covers only works of fine art: paintings, drawings, sculptures and photographs produced for exhibition in a limited signed edition of no more than 200 copies. The VARA does not apply to motion pictures or other audiovisual works, electronic publications, works made for hire or applied artworks such as advertisements or technical drawings.

The VARA gives artists the rights of attribution (the right to be named as author of the work) and integrity (the right to prevent the intentional destruction or modification of the work in a way that harms the artist's reputation). This means that an artist might be able to object if she believes a multimedia developer has distorted or mutilated her work for inclusion in a multimedia product.

An artist's rights under VARA can be waived by contract. It is a good idea to obtain such a waiver whenever possible. Our sample multimedia license agreement contains such a waiver (see Section G2, below). Such a waiver will also be effective in some, but not all, foreign countries.

6. Cartoons

The rights to cartoons are usually handled by distribution syndicates or agents. A flat fee is customarily charged for a limited time use. You should be able to find out who to contact for permission by calling the publication in which the cartoon appeared.

7. Music

The music industry is the only branch of the copyright industry that has in place a standardized process for obtaining permissions. For this reason, obtaining multimedia rights to music is far easier than for any other form of third party material.

> **FURTHER REFERENCE**
>
> Our discussion just scratches the surface of music licensing. For a superb detailed explanation of all the issues involved in music licensing, including a special chapter on multimedia, refer to *The Art of Music Licensing*, by Al and Bob Kohn (Prentice Hall Law & Business, 270 Sylvan Ave, Englewood Cliffs, NJ 07632; 800-223-0231). This book is expensive—about $80—but it's well worth it.

a. Music Copyrights

As we noted in Section E1a, above, a copyright is infinitely divisible. A given piece of music will usually be sold or licensed in a number of different ways.

For example, here are some (but not all) of the different licenses a songwriter can grant for the same song:

- a print license authorizing someone to print the song as sheet music,
- a mechanical license permitting the licensee to reproduce the song in a record, CD, tape, etc.,
- a synchronization license permitting the song to be used in a film, video or other audiovisual work, and
- a performance license authorizing the song to be performed publicly.

Things are made even more complicated by the fact that there are two completely separate copyrights involved in a musical recording:

- *The copyright in the song or other musical composition itself.* The copyright in a song is usually owned solely by a music publisher or co-owned by the publisher and songwriter. Copyrights in songs themselves are sometimes called "publishing rights."
- *The copyright in the recording company's sound recording.* When a song or other musical composition is recorded by a recording company, a new work (a "derivative" work) is created. The recording company usually owns the copyright in a sound recording. Unless the song is in the public domain, the recording company must obtain permission from the copyright owner of the song to record it.

This means that to make a new recording of a song for inclusion in a multimedia work, a developer must obtain permission from the music publisher and perhaps the songwriter. But to use an existing recording, permission must be obtained from the music publisher, perhaps the songwriter *and* the recording company. As outlined below, it's far easier to do the first than the second.

MUSIC SAMPLING

With modern digital audio technology, anyone with access to a digital synthesizer can capture all or part of a previous recording and reuse bits and pieces in new recordings. The unauthorized sampling of even a few seconds of a sound recording can constitute copyright infringement of both the sound recording from which the sample is taken and the underlying song. Particularly if the recording is well-known, there is a real risk of being sued for illegal copying and having to pay substantial damages. This risk is reduced if the sampled sounds are so altered that their original source is not recognizable. But if the source of sampled music is recognizable, permission for the use should be obtained as outlined in this section. A good general rule is, "If you can name the tune, get permission." (For a detailed discussion of sampling, see *The Art of Music Licensing*, by Al and Bob Kohn (Prentice Hall Law & Business).)

b. Making New Recordings of Existing Music

The music industry has developed a highly efficient process for obtaining permission to make a new recording of existing copyrighted music and reproducing it in a multimedia program. The Harry Fox Agency—a subsidiary of the National Music Publishers' Association—issues licenses and collects and distributes royalties on behalf of music publishers who have entered into agreements with Fox for this service. About 80% of all music publishers utilize the Harry Fox Agency.

A software developer need only tell The Harry Fox Agency what music it would like to license. Fox will determine who owns the rights and contact them for a price quotation. There are no set rates for the use of music in multimedia programs. Most music publishers will demand a royalty for the use of their music rather than charge a fixed fee up-front. Currently, the average royalty is 12 cents per unit manufactured and distributed. Thus, if a software developer used eight songs at this rate, it would have to pay 96 cents to the Harry Fox Agency for each program it distributed. However, keep in mind that the 12-cent rate is only an average. Some publishers may demand more, some less. This is a matter for negotiation.

The Harry Fox Agency will help with negotiations. It has developed a multimedia recording license for music, called an MMERL License, for the parties to sign. The agency can be contacted at:

The Harry Fox Agency
205 E. 42nd St.
New York, NY 10017
212-370-5330

The Harry Fox Agency handles what are known as mechanical and synchronization licenses—licenses to record a song or other musical composition and use it in conjunction with still or moving images. This is sufficient for personal use of a multimedia program. However, if a multimedia product containing a musical composition is to be performed publicly, a public performance license must be obtained from the copyright owner as well. Under the Copyright Act, a public performance occurs when a work is performed "at a place open to the public or at any place where a substantial number of persons outside the normal circle of a family and its social acquaintances is gathered" (17 U.S.C. 101). Thus, for example, the developer of a multimedia program designed to be used for sales presentations at conventions, in bars or other public places would need to obtain a performance license for any songs it wanted to include in the work.

Almost all U.S. music publishers and composers use one of three performing rights societies to serve as their agents for the licensing of performance rights. These are (in order of size):

ASCAP (American Society of Composers, Authors & Publishers)
One Lincoln Plaza
New York, NY 10023
212-595-3050

BMI (Broadcast Music, Inc.)
320 W. 57th St.
New York, NY 10019
212-586-2000

SESAC (Society of European State Authors and Composers)
156 W. 56th St.
New York, NY 10019
212-586-3450

Contact ASCAP first. If it does not serve as agent for the music publisher or composer involved, contact BMI. Together, ASCAP and BMI represent 99% of all U.S. music publishers and composers.

c. Using Existing Recordings

Obtaining permission to use an existing recording can be more difficult and expensive than making a new one. First, it is necessary to obtain the mechanical and synchronization rights to the music itself through the Harry Fox Agency, as outlined above. If the multimedia product is to be performed in public, a performance license must also be obtained through the appropriate performing rights society. Permission must also be obtained to use the recording itself (termed "master recording rights") from the owner of the copyright in the recording.

The "special markets division" of the appropriate recording company must be contacted to obtain master recording rights. The recording contract must be examined to see who has the right to grant permission to re-use the recording. This may be the record company or the artist. Recording companies are generally reluctant to permit their recordings to be reused, particularly if a well-known song is performed by a well-known artist. Where obtainable, permission to do so is usually very expensive. Musician union agreements may also require that re-use fees be paid to the musicians, vocalists and others who worked on the recording.

MUSIC CLEARANCE FIRMS

Developers who do not wish to go to the time and trouble of obtaining music permissions themselves can retain the services of music clearance firms. For a fee, these companies will request, negotiate and process music permissions. Using such firms will usually be cheaper than retaining a music attorney, and they are often more effective. These firms are located primarily in New York, Los Angeles and Nashville, the centers of the music business. Two of the best known firms are:

BZ Rights and Permissions, Inc.
125 West 72nd St.
New York, NY 10023
212-580-0615
Fax: 212-769-9224

Clearing House, Ltd.
6605 Hollywood Blvd.
Hollywood, CA 90028
213-469-3186
Fax: 213-469-1213

d. Music Libraries

Probably the cheapest and easiest way to obtain the rights to "generic" music is to license it from music libraries (also called Production Music Libraries or "PML's"). Original music by lesser known artists and sound effects are available from music libraries. Several libraries are listed in the publication *Songwriter's Market* (Writer's Digest Books). Production Music Libraries control the rights to both the recording and the song or other musical composition. This means the multimedia developer need only deal with the music library to obtain all the rights it needs.

8. Software

Multimedia programs often include third-party software—software "engines"— that drive the program and application software programs to support graphics, sound and animation. A license from the copyright owner must be obtained to distribute third party software with a multimedia program. To obtain such a license, contact the software publisher.

In our example above, MultiSolutions Software wanted its program to contain Apple operating system software and HyperCard software. MultiSolutions would need to obtain a license from Apple to do this. (But MultiSolutions would not need Apple's permission to sell a HyperCard "stack," so long as HyperCard itself was not included on the disk.)

F.   Privacy and Publicity Problems

Privacy and publicity problems arise when a multimedia work uses photographs, video, film or other images of an individual's likeness or recordings of a person's voice. This is a complex area of the law and privacy/publicity rights vary from state to state. The following is a brief overview.

FURTHER REFERENCE

You'll find further discussion of privacy and publicity issues in *Multimedia: Law & Practice*, by Michael D. Scott (Prentice Hall Law & Business). The definitive work on these issues is *The Rights of Publicity and Privacy*, by J. Thomas McCarthy (Clark Boardman Callaghan).

1. Right to Privacy

The right to privacy is simply the right to be left alone. The law protects a person from humiliation, embarrassment, loss of self-esteem or other injury to his or her sensibilities caused by the following types of activities:

- using a person's name, likeness or voice for commercial purposes, without authorization—for example, in an advertisement,
- entering or observing a private or secluded area without consent—for example, spying on a person's home or office without permission to take photographs,
- publicly displaying an image which shows or implies something embarrassing and untrue about someone—for example, using a picture of an uninfected person in a work about sexually transmitted diseases in a way that implies that the person has such a disease, or
- publicly disclosing true, but private and embarrassing facts about a person that are of no legitimate public concern—for example, displaying film footage of a person hugging someone other than his or her spouse.

These privacy rights belong primarily to private individuals. Public officials (persons who hold important elective or appointed offices) and "public figures" have little or no right of privacy for acts relating to their public life. Determining if someone qualifies as a public figure can be difficult. Persons who are extremely influential and powerful, frequently appear in the media, or are in the forefront of public controversies all qualify as "public figures." This includes not only people we normally think of as "celebrities"—film and TV stars, rock stars, sports heroes, famous business tycoons, and so forth—but lesser known individuals involved in public affairs—for example, the heads of the ACLU and NRA.

A person's privacy rights cease when he or she dies. Thus, there are no privacy issues presented in using old photos or archival or newsreel footage of people who are dead.

2. Right of Publicity

The right of publicity is the right to control when and how one's name, voice or likeness may be used for purposes of advertising or trade—for example, to advertise or sell a product or service. Public figures—famous athletes or film stars, for example—can earn substantial sums by endorsing products and appearing in commercials. No one would pay for an endorsement if the right of publicity were not legally protected. Only human beings have a right of publicity; corporations, firms and institutions do not.

Unlike the privacy rights discussed above, the right to publicity continues in some states for many years after a celebrity's death. For example, in California, the right to publicity lasts for 50 years after a person's death; in Oklahoma, 100 years. This means, for example, that it is illegal to use a photo of Marilyn Monroe or Elvis Presley for commercial purposes in California or Oklahoma without the consent of their estates. Because most multimedia programs are nationally distributed, permission must be obtained to use a deceased celebrity's name, likeness or voice for commercial purposes. That is, a developer normally cannot restrict distribution only to those states not providing privacy rights after a person dies.

3. First Amendment Limitations on Privacy/Publicity Rights

The rights to privacy and publicity are not absolute. The First Amendment to the U.S. Constitution guarantees freedom of speech and of the press. The First Amendment gives priority to the public's right to know about newsworthy events of public significance. Courts have held that a person's name or likeness may be used without consent where it is done for educational or informational purposes. This enables the news media to publicly disclose a person's name, likeness or other characteristics without permission for newsworthy and editorial purposes.

The First Amendment applies to software developers as well as to the news media. Under the First Amendment, a multimedia developer has broad latitude to use a person's image, voice or name for educational, cultural and artistic purposes. This is particularly true where public figures are involved. But, if your purpose is primarily to sell a product or service, the First Amendment will not protect the use. For example, film footage of General Norman Schwartzkopf could be used in a CD-ROM history of the Persian Gulf War without violating the General's privacy or publicity rights. However, the General's right to publicity would likely be violated if the same footage was used in a multimedia sales presentation at an arms dealer's convention.

4. Releases of Privacy/Publicity Claims

A release is simply a contract by which a person consents to the use of his name, likeness or other element of his persona for the purposes specified in the release. A release should be obtained from any individual whose likeness, voice, name or other identifiable characteristics are used in recognizable form in a multimedia work that has a purely commercial purpose. It may be difficult to determine whether a multimedia work is just commercial in nature or has an educational, artistic or cultural purpose so as to be protected under the First Amendment (as discussed in Section F3, above). In this event, the conservative approach is to obtain privacy/publicity releases. Such releases may even be required to obtain Errors and Omissions insurance coverage. (See the discussion in Section E1e, above.)

In most cases, you'll have to obtain any necessary releases yourself. Unless they happen to already have releases, it's unlikely that most copyright owners will be willing to get them for you. Stock photo and stock footage houses customarily do not provide releases, although some will do so for an additional fee.

Commercial photographers customarily obtain releases from their models, so you might be able to obtain releases from them when you deal directly with a photographer. If a photographer or other copyright owner has obtained a release for the material you wish to use, make sure to ask for a copy and review it. Here's what to look for:

- Make sure the release covers the material you want to use.
- The release should specify that the photographer may sell or assign the right to use the photos or other materials to third parties.
- If you intend to alter or otherwise change or distort the image, make sure the release allows this.
- A release should always be in writing. If the subject is a minor (under 18 years old), the release should be signed by his or her parent or legal guardian.
- Finally, the release should specify that it is irrevocable, otherwise the release could be terminated by the person giving it at any time.

  If these requirements are not met, a new release must be obtained.

Below is a sample of a self-explanatory valid Multimedia Publicity/ Privacy Release, which may be used in connection with any kind of material. The full text of this release is on the forms disk under MULTIREL.TXT. See Chapter 1, Section C, for instructions on using the forms disk.

SAMPLE
MULTIMEDIA PUBLICITY/PRIVACY RELEASE

In consideration of MultiSolutions Software, Inc.'s ("Developer") agreement to incorporate some or all of the Materials identified below (the "Materials") in one or more of its multimedia works (the "Works"), and other good and valuable consideration, the receipt and sufficiency of which is hereby acknowledged, I hereby grant Developer permission to use, adapt, modify, reproduce, distribute, publicly perform and display, in any form now known or later developed, the Materials specified in this release (as indicated by my initials) throughout the world, by incorporating them into one or more Works and/or advertising and promotional materials relating thereto.

This release is for the following Materials: *(initial appropriate line(s)):*

____ Name

____ Voice

____ Visual likeness (on photographs, video, film, etc.)

____ Photographs, graphics or other artwork as specified: _____

_____

_____

____ Film, videotape or other audiovisual materials as specified: _____

_____

_____

____ Music or sound recordings as specified: _____

_____

_____

____ Other: _____

_____

_____

I warrant and represent that the Materials identified above are either owned by me, and/or are original to me and/or that I have full authority from the owner of the Materials to grant this release.

I release Developer, its agents, employees, licensees and assigns from any and all claims I may have now or in the future for invasion of privacy, right of publicity, copyright infringement, defamation or any other cause of action arising out of the use, reproduction, adaptation, distribution, broadcast, performance or display of the Works.

I waive any right to inspect or approve any Works that may be created containing the Materials.

I understand and agree that Developer is and shall be the exclusive owner of all right, title and interest, including copyright, in the Works, and any advertising or promotional materials containing the Materials, except as to preexisting rights in any of the Materials released hereunder.

I am of full legal age and have read this release and am fully familiar with its contents.

By: _____
    (signature)

_____
(typed or printed name)

Date: _____

G. Multimedia License Agreements

Permission to use all or part of a copyrighted work in a multimedia program should always be obtained in writing. Many of the copyright owners you'll be dealing with—publishers, record companies, and stock photo houses, for example—will likely have their own permission forms or license agreements for you to sign. In that case, there may not be much room for you to negotiate changes.

1. Negotiating a Multimedia License Agreement

Following are the most important things you should be aware of when negotiating a multimedia license agreement. A sample Multimedia License Agreement that covers all of these issues is provided in Section G2, below.

a. Definition: Territory

The agreement should state what territory the license covers. A license may be limited to a particular geographical area—the United States or North America, for example—or it may be worldwide. A worldwide license is best for the developer.

Care must be taken that the territory is the same for every license negotiated for a single multimedia work. This is because the license with the narrowest territory will govern the entire project. For example, if MultiSolutions in our example above negotiated 99 worldwide licenses for its Columbus project and one license limited to the U.S., the finished work could only be distributed in the U.S. (otherwise the U.S.-only license would be violated).

b. The License Grant

The developer must make sure that the copyright owner grants it all the rights necessary to use the material in the multimedia product. This should include the right to use, modify and distribute the material as part of the multimedia product. (For an example, see Clause 3 of the Multimedia License Agreement below. It's also contained on the forms disk under MULTILIC.TXT.)

The license grant should also state whether it is exclusive or nonexclusive. An exclusive license means the developer is the only one permitted to exercise the rights granted in the license; obviously, a nonexclusive license means the opposite—in other words, the copyright owner will be able to license the same material on a nonexclusive basis to others.

Depending on the nature of the material being licensed, it may be important for a developer to obtain an exclusive license since it means competitors will not be able to use the same material. For example, a developer of an entertainment program based on a unique cartoon character will likely wish to have the exclusive right to use the character. However, a nonexclusive license is usually adequate when dealing less unique or important materials, such as run-of-the-mill photos, illustrations or stock footage.

Presumably, the copyright owner would require the developer to pay substantially more for an exclusive license, since it's giving up the right to grant multimedia licenses to others. Many copyright owners will simply refuse to grant an exclusive license. For example, stock photo houses rarely grant exclusive licenses to use their materials.

The copyright owner may wish to limit the license to a particular media format or configuration and/or platform, for example, CD-ROM to run only on the Apple Macintosh. Obviously, this is not in the developer's best interests, since it limits the potential market for the product. Moreover, technological advances are rapidly changing the standard formats used for multimedia works.

c. Term

The developer should try to ensure that the term of the license lasts for the life of the multimedia product. When the license expires, the developer will have to negotiate a new one with the licensor or delete the material from its product.

A perpetual license is best, but the licensor may balk at this or demand substantially more money. A fixed term—five or ten years, for example—may be all the developer can obtain.

As with territory, the term of each license should be the same, because the license with the shortest term will govern the entire project.

d. Payment

Payment can take a variety of forms: for example, a fixed fee up-front, a fixed fee paid over time, an up-front fee combined with a royalty or a straight royalty. Royalties can be paid in a number of ways—for example, a fixed sum for each copy of the work that is sold or a percentage of the price of the product. (See Chapter 12, Section B1, for a detailed discussion of various types of royalty provisions.)

e. Use of Licensed Materials

If you intend to edit or otherwise alter the licensed material in any way, make sure the agreement specifically gives you permission to do so. Some copyright owners may demand control over how their materials appear in the multimedia work. This is a matter for negotiation.

As discussed in Section E5a, above, visual artists have certain moral rights in the United States under the Visual Artists Rights Act and all authors have much broader moral rights in many foreign countries. For this reason, a developer should seek to obtain wherever possible a written waiver of all moral rights held by the creator of the materials being licensed. The sample language in this clause provides such a waiver.

f. Representations and Warranties

A representation and warranty is a legally binding promise about a statement of fact. If the promise turns out not to be true, the promisor can be sued for breach of contract.

The developer should seek to obtain a warranty from the copyright owner that it actually owns the rights to the materials it is licensing and that the use of the materials will not violate any third party's copyright or other proprietary rights. The language in this clause includes this kind of warranty.

Some copyright owners will refuse to grant such a warranty. Indeed, the copyright owner of the material a developer wishes to use may require the *developer* to provide it a warranty of noninfringement. In other words, to obtain permission to use the materials, the developer would guarantee the copyright owner that the use will not result in any copyright infringement claims or other intellectual property infringement claims against the owner. The developer may also have to promise that it will obtain any necessary privacy/publicity and other releases. (See the discussion in Section F, above.)

g. Indemnification

An indemnification clause is frequently paired with representations and warranties. An indemnity is a promise by one person to pay specified costs and losses of another party under specified circumstances.

A developer should seek to require the copyright owner to indemnify it if any of the owner's representations and warranties turn out to be untrue. This means that the owner will have to bear or reimburse all costs and expenses, including attorney fees and damages, owed or paid by the developer if, for example, its use of the material results in a claim that it violated a third party's privacy or publicity rights. If a full-blown lawsuit results, these costs could be substantial.

As with warranties, the copyright owner of the material a developer wants to use may refuse to agree to indemnify the developer. Instead, the owner may demand that the developer indemnify it if the owner is sued by a third party as a result of the developer's use of the material in the multimedia work.

A multimedia developer should definitely consider obtaining insurance to cover any potential infringement claims. (See Section E1e for a discussion.)

2. Multimedia License Agreement

The Multimedia License Agreement presented in this section is favorable to the developer. It does not require the developer to make any warranties or indemnify the copyright owner. Some copyright owners may require that these items be added to the agreement.

The full text of the following agreement is on the forms disk under MULTILIC.TXT. See Chapter 1, Sections C and D, for instructions on using the forms disk and preparing a final agreement. The Multimedia License Agreement is self-explanatory; see Section G1, above, for a discussion of key issues.

SAMPLE
MULTIMEDIA LICENSE AGREEMENT

This Agreement is made as of June 19, 199X between Argosy Productions, Inc. (the "Owner") and MultiSolutions Software, Inc. (the "Developer").

1. Background: Owner owns, controls or is in possession of the materials described in Exhibit 1 to this Agreement (the "Licensed Materials"). Developer desires to license all or part of these Licensed Materials for use in a multimedia program (the "Licensed Product"). Accordingly, the parties agree as follows.

2. Definitions: The following definitions shall apply to this Agreement.

"Licensed Materials" means the materials described in detail in Exhibit 1 to this Agreement.

"Licensed Product" means the following multimedia program: An interactive multimedia program entitled "Columbus 'Discovers' America" produced by MultiSolutions Software, Inc.

"Derivative Works" means a work that is based upon one or more preexisting works, such as a revision, modification, translation, abridgment, condensation, expansion or any other form in which such a preexisting work may be recast, transformed or adapted, and that, if prepared without authorization by the owner of the preexisting work, would constitute copyright infringement.

"Territory" means worldwide.

3. License Grant: Owner hereby grants Developer a nonexclusive license in the Territory defined in Clause 2 to:

(a) use, reproduce and create Derivative Works of and from the Licensed Materials;

(b) incorporate the Licensed Materials and/or Derivative Works thereof within the Licensed Product; and

(c) market, promote, sell, license and/or distribute copies of the Licensed Materials and Derivative Works thereof as part of the Licensed Product, both directly to end users and indirectly through distributors, dealers, resellers, agents and other third parties.

Developer shall not distribute or transfer in any way any copy of all or part of the Licensed Materials separate and apart from the Licensed Product.

4. Payment and Delivery: On execution of this Agreement, Developer agrees to pay Owner as follows: $2,000 cash.

Owner shall deliver the Licensed Materials to Developer within 10 days after execution of this Agreement.

5. Term of the License: This license commences on the date it is executed and shall continue for a period of four years unless earlier terminated in accordance with the terms of this Agreement.

6. Termination of the License: Each party has the right to terminate this Agreement if the other party has materially breached any obligation or warranty herein and such breach remains uncured for a period of 30 days after notice of such breach is sent to the other party. Upon termination of this Agreement, Developer shall promptly return to Owner all Licensed Materials and any other property of Owner held by it.

If this Agreement is terminated for any reason other than Developer's uncured material breach of its terms, Developer may continue to distribute existing Licensed Product already in inventory as of the effective date of termination.

7. Use of Licensed Materials: Owner acknowledges and agrees that Developer shall have sole discretion to determine the manner in which Licensed Materials are used in the Licensed Product. Developer may edit or otherwise alter the Licensed Materials and may combine them with other materials as it deems necessary for inclusion in the Licensed Product. Owner waives any and all moral rights Owner may have in the Licensed Materials, including those arising under the Visual Artists Rights Act.

8. Copies of Licensed Materials: Owner acknowledges that in the course of preparing the Licensed Product, Developer may have to make copies and/or other reproductions of the Licensed Materials. Subject to the terms of this Agreement, Owner agrees that Developer shall have the right to possess and use such copies during the term of this Agreement. Developer shall not make any copies or other reproductions of the Licensed Materials after this Agreement terminates.

9. Copyright Notice and Credit Line: The following copyright notice and credit line must appear in connection with Developer's use of the Licensed Materials: "Documentary footage from 'The Logbook of Christopher Columbus,' courtesy of Argosy Productions, Inc. © 1988 by Argosy Production, Inc. All Rights Reserved."

10. Publicity/Privacy Releases: Developer shall obtain all necessary releases to enable Developer to utilize the Licensed Materials pursuant to this Agreement without violating any third party's privacy or publicity rights. This includes, but is not limited to, the releases of all persons or organizations whose name, voice, likeness, portrayal, impersonation or performance is included in the Licensed Materials.

11. Representations and Warranties: Owner hereby represents and warrants to Developer as follows:

(a) Owner is the owner of all right, title and interest, including copyright, in all the Licensed Materials, or has the authority to enter into this Agreement on behalf of the owner.

(b) Owner has not granted any rights or licenses to the Licensed Materials that would conflict with Owner's obligations under this Agreement.

(c) Owner will not enter into any agreement with any third party which would affect Developer's rights under this Agreement, or bind Developer to any third party, without Developer's prior written consent.

(d) Developer's use of the Licensed Materials as authorized by this Agreement will not infringe any existing copyright, trade secret, patent or trademark rights of any third party.

12. Indemnification: Owner shall indemnify Developer against all claims, liabilities and costs, including reasonable attorney fees, of defending any claim or suit arising by reason of Owner's breach of any condition, warranty or representation contained in this Agreement.

13. General Provisions: The following provisions shall apply.

(a) This Multimedia License Agreement is the sole and entire Agreement between the parties relating to the subject matter hereof, and supersedes all prior understandings, agreements and documentation relating to such subject matter. Any modifications to this Agreement must be in writing and signed by both parties.

(b) If any provision in this Agreement is held by a court of competent jurisdiction to be invalid, void or unenforceable, the remaining provisions will continue in full force without being impaired or invalidated in any way.

(c) This Agreement will be governed by the laws of the State of California.

(d) Notices and correspondence to Owner should be sent to: Argosy Productions, Inc., 1411 Melrose Blvd., Hollywood, CA 90021.

(e) Notices and correspondence to Developer should be sent to: MultiSolutions Software, Inc., 18 North Bay Drive, Boston, MA 02110.

(f) This Agreement shall bind and inure to the benefit of both parties and is not assignable by either party without the consent of the other.

Argosy Productions, Inc.

By: _____

Name: _____

Title: _____

Date: _____

MultiSolutions Software, Inc.

By: _____

Name: _____

Title: _____

Date: _____

EXHIBIT 1

The Licensed Materials are as follows: Up to two minutes of S-VHS video footage from documentary entitled "The Logbook of Christopher Columbus"; Argosy catalog #8293. ■

C H A P T E R 1 4

Help Beyond This Book

We hope this book will provide you with most of the information you need about software law and contracts. But you may need additional help, either in the form of more advanced legal resources or an attorney's advice.

In Section A, we introduce you to resources that contain comprehensive information on each area of intellectual property law. In Section B, we list several resources that provide additional software contracts. Finally, in Section C, we give some tips for finding a lawyer specializing in computer law.

A. Further Information on Intellectual Property Law

If you have any questions about intellectual property law (copyright, trade secret, patent or trademark law) that have not been answered by this book, a two-step process is suggested. But before you take these steps, you will need to find a law library. Many law libraries are open to the public and can be found in most federal, state and county courthouses. Law school libraries in public universities also routinely grant access to the public. In addition, it is also often possible to use private law libraries maintained by local bar associations, large law firms, state agencies or large corporations if you know a local attorney or are willing to be persistent in seeking permission from the powers that be.

Law libraries may seem intimidating at first. It may be helpful to know that most librarians have a sincere interest in helping anyone who desires to use their library. While they won't answer your legal questions, they will often put your hands on the materials that will give you a good start.

After you locate a law library, your approach to legal research should proceed along these lines:

- Start by taking a look at one or more discussions by experts in the field to get a background and overview of the topic being researched. You will already have obtained a basic background from this book and will be looking for additional details on a particular topic.

- If you need still more information, read the law itself (cases and statutes) upon which the experts base their opinions. The accompanying sidebar discusses how to research case law in more detail.
- To find out information on recent legal developments, you may want to look at articles that appear in scholarly journals called "law reviews."

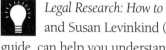 *Legal Research: How to Find and Understand the Law*, by Stephen Elias and Susan Levinkind (Nolo Press), or another basic legal research guide, can help you understand legal citations, use the law library, and understand what you find there.

RESEARCHING COURT DECISIONS

Throughout this book, legal treatises and law review articles are referred to in citations like this: *Apple Computer v. Franklin*, 714 F.2d 1240 (3rd Cir. 1983). This identifies a particular legal decision and tells you where the decision may be found and read. Any case decided by a federal court of appeals is found in a series of books called the Federal Reporter. Older cases are contained in the first series of the Federal Reporter or "F." for short. More recent cases are contained in the second series of the Federal Reporter or "F.2d" for short. To locate the *Apple v. Franklin* case, simply find a law library that has the Federal Reporter, Second Series (almost all do), locate volume 714 and turn to page 1240.

Opinions by the federal district courts (these are the federal trial courts) are in a series called the Federal Supplement or "F.Supp." For example, a case that appears in the Federal Supplement is *Lotus Dev. Corp. v. Paperback Software Int'l.* 740 F.Supp. 37 (D. Mass. 1990).

Cases decided by the U.S. Supreme Court are found in three publications, any of which is fine to use: United States Reports (identified as "U.S."), the Supreme Court Reporter "identified as "S.Ct.") and the Supreme Court Reports, Lawyer's Edition (identified as "L.Ed."). Supreme Court case citations often refer to all three publications—for example—*Diamond v. Diehr,* 450 U.S. 174, 101 S.Ct. 1048, 96 L.Ed. 187 (1985).

1. Copyright Law

For more information about copyright protection for software, you should first consult *Copyright Your Software*, by Stephen Fishman (Nolo Press). It covers in detail all the topics touched on in Chapter 3, *Copyright Protection for Software* and provides step-by-step instructions and all the forms needed to register a software copyright with the Copyright Office.

Legal Treatises

- *Scott on Computer Law*, by Michael D. Scott (Prentice Hall Law & Business). This two-volume treatise contains a detailed discussion of copyright protection for software, including copyright protection in foreign countries.
- *Computer Software*, by L.J. Kutten (Clark Boardman Callaghan), includes a chapter on software copyright.
- *Software, Copyright, & Competition*, by Anthony Lawrence Clapes (Quorum Books), gives one lawyer's view on how software should be protected by the copyright law.
- *Nimmer on Copyright*, by Melville and David (Matthew Bender), is the leading treatise on all aspects of copyright law. This four-volume work covers virtually every legal issue concerning U.S. and foreign copyright law. Its coverage of computer software has recently been expanded, but it is not concerned exclusively with software, like the two treatises cited above.
- *The Law and Business of Computer Software*, edited by D.C. Toedt III (Clark Boardman Callaghan), contains a useful article providing a country-by-country analysis of international copyright protection for software.
- *International Copyright Protection*, edited by David Nimmer and Paul Geller (Matthew Bender), provides exhaustive coverage of copyright protection in other countries.

Copyright Law Reporter

For the most recent information available on copyright, consult the *Copyright Law Reporter*, a weekly loose-leaf service published by Commerce Clearing House (CCH). It contains the full text or summaries of recent copyright-related court decisions and relevant discussions of new developments in copyright law. The first volume of the set contains easy-to-follow instructions on how to use this valuable resource.

Law Review Articles

If you have a very unusual copyright problem that is not covered by books on copyright and/or computer law, or you have a problem in an area in which the law has changed very recently, the best sources of available information may be law review articles. You can find citations to all the law review articles on a particular topic by looking under "copyright" in the *Index to Legal Periodicals* or *Current Law Index*. A key to the abbreviations used in these indices is located at the front of each index volume. Substantial collections of law reviews are usually kept in large public law libraries or university libraries.

Statutes

The primary law governing all copyrights in the United States after January 1, 1978 is the Copyright Act of 1976. You can obtain a free copy of the Copyright Act by calling the Copyright Office forms hotline at (202) 707-9100; ask for *Circular 92*.

The Copyright Act is located in Title 17 of the United States Code. It is contained in:

* *United States Code Annotated* (U.S.C.A.)
* *United States Code Service, Lawyers Edition* (U.S.C.S.)
* *Nimmer on Copyright*, Volume 4, and
* *Copyright Law Reporter*.

To find a specific statute, consult either the index at the end of Title 17, or the index at the end of the entire code.

Regulations

The United States Copyright Office has issued regulations which implement the copyright statutes and establish the procedures which must be followed to register a work. These regulations are located in:

- Title 17 of the *Code of Federal Regulations* (CFR), a paperback service that is updated annually,
- the supplement to Title 17 of the U.S.C.A.,
- *Nimmer On Copyright,* Volume 4, and
- *Copyright Law Reporter.*

Court Decisions

There are several ways to find court decisions on a particular legal issue. This book, legal treatises and law review articles contain many case citations. In addition:

- The *United States Code Annotated* and *United States Code Service* both cite and briefly summarize all the decisions relevant to each section of the Copyright Act of 1976. These are located just after each section of the Act.
- *Federal Practice Digest* (West Publishing Company) provides short summaries of copyright law decisions under the term "copyright." The digest contains a detailed table of contents and a very detailed subject matter index at the end of the set.

To research a particular court decision, see instructions in the sidebar, above.

2. Trade Secret Law

If you want to research trade secret law, here are some resources.

Legal Treatises

- *Milgrim on Trade Secrets*, a comprehensive treatment of trade secret law published by Matthew Bender as Volume 12 of its *Business Organizations* series, is probably the most complete resource regarding trade secret issues, especially if you have a specific or detailed question.
- *Trade Secret Law Handbook*, by Melvin F. Jager (Clark Boardman Callaghan), contains mini-discussions of most tradesecret related concepts, a number of sample agreements and licenses, as well as references to cases and statutes where appropriate.
- *Trade Secrets*, by James Pooley (Osborn/McGraw Hill), is an excellent book written for nonlawyers. You will find this book more accessible than the treatises cited above. It does not contain the extensive citations to primary resource materials (cases and statutes) that the Milgrim and Jager books have, but it does include sample trade secret agreements.

Law Review Articles

Law review articles are often a good place to find information about recent software protection developments. Look under "Trade Secret" in the *Index to Legal Periodicals* or *Current Law Index*. A key to the abbreviations used in these indexes is located at the front of each index volume. Substantial collections of law reviews are usually located in large public law libraries or university libraries.

Statutes

There is no national trade secret law; instead, it consists of individual laws for each state. For direct access to state statutes governing trade secrets, look under "Trade Secret," "Proprietary Information," or "Commercial Secret" in the index accompanying the statutes of the state in question.

In addition, the Uniform Trade Secrets Act, a model statute designed by legal scholars, has been adopted in one version or another by some 26 states. You can find it in Volume 14 of the Uniform Laws Annotated, published by West Publishing Co.

Court Decisions

For summaries of cases involving trade secret principles, consult the West Publishing Company state or regional digests under "Trade Regulation," "Contracts," "Agency" and "Master and Servant."

3. Patent Law

The first source to consult if you have any questions about patent law is *Patent It Yourself*, by David Pressman (Nolo Press). This book explains in detail how the patent system works and how to prepare and file a patent application yourself. *Patent It Yourself* software is also available from Nolo.

Legal Treatises

- *Patent Law Fundamentals*, by Peter Rosenberg (Clark Boardman Callaghan), is the best legal treatise for patent law. This publication is generally considered by patent attorneys to be the bible of patent law. Because it is written for attorneys, it might be somewhat difficult sledding for the nonlawyer. However, if you first obtain an overview of your topic from the Pressman book, you should do fine.
- *Patent Law Handbook*, by C. Bruce Hamburg (Clark Boardman Callaghan), is another useful book. A new edition of that book is issued every year.

Law Review Articles

As mentioned earlier, law review articles are an excellent way to keep abreast of recent legal developments. By looking under "Patents" in the *Index to Legal Periodicals* or *Current Law Index*, you will find frequent references to articles on current patent law developments. A key to the abbreviations used in these indexes is located at the front of each index volume. Substantial collections of law reviews are usually located in large public law libraries or university libraries.

Statutes

The basic U.S. Patent Law is located in Title 35, United States Code, Section 101 and following. This can be found in the *United States Code Annotated* (U.S.C.A.) or *United States Code Service, Lawyers Edition* (U.S.C.S.).

Regulations

The U.S. Patent and Trademark Office has issued regulations contained in Title 37 of the *Code of Federal Regulations* (CFR). These regulations govern such details as what a patent application must contain and how your application is processed by the Patent Office.

Court Decisions

You'll find citations to relevant court decisions in *Patent Law Fundamentals* or a law review article. In addition, the *U.S. Code Annotated* and *U.S. Code Service* both refer to and briefly summarize all the decisions relevant to each section of the patent law. You can also find short summaries of patent law decisions in West Publishing Company's *Federal Practice Digest* under the term "patent."

4. Trademark Law

Before consulting any of the resources cited below, first read *Trademark: How to Name Your Business & Product*, by Kate McGrath and Stephen Elias (Nolo Press). This guide provides an overview of trademark law and explains how to select and register a trademark and conduct trademark searches.

Treatises

- *Trademarks and Unfair Competition*, by J. Thomas McCarthy (Clark Boardman Callaghan), is the most authoritative book on trademark law. This two-volume treatise discusses virtually every legal issue that has arisen regarding trademarks.
- *Trademark Registration Practice*, by James E. Hawes (Clark Boardman Callaghan), provides a detailed guide to trademark registration.
- *Trademark Law—A Practitioner's Guide*, by Siegrun D. Kane (Practicing Law Institute), contains practical advice about trademark disputes and litigation.

Law Review Articles

You can find law review articles on trademark law by looking under "trademark" or "unfair competition" in the *Index to Legal Periodicals* or *Current Law Index*. A key to the abbreviations used in these indexes is located at the front of each index volume. Substantial collections of law reviews are usually located in large public law libraries or university libraries.

Statutes

The main law governing trademarks in the United States is the Lanham Act, also known as the Federal Trademark Act of 1946 (as amended in 1988). It is codified at Title 15, Chapters 1051 through 1127 of the United States Code. You can find it in either of two books:

- *United States Code Annotated* (U.S.C.A.), or
- *United States Code Service, Lawyers Edition* (U.S.C.S.).

All law libraries carry at least one of these series. To find a specific section of the Lanham Act, consult either the index at the end of Title 15, or the index at the end of the entire code.

Regulations

The regulations implementing the Lanham Act consist of the specific rules governing trademark registration. They are found in Title 37, Chapter 1, of the *Code of Federal Regulations* (CFR).

Court Decisions

You'll find citations to relevant court decisions in *Trademarks and Unfair Competition* or a law review article. In addition, the *U.S. Code Annotated* and *U.S. Code Service* both refer to and briefly summarize all the decisions relevant to each section of the Lanham Act. You can also find short summaries of trademark law decisions in West Publishing Company's *Federal Practice Digest* under the term "trademark."

B. Further Information on Software Contracts

If you need a software contract not contained in this book, consult the following sources:

- *Vendor's Guide to Computer Contracting,* by Friedman, Hildebrand and Lipner (Prentice Hall Law & Business). This one-volume guide contains a number of sample contracts designed with a software developer's interests in mind. It includes a sample software license agreement, development agreement, employment and consulting agreements, maintenance and service agreements, marketing/distributing agreements and software escrow agreements. The book was written for nonlawyers and contains clear discussions of what is in the forms and how to use them.

- *Allen & Davis on Computer Contracting: A User's Guide with Forms and Strategies*, by Don A. Allen and Lanny J. Davis (Prentice Hall Law & Business). This book discusses software and hardware contracting from the customer's point of view. It has an extensive discussion of how a customer should organize a system for software contracting and negotiate software and hardware contracts. It includes sample annotated software licensing, development, maintenance and escrow agreements. It also has sample hardware purchase and lease agreements. All the agreements are designed to protect the customer's interests.
- *Computer Software Agreements*, by Ridley, Quittmeyer and Matuszeski (Warren, Gorham & Lamont). This book was written for lawyers and is not as accessible as the two listed above; but it contains a huge number of sample agreements, including multiple development, employment, marketing, distribution, end-user, service bureau, database and backup services agreements.
- *1993 Computer Law Forms Handbook*, by Laurens R. Schwartz (Clark Boardman Company). This rather haphazardly organized trade paperback is relatively inexpensive and contains many sample agreements.

You may be able to find these books in a large university library or law library; otherwise, you'll probably have to order them direct from the publisher. They can all be ordered on 30-day approval, so you can send them back if you don't like them.

C. Finding a Lawyer

If you're faced with a problem you cannot or do not want to handle yourself, you may need to see a lawyer. A large number of lawyers hold themselves out to the public as "computer lawyers." Many of them have a background in intellectual property litigation; others may have worked for a computer software or hardware company or for a law firm that does extensive business advising such companies.

A lawyer with a solid background either working for or advising hi-tech businesses is probably your best bet if you need help with contract drafting. But if you need help filing a patent application or (God forbid) with patent litigation, be aware that patent law is a separate legal specialty. Only lawyers admitted to the federal patent bar can practice patent law. Many patent lawyers specialize in a particular industry; be sure to ask any patent lawyer you considering hiring whether he or she has experience handling software patent applications and/or litigation.

Patent lawyers may also be able to help you with trademark, copyright and trade secret matters. But some patent lawyers don't put much effort into these other areas. So, if you are shopping for a copyright, trademark or trade secret lawyer, do your best to find someone who specializes primarily in these fields.

Finding a good lawyer is no different than finding any other professional to help your business. The best way is always to ask for referrals from friends or colleagues in your industry. If your company has a general business lawyer, ask for a referral as well. Your county bar association may also be able to refer you to someone. If all else fails, look in your local yellow pages under attorneys specializing in "computer law" and "patent, trademark & copyright." ■

A PPENDIX

Abstract of In re Alappat

On July 29, 1994 In re Alappat was decided in the U.S. Circuit Court of Appeals after a hearing involving all of the court's 11 Judges. Judge Rich wrote the majority opinion. Three judges declined to state an opinion and two judges dissented.

After dealing with a major procedural issue, the majority opinion addressed these two questions:

- when software is patentable under 35 USC Section 101 (which defines the broad categories of patentable subject matter) and
- how "means plus function" clauses in the claims to a software invention affect patentability.

The language from the court opinion appears in regular type. Our comments are in bold. All figures referred to in the text are omitted.

92-1381

(Serial No. 09/149,792)

IN RE KURIAPPAN P. ALAPPAT, EDWARD
E. AVERILL and JAMES G. LARSEN

Alexander C. Johnson, Jr., Marger, Johnson, McCollom & Stolowitz, P.C., of Portland, Oregon, argued for appellants. With him on the brief was *Peter J. Meza*. Also on the brief was *Francis I. Gray*, Tektronix, Inc., of Wilsonville, Oregon. *Allen M. Sokal*, Finnegan, Henderson, Farabow, Et Al., of Washington, D.C., argued for Amicus Curiae, Federal Circuit Bar Association. With him on the brief were *Gerald H. Bjorge, Herbert H. Mintz* and *George E. Hutchinson.*

Fred E. McKelvey, Solicitor, Office of the Solicitor, of Arlington, Virginia, argued for appellee. With him on the brief were *Lee E. Barrett* and *Richard E. Schafer*, Associate Solicitor. Of counsel were *Albin F. Drost* and *John W. Dewhirst.*

Herbert C. Wamsley and *Richard C. Witte*, Intellectual Property Owners, Inc., of Washington, D.C., were on the brief for Amicus Curiae, Intellectual Property Owners, Inc.

Richard H. Stern, Graham & James, of Washington, D.C., was on the brief for Amicus Curiae, Seagate Technology, Inc. Also on the brief was *Edward P. Heller, III*, Patent Counsel.

Fred I. Koenigsberg and *Nancy J. Linck*, Cushman, Darby & Cushman, of Washington, D.C., were on the brief for Amicus Curiae, American Intellectual Property Law Association. Also on the brief were *Harold C. Wegner* and *H. Robb Workman*, Wegner, Cantor, Mueller & Player, of Washington, D.C. Of counsel was *William S. LaFuze.*

Appealed from: U.S. Patent and Trademark Office
Board of Patent Appeals and Interferences

92-1381
(Serial No. 07/149,792)

IN RE KURIAPPAN P. ALAPPAT, EDWARD
E. AVERILL and JAMES G. LARSEN

DECIDED: July 29, 1994

Before ARCHER, *Chief Judge*, and RICH, NIES, NEWMAN, MAYER, MICHEL,
    PLAGER, LOURIE, CLEVENGER, RADER and SCHALL, *Circuit Judges*.

RICH, *Circuit Judge*, with whom:

> as to Part I (Jurisdiction): NEWMAN, LOURIE and RADER, *Circuit Judges*, join;
> ARCHER, *Chief Judge*, NIES and PLAGER, *Circuit Judges*, concur in conclusion;
> and MAYER, MICHEL, CLEVENGER and SCHALL, *Circuit Judges*, dissent; and

> as to Part II (Merits): NEWMAN, LOURIE, MICHEL, PLAGER and RADER,
> *Circuit Judges*, join; ARCHER, *Chief Judge*, and NIES, *Circuit Judge*, dissent; and
> MAYER, CLEVENGER and SCHALL, *Circuit Judges*, take no position.

Kuriappan P. Alappat, Edward E. Averill, and James G. Larsen (collectively Alappat) appeal the
April 22, 1992, reconsideration decision of the Board of Patent Appeals and Interferences
(Board) of the United States Patent and Trademark Office (PTO), Ex Parte Alappat, 23 USPQ2d
1340 (BPAI, 1992), which sustained the Examiner's rejection of claims 15-19 of application
Serial No. 07/149,792 ('792 application) as being unpatentable under 35 U.S.C. § 101 (1988).
    **First, the Court addressed the question of whether the Court had legal authority
(jurisdiction) to consider the issue before it. Because the Court's jurisdiction is not within
the scope of this book, we delete that discussion.**

II. THE MERITS
    *Our conclusion is that the appealed decision should be reversed because the appealed claims are
directed to a "machine" which is one of the categories named in 35 U.S.C. § 101, as the first panel of the Board
held.*
    **Alappat's invention is about the conversion of input analog data to an oscilloscope to
output digital waveform data sequence recognizable as a wave on the oscilloscope screen.**

A. *Alappat's Invention*
    Alappat's invention relates generally to a means for creating a smooth waveform display in a
digital oscilloscope. The screen of an oscillosope is the front of a cathode-ray tube (CRT), which
is like a TV picture tube, whose screen, when in operation, presents an array (or raster) of pixels
arranged at intersections of vertical columns and horizontal rows, a pixel being a spot on the
screen which may be illuminated by directing an electron beam to that spot, as in TV. Each
column in the array represents a different time period, and each row represents a different
magnitude. An input signal to the oscilloscope is sampled and digitized to provide a waveform
data sequence (vector list), wherein each successive element of the sequence represents the
magnitude of the waveform at a successively later time. The waveform data sequence is then
processed to provide a bit map, which is a stored data array indicating which pixels are to be

illuminated. The waveform ultimately displayed is formed by a group of vectors, wherein each vector has a straight line trajectory between two points on the screen at elevations representing the magnitudes of two successive input signal samples and at horizontal positions representing the timing of the two samples.

Because a CRT screen contains a finite number of pixels, rapidly rising and falling portions of a waveform can appear discontinuous or jagged due to differences in the elevation of horizontally contiguous pixels included in the waveform. In addition, the presence of "noise" in an input signal can cause portions of the waveform to oscillate between contiguous pixel rows when the magnitude of the input signal lies between values represented by the elevations of the two rows. Moreover, the vertical resolution of the display may be limited by the number of rows of pixels on the screen. The noticeability and appearance of these effects is known as *aliasing*.

To overcome these effects, *Alappat's invention employs an anti-aliasing system* wherein each vector making up the waveform is represented by modulating the illumination intensity of pixels having center points bounding the trajectory of the vector. The intensity at which each of the pixels is illuminated depends upon the distance of the center point of each pixel from the trajectory of the vector. Pixels lying squarely on the waveform trace receive maximum illumination, whereas pixels lying along an edge of the trace receive illumination decreasing in intensity proportional to the increase in the distance of the center point of the pixel from the vector trajectory. Employing this *anti-aliasing* technique eliminates any apparent discontinuity, jaggedness, or oscillation in the waveform, *thus giving the visual appearance of a smooth continuous waveform*. In short, and in lay terms, the invention is an improvement in an oscilloscope comparable to a TV having a clearer picture.

Reference to Fig. 5A of the '792 application, reproduced below, better illustrates the manner in which a smooth appearing waveform is created.

Each square in this figure represents a pixel, and the intensity level at which each pixel is illuminated is indicated in hexadecimal notation by the number or letter found in each square. Hexadecimal notation has sixteen characters, the numbers 0-9 and the letters A-F, wherein A represents 10, B represents 11, C represents 12, D represents 13, E represents 14, and F represents 15. The intensity at which each pixel is illuminated increases from 0 to F. Accordingly, a square with a 0 (zero) in it represents a pixel having no illumination, and a square with an F in it represents a pixel having maximum illumination. Although hexadecimal notation is used in the figure to represent intensity illumination, the intensity level is stored in the bit map of Alappat's system as a 4-bit binary number, with 0000 representing a pixel having no illumination and 1111 representing a pixel having maximum illumination.

Points 54 and 52 in Fig. 5A represent successive observation points on the screen of an oscilliscope. Without the benefit of Alappat's anti-aliasing system, points 54 and 52 would appear on the screen as separate, unconnected spots. In Alappat's system, the different intensity level at which each of the pixels is illuminated produces the appearance of the line 48, a so-called vector.

The intensity at which each pixel is to be illuminated is determined as follows, using pixel 55 as an example. First, the vertical distance between the Y coordinates of observation points 54 and 52 ($\breve{Y}y_i$) is determined. In this example, this difference equals 7 units, with one unit representing the center-to-center distance of adjacent pixels. Then, the elevation of pixel 55 above pixel 54 ($\breve{Y}y_{ij}$) is determined, which in this case is 2 units. The $\breve{Y}y_i$ and $\breve{Y}y_{ij}$ values are then "normalized," which Alappat describes as converting these values to larger values which are easier to use in mathematical calculations. In Alappat's example, a barrel shifter is used to shift the binary input to the left by the number of bits required to set the most significant (leftmost) bit of its output signal to "1." The $\breve{Y}y_i$

and $\ddot{Y}y_{ij}$ values are then plugged into a mathematical equation for determining the intensity at which the particular pixel is to be illuminated. In this particular example, the equation $I'(i,j) = [1-(\ddot{Y}y_{ij}/\ddot{Y}y_i)]F$, wherein F is 15 in hexadecimal notation, suffices. The intensity of pixel 55 in this example would thus be calculated as follows:

$$[1-(2/7)]15 = (5/7)15 = 10.71 \sim 11 \text{ (or B)}.$$

Accordingly, pixel 55 is illuminated at 11/15 of the intensity of the pixels in which observation points 54 and 52 lie. Alappat discloses that the particular formula used will vary depending on the shape of the waveform.

B. The Rejected Claims

Claim 15, the only independent claim in issue, reads:

A rasterizer for converting vector list data representing sample magnitudes of an input waveform into anti-aliased pixel illumination intensity data to be displayed on a display means comprising:

(a) means for determining the vertical distance between the endpoints of each of the vectors in the data list;

(b) means for determining the elevation of a row of pixels that is spanned by the vector;

(c) means for normalizing the vertical distance and elevation; and

(d) means for outputting illumination intensity data as a predetermined function of the normalized vertical distance and elevation.

Each of claims 16-19 depends directly from claim 15 and more specifically defines an element of the rasterizer claimed therein. Claim 16 recites that means (a) for determining the vertical distance between the endpoints of each of the vectors in the data list, $\ddot{Y}y_i$ described above, comprises an *arithmetic logic circuit* configured to perform an absolute value function. Claim 17 recites that means (b) for determining the elevation of a row of pixels that is spanned by the vector, $\ddot{Y}y_{ij}$ described above, comprises an *arithmetic logic circuit* configured to perform an absolute value function. Claim 18 recites that means (c) for normalizing the vertical distance and elevation comprises *a pair of barrel shifters*. Finally, claim 19 recites that means (d) for outputting comprises *a read only memory (ROM)* containing illumination intensity data. As the first Board panel found, each of (a)—(d) was a device known in the electronics arts before Alappat made his invention.

C. The Examiner's Rejection and Board Reviews

The Examiner's final rejection of claims 15-19 was under 35 U.S.C. § 101 "because the claimed invention is non statutory subject matter," and the original three-member Board panel reversed this rejection. That Board panel held that, although claim 15 *recites* a mathematical algorithm, *the claim as a whole is directed to a machine* and thus to statutory subject matter named in § 101. In reaching this decision, the original panel construed the means clauses in claim 15 pursuant to 35 U.S.C. § 112, paragraph six (§ 112 ¶ 6), as corresponding to the respective structures disclosed in the specification of Alappat's application, and equivalents thereof.

In its reconsideration decision, the five-member majority of the expanded, eight-member Board panel "modified" the decision of the original panel and affirmed the Examiner's § 101 rejection. The majority *held that the PTO need not apply §112 ¶ 6 in rendering patentability determinations*, characterizing this court's statements to the contrary in *In re Iwahashi*, 888 F.2d 1370, 1375, 12 USPQ2d 1908, 1912 (Fed. Cir. 1989), "as dicta," and dismissing this court's discussion of § 112 ¶ 6 in *Arrhythmia Research Technology, Inc. v. Corazonix Corp.*, 958 F.2d 1053, 1060, 22 USPQ2d 1033,

1038 (Fed. Cir. 1992) on the basis that the rules of claim construction in infringement actions differ from the rules for claim interpretation during prosecution in the PTO. The majority stated that, during examination, the PTO gives means-plus-function clauses in claims their broadest interpretation and does not impute limitations from the specification into the claims. *See Applicability of the Last Paragraph of 35 USC §112 to Patentability Determinations Before the Patent and Trademark Office,* 1134 TMOG 633 (1992); *Notice Interpreting In Re Iwahashi (Fed. Cir. 1989),* 1112 OG 16 (1990). Accordingly, the majority held that each of the means recited in claim 15 reads on any and every means for performing the particular function recited.

The majority further held that, because claim 15 is written completely in "means for" language and because these means clauses are read broadly in the PTO to encompass each and every means for performing the recited functions, claim 15 amounts to nothing more than a process claim wherein each means clause represents only a step in that process. The majority stated that each of the steps in this postulated process claim recites a mathematical operation, which steps combine to form a "mathematical algorithm for computing pixel information," *Alappat,* 23 USPQ2d at 1345, and that, "when the claim is viewed without the steps of this mathematical algorithm, no other elements or steps are found." *Alappat,* 23 USPQ2d at 1346. The majority thus concluded that the claim was directed to nonstatutory subject matter.[1/]

In its analysis, the majority further stated:

> It is further significant that claim 15, as drafted, reads on a digital computer "means" to perform the various steps under program control. In such a case, it is proper to treat the claim as if drawn to a method. We will not presume that a stored program digital computer is not within the § 112 ¶ 6 range of equivalents of the structure disclosed in the specification. The disclosed ALU, ROM and shift registers are all common elements of stored program digital computers. Even if appellants were willing to admit that a stored program digital computer were not within the range of equivalents, § 112 ¶ 2 requires that this be clearly apparent from the claims based upon limitations recited in the claims.

Alappat, 23 USPQ2d at 1345.[2/] The Board majority also stated that dependent claims 16-19 were not before them for consideration because they had not been argued by Alappat and thus not addressed by the Examiner or the original three-member Board panel. *Alappat,* 23 USPQ2d at 1341 n.1.[3/]

The Court set out the questions before it in this manner:
- **Was the invention as described in claim 15 a machine and patentable under 35 USC Section 101 or was it an unpatentable mathematical algorithm?**
- **For patentability purposes, should means plus function clauses be read in light of information provided in the specification examples and their equivalents, or should means plus function clauses be read as broadly as possible (which increases the likelihood that the claims with means plus function clauses are not patentable over (in light of) prior art?**

First, the Court decided that the means plus function clauses in claims should be read, for patentability purposes, in light of the specific examples given in the specification (and equivalents of these examples) which perform the functions described in the clauses. When read in this manner, claim 15 unquestionably recited an invention which is made up of a combination of known electronic circuitry elements.

D. Analysis

   (1) *Section 112, Paragraph Six*

As recently explained in In re Donaldson, 16 F.3d 1189, 1193, 29 USPQ2d 1845, 1050 (Fed. Cir. 1994), the PTO is not exempt from following the statutory mandate of § 112 ¶ 6, which reads:
An element in a claim for a combination may be expressed as *a means* or step for performing a specified function without the recital of structure, material, or acts in support thereof, and such claim *shall be construed* to cover the corresponding structure, material, or acts described in the specification and equivalents thereof.

35 U.S.C. § 112, paragraph 6 (1988) (emphasis added).[4/] The Board majority therefore erred as a matter of law in refusing to apply § 112 ¶ 6 in rendering its § 101 patentable subject matter determination.

Given Alappat's disclosure, it was error for the Board majority to interpret each of the means clauses in claim 15 so broadly as to "read on any and every means for performing the functions" recited, as it said it was doing, and then to conclude that claim 15 is nothing more than a process claim wherein each means clause represents a step in that process. Contrary to suggestions by the Commissioner, this court's precedents do not support the Board's view that the particular apparatus claims at issue in this case may be viewed as nothing more than process claims. The cases relied upon by the Commissioner, namely, *In re Abele*, 684 F.2d 902, 214 USPQ 682 (CCPA 1982), *In re Pardo*, 684 F.2d 912, 214 USPQ 673 (CCPA 1982), *In re Meyer*, 688 F.2d 789, 215 USPQ 193 (CCPA 1982), *In re Walter*, 618 F.2d 758, 205 USPQ 397 (CCPA 1980), and *In re Maucorps*, 609 F.2d 481, 203 USPQ 812 (CCPA 1979), differ from the instant case. In *Abele, Pardo,* and *Walter,* given the apparent lack of any supporting structure in the specification corresponding to the claimed "means" elements, the court reasonably concluded that the claims at issue were in effect nothing more than process claims in the guise of apparatus claims. This is clearly not the case now before us. As to *Maucorps* and *Meyer*, despite suggestions therein to the contrary, the claimed means-plus-function elements at issue in those cases were not construed as limited to those means disclosed in the specification and equivalents thereof. As reaffirmed in *Donaldson*, such claim construction is improper, and therefore, those cases are of limited value in dealing with the issue presently before us. We further note that *Maucorps* dealt with a business methodology for deciding how salesmen should best handle respective customers and *Meyer* involved a "system" for aiding a neurologist in diagnosing patients. Clearly, neither of the alleged "inventions" in those cases falls within any § 101 category.

When independent claim 15 is construed in accordance with § 112 ¶ 6, claim 15 reads as follows, the subject matter in brackets representing the structure which Alappat discloses in his specification as corresponding to the respective means language recited in the claims:
A rasterizer [a "machine"] for converting vector list data representing sample magnitudes of an input waveform into anti-aliased pixel illumination intensity data to be displayed on a display means comprising:
(a) [an arithmetic logic *circuit* configured to perform an absolute value function, or an equivalent thereof] for determining the vertical distance between the endpoints of each of the vectors in the data list;
(b) [an arithmetic logic *circuit* configured to perform an absolute value function, or an equivalent thereof] for determining the elevation of a row of pixels that is spanned by the vector;
(c) [a pair of *barrel shifters*, or equivalents thereof] for normalizing the vertical distance and elevation; and

(d) [a *read only memory (ROM)* containing illumination intensity data, or an equivalent thereof] for outputting illumination intensity data as a predetermined function of the normalized vertical distance and elevation.

As is evident, claim 15 unquestionably recites a machine, or apparatus, made up of a combination of known electronic circuitry elements.

Despite suggestions by the Commissioner to the contrary, each of dependent claims 16-19 serves to *further limit* claim 15. Section 112 ¶ 6 requires that each of the means recited in independent claim 15 be construed to cover at least the structure disclosed in the specification corresponding to the "means." Each of dependent claims 16-19 is in fact limited to one of the structures disclosed in the specification.

The ruling that results from this case on this issue is a boon for software patent claim drafters. It allows detailed examples of a software-based invention to be given in the specification while at the same time allowing the inventive ideas to be described in a means plus function clause, as an element of the machine, using substantially less words.

Example: In this case, a rasterizer with four elements was described in claim 15. Each of the four elements was described in means plus function language. So a proper interpretation of the scope of the claim was determined by reading the examples in the specification. In this case, from the specification, we find that the invention is to a rasterizer comprising an arithmetic logic circuit configured to perform an absolute value function, or its equivalent, for determining the vertical distance between endpoints of each of the vectors in the data list, and so on for the other 3 elements of the claim (15 b, c, and d). Each element of the claim is given tangibility and specificity by reference to the more detailed description of the element in the specification.

The Court's ruling on this issue also means that persons drafting claims in means plus function format must be sure to give adequate examples in the specification of how exactly they envision that function being performed. Without reference to the specific examples, an element described in means plus function format will be construed to read on every means for achieving that function and will probably be considered too broad to be patentable (that is, will "read on" prior art).

The moral of the story is that if you want to use means plus function clauses in your claims, give examples in the specification that describe how you have achieved that function, that is, what means you used. Your patent will cover your description of a means to achieve that function, and equivalent means for achieving the same function.

The Court then turned to the issue of when a software-based invention is a machine and when it is an unpatentable algorithm. As mentioned in Chapter 5, a machine is one of the four categories of patentable subject matter. However, laws of nature, natural phenomena, abstract ideas, and certain mathematical subject matter are not, standing alone, considered to fit within any of the four categories. That is, they are not considered to be patentable subject matter.

The Court's opinion first points out that claims are to be read "as a whole", so that it is not necessary to determine whether the claim contains, as merely a part of the whole, any mathematical subject matter which standing alone would not be entitled to patent protection. Another way to say this is that a claim which uses a mathematical formula (equation or algorithm), computer program or digital computer, but which otherwise describes an invention which fits into one of those four statutory categories (that is a machine or process) should not—on the basis of the algorithm alone—be considered unpatentable.

(2) Section 101

The reconsideration Board majority affirmed the Examiner's rejection of claims 15-19 on the basis that these claims are not directed to statutory subject matter as defined in § 101, which reads:

Whoever invents or discovers any new and useful process, *machine*, manufacture, or composition of matter, or any new and useful improvement thereof, may obtain a patent therefor, subject to the conditions and requirements of this title. [Emphasis ours.]

As discussed in section II.D.(1), supra, claim 15, properly construed, claims a machine, namely, a rasterizer "for converting vector list data representing sample magnitudes of an input waveform into anti-aliased pixel illumination intensity data to be displayed on a display means," which machine is made up of, at the very least, the specific structures disclosed in Alappat's specification corresponding to the means-plus-function elements (a)-(d) recited in the claim. According to Alappat, the claimed rasterizer performs the same overall function as prior art rasterizers,[5/] but does so in a different way, which is represented by the combination of four elements claimed in means-plus-function terminology.[6/] Because claim 15 is directed to a "machine," which is one of the four categories of patentable subject matter enumerated in § 101, claim 15 appears on its face to be directed to § 101 subject matter.

This does not quite end the analysis, however, because the Board majority argues that the claimed subject matter falls within a judicially created exception to § 101 which the majority refers to as the "mathematical algorithm" exception. Although the PTO has failed to support the premise that the "mathematical algorithm" exception applies to true apparatus claims, we recognize that our own precedent suggests that this may be the case. See *In re Johnson*, 589 F.2d 1070, 1077, 200 USPQ 199, 206 (CCPA 1978) ("*Benson* [referring to *Gottschalk v. Benson*, 409 U.S. 63 (1972)] applies equally whether an invention is claimed as an apparatus or process, because the form of the claim is often an exercise in drafting."). Even if the mathematical subject matter exception to § 101 does apply to true apparatus claims, the claimed subject matter in this case does not fall within that exception.

(a)

The plain and unambiguous meaning of § 101 is that any new and useful process, machine, manufacture, or composition of matter, or any new and useful improvement thereof, may be patented if it meets the requirements for patentability set forth in Title 35, such as those found in §§ 102, 103, and 112. The use of the expansive term "any" in § 101 represents Congress's intent not to place any restrictions on the subject matter for which a patent may be obtained beyond those specifically recited in § 101 and the other parts of Title 35. Indeed, the Supreme Court has acknowledged that Congress intended § 101 to extend to "anything under the sun that is made by man." *Diamond v. Chakrabarty*, 447 U.S. 303, 309 (1980), *quoting* S. Rep. No. 1979, 82nd Cong., 2nd Sess., 5 (1952); H.R. Rep. No. 1923, 82nd Cong., 2nd Sess., 6 (1952). Thus, it is improper to read into § 101 limitations as to the subject matter that may be patented where the legislative history does not indicate that Congress clearly intended such limitations. *See Chakrabarty*, 447 U.S. at 308 ("We have also cautioned that courts 'should not read into the patent laws limitations and conditions which the legislature has not expressed.'"), *quoting United States v. Dubilier Condenser Corp.*, 289 U.S. 178, 199 (1933).

Despite the apparent sweep of § 101, the Supreme Court has held that certain categories of subject matter are not entitled to patent protection. In *Diehr*, its most recent case addressing § 101, the Supreme Court explained that there are three categories of subject matter for which one may not obtain patent protection, namely "laws of nature, natural phenomena, and abstract ideas." *Diehr*, 450 U.S. at 185.[7/] Of relevance to this case, the Supreme Court also has held that certain mathematical subject matter is not, standing alone, entitled to patent protection. *See Diehr*, 450 U.S. 175; *Parker v. Flook*, 437 U.S. 584; *Gottschalk v. Benson*, 409 U.S. 63.[8/] A close analysis of *Diehr*, *Flook*, and *Benson* reveals that the Supreme Court never intended to create an overly broad, fourth category of subject matter excluded from § 101. Rather, at the core of the Court's analysis in each of these cases lies an attempt by the Court to explain a rather straightforward concept, namely, that certain types of mathematical subject matter, standing alone, represent nothing more than *abstract ideas* until reduced to some type of practical application, and thus that subject matter is not, in and of itself, entitled to patent protection.[9/]

Diehr also demands that the focus in any statutory subject matter analysis be on the claim as a whole. Indeed, the Supreme Court stated in *Diehr*:

[W]hen a claim containing a mathematical formula [, mathematical equation, mathematical algorithm, or the like,] implements or applies that formula [, equation, algorithm, or the like,] in a structure or process which, when considered *as a whole*, is performing a function which the patent laws were designed to protect (e.g., transforming or reducing an article to a different state or thing), then the claim satisfies the requirements of § 101.

Diehr, 450 U.S. at 192 (emphasis added). *In re Iwahashi*, 888 F.2d at 1375, 12 USPQ2d at 1911; *In re Taner*, 681 F.2d 787, 789, 214 USPQ 678, 680 (CCPA 1982). It is thus not necessary to determine whether a claim contains, as merely a part of the whole, any mathematical subject matter which standing alone would not be entitled to patent protection. Indeed, because the dispositive inquiry is whether the claim *as a whole* is directed to statutory subject matter, it is irrelevant that a claim may contain, as part of the whole, subject matter which would not be patentable by itself.[10/] "A claim drawn to subject matter otherwise statutory does not become nonstatutory simply because it uses a mathematical formula, [mathematical equation, mathematical algorithm,] computer program or digital computer." *Diehr*, 450 U.S. at 187.

The court concluded that the invention claimed in claim 15, *as a whole*, **was directed to a combination of interrelated elements which combine to form a machine for converting discrete waveform data samples into anti-aliased pixel illumination intensity data to be displayed on a display means (the oscilloscope screen). This conclusion was reached in spite of the fact that many of the means elements recited in claim 15 represented circuitry elements that perform mathematical calculations, something the court pointed out is essentially true of all digital electrical circuits.**

Finally, the Court concluded that Alappat's rasterizer was not a disembodied mathematical concept which could be characterized as an abstract idea, but rather a specific machine to produce a useful, concrete, and tangible result.

(b)

Given the foregoing, the proper inquiry in dealing with the so called mathematical subject matter exception to § 101 alleged herein is to see whether the claimed subject matter *as a whole* is a disembodied mathematical concept, whether categorized as a mathematical formula, mathematical equation, mathematical algorithm, or the like, which in essence represents nothing more than a "law of nature," "natural phenomenon," or "abstract idea." If so, *Diehr* precludes the patenting of that subject matter. That is not the case here.

Although many, or arguably even all,[11/] of the means elements recited in claim 15 represent circuitry elements that perform mathematical calculations, which is essentially true of all digital electrical circuits, the claimed invention as a whole is directed to a combination of interrelated elements which combine to form a machine for converting discrete waveform data samples into anti-aliased pixel illumination intensity data to be displayed on a display means.[12/] This is not a disembodied mathematical concept which may be characterized as an "abstract idea," but rather a specific machine to produce a useful, concrete, and tangible result.

The fact that the four claimed means elements function to transform one set of data to another through what may be viewed as a series of mathematical calculations does not alone justify a holding that the claim as a whole is directed to nonstatutory subject matter. *See In re Iwahashi*, 888 F.2d at 1375, 12 USPQ2d at 1911.[13/] Indeed, claim 15 as written is not "so abstract and sweeping" that it would "wholly pre-empt" the use of any apparatus employing the combination of mathematical calculations recited therein. *See Benson*, 409 U.S. at 68-72 (1972). Rather, claim 15 is limited to the use of a particularly claimed combination of elements performing the particularly claimed combination of calculations to transform, i.e., rasterize, digitized waveforms (data) into anti-aliased, pixel illumination data to produce a smooth waveform.

Furthermore, the claim preamble's recitation that the subject matter for which Alappat seeks patent protection is a rasterizer for creating a smooth waveform is not a mere field-of-use label having no significance. Indeed, the preamble specifically recites that the claimed rasterizer converts waveform data into output illumination data for a display, and the means elements recited in the body of the claim make reference not only to the inputted waveform data recited in the preamble but also to the output illumination data also recited in the preamble. Claim 15 thus defines a combination of elements constituting a machine for producing an anti-aliased waveform.

The reconsideration Board majority also erred in its reasoning that claim 15 is unpatentable merely because it "reads on a general purpose digital computer 'means' to perform the various steps under program control."[14/] *Alappat*, 23 USPQ2d at 1345. The Board majority stated that it would "not presume that a stored program digital computer is not within the § 112 ¶ 6 range of equivalents of the structure disclosed in the specification."[15/] *Alappat*, 23 USPQ2d at 1345. Alappat admits that claim 15 would read on a general purpose computer programmed to carry out the claimed invention, but argues that this alone also does not justify holding claim 15 unpatentable as directed to nonstatutory subject matter. We agree. We have held that such programming creates a new machine, because a general purpose computer in effect becomes a special purpose computer once it is programmed to perform particular functions pursuant to instructions from program software. *In re Freeman*, 573 F.2d 1237, 1247 n.11, 197 USPQ 464, 472 n.11 (CCPA 1978); *In re Noll*, 545 F.2d 141, 148, 191 USPQ 721, 726 (CCPA 1976); *In re Prater,* 415 F.2d at 1403 n.29, 162 USPQ at 549-50 n.29.

Under the Board majority's reasoning, a programmed general purpose computer could never be viewed as patentable subject matter under § 101. This reasoning is without basis in the law. The Supreme Court has never held that a programmed computer may never be entitled to patent protection. Indeed, the *Benson* court specifically stated that its decision therein did not preclude "a patent for any program servicing a computer." *Benson*, 409 U.S. at 71. Consequently, a computer operating pursuant to software *may* represent patentable subject matter, provided, of course, that the claimed subject matter meets all of the other requirements of Title 35. In any case, a computer, like a rasterizer, is apparatus not mathematics.

CONCLUSION

For the foregoing reasons, the appealed decision of the Board affirming the examiner's rejection is

REVERSED

Notes

[1]/ *See also Patent and Trademark Practice is Reviewed at PTO Day*, 45 PTCJ 245, 246 (1993); *IP Laws Attempt to Adapt to Changes of New Technologies*, 45 PTCJ 49 (1993); *Federal Circuit Will Hear In Re Alappat Case En Banc*, 45 PTCJ 56 (1992); *"Means For" Claim Recites Non-Statutory Algorithm When Treated as Method Claim*, 44 PTCJ 69 (1992); MPEP § 2110.

[2]/ *See also PTO Report on Patentable Subject Matter: Mathematical Algorithms and Computer Programs*, 1106 TMOG 5 (1989), *reprinted in* 38 PTCJ 551, 563 (1989).

[3]/ Nevertheless, we note that the Examiner stated during prosecution: "the use of physical elements to provide the 'number crunching' is not considered patentable. The mere display of illumination intensity data is not considered significant post solution activity." *12/05/89 Office action*, pg. 4. Thus, even if the specific structures recited in dependent claims 16-19 had been incorporated into claim 15, the Examiner presumably would have found claim 15 to be directed to nonstatutory subject matter.

[4]/ *Accord, In re Bond*, 910 F.2d 831, 833, 15 USPQ2d 1566, 1568 (Fed. Cir. 1990); *In re Iwahashi*, 888 F.2d 1370, 1375, 12 USPQ2d 1908, 1912 (Fed. Cir. 1990); *In re Meyer*, 688 F.2d 789, 796, 215 USPQ 193, 199 (CCPA 1982); *In re Knowlton*, 481 F.2d 1357, 1366, 178 USPQ 486, 492-93 (CCPA 1973); *In re Foster*, 438 F.2d 1011, 1014, 169 USPQ 99, 102 (CCPA 1971); *In re Bernhart*, 417 F.2d 1395, 1399, 163 USPQ 611, 615 (CCPA 1969); *In re Prater*, 415 F.2d 1393, 1406, 162 USPQ 541, 551-52 (CCPA 1969). *See also generally* R. Carl Moy, *The Interpretation of Means Expressions During Prosecution*, 68 JPOS 246 (1986).

[5]/ Representative examples of prior art rasterizers are illustrated in U.S. Patent No. 4,215,414, U.S. Patent No. 4,540,938, U.S. Patent No. 4,586,037, and U.S. Patent No. 4,672,369.

[6]/ Alappat further notes that the Examiner found the particularly claimed combination to be patentably distinct from prior art rasterizers.

[7]/ Laws of nature and natural phenomena are in essence "manifestatations of . . . nature [i.e., not "new"], free to all men and reserved exclusively to none," *see Chakrabarty* 447 U.S. at 309, *quoting Funk Bros. Seed Co. v. Kalo Inoculant Co.*, 333 U.S. 127, 130 (1948), whereas abstract ideas constitute disembodied concepts or truths which are not "useful" from a practical standpoint standing alone, i.e., they are not "useful" until reduced to some practical application. Of course, a process, machine, manufacture, or composition of matter employing a law of nature, natural phenomenon, or abstract idea may be patentable even though the law of nature, natural phenomenon, or abstract idea employed would not, by itself, be entitled to such protection. *See e.g. Parker v. Flook*, 437 U.S. 584, 590 (1978) ("a process is not unpatentable simply because it contains a law of nature or a mathematical algorithm."); *Funk Bros. Seed*, 333 U.S. at 130 ("He who discovers a hitherto unknown phenomenon of nature has no claim to a monopoly of it which the law recognizes. If there is to be invention from such a discovery, it must come from the application of the law to a new and useful end."); *Mackay Radio & Telegraph Co. v. Radio Corp. of America*, 306 U.S. 86, 94 (1939) ("While a scientific truth, or the mathematical expression of it, is not a patentable invention, a novel and useful structure created with the aid of knowledge of scientific truth may be.").

[8]/ The Supreme Court has not been clear, however, as to whether such subject matter is excluded from the scope of § 101 because it represents laws of nature, natural phenomena, or abstract ideas. *See Diehr*, 450 U.S. at 186 (viewed mathematical algorithm as a law of nature); *Benson*, 409 U.S. at 71-72 (treated mathematical algorithm as an "idea"). The Supreme Court also has not been clear as to exactly what kind of mathematical subject matter may not be patented. The Supreme Court has used, among others, the terms "mathematical algorithm," "mathematical formula," and "mathematical equation" to describe types of mathematical subject matter not entitled to patent

protection standing alone. The Supreme Court has not set forth, however, any consistent or clear explanation of what it intended by such terms or how these terms are related, if at all.

[9/] The Supreme Court's use of such varying language as "algorithm," "formula," and "equation" merely illustrates the understandable struggle that the Court was having in articulating a rule for mathematical subject matter, given the esoteric nature of such subject matter and the various definitions that are attributed to such terms as "algorithm," "formula," and "equation," and not an attempt to create a broad fourth category of excluded subject matter.

[10/] We note, however, that an analysis wherein one attempts to identify whether any part of a claim recites mathematical subject matter which would not by itself be patentable is not an improper analysis. Such a dissection of a claim may be helpful under some circumstances to more fully understand the claimed subject matter. Nevertheless, even in those cases wherein courts have applied a variant of the two-part analysis of *In re Freeman*, 573 F.2d 1237, 197 USPQ 464 (CCPA 1978), as amended by *In re Walter*, 618 F.2d 758, 205 USPQ 397, the ultimate issue always has been whether the claim as a whole is drawn to statutory subject matter. *See e.g. In re Grams*, 888 F.2d at 838, 12 USPQ2 at 1827; *In re Meyer*, 688 F.2d at 796, 215 USPQ at 198; *In re Pardo*, 684 F.2d at 915, 214 USPQ at 676; *In re Abele*, 684 F.2d at 907, 214 USPQ at 687; *In re Walter*, 618 F.2d at 767, 205 USPQ at 407. In *In re Pardo*, the CCPA described the *Freeman-Walter* two-part test as follows: "First, the claim is analyzed to determine whether a mathematical algorithm is directly or indirectly recited. Next, if a mathematical algorithm is found, the claim *as a whole* is further analyzed to determine whether the algorithm is 'applied in any manner to physical elements or process steps,' and, if it is, it 'passes muster under § 101.'" *In re Pardo*, 684 F.2d at 915, 214 USPQ at 675-76 (emphasis added) (*quoting In re Walter*, 618 F.2d at 767, 205 USPQ at 407.).

[11/] The Board majority stated that each of the means of claim 15 represents a mathematical operation. The majority failed, however, to point out any particular mathematical equations corresponding to elements (c) and (d) of claim 15. In addition, we note the Board majority's irreconcilable position that it is free to impute mathematical equations from Alappat's specification into claim 15, yet it refuses to impute the electrical structure designed to carry out the arithmetic operations.

[12/] Although means (a) and (b) are independent of each other as claimed, each utilizes the same inputs and is connected to element (c), as means (c) normalizes the output of means (a) and (b). Means (c) is in turn connected to means element (d) which outputs illumination intensity data in response to an input from means (c).

[13/] The Board majority's attempts to distinguish *Iwahashi* on the basis that the claim at issue in that case recited a ROM are unavailing. The *Iwahashi* court clearly did not find patentable subject matter merely because a ROM was recited in the claim at issue; rather the court held that the claim as whole, directed to the combination of the claimed means elements, including the claimed ROM as one element, was directed to statutory subject matter. It was not the ROM alone that carried the day.

[14/] The Board majority argued that the fact that claim 15 reads on a programmed digital computer further justifies treating claim 15 as a process claim. We disagree. Our discussion in section II.D.(1) sufficiently sets forth why claim 15 must be construed as an apparatus claim as it is illustrated in section II.D.(2).

[15/] The disclosed ALU, ROM and shift registers are all common elements of stored program digital computers.

Index

C A T A L O G

...more books from Nolo Press

The Independent Paralegal's Handbook

Attorney Ralph Warner. Nat'l 3rd ed.
Provides legal and business guidelines for anyone who wants to go into business as an independent paralegal helping consumers with routine legal tasks.
$29.95 PARA

books with disk

How to Form a Nonprofit Corporation

Attorney Anthony Mancuso. Nat'l 2nd ed.
Explains the legal formalities involved and provides detailed information on the differences in the law among all 50 states. It also contains forms for the Articles, Bylaws and Minutes you need, along with complete instructions for obtaining federal 501(c)(3) tax exemptions and qualifying for public charity status. Includes incorporation forms on disk.
DOS $39.95/NNP

How to Form Your Own Corporation

Attorney Anthony Mancuso.
Step-by-step guide to forming your own corporation. Provides clear instructions and all the forms you need including Articles, Bylaws, Minutes and Stock Certificates. Includes all incorporation forms on disk.
Florida DOS $39.95/FLCO
New York DOS $39.95/NYCO
Texas DOS $39.95/TCI

Taking Care of Your Corporation, Vol. 1: Director and Shareholder Meetings Made Easy

Attorney Anthony Mancuso. Nat'l 1st ed.
This book takes the drudgery out of the necessary task of holding meetings of the board of directors and shareholders. It shows how to comply with state laws for holding meetings, how to prepare minutes for annual and special meetings, take corporate action by written consent, hold real or paper meetings and handle corporate formalities using e-mail, computer bulletin boards, fax and telephone and video conferencing. Includes all corporate forms on disk.
DOS $26.95/CORK

How to Form Your Own California Corporation With Corporate Records Binder & Disk

Attorney Anthony Mancuso. CA 1st Ed.
How to Form Your Own California Corporation is also available in a handy new format. It includes all the forms and instructions you need to form your own corporation, a corporate records binder, stock certificates and all incorporation forms on disk.
$39.95/CACI

The California Nonprofit Corporation Handbook

Attorney Anthony Mancuso. Version 1.0
This book with disk package shows you step-by-step how to form and operate a nonprofit corporation in California. Included on disk are the forms for the Articles, Bylaws and Minutes.
DOS $39.95 NPI
MACINTOSH $39.95 NPM

Software Development: A Legal Guide

Attorney Stephen Fishman. Nat'l 1st ed.
Clearly explains patent, copyright, trademark and trade secret protection and shows how to draft development contracts and employment agreements. Includes all contracts and agreements on disk.
DOS $44.95/SFT

software

Nolo's Partnership Maker

Version 1.0
Prepares a legal partnership agreement for doing business in any state. Select and assemble the standard partnership clauses provided or create your own customized agreement. Includes on-line legal help screens, glossary and tutorial, and a manual that takes you through the process step-by-step.
DOS $129.95/PAGI1

California Incorporator

Version 1.0 (good only in CA)
Answer the questions on the screen and this software program will print out the 35-40 pages of documents you need to make your California corporation legal. A 200-page manual explains the incorporation process.
DOS $129.00/INCI

How to Start Your Own Business: Small Business Law

Attorney Ralph Warner with Joanne Greene. Nat'l 1st ed. 60 minutes
This tape covers what every small business owner needs to know about organizing as a sole proprietorship, partnership or corporation, protecting the business name, renting space, hiring employees and paying taxes.
$14.95/TBUS

Getting Started as an Independent Paralegal

Attorney Ralph Warner. Nat'l 2nd ed. Two tapes, approximately 2 hrs.
Practical and legal advice on going into business as an independent paralegal from the author of *The Independent Paralegal's Handbook*.
$44.95/GSIP

ESTATE PLANNING & PROBATE

Plan Your Estate

Attorney Denis Clifford. Nat'l 3rd ed.
Thoroughly revised and updated, this is the most comprehensive estate planing book available. It covers everything from basic estate planning to sophisticated tax saving stratagies. Includes information on federal estate and gift taxes, estate tax saving trusts, trusts used to control property left to beneficiaries, charitable remainder trusts, durable powers of attorney, living wills, funerals and burials. Good in all states except Lousiana.
$24.95/NEST

Make Your Own Living Trust

Attorney Denis Clifford. Nat'l 1st ed.
Find out how a living trust works, how to create one, and how to determine what kind of trust is right for you. Contains all the forms and instructions you need to prepare a basic living trust to avoid probate, a marital life estate trust (A-B trust) to avoid probate and estate taxes, and a back-up will. Good in all states except Louisiana.
$19.95/LITR

Nolo's Simple Will Book

Attorney Denis Clifford. Nat'l 2nd ed.
It's easy to write a legally valid will using this book. Includes all the instructions and sample forms you need to name a personal guardian for minor children, leave property to minor children or young adults and update a will when necessary. Good in all states except Louisiana.
$17.95/SWIL

Who Will Handle Your Finances If You Can't?

Attorneys Denis Clifford & Mary Randolph. Nat'l 1st ed.
Give a trusted person legal authority to handle your financial matters if illness or old age makes it impossible for you to handle them yourself. Create a durable power of attorney for finances with the step-by-step instructions and fill-in-the-blank forms included in this book.
$19.95/FINA

The Conservatorship Book

Lisa Goldoftas & Attorney Carolyn Farren. CA 2nd ed.
Provides forms and all instructions necessary to file conservatorship documents, appear in court, be appointed conservator and end a conservatorship.
$29.95/CNSV

How to Probate an Estate

Julia Nissley. CA 8th ed.
Save costly attorneys' fees by handling the probate process yourself. This book shows you step-by-step how to settle an estate. It also explains the simple procedures you can use to transfer assets that don't require probate. Forms included.
$34.95/PAE

5 Ways to Avoid Probate

Attorney Ralph Warner with Joanne Greene. Nat'l 1st ed. 60 minutes
Provides clear, in-depth explanations of the principal probate avoidance techniques: joint tenancy, insurance, living trusts, savings account trusts and pension plans.
$14.95/KWL

Write Your Will

Attorney Ralph Warner with Joanne Greene. Nat'l 1st ed. 60 minutes
If you're getting ready to write your will, this tape is a good place to start. It answers the most frequently asked questions about writing a will and covers all key issues.
$14.95/TWYW

Nolo's Law Form Kit: Wills

Attorney Denis Clifford & Lisa Goldoftas. Nat'l 1st ed.
All the forms and instructions you need to create a legally valid will, quickly and easily.
$14.95/KWL

software

Living Trust Maker

Version 2.0
Put your assets into a trust and save your heirs the headache, time and expense of probate with this easy-to-use software. Use it to set up an individual or shared marital trust, transfer property to the trust, and change or revoke the trust at any time. Its manual guides you through the process, and legal help screens and an on-line glossary explain key legal terms and concepts. Good in all states except Louisiana.
WINDOWS $79.95/LTWI2
MACINTOSH $79.95/LTM2

WillMaker®

Version 5.0
Make your own legal will and living will (healthcare directive)—and thoroughly document your final arrangements—with *WillMaker 5*. It's easy-to-use interview format takes you through each document step-by-step. On-line legal help is available throughout the program. Name a guardian for your children, make up to 100 property bequests, direct your healthcare in the event of coma or terminal illness, and let your loved ones know your wishes around your own final arrangements.
WINDOWS $69.95/WIW5
DOS $69.95/WI5
MACINTOSH $69.95/WM5

Nolo's Personal RecordKeeper

Version 3.0
Finally, a safe, accessible place for your important records. Over 200 categories and subcategories to organize and store your important financial, legal and personal information, compute your net worth and create inventories for insurance records. Export your net worth and home inventory data to Quicken®.
DOS $49.95/FRI3
MACINTOSH $49.95/FRM3

GOING TO COURT

How to Change Your Name

Attorneys David Loeb & David Brown. CA 6th ed.
All the forms and instructions you need to change your name in California.
$24.95/NAME

Represent Yourself in Court

Attorneys Paul Bergman & Sara Berman-Barrett. Nat'l 1st ed.
Handle your own civil court case from start to finish without a lawyer with the most thorough guide to contested court cases ever published for the non-lawyer. Covers all aspects of civil trials.
$29.95/RYC

Everybody's Guide to Municipal Court

Judge Roderic Duncan. CA 1st ed.
Sue and defend cases for up to $25,000 in California Municipal Court. Gives step-by-step instructions for preparing and filing forms, gathering evidence and appearing in court.
$29.95/MUNI

Everybody's Guide to Small Claims Court

Attorney Ralph Warner. Nat'l 5th ed. CA 11th ed.
These books will help you decide if you should sue in Small Claims Court, show you how to file and serve papers, tell you what to bring to court and how to collect a judgment.
National $18.95/NSCC
California $18.95/CSCC

Fight Your Ticket

Attorney David Brown. CA 5th ed.
Shows you how to fight an unfair traffic ticket—when you're stopped, at arraignment, at trial and on appeal.
$18.95/FYT

Collect Your Court Judgment

Gini Graham Scott, Attorney Stephen Elias & Lisa Goldoftas. CA 2nd ed.
Contains step-by-step instructions and all the forms you need to collect a court judgment from the debtor's bank accounts, wages, business receipts, real estate or other assets.
$19.95/JUDG

The Criminal Records Book

Attorney Warren Siegel. CA 3rd ed.
Shows you step-by-step how to seal criminal records, dismiss convictions, destroy marijuana records and reduce felony convictions.
$19.95/CRIM

---

audio cassette tapes

Winning in Small Claims Court

Attorney Ralph Warner with Joanne Greene. Nat'l 1st ed. 60 minutes
Guides you through all the major issues involved in preparing and winning a small claims court case—deciding if there is a good case, assessing whether you can collect if you win, preparing your evidence, and arguing before the judge.
$14.95/TWIN

THE NEIGHBORHOOD

Dog Law

Attorney Mary Randolph. Nat'l 2nd ed.
A practical guide to the laws that affect dog owners and their neighbors. Answers common questions about biting, barking, veterinarians and more.
$12.95/DOG

Neighbor Law: Fences, Trees, Boundaries & Noise

Attorney Cora Jordan. Nat'l 2nd ed.
Answers common questions about the subjects that most often trigger disputes between neighbors: fences, trees, boundaries and noise. It explains how to find the law and resolve disputes without a nasty lawsuit.
$16.95/NEI

Safe Homes, Safe Neighborhoods: Stopping Crime Where You Live

Stephanie Mann with M.C. Blakeman. Nat'l 1st ed.
Learn how you and your neighbors can work together to protect yourselves, your families and property from crime. Explains how to form a neighborhood crime prevention group; avoid burglaries, car thefts, muggings and rapes; combat gangs and drug dealing; improve home security and make the neighborhood safer for children.
$14.95/SAFE

FAMILY MATTERS

The Living Together Kit

Attorneys Toni Ihara & Ralph Warner. Nat'l 7th ed.
A detailed guide designed to help the increasing number of unmarried couples living together understand the laws that affect them. Sample agreements and instructions are included.
$24.95/LTK

Nolo's Pocket Guide to Family Law

Attorneys Robin Leonard & Stephen Elias. Nat'l 3rd ed.
Here's help for anyone who has a question or problem involving family law—marriage, divorce, adoption or living together.
$14.95/FLD

A Legal Guide for Lesbian and Gay Couples

Attorneys Hayden Curry, Denis Clifford & Robin Leonard. Nat'l 8th ed.
This book shows lesbian and gay couples how to write a living-together contract, plan for medical emergencies, understand the practical and legal aspects of having and raising children and plan their estates. Includes forms and sample agreements.
$24.95/LG

Divorce: A New Yorker's Guide to Doing it Yourself

Bliss Alexandra. New York 1st ed.
Step-by-step instructions and all the forms you need to do your own divorce and save thousands of dollars in legal fees. Shows you how to divide property, arrange custody of the children, set child support and maintenance (alimony), draft a divorce agreement and fill out and file all forms.
$24.95/NYDIV

Divorce & Money

Violet Woodhouse & Victoria Felton-Collins with M.C. Blakeman. Nat'l 2nd ed.
Explains how to evaluate such major assets as family homes and businesses, investments, pensions, and how to arrive at a division of property that is fair to both sides.
$21.95/DIMO

How to Raise or Lower Child Support in California

Judge Roderic Duncan & Attorney Warren Siegal. CA 2nd ed.
Appropriate for parents on either side of the support issue. All the forms and instructions necessary to raise or lower an existing child support order.
$17.95/CHLD

The Guardianship Book

Lisa Goldoftas & Attorney David Brown. CA 1st ed.
Provides step-by-step instructions and the forms needed to obtain a legal guardianship of a minor without a lawyer.
$19.95/GB

How to Adopt Your Stepchild in California

Frank Zagone & Attorney Mary Randolph. CA 4th ed.
Provides sample forms and step-by-step instructions for completing a simple uncontested stepparent adoption in California.
$22.95/ADOP

Smart Ways to Save Money During and After Divorce

Victoria F. Collins & Ginita Wall. Nat'l 1st ed.
If you're going through a divorce, most likely you're faced with an overwhelming number of financial decisions. Here's a book packed with information on how to save money before, during and after divorce. It covers how to keep attorney's fees low, save on taxes, divide assets fairly, understand child support and alimony obligations and put aside money now for expenses later.
$14.95/SAVMO

California Marriage & Divorce Law

Attorneys Ralph Warner, Toni Ihara & Stephen Elias. CA 11th ed.
Explains community property, pre-nuptial contracts, foreign marriages, buying a house, getting a divorce, dividing property, and more. Pre-nuptial contracts included.
$19.95/MARR

Practical Divorce Solutions

Attorney Charles Sherman. Nat'l 1st ed.
Covers the emotional aspects of divorce and provides an overview of the legal and financial considerations.
$14.95/PDS

How to Do Your Own Divorce

Attorney Charles Sherman (Texas ed. by Sherman & Simons).
CA 19th ed. & Texas 5th ed.
These books contain all the forms and instructions you need to do your own uncontested divorce without a lawyer.
California $21.95/CDIV
Texas $17.95/TDIV

MONEY MATTERS

Stand Up to the IRS

Attorney Fred Daily. Nat'l 2nd ed.
Gives detailed strategies on surviving an audit, appealing an audit decision, going to Tax Court and dealing with IRS collectors. It also discusses filing delinquent tax returns, tax crimes, concerns of small business people and getting help from the IRS ombudsman.
$21.95/SIRS

How to File for Bankruptcy

Attorneys Stephen Elias, Albin Renauer & Robin Leonard. Nat'l 4th ed.
Trying to decide whether or not filing for bankruptcy makes sense? This book contains an overview of the process and all the forms plus step-by-step instructions you need to file for Chapter 7 Bankruptcy.
$25.95/HFB

Money Troubles: Legal Strategies to Cope With Your Debts

Attorney Robin Leonard. Nat'l 2nd ed.
Essential for anyone who has gotten behind on bills. It shows how to obtain a credit file, negotiate with persistent creditors, challenge wage attachments, contend with property repossessions and more.
$16.95/MT

Simple Contracts for Personal Use

Attorney Stephen Elias & Marcia Stewart. Nat'l 2nd ed.
Contains clearly written legal form contracts to buy and sell property, borrow and lend money, store and lend personal property, release others from personal liability, or pay a contractor to do home repairs. Includes agreements to arrange child care and other household help.
$16.95/CONT

law form kits

Nolo's Law Form Kit: Power of Attorney

Attorneys Denis Clifford & Mary Randolph and Lisa Goldoftas. Nat'l 1st ed.
Create a conventional power of attorney to assign someone you trust to take of your finances, business, real estate or children when you are away or unavailable. Provides all the forms with step-by-step instructions.
$14.95/KPA

Nolo's Law Form Kit: Loan Agreements

Attorney Stephen Elias, Marcia Stewart & Lisa Goldoftas. Nat'l 1st ed.
Provides all the forms and instructions necessary to create a legal and effective promissory note. Shows how to decide on an interest rate, set a payment schedule and keep track of payments.
$14.95/KLOAN

Nolo's Law Form Kit: Buy and Sell Contracts

Attorney Stephen Elias, Marcia Stewart & Lisa Goldoftas. Nat'l 1st ed.
Step-by-step instructions and all the forms necessary for creating bills of sale for cars, boats, computers, electronic equipment, household appliances and other personal property.
$9.95/KCONT

Nolo's Law Form Kit: Personal Bankruptcy

Attorneys Steve Elias, Albin Renauer & Robin Leonard and Lisa Goldoftas. Nat'l 1st ed.
All the forms and instructions you need to file for Chapter 7 bankruptcy.
$14.95/KBNK

Nolo's Law Forms Kit: Rebuild Your Credit

Attorney Robin Leonard. Nat'l 1st ed.
Provides strategies for dealing with debts and rebuilding your credit. Shows you how to negotiate with creditors and collection agencies, clean up your credit file, devise a spending plan and get credit in your name.
$14.95/KCRD

PATENT, COPYRIGHT & TRADEMARK

Trademark: How to Name Your Business & Product

Attorneys Kate McGrath & Stephen Elias, with Trademark Attorney Sarah Shena. Nat'l 1st ed.
Learn how to choose a name or logo that others can't copy, conduct a trademark search, register a trademark with the U.S. Patent and Trademark Office and protect and maintain the trademark.
$29.95/TRD

Patent It Yourself

Attorney David Pressman. Nat'l 3rd ed.
From the patent search to the actual application, this book covers everything including the use and licensing of patents, successful marketing and how to deal with infringement. Includes all necessary forms and instructions.
$39.95/PAT

The Inventor's Notebook

Fred Grissom & Attorney David Pressman. Nat'l 1st ed.
Helps you document the process of successful independent inventing by providing forms, instructions, references to relevant areas of patent law, a bibliography of legal and non-legal aids and more.
$19.95/INOT

The Copyright Handbook

Attorney Stephen Fishman. Nat'l 2nd ed.
Provides forms and step-by-step instructions for protecting all types of written expression under U.S. and international copyright law. Covers copyright infringement, fair use, works for hire and transfers of copyright ownership.
$24.95/COHA

software

Patent It Yourself Software

Version 1.0
Patent It Yourself is also available in software. With separate tracks for novice and expert users, it takes you through the process step-by-step. It shows how to evaluate patentability of your invention, how to prepare and file your patent application and how to generate all the forms you need to protect and exploit your invention.
Windows $229.95/PYW1

HOMEOWNERS

How to Buy a House in California

Attorney Ralph Warner, Ira Serkes & George Devine. CA 3rd ed.
Effective strategies for finding a house, working with a real estate agent, making an offer and negotiating intelligently. Includes information on all types of mortgages as well as private financing options.
$24.95/BHCA

For Sale By Owner

George Devine. CA 2nd ed.
Everything you need to know to sell your own house, from pricing and marketing, to writing a contract and going through escrow. Disclosure and contract forms included.
$24.95/FSBO

Homestead Your House

Attorneys Ralph Warner, Charles Sherman & Toni Ihara.
Shows you how to file a Declaration of Homestead and includes complete instructions and tear-out forms.
$9.95/HOME

The Deeds Book

Attorney Mary Randolph. CA 3rd ed.
Shows you how to fill out and file the right kind of deed when transferring property. Outlines the legal requirements of real property transfer.
$16.95/DEED

LANDLORDS & TENANTS

The Landlord's Law Book, Vol. 1: Rights & Responsibilities

Attorneys David Brown & Ralph Warner. CA 4th ed.
Essential for every California landlord. Covers deposits, leases and rental agreements, inspections (tenants' privacy rights), habitability (rent withholding), ending a tenancy, liability and rent control. Forms included.
$32.95/LBRT

The Landlord's Law Book, Vol. 2: Evictions

Attorney David Brown. CA 4th ed.
Shows step-by-step how to go to court and evict a tenant. Contains all the tear-out forms and necessary instructions.
$32.95/LBEV

Nolo's Law Form Kit: Leases & Rental Agreements

Attorney Ralph Warner & Marcia Stewart. CA 1st ed.
With these easy-to-use forms and instructions, California landlords can prepare their own rental application, fixed term lease, month-to-month agreement and notice to pay rent or quit.
$14.95/KLEAS

Tenants' Rights

Attorneys Myron Moskovitz & Ralph Warner. CA 12th ed.
This practical guide to dealing with your landlord explains your rights under federal law, California law and rent control ordinances. Forms included.
$18.95/CTEN

JUST FOR FUN

Nolo's Favorite Lawyer Jokes on Disk

Over 200 jokes and hilariously nasty remarks about lawyers organized by categories (Lawyers as Vultures, Nobody Loves a Lawyer, Lawyers in Love...). 100% guaranteed to produce an evening of chuckles and drive every lawyer you know nuts.
IBM PC $9.95/JODI
MACINTOSH $9.95/JODM

Devil's Advocates: The Unnatural History of Lawyers

by Andrew & Jonathan Roth. Nat'l 1st ed.
A hilarious look at the history of the legal profession.
$12.95/DA

Poetic Justice: The Funniest, Meanest Things Ever Said About Lawyers

Edited by Jonathan & Andrew Roth. Nat'l 1st ed.
A great gift for anyone in the legal profession who has managed to maintain a sense of humor.
$9.95/PJ

29 Reasons Not to Go to Law School

Attorneys Ralph Warner & Toni Ihara. Nat'l 4th ed.
Filled with humor, this book can save you three years, $150,000 and your sanity.
$9.95/29R

OLDER AMERICANS

Social Security, Medicare & Pensions

Attorney Joseph Matthews with Dorothy Matthews Berman. Nat'l 5th ed.
Offers invaluable guidance through the current maze of rights and benefits for those 55 and over, including Medicare, Medicaid and Social Security retirement and disability benefits, and age discrimination protections.
$18.95/SOA

Beat the Nursing Home Trap: A Consumer's Guide to Choosing and Financing Long-term Care

Attorney Joseph Matthews. Nat'l 1st ed.
Guides you in choosing and paying for long-term care, alerting you to practical concerns and explaining laws that may affect your decisions.
$18.95/ELD

REFERENCE

Legal Research: How to Find and Understand the Law

Attorneys Stephen Elias & Susan Levinkind. Nat'l 3rd ed.
A valuable tool on its own or as a companion to just about every other Nolo book. Gives easy-to-use, step-by-step instructions on how to find legal information.
$19.95/LRES

Legal Research Made Easy: A Roadmap Through the Law Library Maze

2-1/2 hr. videotape and 40-page manual.
Nolo Press/Legal Star Communications. Nat'l 1st ed.
Professor Bob Berring explains how to use all the basic legal research tools in your local law library with an easy-to-follow six-step research plan and a sense of humor.
$89.95/LRME

CONSUMER/REFERENCE

Nolo's Pocket Guide to California Law on Disk

This handy resource is also availaable on disk. With this new format you can rapidly search through California law by topic and subtopic, or by using the key-word index. The program tracks and saves searches, and allows you to save text to a file for later use.
Windows $24.95/CLWIN
Macintosh $24.95/CLM

Nolo's Pocket Guide to California Law

Attorney Lisa Guerin & Nolo Press Editors. CA 2nd ed.
Get quick clear answers to questions about child support, custody, consumer rights, employee rights, government benefits, divorce, bankruptcy, adoption, wills and much more.
$10.95/CLAW

Nolo's Pocket Guide to Consumer Rights

Barbara Kaufman. CA 2nd ed.
Practical advice on hundreds of consumer topics. Shows Californians how and where to complain about everything from accountants, misleading advertisements and lost baggage to vacation scams and dishonored warranties.
$14.95/CAG

Nolo's Law Form Kit: Hiring Child Care & Household Help

Attorney Barbara Kate Repa & Lisa Goldoftas. Nat'l 1st ed.
All the necessary forms and instructions for fulfilling your legal and tax responsibilities. Includes employment contracts, application forms and required IRS forms.
$14.95/KCHLD

How to Win Your Personal Injury Claim

Attorney Joseph Matthews. Nat'l 1st ed.
Armed with the right information anyone can handle a personal injury claim. This step-by-step guide shows you how to avoid insurance company run-arounds, evaluate what your claim is worth, obtain a full and fair settlement and save for yourself what you would pay a lawyer.
$24.95/PICL

Fed Up with the Legal System: What's Wrong and How to Fix It

Attorneys Ralph Warner & Stephen Elias. Nat'l 2nd ed.
Forty common-sense proposals to make our legal system fairer, faster, cheaper and more accessible.
$9.95/LEG

IMMIGRATION

How to Get a Green Card: Legal Ways to Stay in the U.S.A.

Attorney Loida Nicolas Lewis with Len T. Madlanscay. Nat'l 1st ed.
Written by a former INS attorney, this book clearly explains the steps involved in getting a green card. It covers who can qualify, what documents to present, and how to fill out all the forms and have them processed. Tear-out forms included.
$22.95/GRN

Como Obtener La Tajeta Verde: Maneras Legitimas de Permanacer en los EE.UU.

Attorney Loida Nicolas Lewis with Len T. Madlanscay. Nat'l 1st ed.
The Spanish edition of *How to Get a Green Card.*
$24.95/VERDE

ORDER FORM

Name

Address (UPS to street address, Priority Mail to P.O. boxes)

Catalog Code	Quantity	Item	Unit Price	Total
			Subtotal	

In California add appropriate Sales Tax

Shipping & Handling (add $4 for 1 item, $5 for 2-3 items and 50¢ for each additional item)

2nd day UPS Delivery (add $5, $8 for AK and HI)

TOTAL

METHOD OF PAYMENT

☐ Check enclosed   ☐ VISA   ☐ MasterCard   ☐ Discover Card   ☐ American Express

Account #   Expiration Date

Signature   Phone

FOR FASTER SERVICE, USE YOUR CREDIT CARD AND OUR TOLL-FREE NUMBERS

Call our toll-free number between 7am and 6 pm Pacific Time Monday through Friday.

ORDER LINE   **1-800-992-6656**
GENERAL INFORMATION   **1-510-549-1976**
FAX US YOUR ORDER   **1-800-645-0895**

Or mail your order with a check or money order made payable to:
Nolo Press, 950 Parker Street, Berkeley, CA 94710

VISIT OUR STORE

If you live in the Bay Area, be sure to visit the Nolo Press Bookstore on the corner of 9th & Parker Streets in west Berkeley. You'll find our complete line of books and software—all at a discount. CALL 1-510-704-2248 for hours.

ALLOW 2-3 WEEKS FOR DELIVERY. PRICES SUBJECT TO CHANGE.   SOFT 1.2

When you register, we'll send you our quarterly newspaper, the *Nolo News*, free for two years. (U.S. addresses only.) Here's what you'll get in every issue:

■ INFORMATIVE ARTICLES

Written by Nolo editors, articles provide practical legal information on issues you encounter in everyday life: family law, wills, debts, consumer rights, and much more.

■ UPDATE SERVICE

The *Nolo News* keeps you informed of legal changes that affect any Nolo book and software program.

■ BOOK AND SOFTWARE REVIEWS

We're always looking for good legal and consumer books and software from other publishers. When we find them, we review them and offer them in our mail order catalog.

■ ANSWERS TO YOUR LEGAL QUESTIONS

Our readers are always challenging us with good questions on a variety of legal issues. So in each issue, "Auntie Nolo" gives sage advice and sound information.

■ COMPLETE NOLO PRESS CATALOG

The *Nolo News* contains an up-to-the-minute catalog of all Nolo books and software, which you can order using our "800" toll-free order line. And you can see at a glance if you're using an out-of-date version of a Nolo product.

■ LAWYER JOKES

Nolo's famous lawyer joke column continually gets the goat of the legal establishment. If we print a joke you send in, you'll get a $20 Nolo gift certificate.

We promise *never* to give your name and address to any other organization.

SOFTWARE DEVELOPMENT: A LEGAL GUIDE　　　　　　　Registration Card

We'd like to know what you think! Please take a moment to fill out and return this postage paid card for a free two year subscription to the *Nolo News*. If you already receive the *Nolo News*, we'll extend your subscription.

Name _____ Ph.(　　) _____

Address _____

City _____ State _____ Zip _____

Where did you hear about this book? _____

For what purpose did you use this book? _____

Did you consult a lawyer?	Yes	No		Not Applicable		
Was it easy for you to use this book?	(very easy)	5	4	3	2	1	(very difficult)
Did you find this book helpful?	(very)	5	4	3	2	1	(not at all)

Comments _____

_____

_____

_____

_____

COMPLETE AND MAIL TODAY

THANK YOU

SFT 1.2